Lecture Notes in Computer Science 1291

Edited by G. Goos, J. Hartmanis and J. van Leeuwen

Advisory Board: W. Brauer   D. Gries   J. Stoer

Springer
Berlin
Heidelberg
New York
Barcelona
Budapest
Hong Kong
London
Milan
Paris
Santa Clara
Singapore
Tokyo

Dror G. Feitelson   Larry Rudolph (Eds.)

Job Scheduling Strategies for Parallel Processing

IPPS '97 Workshop
Geneva, Switzerland, April 5, 1997
Proceedings

 Springer

Series Editors

Gerhard Goos, Karlsruhe University, Germany
Juris Hartmanis, Cornell University, NY, USA
Jan van Leeuwen, Utrecht University, The Netherlands

Volume Editors

Dror G. Feitelson
Larry Rudolph
The Hebrew University, Institute of Computer Science
91904 Jerusalem, Israel
E-mail: (feit/rudolph)@cs.huji.ac.il

Cataloging-in-Publication data applied for

Die Deutsche Bibliothek - CIP-Einheitsaufnahme

Job scheduling strategies for parallel processing : proceedings / IPPS '97
workshop, Geneva, Switzerland, April 5, 1997 / Dror G. Feitelson ; Larry
Rudolph (ed.). - Berlin ; Heidelberg ; New York ; Barcelona ; Budapest ; Hong
Kong ; London ; Milan ; Paris ; Santa Clara ; Singapore ; Tokyo : Springer,
1997
   (Lecture notes in computer science ; Vol. 1291)
   ISBN 3-540-63574-2

CR Subject Classification (1991): D.4, D.1.3, F.2.2, C.1.2, B.2.1, B.6.1, F.1.2

ISSN 0302-9743
ISBN 3-540-63574-2 Springer-Verlag Berlin Heidelberg New York

© Springer-Verlag Berlin Heidelberg 1997
Printed in Germany

Typesetting: Camera-ready by author
SPIN 10546406   06/3142 – 5 4 3 2 1 0   Printed on acid-free paper

Preface

This volume contains the papers presented at the third workshop on Job Scheduling Strategies for Parallel Processing, which was held in conjunction with IPPS '97 in Geneva, Switzerland, on April 5, 1997. All the papers have gone through the usual refereeing process, with the full version being read and evaluated by five or six members of the program committee in most cases. We would like to take this opportunity to thank the program committee, Nawaf Bitar, David Black, Atsushi Hori, Mal Kalos, Richard Lagerstrom, Miron Livny, Virginia Lo, Reagan Moore, Bill Nitzberg, Uwe Schwiegelshohn, Ken Sevcik, Mark Squillante, and John Zahorjan, for an excellent job. Thanks are also due to the authors for their submissions, presentations, and final revisions for this volume. Finally, we would like to thank the MIT Laboratory for Computer Science and the Computer Science Institute at Hebrew University for the use of their facilities in preparation of these proceedings.

As multi-user parallel supercomputers become more widespread, job scheduling takes on a crucial role. The number of users of parallel supercomputers is growing at an even faster pace and so there is an increasing number of users who must share a parallel computer's resources. Job scheduling strategies must address this need.

There is a spectrum of groups that are interested in job scheduling strategies for parallel processors. At one end are the vendors of parallel supercomputers who supply the scheduling software for managing jobs on their machines. In the middle are researchers in academia, National Labs, and industrial research labs who propose new scheduling strategies and methods for evaluating and comparing them. At the other end of the spectrum are the users and system administrators of parallel processing facilities who have a set of demands and requirements.

The goal of the workshop was to bring together people from all three groups, in order to exchange ideas and discuss ongoing work. Indeed, many interesting discussions took place, and the workshop was quite lively. We were encouraged by this since we believe it is important to increase communication so that academics work on the right problems and vendors and computation centers make the best use of the novel solutions. We hope these proceedings help parallel supercomputing to achieve its fundamental goal of satisfying the needs of the user.

This was the third annual workshop in this series, which reflects the continued interest in this field. The previous two were held in conjunction with IPPS '95 and IPPS '96, in Santa Barbara and Honolulu, respectively. Their proceedings are available from Springer-Verlag as volumes 949 and 1162 in the Lecture Notes in Computer Science series.

Jerusalem, June 1997

Dror Feitelson
Larry Rudolph

Contents

Theory and Practice
in Parallel Job Scheduling

Dror G. Feitelson[1], Larry Rudolph[1], Uwe Schwiegelshohn[2], Kenneth C.
Sevcik[3], and Parkson Wong[4]

[1] Institute of Computer Science
The Hebrew University, 91904 Jerusalem, Israel
{feit,rudolph}@cs.huji.ac.il
[2] Computer Engineering Institute
University Dortmund, 44221 Dortmund, Germany
uwe@carla.e-technik.uni-dortmund.de
[3] Department of Computer Science
University of Toronto, Toronto, Ontario, Canada M5S 3G4
kcs@cs.toronto.edu
[4] MRJ, Inc., NASA Contract NAS 2-14303
Moffett Field, CA 94035-1000, USA
parkson@nas.nasa.gov

Abstract. The scheduling of jobs on parallel supercomputer is becoming the subject of much research. However, there is concern about the divergence of theory and practice. We review theoretical research in this area, and recommendations based on recent results. This is contrasted with a proposal for standard interfaces among the components of a scheduling system, that has grown from requirements in the field.

1 Introduction

The scheduling of jobs on parallel supercomputers is becoming the subject of much research activity. See, for example the proceedings of three workshops [40], and a survey of a large number of proposed and implemented approaches [19]. It has become a distinct research topic from the largely unrelated, but better known problem of DAG scheduling [1]. DAG scheduling assumes that all tasks have fixed and specified dependencies, whereas job scheduling assumes that the jobs are mostly independent.

This paper is about scheduling jobs on distributed memory massively parallel processors (MPPs), which currently dominate the supercomputing arena. In terms of scheduling, on such machines memory is typically allocated in conjunction with the processors, rather than being treated as a distinct resource. However, this does not preclude a shared address space model of computation, and indeed many recent systems provide hardware support for different levels of memory sharing.

There are a growing number of high performance computing facilities that support large diverse workloads of parallel jobs on multicomputers that have tens to thousands of processors. The typical way that they are currently used is that:

1. The system is divided into "partitions" consisting of different numbers of processors. Most processors are allocated to partitions devoted to serving parallel jobs. One partition is typically set aside for support of interactive work through time-slicing of its processors. Another may be devoted to service tasks, such as running a parallel file system. The configuration of partitions may be changed on a regular basis (for example, by providing larger partitions for parallel jobs at night or over weekends, at the expense of the interactive partition).

2. A (large) number of queues are established, each one corresponding to a specific combination of job characteristics. (For example, one queue might correspond to jobs that require as many as 32 processors, and are expected to run no longer than 15 minutes.) Some queues are served at higher priority than others, so the user tends to submit a job to the highest priority queue for which the job qualifies based on its expected resource requirements.

3. Each partition is associated with one or more queues, and its processors serve as a pool for those queues. Whenever some processors are free, the associated queues are searched in order of priority for one that is non-empty. The first job in that non-empty queue is then activated in the partition, and it runs until it completes, provided the number of free processors is sufficient. Within each queue jobs are processed strictly in first-come-first-served order.

Thus:

- the number of processors assigned to a job is fixed by the user;
- once initiated the job runs to completion.

While there exist some innovations that have been introduced into production systems, such as non-FCFS service and support for swapping, the general trend is to retain the same framework, and moreover, to cast it into a standard. Many studies, however, show that more flexibility in both the scheduler actions and the way programs make use of parallelism result in better performance. But there is hope for convergence [25]. For example, theoretical analysis underscores the effectiveness of preemption in achieving low average response times, and also shows that considerable benefits are possible if the scheduler is allowed to tailor the partition sizes in accordance with the current system load. Notably, much of this work is based on workload models that are derived from measurements at supercomputer installations.

We survey the theoretical background in Section 2, and the specific recommendations that are made in Section 3. The standardization effort based on practical work at large installations is reviewed in Section 4. Finally, we discuss this state of affairs and present our conclusions in Section 5.

2 Survey of Theoretical Results

Various kinds of scheduling or sequencing problems have been addressed since the fifties by theoretical researchers from the areas of computer science, operations research, and discrete mathematics. The challenge of efficient job management on computers has frequently been named as a key reason to address this kind of problems. This is especially true for job scheduling on parallel systems with a large number of processors or nodes. Hence a direct use of many of these theoretical results in real applications would seem to be natural. However, many of these theoretical resutls rely on a creative set of assumptions, in order to make their proofs tractable. This divergence from reality not only make them hard to use in practice, but also the diversity of divergence makes them hard to compare with each other.

2.1 The Diversity of Divergence

This section covers many of the assumptions of theoretical work, by presenting a rough classification of different theoretical models. This includes different cost metrics, different features and operations available on the modeled system, and different algorithmic approaches.

Cost metrics For the discussion of the various cost metrics we use the following notations:

$$t_i = \text{completion time of job } i$$
$$s_i = \text{release time of job } i$$
$$w_i = \text{weight of job } i$$
$$d_i = \text{deadline of job } i$$

The *completion* time t_i is the time when the computer system has finally completed work on this job. Note that no information is provided on whether the job has been successfully completed or whether it has been removed from the system for other reasons. The *release* time s_i is the earliest time the computer system can start working on job i. Usually, the release time of a job is identical with its submital or arrival time, i.e. the first time when the system becomes aware of the new job. However, sometimes it is assumed that the scheduling system is aware of all jobs at time 0, but job i cannot be started before some time $s_i \geq 0$. The *weight* w_i of a job is a way to prioritize one job over another. The *deadline* d_i is the time by which a job must complete its execution. There is no generally accepted definition as to what happens if the deadline is not met for a specific job, i.e. $t_i > d_i$.

Obviously, the role of the scheduler is the allocation of limitted system resources to competing jobs. A job should somehow be charged for its resource comsumption. Often the cost of a schedule is simply the sum of the individual job costs. This cost function serves as basis to compare and evaluate different schedules. Assuming a job system τ the following metrics are commonly used:

$$\max_{i \in \tau} t_i \qquad\qquad = \text{Makespan (throughput)}$$

$$|\{i \in \tau | t_i > d_i\}| \qquad = \text{Deadline misses}$$

$$\sum_{i \in \tau} w_i t_i \qquad\qquad = \text{Weighted completion time}$$

$$\sum_{i \in \tau} w_i(t_i - s_i) \qquad = \text{Weighted flow (response) time}$$

$$\sum_{i \in \tau} w_i \max\{0, t_i - d_i\} = \text{Weighted tardiness}$$

Note that response time and flow time usually have the same meaning. The origin of these criteria often goes back to the fifties. For instance Smith [82] showed in 1956 that the sum of the weighted completion times for a system of jobs on a single processor can be minimized if the tasks are scheduled by increasing execution time to weight ratio, the so called Smith ratio. If all jobs have unit weight this algorithm becomes the well known shortest-job first method.

These metrics allow a relatively simple evaluation of algorithms which may be one reason for their popularity, but there are some subtle difference in them. A schedule with optimal weighted completion time also has the optimal weighted flow time. This equality does not hold, however, when they deviate by even a constant factor from the optimum as shown by Kellerer et al. [42] and by Leonardi and Raz [47].

In reality, the metrics attempt to formalize the real goals of a scheduler:

1. Satisfy the users.
2. Maximize the profit.

For instance, a reduction of the job response time will most likely improve user satisfaction.

Example 1. Assume that a job i needs approximately 3 hours of computation time. If the user submits the job in the morning (9am) he may expect to receive the results after lunch. It probably does not matter to him whether the job is started immediately or delayed for an hour as long as it is done by 1pm. Any delay beyond 1pm may cause annoyance and thus reduce user satisfaction, i.e. increase costs. This corresponds to tardiness scheduling. However, if the job is not completed before 5pm it may be sufficient if the user gets his results early next morning. Moreover, he may be able to deal with the situation easily if he is informed at the time of submital that execution of the job by 5pm cannot be expected. Also, if the user is charged for the use of system resources, he may be willing to postpone execution of his job until nighttime when the charge is reduced.

The use of metrics such as throughput and response time in many commercial installations may be due to the simplicity of the evaluation, or it may be a sign of some non-obvious influence from theory. On the other hand, a good management policy for a commercial system may require that different metrics are used during different times of the day: During daytime many users will actually wait for the completion of their submitted jobs. Thus a response time metric is appropriate. However, during the night it is best to maximize the throughput of jobs.

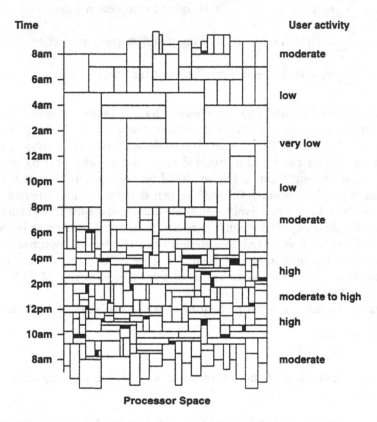

Fig. 1. *Workload of a parallel computer over the course of a day.*

Fig. 1 shows the load of a multiprocessor over the course of a day. For reasons of simplicity each job is described as a rectangle. Black rectangles denote idle processors due to fragmentation. However, note that multiprocessors do not necessarily require a linear one-dimensional processor space. But this way it is easier to visualize jobs. As shown in the figure, during periods of high user activity small jobs are given preference even if some processors remain idle due to fragmentation of the processor space. Jobs are allocated resources such that the shortest response time is achieved. On the other hand during periods of low user activity large batch jobs are started. Also moldable jobs are run in a way to increase efficiency, i.e. using fewer processors while requiring longer execution time.

Recent studies, e.g. Charkrabarti et al. [7], explicitly address the problem of bicriteria scheduling where scheduling methods are introduced which generate good schedules with respect to the makespan and the weighted completion time metric.

The Model A large variety of different machine and scheduling models have been used in studies of scheduling problems. The constraints incorporated into these models directly affect operations of the scheduler. They are at least partly inspired by the way real systems are managed and how parallel applications are written. The following roughly classifies these models according to five criteria:

1. Partition Specification Each parallel job is executed in a *partition* that consists of a number of processors. The size of such a partition may depend on the multiprocessor, the application, and the load of multiprocessor [25]. Moreover, the size of the partition of a specific job may change during the lifetime of this job in some models:

- **Fixed.** The partition size is defined by the system administrator and can be modified only by reboot.
- **Variable.** The partition size is determined at submission time of the job based on user request.
- **Adaptive.** The partition size is determined by the scheduler at the time the job is initiated, based on the system load, and taking the user request into account.
- **Dynamic.** The partition size may change during the execution of a job, to reflect changing requirements and system load.

Feldmann et al. [26] have considered fixed partitions generated by different architectures such as hypercubes, trees, or meshes. Many other authors use the variable partitioning paradigm, in which each job requires a specific number of processors but can be scheduled on any subset of processors of the system. An example of a theoretical study based on the adaptive approach is the work of Turek et al. [88]. Here, the application does not require a specific number of processors, but can use different numbers. However, once a partition for a job has been selected its size cannot change anymore. Finally, in dynamic partitioning the size of a partition may change at run time. This model has, for instance, been used by Deng et al. [11].

2. Job Flexibility As already mentioned advanced partitioning methods must not only be supported by the multiprocessor system but by the application as well. Therefore, Feitelson and Rudolph [25] characterize applications as follows:

- **Rigid jobs.** The number of processors assigned to a job is specified external to the scheduler, and precisely that number of processors are made available to the job throughout its execution.
- **Moldable jobs.** The number of processors assigned to a job is determined by the system scheduler within certain constraints when the job is first activated, and it uses that many processors throughout its execution.

- **Evolving jobs.** The job goes through different phases that require different numbers of processors, so the number of processors allocated may change during the job's execution in response to the job requesting more processors or relinquishing some. Each job is allocated at least the number of processors it requires at each point in its execution (but it may be allocated more to avoid the overheads of reallocation at each phase).
- **Malleable jobs.** The number of processors assigned to a job may change during the job's execution, as a result of the system giving it additional processors or requiring that the job release some.

The manner in which an application is written determines which of the four types is used[1]. The more effort devoted to writing the application with the intention of promoting it to one of the later types, the better a good scheduler can perform with respect to both the particular job, and the whole workload. Generally, a scheduler can start a job sooner if the job is moldable or even malleable than if it is rigid [87].

If jobs are *moldable*, then processor allocations can be selected in accordance with the current system load, which delays the onset of saturation as system load increases [25]. It is generally not difficult to write an application so that it is moldable, and is able to execute with processor allocations over some range (e.g., any power of two from four to 256). *Evolving* jobs arise when applications go through distinct phases, and their natural parallelism is different in different phases. For such jobs, system calls are inserted at the appropriate points in the application code to indicate where parallelism changes [96].

Certain parallel applications, such as those based on the "work crew" model[2], can be modified to be *malleable* relatively easily. An increased processor allocation allows more processors to take work from the queue, while a reduction means that some processors cease picking up work and are deallocated [67]. In most cases, however, it is more difficult to support malleability in the way an application is written. One way of attaining a limited form of malleability is by creating as many threads in a job as the largest number of processors that would ever be used, and then using multiplexing (or *folding* [51,38]) to have the job execute on a lesser number of processors. Alternatively, a job can be made malleable by inserting application specific code at particular synchronization points to repartition the data in response to any change in processor allocation. The latter approach is somewhat more effective, but it requires more effort from the application writer, as well as significantly more system support. Much of the required mechanisms for supporting malleable job scheduling is present in facilities for checkpointing parallel jobs [66]. Hence, a combined benefit can be derived if processor allocations are changed only at times when checkpoints are taken.

---

[1] Some theoretical studies use different terminology. For example, Ludwig and Tiwari [50] speak about "malleable" jobs which are equivalent to moldable jobs in our terminology.

[2] In the "work crew" model, processors pick up relatively small and independent units of computation from a central queue.

For stable applications that are widely and frequently used by many users, the effort required to make them malleable may be well justified. Otherwise, it is probably not worthwhile to write applications so that they are malleable.

3. Level of Preemption Supported Another issue is the extent to which individual threads or entire jobs can be preempted and potentially relocated during the execution of a job:

- **No Preemption.** Once a job is initiated it runs to completion while holding all its assigned processors throughout its execution.
- **Local Preemption.** Threads of a job may be preempted, but each thread can only be resumed later on the same processor. This kind of preemption does not require any data movement between processors.
- **Migratable Preemption.** Threads of a job may be suspended on one processor and subsequently resumed on another.
- **Gang Scheduling.** All active threads of a job are suspended and resumed simultaneously. Gang scheduling may be implemented with or without migration.

While many theoretical scheduling studies only use a model without preemption, more recently preemption has also been taken into account. Schwiegelshohn [71] uses a gang scheduling model without migration. The work of Deng et al. [11] is based upon migratable preemption.

In a real system the preemption of a job requires that all the job's threads be stopped in a consistent state (i.e., without any messages being lost), and the full state of each thread must be preserved. The memory contents associated with the job may be either explicitly written out of memory, or may be implicitly removed over time by a process such as page replacement. Whether or not the data of a job is removed from memory when the job is preempted depends in part on the memory requirements of the preempting job and the total amount of memory available.

In addition migratable preemption needs the mechanism of moving a thread from one processor to another, while preserving all existing communication paths to other threads. Also, when a thread is migrated, its associated data must follow. In message passing systems, this requires that the data be copied from one processor to another. In shared memory systems, the data can be transferred a cache line or page at a time as it is referenced. Preemption may have great benefit in leading to improved performance, even if it is used infrequently and on only a small fraction of all jobs.

Preemption in real machines has an overhead cost, e.g. Motwani et al. [55] address the overhead by minimizing the number of preemptions. In order to compare a preemptive schedule with non-preemptive ones Schwiegelshohn [71] includes a time penalty for each preemption.

4. Amount of Job and Workload Knowledge Available Systems differ in the type, quantity, and accuracy of information available to and used by the scheduler.

Characteristics of individual jobs that are useful in scheduling include (i) the total processing requirement, and (ii) the speedup characteristics of the job. Full knowledge of the latter requires knowing the execution time of the job for each number of processors on which it might be executed. Partial knowledge is provided by characteristics such as average parallelism (the average number of processors busy when the job is allocated ample processors), and maximum parallelism (the largest number of processors that a job can make use of at any point in its execution).

Workload information is also useful in choosing a scheduling policy. For example, workload measurements at a number of high-performance computing facilities have indicated that the variability in processing requirements among jobs is extreme, with most jobs having execution times of a few seconds, but a small number having execution times of many hours. The coefficient of variation[3], or CV, of the service times of jobs has been observed to be in the four to seventy range at several centers [8,64,21]. This implies that a mechanism to prevent short jobs from being delayed by long jobs is mandatory.

The knowledge available to the scheduler may be at one of the following levels:

- **None.** No prior knowledge is available or used in scheduling, so all jobs are treated the same upon submission.
- **Workload.** Knowledge of the overall distribution of service times in the workload is available, but no specific knowledge about individual jobs. Again, jobs are treated the same, but policy attributes and parameters can be tuned to fit the workload.
- **Class.** Each submitted job is associated with a "class", and some key characteristics of jobs in the class are known, including, for example, estimates of processing requirement, maximum parallelism, average parallelism, and possibly more detailed speedup characteristics.
- **Job.** The execution time of the job on any given number of processors is known exactly.

Job knowledge, which is defined to be exact, is unrealistic in practice. However, assuming omniscience in modeling studies makes it possible to obtain an optimistic bound on performance that is not attainable in practice. Presuming job knowledge in modeling studies sets a standard in performance against which practically realizable scheduling algorithms, which use class knowledge at most, can be compared.

On-line scheduling has been addressed more frequently in recent years. For instance Shmoys et al. [78] discussed makespan scheduling if the job characteristics are not known until the release time and the execution time requirements of the job are also not available before the job has been executed to completion. They show that any algorithm with all jobs available at time 0 can be converted

---

[3] The coefficient of variation of a distribution is its standard deviation divided by its mean.

to an algorithm that handles dynamic arrivals with a competitive factor at most twice larger.

Many systems make no effort at all to use information that accompanies a job submission to estimate the resource requirements of the job. However, smallest demand type disciplines (e.g., "Least Work First" (LWF)) can be used to yield low average response times if the resource demand of each job is known (precisely or approximately). For example, in many current systems jobs are submitted to one of a large number of queues, and the queue selected indicates such information as the number of processors needed, a limit on the execution time, and other parameters. Thus, each queue corresponds to a job class. In these systems, this information can be used implicitly through the way queues are assigned to (fixed) partitions, and the relative priorities assigned to the queues.

Any information provided by the user relating to job resource requirements must be used carefully both because it is prohibitively difficult for the user to consistently provide information with high accuracy, and also because the user may be motivated to deceive the scheduler intentionally. Thus, sources from which to gain knowledge about job resource requirements must be broadened to include:

- consider user provided information (while recognizing that it is historically quite unreliable, in part because users aren't careful about making good estimates);
- measure efficiency during execution and increase processor allocations only for jobs that are using their currently allocated processors effectively;
- keep track of execution time and speedup knowledge from past executions on a class by class basis, and use that information.

All identifying characteristics associated with the submital of a job can potentially be used to determine its class. These characteristics include the user id, the file to be executed, the memory size specified, and possibly others. An estimate of the efficiency [59] or the execution time [31] of a job being scheduled can be obtained from retained statistics on the actual resource usage of jobs from the same (or a similar) class that have been previously submitted and executed. A small database can be kept to record resource consumption of jobs on a class by class basis. This is very useful particularly for large jobs that are executed repeatedly.

5. Memory Allocation For high performance applications, memory is usually the critical resource.

This is particularly true in shared-memory systems, where the allocation of memory is relatively decoupled from the allocation of processors. Thus there are two types of memory to consider:

- **Distributed Memory.** Typically each processor and its associated memory is allocated as a unit. Message passing is used to access data in remote memory.

– **Shared Memory.** Access cost to shared memory can either be uniform (UMA) or nonuniform (NUMA) for all the processors. With UMA, there is the potential for more equitable allocation of the memory resources. With NUMA, the performance is sensitive to the allocation of a job to processors and its data to memories.

Mostly, memory requirements have been ignored in real scheduling systems and are not even part of the model in theoretical studies, although this is changing [65,73,62,61].

Algorithmic Methods The intractability for many scheduling problems has been well studied [28]. Examples in the specific area of parallel job scheduling include preemptive and non-preemptive gang scheduling by Du and Leung [13] using makespan, and Bruno, Coffman, and Sethi [6] and McNaughton [53] who use weighted completion time as optimization criterion.

With the intractability of many scheduling problems being established, polynomial algorithms guaranteeing a small deviation from the optimal schedule appear more attractive. Some polynomial algorithms are still very complex, [70], while others are particular simple algorithms, like list scheduling methods [41,95]. The latter promises to be of the greatest help for the selection of scheduling methods in real systems.

Although many of the approximation algorithms have a low computational complexity and produce schedules that are close to the optimum, they are usually not the method of choice in commercial installations.

The worst case approximation factor is usually of little relevance to a practical problem since a schedule that approaches the worst case is often unacceptable for a production schedule. For instance, the makespan approximation factor for list schedules of non-preemptive parallel job schedules is 2. In other words, up to 50% of the nodes of a multiprocessor system may be left idle. However, these high costs are only encountered for a few job systems which may never be part of real workloads.

Turek et al. [89] proposed "SMART" schedules for the off-line non-preemptive completion time scheduling of parallel jobs. They prove an approximation factor of 8 [72] and give a worst case example with a deviation of 4.5. However, applying the algorithm on job systems obtained from the traces of the Intel Paragon at the San Diego Supercomputing Center gave an average deviation from the optimum by 2. This result was further improved to the factor 1.4 by using the job order of the SMART schedule as input for a list schedule [33]. But note that SMART generates non-preemptive off-line schedules and requires the knowledge of the execution time of all jobs. The consideration of more complex constraints may make any general approximation algorithm impossible [42,47].

The evaluation of any scheduler can be either done by comparing its schedule against the optimal schedule or against schedules generated by other methods. Sleator and Tarjan [80] introduced the notion of competitive analysis. An on-line algorithm is competitive if it is guaranteed to produce a result that is within a constant factor of the optimal result. Only the deviation from the optimal schedule can determine whether there is enough room for improvement to motivate further algorithmic research. Unfortunately, the optimal schedule cannot be obtained easily, but an analysis of an approximation algorithm can use lower bounds for the optimal schedule to determine the competitive factor, e.g. the squashed area bound introduced by Turek et al. [89].

Moreover, the theoretical analysis may be able to pinpoint the conditions which may lead to a bad schedule. These methods can also be applied to any practical approach and help to determine critical workloads. If the evaluation of real traces reveals that such critical workloads rarely or even never occur then they can either be ignored or the approach can be enhanced with a procedure to specifically handle those situations.

For instance Kawaguchi and Kyan's LRF schedule [41] can be easily extended to parallel jobs. As long as no parallel job requires more than 50% of the processors, this will only increase the approximation factor from 1.21 to 2 [87]. However, if jobs requiring more processors are allowed in addition, no constant approximation factor can be guaranteed.

2.2 Some Specific Studies

Workload Characterization Several workload characterization studies of production high-performance computing facilities have been carried out. They reveal characteristics of actual workloads that can be exploited in scheduling.

Feitelson and Nitzberg [21] noted that repeated runs of the same application occurred frequently, and later runs tended to have similar resource consumption patterns as the corresponding earlier ones. Hotovy [37] studied a quite different system, yet found many of the same observations to hold. Gibbons [30] also analyzed workload data from the Cornell site in addition to two sites where parallel applications are executed on a network of workstations, concluding that in all three systems classifying the jobs by user, execution script, and requested degree of parallelism led to classes of jobs in which execution time variability is much lower than in the overall workload. The common conclusion is that much information about a job's resource requirements can be uncovered without demanding the user's cooperation.

Feitelson [17] studied the memory requirements of parallel jobs in a CM-5 environment. He found that memory is a significant resource in high-performance computing, although he observed that users typically request more processors than naturally correspond to their memory requirements.

Jann et al. [39] have produced a workload model based on measurements of the workload on the Cornell Theory Center SP2 machine. This model is intended to be used by other researchers, leading to easier and more meaningful comparison of results. Nguyen at al. [58] have measured the speedup characteristics of a variety of applications.

Batch Job Scheduling In an effort to improve the way current schedulers behave, several groups have modified NQS implementations to allow queue reordering in order to achieve better packing. Lifka et al. [49,79] have developed a scheduler on top of LoadLeveler with the feature that the strict FCFS order of activating jobs is relaxed. In this scheduler, known as "EASY", jobs are scheduled in a FCFS order to run at the earliest time that a sufficient number of processors are available for them. However, this can mean that smaller jobs may be executed before bigger jobs that arrived earlier, whenever they can do so without delaying the previously scheduled jobs[4]. It was found that user satisfaction was greatly increased since smaller jobs tended to get through faster, because they could bypass the very big ones.

Henderson [35] describes the Portable Batch System (PBS), another system in which performance gains are achieved by moving away from strict FCFS scheduling. Wan et al. [92] also implement a non-FCFS scheduler that uses a variation of a 2-D buddy system to do processor allocation for the Intel Paragon.

Thread-oriented scheduling Nelson, Towsley, and Tantawi [57] compare four cases in which parallel jobs are scheduled in either a *centralized* or *de-centralized* fashion, and the threads of a job are either spread across all processors or all executed on one processor. They found that best performance resulted from centralized scheduling and spreading the threads across processors. Among the other options, decentralized scheduling of split tasks beat centralized scheduling with no splitting under light load, but the reverse is true under heavy load.

Dynamically Changing A Job's Processor Allocation Because the efficiency of parallel jobs generally decreases as their processor allocation increases, it is necessary to decrease processor allocations to moldable jobs as the overall system load increases in order to avoid system saturation (see Sevcik [77]). Zahorjan and McCann [97] found that allocating processors to evolving jobs according to their dynamic needs led to much better performance than either run-to-completion with a rigid allocation or round-robin. For the overhead parameters they chose, round-robin beat run-to-completion only at quite low system loads.

Ghosal et al. [29] propose several processor allocation schemes based on the *processor working set* (PWS), which is the number of allocated processors for which the ratio of execution time to efficiency is minimized. (The PWS differs from the average parallelism of the job by at most a factor of two [16].) The best of the variants of PWS gives jobs at most their processor working set, but under heavy load gives fewer and fewer processors to each job, thus increasing efficiency and therefore system capacity.

Setia, Squillante, and Tripathi [74] use a queuing theoretic model to investigate how parallel processing overheads cause efficiency to decrease with larger processor allocations. In a later study [75], they go on to show that dynamic partitioning of the system beats static partitioning at moderate and heavy loads. Naik, Setia and Squillante [56] show that dynamic partitioning allows much better performance than fixed partitioning, but that much of the difference in

---

[4] Actually, EASY only guarantees that the *first* job in the queue will not be delayed.

performance can be obtained by using knowledge of job characteristics, and assigning non-preemptive priorities to certain job classes for admission to fixed partitions.

McCann and Zahorjan [51] found that "efficiency-preserving" scheduling using folding allowed performance to remain much better than with equipartitioning (EQUI) as load increases. Padhye and Dowdy [60] compare the effectiveness of treating jobs as moldable to that of exploiting their malleability by folding. They find that the former approach suffices unless jobs are irregular (i.e., evolving) in their pattern of resource consumption. Similarly, in the context of quantum-based allocation of processing intervals, Chiang et al. [9] showed that static processor allocations (for which jobs need only be moldable) led to performance nearly as good as that obtained by dynamic processor allocation (which requires that jobs be malleable).

Foregoing Optimal Utilization Downey [12] studies the problem of scheduling in an environment where moldable jobs are activated from an FCFS queue, and run to completion. He suggests how to use predictions of the expected queuing time for awaiting the availability of different numbers of processors in order to decide when a particular job should be activated. The tradeoff is between starting a job sooner with fewer processors and delaying its start (causing processors to be left idle) until a larger number of processors is available. Algorithms that leave processors idle in anticipation of future arrivals were also investigated by Rosti et al. [69] and Smirni et al. [81].

The Need for Preemption A number of studies have demonstrated that despite the overheads of preemption, the flexibility derived from the ability to preempt jobs allows for much better schedules.

The most often quoted reason for using preemption is that time slicing gives priority to short running jobs, and therefore approximates the Shortest-Job First policy, which is known to reduce the average response time. This is especially true when the workload has a very high variability (which is the case in real production systems). Parsons and Sevcik [64] show the importance of preemption under high variance by comparing versions with and without preemption of the same policy. Good support for short running jobs is important because it allows for interactive feedback.

Another use of preemption that is also known from conventional uniprocessor systems is that it allows the overlap of computation and I/O. This is especially important in large scale systems that perform I/O to mass storage devices, an operation that may take several minutes to complete. Lee et al. [45] have shown that some jobs are more sensitive to perturbations than others, therefore some jobs have a stronger requirement for gang scheduling. However, all parallel jobs benefit from *rate-equivalent* scheduling, that is all threads get to run for the same fraction of the wallclock time, but not necessarily simultanously.

Preemption is also useful to control the share of resources allocated to competing jobs. Stride and lottery scheduling use the notion of tickets to fairly allocate resources, including CPU time [90,91]. Each job gets a proportion of the CPU, according to the proportion of tickets assigned to the job. A time line is then produced for each job containing the periods when the job is scheduled to run. That is, the time quantums are placed at strides along the timeline. The timelines from all the jobs are pushed down onto a single timeline, and idle time squeezed out.

In parallel systems, preemption is also useful in reducing fragmentation. For example, with preemption it is not necessary to accumulate idle processors in order to run a large job. Feitelson and Jette [20] demonstrate that the preemptions inherent in time-slicing allow the system to escape from bad processor allocation decisions, boosting utilization over space-slicing for rigid jobs, and avoiding the need for non-work conserving algorithms. Also, preemtion is needed in order to migrate processes to actively counter fragmentation.

Finally, in many computing centers it was noted that a non-negligible number of parallel batch jobs failed to run more than a minute due to reasons such as an incorrectly specified data file. Therefore, it might be reasonable that jobs should be started immediately after submission, then interrupted after 1 minute and finally resumed and completed at a later time.

Time-Slicing and Space-Slicing Scheduling Many variations of scheduling algorithms based on time-slicing and space-slicing have been proposed and evaluated. Time-slicing is motivated by the high variability and imperfect knowledge of service times, as described above, while space-slicing is motivated by the goal of having processors used with high efficiency.

Time slicing is typically implemented by gang scheduling, that is, all the threads in a job are scheduled (and de-scheduled) simultaneously. Gang scheduling is compared to local scheduling and is found to be superior by Feitelson and Rudolph [24]. Squillante et al. [85] and Wang et al. [94] have analyzed a variation of gang scheduling that involves providing service cyclically among a set of fixed partition configurations, each having a number of partitions equal to some power of two. They find that long jobs benefit substantially from this approach, but only at the cost of longer response times for short jobs. Feitelson and Rudolph [23] and Hori et al. [36] analyze a more flexible policy in which there is time slicing among multiple active sets of partitions. Lee et al. [45] study the interaction of gang scheduling and I/O, and found that many jobs may tolerate the perturbations caused by I/O, that I/O bound jobs suffer under gang scheduling, and therefore argue in favor a flexible gang scheduling.

Several studies have revealed that EQUI does very well, even when some moderate charge for the overhead of frequent preemptions is made [86,48]. Squillante [84] provides an analysis of the performance of dynamic partitioning. Deng et al. show that EQUI is optimally competitive [11]. Dussa et al. [14] compares space-slicing against no partitioning, and finds that space-partitioning pays off.

Knowledge-Based Scheduling Majumdar, Eager and Bunt showed that, under high variability service time distributions, round-robin (RR) was far better than FCFS, but that policies based on knowledge of the processing requirement (such as least work first) were still better. Knowledge of the average parallelism of a job makes it possible to allocate each job an appropriate number of processors to make it operate at a near-optimal ratio of execution time to efficiency [16]. With the knowledge of how many processors each job uses, policies for packing the jobs into frames for gang scheduling are investigated by Feitelson [18]. Feitelson and Rudolph [22] describe a discipline in which processes that communicate frequently are identified, and it is assured that the corresponding threads are all activated at the same time. Similar schemes in which co-scheduling is triggered by communication events were described by Sobalvarro and Weihl [83] and by Dusseau, Arpaci, and Culler [15].

Taking system load and minimum and maximum parallelism of each job into account as well, still higher throughputs can be sustained [77]. Chiang et al. [8] show that use of knowledge of some job characteristics plus permission to use a single preemption per job allows run-to-completion policies to approach ideal (i.e., no overhead) EQUI, and Anastasiadis et al. [3] show that, by setting the processor allocation of moldable jobs based on some known job characteristics, disciplines with little or no preemption can do nearly as well as EQUI.

Other Factors in Scheduling McCann and Zahorjan [52] studied the scheduling problem where each job has a minimum processor allocation due to its memory requirement. They find that a discipline based on allocation by a buddy system consistently does well. Alverson et al. [2] describe the scheduling policy for the Tera MTA, which includes consideration of memory requirements. Brecht [5] has carried out an experimental evaluation of scheduling in systems where processors are identified with clusters or *pools*, and intracluster memory access is faster than intercluster access. A surprising result is that *worst-fit* scheduling, where each job is allocated to the pool with the most available processors, beats *best-fit* scheduling, where jobs are placed where they come closest to filling out a pool. This is a result of using a model of evolving jobs, where it is best to leave these jobs space to grow. Yue [96] describes the creation of evolving jobs by selecting (in the compiler) at the top of each loop what degree of parallelism should be used for that loop.

Experiments with Parallel Scheduling Many of the results of the modeling studies described above have been corroborated by experimental studies in which various policies were implemented in real systems.

Gibbons has experimented with a number of scheduling disciplines for scheduling rigid jobs in a network of workstations environment. His conclusions include:

- Activating jobs in Least Expected Work First (LEWF) order rather than FCFS reduces the resulting average response time by factors from two to six in various circumstances.
- If service times are unknown or if only estimates are available, then "backfilling" (as in EASY) reduces average response times by a factor of two or

more. (If service times are known exactly, then back-filling has less relative benefit.)

- Whether back-filling is used or not, knowledge of service times is very helpful (particularly if preemption is supported). Having job knowledge and using it leads to response times that are a factor of three to six smaller than for the case of no knowledge. When the knowledge is restricted to class knowledge based on the a small database that records execution characteristics of jobs, the average response times are roughly half those with no knowledge.
- If some knowledge (class or job) is available, then preemption is much less valuable than in the case where no knowledge is available and bad decisions are made (which can only be corrected by preemption).

Parsons has experimented with a broader class of disciplines, most of which exploit moldable and malleable jobs. His positive observations include:

- If migratable preemption is supported at low cost, then very good performance can be achieved, even if no service time knowledge is available. (Also, malleability is not of much additional benefit.)
- If only local preemption is supported, then class knowledge of service times is needed in order to do well by using LEWF order for activation.
- When preemption is not supported, class knowledge and LEWF order are helpful (roughly halving average response times), but not as much as with local preemption supported.
- In (typical) environments where the distribution of service times has very high variance, LERWF does very well when some service time knowledge is available; otherwise, if malleability doesn't lead to excessive overhead, then a simple rule like EQUI does well.

Some additional observations on the negative side are:

- The value of local preemption is restricted by the fragmentation that occurs because jobs must be restarted on the same set of processors on which they previously ran. (In this case, either clever packing strategies or even fixed partitioning are beneficial, because the dependencies among jobs are then limited [25].)
- Even with moldable jobs, performance is poor unless preemption is supported, because if inappropriate allocations are occasionally made to very long jobs, then only preemption can remedy the situation.

3 Recommendations and Future Directions

The current state-of-the-art regarding scheduling on large-scale parallel machines is to use simple and inflexible mechanisms. In essence, the number of processors used for each job is chosen by the user, some sufficiently large partition acquired, and the job is run to completion. A few recent systems support preemption, so that a parallel job can be interrupted and possibly swapped out of memory, but many installations choose not to use this option due to high associated overheads and lack of adequate I/O facilities.

This section presents six recommendations to improve the performance of state-of-the-art schedulers. The recommendations are based on the conclusions of the investigations, analysis, and simulations described above.

A great deal has been learned about how "in theory" multiprogrammed multiprocessor scheduling should be done. As always, it is not easy and sometimes impossible to put theoretical results into practice, especially in production environments. Note, however, that all of the following suggested approaches have been demonstrated to be feasible through prototype implementations and experimentation.

Recommendation 1: Provide system support for parallel job preemption. Preemption is crucial to obtaining the best performance. However, this should be coordinated across the nodes running the job. One such form of coordination is gang scheduling, where all the threads run simultaneously on their respective nodes. Alternatively, rate-equivalent scheduling can be used, meaning that all threads get to run for the same fraction of the wallclock time, but not necessarily simultanously. Note that gang scheduling implies rate-equivalent scheduling.

Preemption is also a precondition for changing the number and identity of processors assigned to a job during runtime which is desirable to best handle evolving and malleable jobs, but the marginal gain in performance is not substantial. Hence it is justified only if it can be provided with little additional effort (as a part of checkpointing procedures, for example).

Recommendation 2: Write applications to be moldable and, if it is natural, then to be evolving. Since system loads vary with time, and users generally do not know when they submit a job what the load conditions will be at the time the job is activated, it is desirable that jobs be moldable rather than rigid, so that available processors can be fully exploited at light load, but still efficient use of processors can be assured at heavy load.

If jobs are naturally evolving (such as a cyclic fork join structure, with relatively long sequential periods), then writing the job as evolving (with annotations or commands to dynamically acquire and release processors) makes it possible to greatly increase the efficiency with which the job utilizes the processors assigned to it.

Writing jobs to be malleable is much more work, and this is typically justified only for applications that consume a significant portion of a system's capacity, because they are either very large or invoked very frequently.

Recommendation 3: When system efficiency is of utmost importance, then base processor allocations on both job characteristics and the current load on the system. Jobs make more efficient use of their assigned processors when they have fewer than when they have more. Hence, as the workload volume increases, it may be necessary to reduce the number of processors assigned on average to each job. At light load, processor availability is not an issue, so each job can be given as many processors as it can use, even if they are not being used at high efficiency. At heavy load, the multiprocessing overhead merely detracts from the overall system capacity, so giving jobs a small number of processors (even one in the limit as long as memory requirements don't preclude this extreme possibility) is the most appropriate action. By doing this, the throughput capacity of the system can be maximized.

When specific processor allocations are selected by users, they tend to be overly aggressive or optimistic. The numbers selected by users are typically suitable for light load conditions, but they lead to unacceptably low processor efficiency at heavy load. Consider a case where there are N statistically identical jobs to run on P processors. Assuming the jobs are moldable, the scheduler has the options to either (1) run them one at a time with all P processors, or (2) run them in pairs with half the processors each. Both the mean and the variance of the response times are lower with the latter approach unless [76]:

$$S(P) > \left[2 - \frac{2}{N+2}\right] \cdot S(P/2)$$

This condition seldom holds when either the number of processors or the number of jobs is moderately large.

Since users cannot practically know the load on the system at the time they submit a job, it is best if they identify a range of acceptable processor allocations, and then leave the choice within that range to the scheduler. The current workload volume can be taken into account either by just observing the occupancy of the queues in which jobs await initiation, or by tracking some prediction of overall load as it varies in daily or weekly cycles.

Recommendation 4: To improve average response times, give priority to jobs that are most likely to complete soon, using preemption when necessary. In uniprocessor scheduling, it is known that RR scheduling protects against highly variable service time distributions by making average response time independent of the service time distribution (assuming preemption overhead is negligible). Further, if the service time distribution is know to have high variability, then feedback (FB) disciplines can exploit this, and yield lower average response times as the variability of the service time distribution grows [10].

When no knowledge of service times is available and malleability can be exploited, the ideal EQUI discipline, which attempts to assign an equal number of processors to each job available for execution is optimal. EQUI is analogous to RR in a uniprocessor context in its ability to schedule relatively well even with no service time knowledge. If malleability is impractical due to lack of system support or jobs aren't written to exploit it, then some form of preemptive scheduling based on time-slicing, such as gang-scheduling, should be used.

In current practice, if queues for jobs with smaller execution times tend to have higher priority, then this is consistent with the idea of using available service time knowledge to favor the jobs that are expected to complete most promptly. If better knowledge of job service times than queue identities is available, then it is best to try to activate the jobs in order of increasing expected remaining service time [63]. If the service times are known to be highly variable, but the service times of individual jobs cannot be predicted in advance, then the discipline that executes the job with least acquired service first is best because it emulates the behavior of least expected remaining work first.

Recommendation 5: Make use of information about job characteristics that is either provided directly, or measured, or remembered. Users already provide information about the execution characteristics of their jobs, in the encoded form of a queue identifier. User supplied estimates cannot be directly believed, but the information is generally positively correlated with truth, and that is sufficient to make better scheduling possible. (A good scheduling policy will penalize users who intentionally misestimate the characteristics of the jobs they submit.)

Assuming malleable jobs, some job characteristics (such as efficiency) can be measured while the job is executing and the system can take appropriate action with respect to giving additional processors, or taking some away from the job. Finally, if some historical information is retained, then observed behavior of previous jobs with certain characteristics can be used to predict (approximately) the behavior of new jobs with similar characteristics.

Recommendation 6: Develop New Models Based on the behavior and shortcomings of real machines, new models should capture relevant aspects such as the following:

1. different preemption penalty costs associated with local preemption and job migration,
2. a relation between execution time and allocated processors for moldable, evolving, and malleable jobs,
3. prevention of job starvation by guaranteeing a completion time for each job at the submission time of the job,
4. pricing policies that are based on some combination of resource consumption by the job, and job characteristics that may or may not be known at the time the job is submitted,
5. cyclic load patterns that motivate delaying some large jobs to time periods of lower overall demand (e.g., "off hours").

4 The PSCHED Standard Proposal

Theoretical research like that described in Section 2 tends to focus on algorithmics and easily measurable metrics, while abstracting away from the details. System administrators, on the other hand, cannot abstract away from real-life concerns. They are also faced with unmeasurable costs and constraints, such as interoperability (will machines work together?) and software lifetime (how soon will parts of the system need to be replaced?). Moreover, achieving the maturity and stability required of production software is much harder than building a prototyope. Finally, they need to cater to users and administrators with many different needs, leading to the creation of rather elaborate systems [4,44].

As a result of such concerns, there is much interest in standardizing various software components. In recent years, message passing libraries were standardized through the MPI effort. Similarly, the PSCHED proposal aims at standardizing the interactions among various components involved in parallel job scheduling.

4.1 Background

Deferred processing of work under the control of a scheduler has been a feature of most proprietary operating systems from the earliest days of multi-user systems in order to maximize utilization of the computer.

The arrival of the UNIX system proved to be a dilemma to many hardware providers and users because it did not include the sophisticated batch facilities offered by the proprietary systems. This omission was rectified in 1986 by NASA Ames Research Center who developed the Network Queuing System (NQS) as a portable Unix application that allows the routing and processing of batch "jobs" in a network. To encourage its usage, the product was later put into the public domain.

The supercomputing technical committee began as a "Birds Of a Feather" (BOF) at the January 1987 Usenix meeting. There was enough general interest to form a supercomputing attachment to the /usr/group working groups. The /usr/group working groups later turned into the IEEE POSIX standard effort.

Due to the strong hardware provider and customer acceptance of NQS, it was decided to use NQS as the basis for the POSIX Batch Environment amendment in 1987. Other batch systems considered at the time included CTSS, MDQS, and PROD. None were thought be have both the functionality and acceptability of NQS. This effort was finally approved as a formal standard on December 13, 1994 as IEEE POSIX 1003.2d. The standard committee decided to postpone addressing issues such as programmatic interface and resource control. The supercomputing working group has since been inactive.

PBS was developed at NASA Ames Research Center as a second generation batch queue system that conforms to the IEEE Std. 1003.2d-1994. The project started in June 1993, and was first released in June 1994 [35].

However, both NQS and PBS were designed to schedule serial jobs, and have no understanding of the needs of parallel jobs. The only support for parallelism is regarding "processors" as another resource during allocation, on the same standing as time, memory, or software licenses. To run efficiently, all parts of a parallel job needed to be scheduled to run at the same time. Without support from the batch queue system, most of the large installation of MPP systems had reverted to space slicing and an "all jobs run to completion" policy.

4.2   Outline of Psched

The idea of creating a metacenter is the force behind the PSCHED project at NASA Ames Research Center. A metacenter is a computing resource where jobs can be scheduled and run on a variety of machines physically located in different facilities [34]. This concept ran into several road blocks:

- Some schedulers are tightly integrated with the message passing library: Condor and PVM.
- Almost all schedulers are tightly integrated with the batch queue system.
- Lack of support for parallel jobs.

The Numerical Aerospace Simulation facility (NAS), as part of a Cooperative Research Agreement involving several NASA centers, IBM, Pratt and Whitney, Platform Computing and others, has formed an informal group with the goal of developing a set of "standard" API calls relating to job and resource management systems. The goal of the PSCHED API is to allow a site to write a scheduler that could schedule a variety of parallel jobs: MPI-2, PVM, and SMP multi-tasking jobs to run on a collection of different machines.

To achieve this goal, we intend to standardize the interfaces between the different modules: message passing libraries, task manager, resource manager, and scheduler (see Fig. 2). The specific roles of these components are

Task Manager: An entity that provides task management services such as: spawn a task on a node, local or remote; deliver a signal from one task to another task within the same parallel application; and interface with a resource management function to provide information about nodes assigned to the set of tasks which make up a parallel application, to obtain additional resources (nodes), to free resources (nodes) no longer required, and to notify tasks of the need to checkpoint, suspend, and/or migrate.

Resource Manager: An entity that provides resource management services such as: monitor the resources available in the system, reserve or allocate resources for tasks, and release or deallocate resources no longer needed by tasks.

Scheduler: An entity that schedules jobs. The scheduler is responsible for determining which task should be run on the system according to some site specific policy and the resources available in the system.

The PSCHED API is not an effort to standardize how any of these modules should be implemented. It is an effort to identify the minimal functionality needed from each module and then standardize its interface. For example, the scheduler is a user of the interfaces provided by the task manager and the resource manager. The scheduler waits for scheduling events from the task manager.

The PSCHED API is divided into two areas:

- A set of calls for use by parallel processing jobs to spawn, control, monitor, and signal tasks under the control or management of the job/resource management system. This set of calls should meet the needs of MPI-II, PVM, and other message passing implementations.

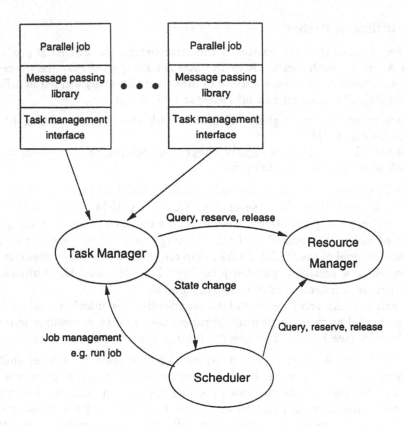

Fig. 2. *Components of the PSCHED environment.*

- A set of calls to be used by batch job schedulers. These calls will allow the development of consistent job/resource schedulers independent of the job/resource management system used. The calls are intended to provide a standard means of obtaining information about the resources available in the processing environment and about the supply of jobs and their requirements.

Let us take a look at an example of how a parallel job would spawn a subtask, adding more nodes to the running job. The job will call the message passing library, for example MPI_Spawn in MPI-II. The message passing library will interface with the task manager to spawn the new task to add more nodes to the existing task. The task manager will inform the scheduler of the request. The scheduler will make a decision based on its scheduling policy. If the policy allows the job to expand, the scheduler will request additional resources from the resource manager, then inform the task manager to start the new sub-task and allow the job to proceed.

```
main()
{
    tm_handle handle[3];

    /* connect to 3 different machines */
    tm_connect(server_1, NULL, &handle[0]);
    tm_connect(server_2, NULL, &handle[1]);
    tm_connect(server_3, NULL, &handle[2]);

    while (1) {
        /* wait for events from any of the servers */
        tm_get_event(handle, 3, &which_handle, &event, &job_id, &args);
        ack = process_event(handle[which_handle], event, job_id, args);
        /* acknowledge the event */
        tm_ack_event(handle[which_handle], event, job_id, ack);
    }
}

process_event(handle, tm_event, job_id, ...)
{
    switch (tm_event) {
        PSCHED_EVENT_JOB_ARRIVED:
            /* call policy routine */
            scheduler_policy(job_id, &run_this_job, resource_needed);
            /* if decided to run job, reserve the resources needed
             * and run the job */
            if (run_this_job) {
                rm_reserve(resource_list, &resource);
                tm_run_job(handle, job_id, resource);
            }
            break;
        PSCHED_EVENT_JOB_EXITED:
            /* release the reources */
            if (resource != PSCHED_RESOURCE_NULL)
                rm_release(resource);
            /* pick a new job to run */
            break;
        PSCHED_EVENT_YIELD:
            /* job is ready to yield some resource, determine
             * whether we want to shrink or expand the job.
             * call the task manager if any action is taken. */
            break;
        PSCHED_EVENT_CHECKPOINT:
            /* a good time to migrate the job if we wanted to */
            break;
        PSCHED_EVENT_REQUEUED:
            /* pick a new job to run */
            break;
```

Fig. 3. *Example skeleton of PSCHED code components.*

```
        PSCHED_EVENT_ADD_RESOURCE:
            /* run policy routines */
            scheduler_policy(job_id, &run_this_job, additional_resource);
            if (run_this_job) {
                    rm_reserve(resource_list, &resource);
                    tm_add_resource(handle, job_id, resource);
            } else {
                    /* tell server we can't fulfill the request
                     * or suspend the run and wait for the resource */
            }
            break;
        PSCHED_EVENT_RELEASE_RESOURCE:
            rm_release(rm_handle, resource);
            break;
        default:
            return UNKNOWN_EVENT;
    }
    return SUCCESS;
}

scheduler_policy(...)
{
    /* this is what the scheduler writters will concentrate on */
}
```

Fig. 3. (cont.)

4.3 Implication on the Programming and Scheduling of Parallel Jobs

Obvious benefits of a standard like PSCHED include:

- real traces can be used in simulations to develop better algorithms
- new algorithms could be directly applied to running systems
- modularity of very complex pieces of software allows a mix and match of:
  - batch / task management system
  - scheduler
  - communication library (e.g., MPI, PVM)
  - scheduling simulators

The PSCHED API will be flexible enough to address some of the problems identified in Section 3 such as shrinking and expanding jobs, checkpointing and migrating jobs.

Hopefully this set of "standard" interfaces will free researchers from the need to port their work to different systems and let them concentrate on innovative scheduling algorithm and scheduler design. This will also make production machines more readily available for researchers. An example of such a scheduler is given in Fig. 3. Once written it should be very easily ported to another environment. The tm_ and rm_ calls are interfaces to the task manager and the resource manager respectively.

Areas that need standardization but are not currently addressed by PSCHED include:

- Moving jobs from one batch queue system to another.
- The accounting information kept by the batch queue system.

5 Discussion and Conclusions

The relationship between theory and practice is an interesting one. Sometimes theory is ahead of practice, and suggests novel approaches and solutions that greatly enhance the state of the art. Sometimes theory straggles behind, and only provides belated justification for well known practices. It is not yet clear what role it will play in the field of parallel job scheduling.

The question of how much theory contributes to practice also depends on the metrics used to measure performance and quality. In the field of job scheduling, the three most common metrics are throughput, utilization, and response time. Throughput and utilization are actually related to each other: if we assume that the statistics of the workload are essentially static, then executing more jobs per unit time on average also leads to a higher utilization. This can go on until the system saturates. If users are satisfied with the system, and the system does not saturate, more jobs will be submitted, leading to higher utilization and throughput. The role of the scheduler is therefore to delay the onset of saturation, by reducing fragmentation and assuring efficient usage of processors [25]. Also, good support for batch jobs can move some of the load to off hours, further increasing the overall utilization.

In practice utilization is a very commonly used metric, as it is easy to measure and reflects directly on the degree to which large investments in parallel hardware are used efficiently. Throughput figures are hardly ever used. Reported utilization figures vary from 50% for the NASA Ames iPSC/860 hypercube [21], through around 70% for the CTC SP2 [37], 74% for the SDSC Paragon [92] and 80% for the Touchstone Delta [54], up to more than 90% for the LLNL Cray T3D [20]. Utilization figures in the 80–90% range are now becoming more common, due to the use of more elaborate batch queueing mechanisms [49,79,92] and gang scheduling [20]. These figures seem to leave only little room for improvement.

However, it should be noted that these figures only reflect one factor contributing to utilization. The real utilization of the hardware is the product of two factors: the fraction of PEs allocated to users, and the efficiency with which these PEs are used. The figures above relate to the first factor, and depend directly on the scheduling policies; they show that current systems can allocate nearly all the resources, with little loss to fragmentation. But the efficiency with which the allocated resources are used depends more on the application being run, and can be quite low. However, the system can still have an effect, because in most applications the efficiency trails off as processors are added. Thus allocating less processors under high loads should improve the second factor, and lead to higher overall utilization [43,68,51]. This is possible with moldable or malleable jobs, but not with rigid ones.

The case of the response time metric is more complex, because little direct evidence exists. Theory suggests that preemption be used to ensure good response times for small jobs [64], especially since workloads have a high variability in computational requirements [21]. This comes close on the heels of actual systems that implement gang scheduling for just this reason [46,32,27,20].

Actually two metrics may be used to gauge the responsiveness of a system: the actual response time (or turnaround time, i.e. the time from submittal to termination), or the slowdown (the ratio of the response time on a loaded system to the response time on a dedicated system). Using actual response times places more weight on long jobs, and "doesn't care" if a short job waits a few minutes, so it may not reflect the users' notion of responsiveness. Slowdown reflects the rather reasonable notion that responsiveness should be measured against requirements, meaning that users should expect their jobs to take time that is proportional to the computation performed. However, for very short jobs, the denominator becomes very small, leading to a large slowdown, even though the actual response time may be quite short, well within the interactive range. It may therefore be best to combine the two metrics. Let T represent the response time on the loaded system, T_d the response time on a dedicated system, and T_h the threshold of interactivity (i.e. the time users are willing to wait). The combined metric for responsiveness as percieved by users would then be

$$R = \begin{cases} T/T_d & \text{if } T_d > T_h \\ T/T_h & \text{if } T_d < T_h \end{cases}$$

For long jobs, this is the normal slowdown. For short jobs, this is the slowdown *relative to the interactivity threshold*, rather than relative to the very short runtime on a dedicated system. If we use T_h as the unit of time, then for short jobs the expression degenerates to the response time. We suggest the name "bounded slowdown" for this metric, as it is similar to the slowdown metric, but bounded away from high values for very short jobs.

Two possible roles for theory, that have relatively few parallels in practice, are how to use knowledge about specific jobs [76], and how to tune algorithmic parameters [93]. In practice, knowledge about jobs is limited to that supplied by the users, typically in the form of choosing a queue with a certain combination of resource limits. This approach has two main drawbacks: first, it leads to a combinatorical explosion of queues, that are hard to deal with. Second, even with very many queues, the resolution in which requirements are expressed is necessarily very coarse, and user estimates are notoriously inaccurate anyway. Recent more theoretical work shows how data can be acquired automatically by the system, rather than relying on the users [59,31,12].

At the same time that theoretical work is focusing, at least to some degree, on practical concerns, practice in the field seems to be rather oblivious of this development. One reason is that the larger and more advanced installations have been developing rather elaborate scheduling facilities, which achieve reasonable results, so the pressure for searching for additional improvements outside is diminished. Another reason is the overwhelming concern for backwards compatability, portability, and interoperability, which leads to standards based on common practices and discourages innovations. It should be hoped, however, that the developed standards will be flexible enough to allow unanticipated advances to be incorporated in the future.

References

1. I. Ahmad, *"Editorial: resource management of parallel and distributed systems with static scheduling: challenges, solutions, and new problems"*. *Concurrency — Pract. & Exp.* **7(5)**, pp. 339–347, Aug 1995.
2. G. Alverson, S. Kahan, R. Korry, C. McCann, and B. Smith, *"Scheduling on the Tera MTA"*. In *Job Scheduling Strategies for Parallel Processing*, D. G. Feitelson and L. Rudolph (eds.), pp. 19–44, Springer-Verlag, 1995. Lecture Notes in Computer Science Vol. 949.
3. S. V. Anastiadis and K. C. Sevcik, *"Parallel application scheduling on networks of workstations"*. *J. Parallel & Distributed Comput.*, Jun 1997. (to appear).
4. J. M. Barton and N. Bitar, *"A scalable multi-discipline, multiple-processor scheduling framework for IRIX"*. In *Job Scheduling Strategies for Parallel Processing*, D. G. Feitelson and L. Rudolph (eds.), pp. 45–69, Springer-Verlag, 1995. Lecture Notes in Computer Science Vol. 949.
5. T. B. Brecht, *"An experimental evaluation of processor pool-based scheduling for shared-memory NUMA multiprocessors"*. In *Job Scheduling Strategies for Parallel Processing*, D. G. Feitelson and L. Rudolph (eds.), Springer Verlag, 1997. Lecture Notes in Computer Science (this volume).
6. J. Bruno, E. G. Coffman, Jr., and R. Sethi, *"Scheduling independent tasks to reduce mean finishing time"*. *Comm. ACM* **17(7)**, pp. 382–387, Jul 1974.
7. S. Chakrabarti, C. Phillips, A. S. Achulz, D. B. Shmoys, C. Stein, and J. Wein, *"Improved approximation algorithms for minsum criteria"*. In *Intl. Colloq. Automata, Lang., & Prog.*, pp. 646–657, Springer-Verlag, 1996. Lecture Notes in Computer Science Vol. 1099.
8. S-H. Chiang, R. K. Mansharamani, and M. K. Vernon, *"Use of application characteristics and limited preemption for run-to-completion parallel processor scheduling policies"*. In *SIGMETRICS Conf. Measurement & Modeling of Comput. Syst.*, pp. 33–44, May 1994.
9. S-H. Chiang and M. K. Vernon, *"Dynamic vs. static quantum-based parallel processor allocation"*. In *Job Scheduling Strategies for Parallel Processing*, D. G. Feitelson and L. Rudolph (eds.), pp. 200–223, Springer-Verlag, 1996. Lecture Notes in Computer Science Vol. 1162.
10. R. W. Conway, W. L. Maxwell, and L. W. Miller, *Theory of Scheduling*. Addison-Wesley, 1967.
11. X. Deng, N. Gu, T. Brecht, and K. Lu, *"Preemptive scheduling of parallel jobs on multiprocessors"*. In *7th SIAM Symp. Discrete Algorithms*, pp. 159–167, Jan 1996.
12. A. B. Downey, *"Using queue time predictions for processor allocation"*. In *Job Scheduling Strategies for Parallel Processing*, D. G. Feitelson and L. Rudolph (eds.), Springer Verlag, 1997. Lecture Notes in Computer Science (this volume).
13. J. Du and J. Y-H. Leung, *"Complexity of scheduling parallel task systems"*. *SIAM J. Discrete Math.* **2(4)**, pp. 473–487, Nov 1989.

14. K. Dussa, K. Carlson, L. Dowdy, and K-H. Park, "Dynamic partitioning in a transputer environment". In SIGMETRICS Conf. Measurement & Modeling of Comput. Syst., pp. 203–213, May 1990.

15. A. Dusseau, R. H. Arpaci, and D. E. Culler, "Effective distributed scheduling of parallel workloads". In SIGMETRICS Conf. Measurement & Modeling of Comput. Syst., pp. 25–36, May 1996.

16. D. L. Eager, J. Zahorjan, and E. D. Lazowska, "Speedup versus efficiency in parallel systems". IEEE Trans. Comput. 38(3), pp. 408–423, Mar 1989.

17. D. G. Feitelson, "Memory usage in the LANL CM-5 workload". In Job Scheduling Strategies for Parallel Processing, D. G. Feitelson and L. Rudolph (eds.), Springer Verlag, 1997. Lecture Notes in Computer Science (this volume).

18. D. G. Feitelson, "Packing schemes for gang scheduling". In Job Scheduling Strategies for Parallel Processing, D. G. Feitelson and L. Rudolph (eds.), pp. 89–110, Springer-Verlag, 1996. Lecture Notes in Computer Science Vol. 1162.

19. D. G. Feitelson, A Survey of Scheduling in Multiprogrammed Parallel Systems. Research Report RC 19790 (87657), IBM T. J. Watson Research Center, Oct 1994.

20. D. G. Feitelson and M. A. Jette, "Improved utilization and responsiveness with gang scheduling". In Job Scheduling Strategies for Parallel Processing, D. G. Feitelson and L. Rudolph (eds.), Springer Verlag, 1997. Lecture Notes in Computer Science (this volume).

21. D. G. Feitelson and B. Nitzberg, "Job characteristics of a production parallel scientific workload on the NASA Ames iPSC/860". In Job Scheduling Strategies for Parallel Processing, D. G. Feitelson and L. Rudolph (eds.), pp. 337–360, Springer-Verlag, 1995. Lecture Notes in Computer Science Vol. 949.

22. D. G. Feitelson and L. Rudolph, "Coscheduling based on runtime identification of activity working sets". Intl. J. Parallel Programming 23(2), pp. 135–160, Apr 1995.

23. D. G. Feitelson and L. Rudolph, "Evaluation of design choices for gang scheduling using distributed hierarchical control". J. Parallel & Distributed Comput. 35(1), pp. 18–34, May 1996.

24. D. G. Feitelson and L. Rudolph, "Gang scheduling performance benefits for fine-grain synchronization". J. Parallel & Distributed Comput. 16(4), pp. 306–318, Dec 1992.

25. D. G. Feitelson and L. Rudolph, "Toward convergence in job schedulers for parallel supercomputers". In Job Scheduling Strategies for Parallel Processing, D. G. Feitelson and L. Rudolph (eds.), pp. 1–26, Springer-Verlag, 1996. Lecture Notes in Computer Science Vol. 1162.

26. A. Feldmann, J. Sgall, and S-H. Teng, "Dynamic scheduling on parallel machines". Theoretical Comput. Sci. 130(1), pp. 49–72, Aug 1994.

27. H. Franke, P. Pattnaik, and L. Rudolph, "Gang scheduling for highly efficient distributed multiprocessor systems". In 6th Symp. Frontiers Massively Parallel Comput., pp. 1–9, Oct 1996.

28. M. R. Garey and D. S. Johnson, Computers and Intractability: A Guide to the Theory of NP-Completeness. Freeman, 1979.

29. D. Ghosal, G. Serazzi, and S. K. Tripathi, "The processor working set and its use in scheduling multiprocessor systems". IEEE Trans. Softw. Eng. 17(5), pp. 443–453, May 1991.

30. R. Gibbons, A Historical Application Profiler for Use by Parallel Schedulers. Master's thesis, Dept. Computer Science, University of Toronto, Dec 1996. Available as Technical Report CSRI-TR 354.

31. R. Gibbons, *"A historical application profiler for use by parallel schedulers"*. In *Job Scheduling Strategies for Parallel Processing*, D. G. Feitelson and L. Rudolph (eds.), Springer Verlag, 1997. Lecture Notes in Computer Science (this volume).

32. B. Gorda and R. Wolski, *"Time sharing massively parallel machines"*. In *Intl. Conf. Parallel Processing*, vol. II, pp. 214–217, Aug 1995.

33. R. L. Graham, *"Bounds on multiprocessing timing anomalies"*. *SIAM J. Applied Mathematics* 17(2), pp. 416–429, Mar 1969.

34. A. S. Grimshaw, J. B. Weissman, E. A. West, and E. C. Loyot, Jr., *"Metasystems: an approach combining parallel processing and heterogeneous distributed computing systems"*. *J. Parallel & Distributed Comput.* 21(3), pp. 257–270, Jun 1994.

35. R. L. Henderson, *"Job scheduling under the portable batch system"*. In *Job Scheduling Strategies for Parallel Processing*, D. G. Feitelson and L. Rudolph (eds.), pp. 279–294, Springer-Verlag, 1995. Lecture Notes in Computer Science Vol. 949.

36. A. Hori et al., *"Time space sharing scheduling and architectural support"*. In *Job Scheduling Strategies for Parallel Processing*, D. G. Feitelson and L. Rudolph (eds.), pp. 92–105, Springer-Verlag, 1995. Lecture Notes in Computer Science Vol. 949.

37. S. Hotovy, *"Workload evolution on the Cornell Theory Center IBM SP2"*. In *Job Scheduling Strategies for Parallel Processing*, D. G. Feitelson and L. Rudolph (eds.), pp. 27–40, Springer-Verlag, 1996. Lecture Notes in Computer Science Vol. 1162.

38. N. Islam, A. Prodromidis, and M. S. Squillante, *"Dynamic partitioning in different distributed-memory environments"*. In *Job Scheduling Strategies for Parallel Processing*, D. G. Feitelson and L. Rudolph (eds.), pp. 244–270, Springer-Verlag, 1996. Lecture Notes in Computer Science Vol. 1162.

39. J. Jann, P. Pattnaik, H. Franke, F. Wang, J. Skovira, and J. Riodan, *"Modeling of workload in mpps"*. In *Job Scheduling Strategies for Parallel Processing*, D. G. Feitelson and L. Rudolph (eds.), Springer Verlag, 1997. Lecture Notes in Computer Science (this volume).

40. *Job Scheduling Strategies for Parallel Processing*, D. G. Feitelson and L. Rudolph (eds.), Springer-Verlag, 1995. Lecture Notes in Computer Science Vol. 949. *Job Scheduling Strategies for Parallel Processing*, D. G. Feitelson and L. Rudolph (eds.), Springer-Verlag, 1996. Lecture Notes in Computer Science Vol. 1162. *Job Scheduling Strategies for Parallel Processing*, D. G. Feitelson and L. Rudolph (eds.), Springer-Verlag, 1997. Lecture Notes in Computer Science (this volume).

41. T. Kawaguchi and S. Kyan, *"Worst case bound of an LRF schedule for the mean weighted flow-time problem"*. *SIAM J. Comput.* 15(4), pp. 1119–1129, Nov 1986.

42. H. Kellerer, T. Tautenhahn, and G. J. Wöginger, *"Approximability and nonapproximability results for minimizing total flow time on a single machine"*. In *28th Ann. Symp. Theory of Computing*, pp. 418–426, 1996.

43. R. Krishnamurti and E. Ma, *"An approximation algorithm for scheduling tasks on varying partition sizes in partitionable multiprocessor systems"*. *IEEE Trans. Comput.* 41(12), pp. 1572–1579, Dec 1992.

44. R. N. Lagerstrom and S. K. Gipp, *"PScheD: political scheduling on the CRAY T3E"*. In *Job Scheduling Strategies for Parallel Processing*, D. G. Feitelson and L. Rudolph (eds.), Springer Verlag, 1997. Lecture Notes in Computer Science (this volume).

45. W. Lee, M. Frank, V. Lee, K. Mackenzie, and L. Rudolph, *"Implications of I/O for gang scheduled workloads"*. In *Job Scheduling Strategies for Parallel Processing*, D. G. Feitelson and L. Rudolph (eds.), Springer Verlag, 1997. Lecture Notes in Computer Science (this volume).

46. C. E. Leiserson, Z. S. Abuhamdeh, D. C. Douglas, C. R. Feynman, M. N. Ganmukhi, J. V. Hill, W. D. Hillis, B. C. Kuszmaul, M. A. St. Pierre, D. S. Wells, M. C. Wong-Chan, S-W. Yang, and R. Zak, *"The network architecture of the Connection Machine CM-5"*. *J. Parallel & Distributed Comput.* **33(2)**, pp. 145–158, Mar 1996.

47. S. Leonardi and D. Raz, *"Approximating total flow time on parallel machines"*. In 29th *Ann. Symp. Theory of Computing*, 1997.

48. S. T. Leutenegger and M. K. Vernon, *"The performance of multiprogrammed multiprocessor scheduling policies"*. In *SIGMETRICS Conf. Measurement & Modeling of Comput. Syst.*, pp. 226–236, May 1990.

49. D. Lifka, *"The ANL/IBM SP scheduling system"*. In *Job Scheduling Strategies for Parallel Processing*, D. G. Feitelson and L. Rudolph (eds.), pp. 295–303, Springer-Verlag, 1995. Lecture Notes in Computer Science Vol. 949.

50. W. Ludwig and P. Tiwari, *"Scheduling malleable and nonmalleable parallel tasks"*. In 5th *SIAM Symp. Discrete Algorithms*, pp. 167–176, Jan 1994.

51. C. McCann and J. Zahorjan, *"Processor allocation policies for message passing parallel computers"*. In *SIGMETRICS Conf. Measurement & Modeling of Comput. Syst.*, pp. 19–32, May 1994.

52. C. McCann and J. Zahorjan, *"Scheduling memory constrained jobs on distributed memory parallel computers"*. In *SIGMETRICS Conf. Measurement & Modeling of Comput. Syst.*, pp. 208–219, May 1995.

53. R. McNaughton, *"Scheduling with deadlines and loss functions"*. *Management Science* **6(1)**, pp. 1–12, Oct 1959.

54. P. Messina, *"The Concurrent Supercomputing Consortium: year 1"*. *IEEE Parallel & Distributed Technology* **1(1)**, pp. 9–16, Feb 1993.

55. R. Motwani, S. Phillips, and E. Torng, *"Non-clairvoyant scheduling"*. *Theoretical Comput. Sci.* **130(1)**, pp. 17–47, Aug 1994.

56. V. K. Naik, S. K. Setia, and M. S. Squillante, *"Performance analysis of job scheduling policies in parallel supercomputing environments"*. In *Supercomputing '93*, pp. 824–833, Nov 1993.

57. R. Nelson, D. Towsley, and A. N. Tantawi, *"Performance analysis of parallel processing systems"*. *IEEE Trans. Softw. Eng.* **14(4)**, pp. 532–540, Apr 1988.

58. T. D. Nguyen, R. Vaswani, and J. Zahorjan, *"Parallel application characterization for multiprocessor scheduling policy design"*. In *Job Scheduling Strategies for Parallel Processing*, D. G. Feitelson and L. Rudolph (eds.), pp. 175–199, Springer-Verlag, 1996. Lecture Notes in Computer Science Vol. 1162.

59. T. D. Nguyen, R. Vaswani, and J. Zahorjan, *"Using runtime measured workload characteristics in parallel processor scheduling"*. In *Job Scheduling Strategies for Parallel Processing*, D. G. Feitelson and L. Rudolph (eds.), pp. 155–174, Springer-Verlag, 1996. Lecture Notes in Computer Science Vol. 1162.

60. J. D. Padhye and L. Dowdy, *"Dynamic versus adaptive processor allocation policies for message passing parallel computers: an empirical comparison"*. In *Job Scheduling Strategies for Parallel Processing*, D. G. Feitelson and L. Rudolph (eds.), pp. 224–243, Springer-Verlag, 1996. Lecture Notes in Computer Science Vol. 1162.

61. E. W. Parsons and K. C. Sevcik, *"Benefits of speedup knowledge in memory-constrained multiprocessor scheduling"*. *Performance Evaluation* **27&28**, pp. 253–272, Oct 1996.

62. E. W. Parsons and K. C. Sevcik, *"Coordinated allocation of memory and processors in multiprocessors"*. In *SIGMETRICS Conf. Measurement & Modeling of Comput. Syst.*, pp. 57–67, May 1996.

63. E. W. Parsons and K. C. Sevcik, *"Implementing multiprocessor scheduling disciplines"*. In *Job Scheduling Strategies for Parallel Processing*, D. G. Feitelson and L. Rudolph (eds.), Springer Verlag, 1997. Lecture Notes in Computer Science (this volume).

64. E. W. Parsons and K. C. Sevcik, *"Multiprocessor scheduling for high-variability service time distributions"*. In *Job Scheduling Strategies for Parallel Processing*, D. G. Feitelson and L. Rudolph (eds.), pp. 127–145, Springer-Verlag, 1995. Lecture Notes in Computer Science Vol. 949.

65. V. G. J. Peris, M. S. Squillante, and V. K. Naik, *"Analysis of the impact of memory in distributed parallel processing systems"*. In *SIGMETRICS Conf. Measurement & Modeling of Comput. Syst.*, pp. 5–18, May 1994.

66. J. Pruyne and M. Livny, *"Managing checkpoints for parallel programs"*. In *Job Scheduling Strategies for Parallel Processing*, D. G. Feitelson and L. Rudolph (eds.), pp. 140–154, Springer-Verlag, 1996. Lecture Notes in Computer Science Vol. 1162.

67. J. Pruyne and M. Livny, *"Parallel processing on dynamic resources with CARMI"*. In *Job Scheduling Strategies for Parallel Processing*, D. G. Feitelson and L. Rudolph (eds.), pp. 259–278, Springer-Verlag, 1995. Lecture Notes in Computer Science Vol. 949.

68. E. Rosti, E. Smirni, L. W. Dowdy, G. Serazzi, and B. M. Carlson, *"Robust partitioning schemes of multiprocessor systems"*. *Performance Evaluation* 19(2-3), pp. 141–165, Mar 1994.

69. E. Rosti, E. Smirni, G. Serazzi, and L. W. Dowdy, *"Analysis of non-work-conserving processor partitioning policies"*. In *Job Scheduling Strategies for Parallel Processing*, D. G. Feitelson and L. Rudolph (eds.), pp. 165–181, Springer-Verlag, 1995. Lecture Notes in Computer Science Vol. 949.

70. S. K. Sahni, *"Algorithms for scheduling independent tasks"*. *J. ACM* 23(1), pp. 116–127, Jan 1976.

71. U. Schwiegelshohn, *"Preemptive weighted completion time scheduling of parallel jobs"*. In 4th *European Symp. Algorithms*, pp. 39–51, Springer-Verlag, Sep 1996. Lecture Notes in Computer Science Vol. 1136.

72. U. Schwiegelshohn, W. Ludwig, J. L. Wolf, J. J. Turek, and P. Yu, *"Smart SMART bounds for weighted response time scheduling"*. *SIAM J. Comput.* To appear.

73. S. K. Setia, *"The interaction between memory allocation and adaptive partitioning in message-passing multicomputers"*. In *Job Scheduling Strategies for Parallel Processing*, D. G. Feitelson and L. Rudolph (eds.), pp. 146–165, Springer-Verlag, 1995. Lecture Notes in Computer Science Vol. 949.

74. S. K. Setia, M. S. Squillante, and S. K. Tripathi, *"Analysis of processor allocation in multiprogrammed, distributed-memory parallel processing systems"*. *IEEE Trans. Parallel & Distributed Syst.* 5(4), pp. 401–420, Apr 1994.

75. S. K. Setia, M. S. Squillante, and S. K. Tripathi, *"Processor scheduling on multiprogrammed, distributed memory parallel computers"*. In *SIGMETRICS Conf. Measurement & Modeling of Comput. Syst.*, pp. 158–170, May 1993.

76. K. C. Sevcik, *"Application scheduling and processor allocation in multiprogrammed parallel processing systems"*. *Performance Evaluation* 19(2-3), pp. 107–140, Mar 1994.

77. K. C. Sevcik, *"Characterization of parallelism in applications and their use in scheduling"*. In *SIGMETRICS Conf. Measurement & Modeling of Comput. Syst.*, pp. 171–180, May 1989.

78. D. Shmoys, J. Wein, and D. Williamson, *"Scheduling parallel machines on-line"*. *SIAM J. Comput.* 24(6), pp. 1313–1331, Dec 1995.

79. J. Skovira, W. Chan, H. Zhou, and D. Lifka, "*The EASY - LoadLeveler API project*". In *Job Scheduling Strategies for Parallel Processing*, D. G. Feitelson and L. Rudolph (eds.), pp. 41–47, Springer-Verlag, 1996. Lecture Notes in Computer Science Vol. 1162.

80. D. D. Sleator and R. E. Tarjan, "*Amortized efficiency of list update and paging rules*". *Comm. ACM* **28(2)**, pp. 202–208, Feb 1985.

81. E. Smirni, E. Rosti, G. Serazzi, L. W. Dowdy, and K. C. Sevcik, "*Performance gains from leaving idle processors in multiprocessor systems*". In *Intl. Conf. Parallel Processing*, vol. III, pp. 203–210, Aug 1995.

82. W. Smith, "*Various optimizers for single-stage production*". *Naval Research Logistics Quarterly* **3**, pp. 59–66, 1956.

83. P. G. Sobalvarro and W. E. Weihl, "*Demand-based coscheduling of parallel jobs on multiprogrammed multiprocessors*". In *Job Scheduling Strategies for Parallel Processing*, D. G. Feitelson and L. Rudolph (eds.), pp. 106–126, Springer-Verlag, 1995. Lecture Notes in Computer Science Vol. 949.

84. M. S. Squillante, "*On the benefits and limitations of dynamic partitioning in parallel computer systems*". In *Job Scheduling Strategies for Parallel Processing*, D. G. Feitelson and L. Rudolph (eds.), pp. 219–238, Springer-Verlag, 1995. Lecture Notes in Computer Science Vol. 949.

85. M. S. Squillante, F. Wang, and M. Papaefthymiou, "*Stochastic analysis of gang scheduling in parallel and distributed systems*". *Performance Evaluation* **27&28**, pp. 273–296, Oct 1996.

86. A. Tucker and A. Gupta, "*Process control and scheduling issues for multiprogrammed shared-memory multiprocessors*". In *12th Symp. Operating Systems Principles*, pp. 159–166, Dec 1989.

87. J. Turek, W. Ludwig, J. L. Wolf, L. Fleischer, P. Tiwari, J. Glasgow, U. Schwiegelshohn, and P. S. Yu, "*Scheduling parallelizable tasks to minimize average response time*". In *6th Symp. Parallel Algorithms & Architectures*, pp. 200–209, Jun 1994.

88. J. Turek, J. L. Wolf, and P. S. Yu, "*Approximate algorithms for scheduling parallelizable tasks*". In *4th Symp. Parallel Algorithms & Architectures*, pp. 323–332, Jun 1992.

89. J. J. Turek, U. Schwiegelshohn, J. L. Wolf, and P. Yu, "*Scheduling parallel tasks to minimize average response time*". In *5th ACM-SIAM Symp. Discrete Algorithms*, pp. 112–121, Jan 1994.

90. C. A. Waldspurger and W. E. Weihl, "*Lottery scheduling: flexible proportional-share resource management*". In *1st Symp. Operating Systems Design & Implementation*, pp. 1–11, USENIX, Nov 1994.

91. C. A. Waldspurger, *Lottery and Stride Scheduling: Flexible Proportional-Share Resource Management*. Ph.D. dissertation, Massachusetts Institute of Technology, Technical Report MIT/LCS/TR-667, Sep 1995.

92. M. Wan, R. Moore, G. Kremenek, and K. Steube, "*A batch scheduler for the Intel Paragon with a non-contiguous node allocation algorithm*". In *Job Scheduling Strategies for Parallel Processing*, D. G. Feitelson and L. Rudolph (eds.), pp. 48–64, Springer-Verlag, 1996. Lecture Notes in Computer Science Vol. 1162.

93. F. Wang, H. Franke, M. Papaefthymiou, P. Pattnaik, L. Rudolph, and M. S. Squillante, "*A gang scheduling design for multiprogrammed parallel computing environments*". In *Job Scheduling Strategies for Parallel Processing*, D. G. Feitelson and L. Rudolph (eds.), pp. 111–125, Springer-Verlag, 1996. Lecture Notes in Computer Science Vol. 1162.

94. F. Wang, M. Papaefthymiou, and M. Squillante, *"Performance evaluation of gang scheduling for parallel and distributed multiprogramming"*. In *Job Scheduling Strategies for Parallel Processing*, D. G. Feitelson and L. Rudolph (eds.), Springer Verlag, 1997. Lecture Notes in Computer Science (this volume).

95. Q. Wang and K. H. Cheng, *"A heuristic of scheduling parallel tasks and its analysis"*. *SIAM J. Comput.* **21(2)**, pp. 281–294, Apr 1992.

96. K. K. Yue and D. J. Lilja, *"Loop-level process control: an effective processor allocation policy for multiprogrammed shared-memory multiprocessors"*. In *Job Scheduling Strategies for Parallel Processing*, D. G. Feitelson and L. Rudolph (eds.), pp. 182–199, Springer-Verlag, 1995. Lecture Notes in Computer Science Vol. 949.

97. J. Zahorjan and C. McCann, *"Processor scheduling in shared memory multiprocessors"*. In *SIGMETRICS Conf. Measurement & Modeling of Comput. Syst.*, pp. 214–225, May 1990.

Using Queue Time Predictions for Processor Allocation

Allen B. Downey

University of California, Berkeley CA 94720

Abstract. When a moldable job is submitted to a space-sharing parallel computer, it must choose whether to begin execution on a small, available cluster or wait in queue for more processors to become available. To make this decision, it must predict how long it will have to wait for the larger cluster. We propose statistical techniques for predicting these queue times, and develop an allocation strategy that uses these predictions. We present a workload model based on observed workloads at the San Diego Supercomputer Center and the Cornell Theory Center, and use this model to drive simulations of various allocation strategies. We find that prediction-based allocation not only improves the turnaround time of individual jobs; it also improves the utilization of the system as a whole.

1 Introduction

Like many shared resources, parallel computers are susceptible to a tragedy of the commons – individuals acting in their own interests tend to overuse and degrade the resource. Specifically, users trying to minimize run times for their jobs might allocate more processors than they can use efficiently. This indulgence lowers the utilization of the system and increases queue times.

A partial solution to this problem is a programming model that supports *adaptive* jobs, that is, jobs that can be configured to run on clusters of various sizes. These jobs improve system utilization by using fewer processors when system load is high, thereby running more efficiently and increasing the number of jobs in the system simultaneously.

But adaptive jobs are not a sufficient solution to the tragedy of the commons, because users have no direct incentive to restrict the cluster sizes of their jobs. Furthermore, even altruistic users might not have the information they need to make the best decisions.

One approach to this problem is a *system-centric* scheduler that chooses cluster sizes automatically, trying to optimize (usually heuristically) a system-wide performance metric like utilization or average turnaround time. We present several problems with this approach, and suggest an alternative, *job-centric* scheduling, in which users (or a system agent acting on their behalf) make scheduling decisions on a job-by-job basis in order to satisfy user-specified goals.

In order to make these decisions, users need to be able to predict the queue time until a given cluster size is available, and the run time of the job as a function of its cluster size. Toward this end we have developed statistical techniques for predicting queue times on space-sharing parallel computers, and a model for using historical information to predict the run times of parallel jobs. The goal of this paper is to evaluate the usefulness of these predictions for processor allocation.

1.1 Adaptive Jobs

Feitelson and Rudolph [8] propose the following classification of adaptive parallel jobs: *rigid* jobs can run only on a fixed cluster size; *moldable* jobs can be configured to run on a range of cluster sizes, but once they begin execution, they cannot change cluster size. *Evolving* jobs change cluster size as they execute; these changes are initiated by the job, and usually correspond to program phases. *Malleable* jobs can also change size dynamically, but unlike evolving jobs, they can respond to system-initiated reconfiguration requests.

Many of the SPMD parallel languages used for scientific computing generate static jobs (rigid or moldable), but few generate dynamic jobs (evolving or malleable). Thus, workloads in current supercomputing environments are made up almost entirely of static jobs. There is some evidence that the fraction of moldable jobs is significant [6], and it is likely to increase as users shift to higher-level programming models. This paper addresses scheduling strategies for moldable jobs.

1.2 System-centric Scheduling

Many simulation and analytic studies have examined the performance of system-centric allocation strategies, that is, strategies designed to maximize an aggregate performance metric without regard for individual jobs. In most cases, this metric is average turnaround time [10] [17] [16] [9] [1] [15], although some studies also consider throughput [13]. Rosti, Smirni et al. use *power*, which is the ratio of throughput to mean response time [14]. In prior work we used a parallel extension of *slowdown*, which is the ratio of the actual response time of a job to the time it would have taken on a dedicated machine [3]. Feitelson and Rudolph use a different formulation of slowdown [7].

There are several common problems with system-centric schedulers:

Starvation: For many system-centric schedulers there is an identifiable class of jobs that receives unacceptable service. For example, utilization-maximizing schedulers tend to starve jobs with low parallel efficiency and odd-sized jobs that cause fragmentation. Turnaround-minimizing schedulers tend to starve large jobs. Although it may be desirable to give different quality of service to different classes of jobs, it is not acceptable for a real system to allow jobs to starve.

One metric fits all: Another problem is that system-centric schedulers are usually based on a single performance metric. In real systems there are often classes of jobs with different performance requirements. For example, users sometimes submit short batch jobs and wait for the results; for these jobs, turnaround time is critical. On the other hand, many users submit jobs before lunch or before leaving for the day and have no interest in turnaround time; in this case the performance goal is to complete before a given deadline. Other scheduling goals include minimizing the completion time of a set of jobs and minimizing the accounting cost of a job.

Perverse incentives: System-centric schedulers often force users to accept decisions that are good for the system as a whole, but contrary to their immediate interests. For example, if there is a job in queue and one idle processor, a utilization-maximizing system might require the job to run, whereas the job might obtain a shorter turnaround time by waiting for more processors. If such strategies are implemented, users will be unsatisfied with the system, and some of them will take steps to subvert it. Since these systems often rely on job information provided by users, it is not hard for a disgruntled user to manipulate the system for his own benefit. In anecdotal reports from supercomputer centers, this sort of behavior is common, and not restricted to malevolent users; rather, it is understood that users will take advantage of loopholes in system policies.

In summary, system-centric schedulers often provide unacceptable service for some jobs, force other jobs to pay for quality of service they do not require, and create incentives for users to subvert the system.

1.3 Job-centric Scheduling

A possible solution to these problems is *job-centric* scheduling, in which the user (or a system agent acting on the user's behalf) makes scheduling decisions on a job-by-job basis in order to satisfy user-specified goals. Some examples are:

1. A user might minimize the cost of a calculation by choosing the smallest cluster size that allows the job to fit in memory.
2. A user might choose a cluster size that yields an acceptable probability that the job will complete before a deadline.
3. A user might choose the cluster size that minimizes the turnaround time of a job (the sum of its queue time and run time).

The strategy we propose in this paper tries to minimize the turnaround time of each job (the third example), but the techniques we develop can be extended to address the other two goals. Thus, job-centric scheduling can solve the one-metric problem.

Also, since the scheduling strategy we propose is based on a FIFO queue, it has no problems with starvation. Compared with some system-centric schedulers, it tends to improve the performance of large, highly-parallel jobs at the expense of smaller jobs, but in supercomputing environments this discrimination is acceptable, if not desirable.

Finally, because job-centric scheduling makes decisions on behalf of individual jobs, it does not create incentives for users to subvert its decisions. As a result this strategy is robust in the presence of self-interested users.

1.4 Why FIFO?

In order to minimize the average turnaround time of a set of jobs, it is optimal to schedule the shortest job first. In supercomputing environments, though, the system seldom knows the run times of jobs *a priori*. Nevertheless, the system can often use information about queued jobs (executable names, user names, queue names) to identify and give priority to short jobs. Such non-FIFO strategies have been shown to improve overall system performance [9][1].

One problem with such strategies is that they tend to starve large jobs; that is, jobs that request a large cluster size might wait in queue indefinitely while smaller jobs run. This problem is not hypothetical, but has been observed frequently at supercomputing sites like the San Diego Supercomputer Center. This situation is particularly problematic because supercomputer centers have a mandate to run large, highly-parallel jobs that cannot run anywhere else. Thus, these sites have been forced to adopt ad hoc measures to expedite large jobs. In some cases, an operator has to override the system's scheduler to rescue starving jobs. It is clear that this is not an appropriate long-term solution.

Another problem with non-FIFO strategies is that they make the system less predictable. Predictability is a useful property because it allows users to decide what jobs (and what problem sizes) to run, when to run them and, in a distributed system, where to run them.

Because of these problems, we have chosen to focus on FIFO queueing strategies. However, there is a natural extension of FIFO scheduling, called backfilling, that has the potential to increase system performance without causing starvation. In a FIFO system, when a large job is waiting at the head of the queue, there may be smaller jobs in queue that could run. Backfilling is the process of allowing these jobs to run, on the condition that they not delay the large job. The EASY scheduler uses this strategy [18] for rigid jobs. In future work we plan to add backfilling to our strategy for moldable jobs.

1.5 Outline

Section 2 presents speedup model we use in Sect. 3 to develop an abstract workload model. This workload is based on observations from the San Diego Supercomputer Center and the Cornell Theory Center. Section 4 describes the statistical techniques we use to predict queue times. Section 5 describes the simulator we use to evaluate various allocation strategies. Section 6 presents our evaluation of these strategies from the job's point of view, and Sect. 7 discusses the effect these strategies have on the system as a whole.

2 Job Model

In order to evaluate the proposed allocation strategies, we will use a simulation based on an *abstract workload model*. On existing systems, we often collect statistics about actual (concrete) workloads; for example, we might know the duration and cluster size of each job. The workloads we observe are the result of interactions between the job mix, the properties of the hardware, and the behavior of the allocation strategy. Thus, it may not be correct to use a concrete workload from one system to simulate and evaluate another. Our goal is to create an abstract workload that separates the characteristics of the job mix from the effect of the system.

Previously [2], we proposed a model of moldable jobs that characterizes each job by three parameters: L, the sequential lifetime of the job, A, the average parallelism, and σ, which measures the job's variance in parallelism. Using this model we can calculate the speedup and run time of a job on any number of processors. This section summarizes our *job model*.

Once we have a model of individual jobs, we can construct a *workload model* that describes the system load, the arrival process, and the distribution of job parameters. Section 3 presents this *abstract workload model*.

2.1 A Model of Moldable Jobs

Our model of parallel speedup is based on a family of curves parameterized by average parallelism, A, and variance in parallelism, V. For given values of these parameters, we construct a hypothetical *parallelism profile*[1] with those values, and use the profile to derive a speedup curve. We use two families of profiles, one for programs with low V, the other for programs with high V. In previous work we showed that this family of speedup profiles captures, at least approximately, the behavior of a variety of parallel scientific applications on a variety of architectures [2].

2.2 Low-variance Model, $\sigma \leq 1$

Figure 1a shows a hypothetical parallelism profile for a program with low variance in parallelism. The degree of parallelism is A for all but some fraction σ of the duration ($0 \leq \sigma \leq 1$). The remaining time is divided between a sequential component and a high-parallelism component. The average parallelism of this profile is A; the variance is $V = \sigma(A-1)^2$.

A program with this profile would have the following speedup as a function of cluster size:

$$S(n) = \begin{cases} \frac{An}{A+\sigma/2(n-1)} & 1 \leq n \leq A \\ \frac{An}{\sigma(A-1/2)+n(1-\sigma/2)} & A \leq n \leq 2A - 1 \\ A & n \geq 2A - 1 \end{cases} \tag{1}$$

---

[1] Sevcik defines the parallelism profile as the distribution of potential parallelism during the execution of a program[17].

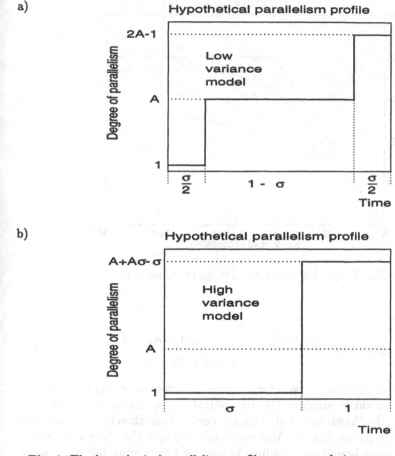

Fig. 1. The hypothetical parallelism profiles we use to derive our speedup model.

2.3 High-variance Model, $\sigma \geq 1$

In the low variance model, σ cannot exceed 1, and thus the variance cannot exceed $V = (A - 1)^2$. In this section, we propose an extended model in which σ can exceed 1 and the variance is unbounded. The two models can be combined naturally because (1) when the parameter $\sigma = 1$, the two models are identical, and (2) for both models the variance is $\sigma(A - 1)^2$.

From the latter property we derive the semantic content of the parameter σ – it is approximately the square of the coefficient of variation of parallelism, CV^2. This approximation follows from the definition of coefficient of variation, $CV = \sqrt{V}/A$. Thus, CV^2 is $\sigma(A - 1)^2/A^2$, which for large A is approximately σ.

Figure 1b shows a hypothetical parallelism profile for a program with high variance in parallelism. A program with this profile would have the following speedup as a function of cluster size:

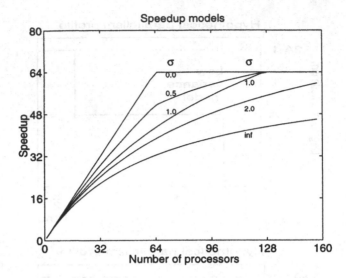

Fig. 2. Speedup curves for a range of values of σ.

$$S(n) = \begin{cases} \frac{nA(\sigma+1)}{\sigma(n+A-1)+A} & 1 \le n \le A + A\sigma - \sigma \\ A & n \ge A + A\sigma - \sigma \end{cases} \qquad (2)$$

Figure 2 shows speedup curves for a range of values of σ (with $A = 64$). When $\sigma = 0$ the curve matches the theoretical upper bound for speedup – bound at first by the "hardware limit" (linear speedup) and then by the "software limit" (the average parallelism A). As σ approaches infinity, the curve approaches the theoretical lower bound on speedup derived by Eager et al. [5]: $S_{min}(n) = An/(A+n-1)$.

Of course, for many jobs there will be ranges of n where this model is inapplicable. For example, a job with large memory requirements will run poorly (or not at all) when n is small. Also, when n is large, speedup may decrease as communication overhead overwhelms computational speedup. Finally, there are some applications that require cluster sizes with specific characteristics; e.g. powers of two and perfect squares. Thus we qualify our job model with the understanding that for each job there may be a limited range of viable cluster sizes.

3 Workload Model

3.1 Distribution of Lifetimes

Ideally, we would like to know the distribution of L, the *sequential lifetime*, for a real workload. Sequential lifetime is the time a job would take on a single processor, so if we knew L, A and σ, we could calculate the speedup, $S(n, A, \sigma)$,

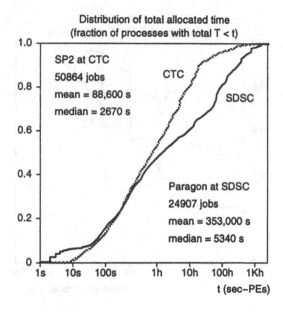

Fig. 3. Distribution of total allocated time for jobs at SDSC and CTC.

on n processors and the run time, L/S. But for most jobs we do not know L; often it is not even defined, because memory requirements prevent some jobs from running on a single processor. On the other hand, we do know the *total allocated time*, T, which is the product of wall clock lifetime and cluster size. For programs with linear speedup, T equals L, but for programs with sublinear speedups, T can be much larger than L.

Figure 3 shows the distribution of total allocated time for jobs from the Intel Paragon at SDSC and the IBM SP2 at CTC. On both machines, the distribution is approximately uniform (linear) in log space, or a *uniform-log distribution*. Thus the cumulative distribution function (cdf) of T has the form:

$$cdf_T(t) = Pr\{T \le t\} = \beta_0 + \beta_1 \ln t \tag{3}$$

where $t_{min} \le t \le t_{max}$, and β_0 and β_1 are the intercept and slope of the observed line. The upper and lower bounds of this distribution are $t_{min} = e^{-\beta_0/\beta_1}$ and $t_{max} = e^{(1.0-\beta_0)/\beta_1}$.

We know of no theoretical reason that the distribution should have this shape, but we believe that it is pervasive among batch workloads, since we have observed similar distributions on the Cray C90 at SDSC, and other authors have reported similar distributions on other systems [6][20].

Depending on the allocation policy, the distribution of T could differ from the distribution of L. For all practical policies, though, the two distributions have the same shape, with different parameters. Thus, in our simulations, we assume that the distribution of L is uniform-log. For the scheduling policies we

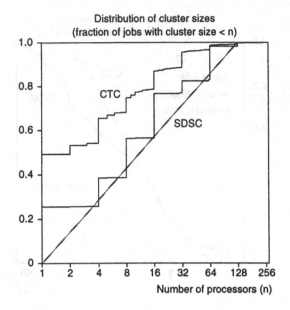

Fig. 4. Distribution of cluster sizes for jobs at SDSC and CTC.

consider, the resulting distribution of T is also uniform-log, excepting a few of the longest and shortest jobs.

In our simulations, L is distributed between e^2 and e^{12} seconds (approximately 7 seconds to 45 hours). The median of this distribution is 18 minutes; the mean is 271 minutes.

3.2 Distribution of Average Parallelism

For our workload model, we would like to know the parallelism profile of the jobs in the workload. But the parallelism profile reflects *potential* parallelism, as if there were an unbounded number of processors available, and in general it is not possible to derive this information by observing the execution of the program.

In the accounting data we have from SDSC and CTC, we do not have information about the average parallelism of jobs. On the other hand, we do know the cluster size the user chose for each job, and we hypothesize that these cluster sizes, in the aggregate, reflect the parallelism of the workload.

Figure 4 shows this distribution for the workloads from SDSC and CTC. In both cases, most jobs have cluster sizes that are powers of two. Neither the Intel Paragon nor the IBM SP2 require power-of-two cluster sizes, but in both cases the interface to the queueing system suggests powers of two and few users have an incentive to resist the combination of suggestion and habit. We believe that the step-wise pattern in the distribution of cluster sizes reflects this habit and not the true distribution of A. Thus for our workload model, we use a uniform-log distribution with parameters $A_{min} = 1$ and $A_{max} = N$, where N is the number of processors in the system. The gray line in the figure shows this model.

Our model fits the SDSC distribution well, but the CTC distribution contains significantly more sequential jobs than the model. This excess is likely due to the fact that the SP2 at CTC has more memory on each node than most workstations, and provides some software that is not available on workstations. Thus, many users submit sequential jobs to the SP2 that they would ordinarily run on workstations. Our workload does not model this behavior because it is not typical of supercomputer sites.

3.3 Distribution of Variance (σ)

In general there is no way to measure the variance in potential parallelism of existing codes explicitly. In previous work, we proposed a way to infer this value from observed speedup curves [2]. To test this technique, we collected speedup curves for a variety of scientific applications running on a variety of parallel computers. We found that the parameter σ, which approximates the coefficient of variance of parallelism, was typically in the range 0–2, with occasional higher values.

Although these observations provide a range of values for σ, they do not tell us its distribution in a real workload. For this study, we use a uniform distribution between 0 and 2.

4 Predicting Queue Times

In previous work we presented statistical techniques for predicting the remaining queue time for a job at the head of the queue [4]. Since we use these predictions in Sect. 6.3, we summarize the techniques here.

We describe the state of the machine at the time of an arrival as follows: there are p jobs running, with ages a_i and cluster sizes n_i (in other words, the ith job has been running on n_i processors for a_i seconds). We would like to predict $Q(n')$, the time until n' additional processors become available, where $n' = n - n_{free}$, n is the number of processors requested, and n_{free} is the number of processors already available. In the next two sections we present ways to estimate the median and mean of $Q(n')$.

4.1 Median Predictor

We can calculate the median of $Q(n')$ exactly by enumerating all possible outcomes (which jobs complete and which are still running), and calculating the probability that the request will be satisfied before a given time t. Then we set this probability to 0.5 and solve for the median queue time. This approach is not feasible when there are many jobs in the system, but it leads to an approximation that is fast to compute and almost as accurate.

We represent each outcome by a bit vector, b, where for each bit, $b_i = 0$ indicates that the ith job is still running, and $b_i = 1$ indicates that the ith job has completed before time t. Since we assume independence between jobs in the system, the probability of a given outcome is the product of the probabilities of each event (the completion or non-completion of a job). The probability of each event comes from the conditional distribution of lifetimes. For a uniform-log distribution of lifetimes, the conditional distribution $cdf_{L|a}$ is

$$
\begin{aligned}
1 - cdf_{L|a}(t) &= Pr\{L > t | L > a\} \\
&= \frac{1 - cdf_L(t)}{1 - cdf_L(a)} \\
&= \frac{1 - \beta_0 - \beta_1 \ln t}{1 - \beta_0 - \beta_1 \ln a}
\end{aligned}
\tag{4}
$$

where $t_{min} \leq a \leq t \leq t_{max}$. Thus, the probability of a given outcome is

$$
Pr\{b\} = \prod_{i | b_i = 0} cdf_{L|a_i}(t) \cdot \prod_{i | b_i = 1} (1 - cdf_{L|a_i}(t))
\tag{5}
$$

For a given outcome, the number of free processors is the sum of the processors freed by each job that completes:

$$
F(b) = \sum_i b_i \cdot n_i
\tag{6}
$$

Thus at time t, the probability that the number of free processors is at least the requested cluster size is the sum of the probabilities of all the outcomes that satisfy the request:

$$
Pr\{F \geq n'\} = \sum_{b | F(b) \geq n'} Pr\{b\}
\tag{7}
$$

Finally, we find the median value of $Q(n')$ by setting $Pr\{F > n'\} = 0.5$ and solving for t.

Of course, the number of possible outcomes (and thus the time for this calculation) increases exponentially with p, the number of running jobs. Thus this is not a feasible approach when there are many running jobs. But when the number of additional processors required (n') is small, it is often the case that there are several jobs running in the system that will single-handedly satisfy the request when they complete. In this case, the probability that the request will be satisfied by time t is dominated by the probability that one of these benefactors will complete before time t.

In other words, the chance that the queue time for n' processors will exceed time t is approximately equal to the probability that none of the benefactors will complete before t:

$$
Pr\{F < n'\} \approx \prod_{i | n_i \geq n'} 1 - cdf_{L|a_i}(t)
\tag{8}
$$

The running time of this calculation is linear in p. Of course, it is only approximately correct, since it ignores the possibility that several small jobs might complete and satisfy the request. Thus, we expect this predictor to be inaccurate when there are many small jobs running in the system, few of which can single-handedly handle the request. The next section presents an alternative predictor that we expect to be more accurate in this case.

4.2 Mean Predictor

When a job is running, we know that at some time in the future it will complete and free all of its processors. Given the age of the job, we can use the conditional distribution (4) to calculate the probability that it will have completed before time t.

We approximate this behavior by a model in which processors are a continuous (rather than discrete) resource that jobs release gradually as they execute. In this case, we imagine that the conditional cumulative distribution indicates what *fraction* of a job's processors will be available at time t.

For example, a job that has been running for 30 minutes might have a 50% chance of completing in the next hour, releasing all of its processors. As an approximation of this behavior, we predict that the job will (deterministically) release 50% of its processors within the next hour.

Thus we predict that the number of free processors at time t will be the sum of the processors released by each job:

$$F = \sum_i n_i \cdot cdf_{L|a_i}(t) \tag{9}$$

To estimate the mean queue time we set $F = n'$ and solve for t.

4.3 Combining the Predictors

Since we expect the two predictors to do well under different circumstances, it is natural to use each when we expect it to be most accurate. In general, we expect the Median Predictor to do well when there are many jobs in the system that can single-handedly satisfy the request (benefactors). When there are few benefactors, we expect the Mean Predictor to be better (especially since, if there are none, we cannot calculate the Median Predictor at all). Thus, in our simulations, we use the Median Predictor when the number of benefactors is 2 or more, and the Mean Predictor otherwise. The particular value of this threshold does not affect the accuracy of the combined predictor drastically.

5 Simulations

To evaluate the benefit of using predicted queue times for processor allocation, we use the models in the previous section to generate workloads, and use a simulator to construct schedules for each workload according to the proposed allocation strategies. We compare these schedules according to several performance metrics.

Our simulations try to capture the daily work cycle that has been observed in several supercomputing environments (the Intel iPSC/860 at NASA Ames and the Paragon at SDSC [6] [20]):

- In early morning there are few arrivals, utilization is at its lowest, and queue lengths are short.
- During the day, the arrival rate increases and jobs accumulate in queue. Utilization is highest late in the day.
- In the evening, the arrival rate falls but the utilization stays high as the jobs in queue begin execution.

To model these variations, we divide each simulated day into two 12-hour phases: during the daytime, jobs arrive according to a Poisson process and either begin execution or join the queue, depending on the state of the system. During the night, no new jobs arrive, but the existing jobs continue to run until all queued jobs have been scheduled.

We choose the day-time arrival rate in order to achieve a specified offered load, ρ. We define the offered load as the total sequential load divided by the processing capacity of the system: $\rho = \lambda \cdot E[L]/N$, where λ is the arrival rate (in jobs per second), $E[L]$ is the average sequential lifetime (271 minutes in our simulations), and N is the number of processors in the system (128 in our simulations). The number of jobs per day is between 160 (when $\rho = 0.5$) and 320 (when $\rho = 1.0$).

6 Results: Job Point-of-view

In this section, we simulate a commonly-proposed, system-centric scheduling strategy and show that this strategy often makes decisions that are contrary to the interests of users. We examine how users might subvert such a system, and measure the potential benefit of doing so.

Our baseline strategy is AVG, which assigns free processors to queued jobs in FIFO order, giving each job no more than A processors, where A is the average parallelism of the job. Several studies have shown that this strategy performs well for a range of workloads [17] [9] [12] [19] [1] [3].

The problem with this strategy is that it forces users to accept decisions that are contrary to their interests. For example, if there is a large job at the head of the queue, it will be forced to run on any available cluster, even a single processor. From the system's point of view, this decision is expected to yield high utilization; from the job's point of view, though, it would be better to wait for a larger cluster.

To see how often this situation arises, we ran 120 simulated days with the AVG strategy and an offered load, ρ, of 0.75 (30421 jobs). Most jobs (63%) are allocated the maximum cluster size, A processors. So there is no reason for users to intervene on behalf of these jobs.

For each of the remaining jobs, we used oracular prediction to find the optimal cluster size. In other words, we found the value of n that minimized the turnaround time $Q(n) + R(n)$, where $Q(n)$ is the queue time until n processors are available, and $R(n)$ is the run time of the job on n processors. As under AVG, n can be no greater than A. We call this strategy OPT.

For the jobs allocated fewer than A processors, most of the time (62%) the best thing is to accept the decision of the system and begin running immediately. Only 38% of these jobs (14% of all jobs) would benefit by waiting for a larger cluster.

But for those jobs, which we call *rebels*, the benefit can be substantial. For each rebel, we calculated the *time savings*, which is the difference between the job's turnaround time on the system-chosen cluster, and the turnaround time it would have on the optimal cluster size. The median savings per rebel is 15 minutes (the median duration of all jobs is only 3 minutes). The average time savings is 1.6 hours (the average duration of all jobs is 1.3 hours). Thus, although most jobs are well-served by system-centric scheduling, many jobs can significantly improve their performance by subverting the system.

In the following sections, we will consider several strategies users might employ to subvert a system-centric scheduler and improve the performance of their jobs. These strategies are based on the assumption that users have the ability to impose minimum cluster sizes on their jobs. It is probably necessary for a real system to provide such a mechanism, because many jobs cannot run on small clusters due to memory constraints.

The metric we use to compare these strategies is *time savings per job*: the total time savings (for all rebels) divided by the number of jobs (including non-rebels). This metric is more meaningful than time savings per rebel – according to the latter metric, it is optimal to choose only one rebel with the largest time savings. The strategy that users would choose is the one that maximizes time savings per job. Under OPT, the average time savings per job is 13.8 minutes.

6.1 STUB: Stubborn Self-interest

Previously [3], we evaluated a simple strategy, STUB, in which users impose a minimum cluster size on their jobs of fA, where f is some fraction between 0 and 1. We believe that this strategy models user behavior in existing supercomputing environments: users choose a fixed cluster size for their jobs that is roughly proportional to the job's available parallelism, but unrelated to current system load. For values of f greater than 0.5, the performance of this strategy degrades drastically.

For this paper, we examine this strategy from the point of view of individual jobs. Testing a range of values of f, we find that the time savings per job peaks at 8.8 minutes, with $f = 0.4$. Under this strategy, 37% of the jobs rebel, of whom 34% end up worse off – their turnaround times would have been shorter if they had not waited. Nevertheless, from the point of view of individual users, STUB is an acceptable if not optimal strategy. Most jobs that hold out for more processors improve their turnaround times by doing so, and the average time savings are significant.

6.2 HEUR: Using Job Characteristics

Using additional information about jobs, we expect that we can identify more successfully the jobs that will benefit by rebelling. Assuming that users know, approximately, the run times of their jobs, we construct a heuristic policy, HEUR, that allows only long jobs with high parallelism to rebel.

Specifically, any job with sequential lifetime greater than L_{thresh} and parallelism greater than A_{thresh} will wait for at least some fraction, f, of its maximum cluster size, A. The parameters A_{thresh}, L_{thresh}, and f must be tuned according to system and workload characteristics.

If we know the run times of jobs, we can make a further improvement to this strategy, which is to cut the losses of a rebel that is waiting too long in queue. To do this, we calculate its potential time savings, $t_{save} = R(n_{free}) - R(fA)$, where n_{free} is the number of free processors, fA is the number of processors the job is waiting for, and $R(n)$ is the job's run time on n processors.

Based on the time savings, we calculate a trial period the rebel is willing to wait, kt_{save}, where k is a free parameter. If this period elapses before the rebel begins execution, the rebel runs on the available processors.

Searching the space of feasible parameters, we find that the following values are best: $L_{thresh} = 0$, $A_{thresh} = 1$, $f = 1.0$ and $k = 0.2$. Thus, contrary to our intuition, job characteristics are not useful for choosing which jobs should rebel; rather, they are most useful for deciding how long a rebel should wait before giving up.

Using these parameters, the average time savings per job is 12.8 minutes, which is 45% higher than under STUB. As under STUB, 37% of the jobs rebel, but twice as many of them (68%) end up worse off. Although the majority of rebels suffer, the overall performance of HEUR is good because the losers lose small and the winners win big. Thus, self-interested users might adopt this strategy, if they are not too averse to risk.

6.3 PRED: Using Predicted Queue Times

In this section we evaluate a strategy, called PRED, that uses the queue time predictors described in Sect. 4. PRED chooses an optimal cluster size for each job in the same way as OPT, except that instead of using deterministic queue times, PRED estimates $Q(n)$ based on the current state of the system.

Under PRED, a rebel may reconsider its decision after some time and, based on a new set of predictions, decide to start running. Because recomputing predictions incurs overhead, it is not clear how often jobs should be prompted to reconsider. In our system, jobs reconsider whenever a job completes or a new job arrives in queue, and whenever the predicted queue time elapses.

The average time savings per job under PRED is 12.8 minutes. Thus, from the point of view of individual jobs, PRED is no better than HEUR. The difference is that PRED is more deft in its selection of rebels. Only 8% of all jobs rebel, and the vast majority of them end up with shorter turnaround times (92%). For the losers the time lost is small (3.7 minutes on average), but for the majority, the benefit is substantial (the median time savings is 55 minutes; the average is 2.7 hours). Thus, risk-averse users would prefer PRED over HEUR.

Another advantage of PRED over HEUR is that it has no free parameters. In a real system, it may be difficult to tune HEUR's four parameters; their values will depend on both system and workload characteristics.

6.4 BIAS: Bias-corrected Prediction

Each time a simulated job uses a prediction to make an allocation decision, we record the prediction and the outcome. Figure 5a shows a scatterplot of these predicted and actual queue times. We measure the quality of the predictions by two metrics, accuracy and bias. Accuracy is the tendency of the predictions and outcomes to be correlated; the coefficient of correlation (CC) of the values in Fig. 5a is 0.48 (calculated under a logarithmic transformation).

Bias is the tendency of the predictions to be consistently too high or too low. The lines in the figure, which track the mean and median of each column, show that short predictions (under ten minutes) are unbiased, but that longer predictions have a strong tendency to be too high. We can quantify this bias by fitting a least-squares line to the scatterplot. For a perfect predictor, the slope of this line would be 1 and the intercept 0; for our predictors the slope is 0.6 and the intercept 1.7.

Fortunately, if we know that a predictor is biased, we can use previous predictions to estimate the parameters of the bias, and apply a corrective transformation to the calculated values. In this case, we estimate the intercept (β_0) and slope (β_1) of the trend line, and apply the transformation $q_{corr} = q * \beta_1 + \beta_0$, where q is the calculated prediction and q_{corr} is the bias-corrected prediction. Figure 5b shows the effect of running the simulator again using this transformation. The slope of the new trend line is 1.01 and the intercept is -0.01, indicating that we have almost completely eliminated the bias.

Although we expected to be able to correct bias, we did not expect this transformation to improve the accuracy of the predictions; the coefficient of correlation should be invariant under an affine transformation. Surprisingly, bias correction raises CC from 0.48 to 0.59. This effect is possible because past predictions influence system state, which influences future predictions; thus the two scatterplots do not represent the same set of predictions. But we do not know why unbiased predictions in the past lead to more accurate predictions in the future.

The improvement in bias and accuracy is reflected in greater time savings. Under BIAS (PRED with bias-corrected prediction) the average time savings per job increases from 12.8 minutes to 13.5 minutes, within 3% of optimal. In practice, the disadvantage of BIAS is that it requires us to record the result of past predictions and estimate the parameters β_0 and β_1 dynamically.

a) Raw predictors

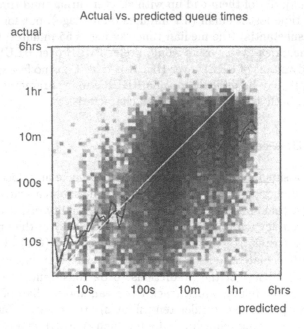

b) Predictors with bias correction

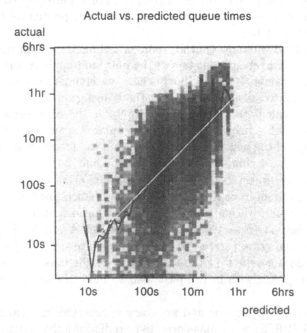

Fig. 5. Scatterplot of predicted and actual queue times (log scale). The white lines show the identity function; i.e. a perfect predictor. The solid lines show the average of the actual queue times in each column; the broken lines show the median.

6.5   Summary of Allocation Strategies

Table 1. Comparison of the strategies (job point-of-view).

	Information used	Average time savings per job (minutes)	Fraction of jobs that rebel	Average time savings per rebel (minutes)	Fraction of rebels that lose
STUB	A	8.8	37%	23.8	34%
HEUR	$A,R(n)$	12.8	37%	34.6	68%
PRED	$A,R(n),E[Q(n)]$	12.8	8%	160	8%
BIAS	$A,R(n),E[Q(n)],\beta_0,\beta_1$	13.5	10%	135	8%
OPT	$A,R(n),Q(n)$	13.8	14%	98.6	0%

Table 1 summarizes the performance of the various allocation strategies. Not surprisingly, the strategies that use more information generally yield better performance.

PRED and BIAS are more conservative than OPT; that is, they choose fewer rebellious jobs. PRED's conservativism is clearly a consequence of the tendency of our predictions to be too long. By overestimating queue times, we discourage jobs from rebelling. But it is not as clear why BIAS, which does not overestimate, is more conservative than OPT. In any case, both prediction-based strategies do a good job of selecting successful rebels; only 8% of rebels ended up spending more time in queue than they save in run time.

7   Results: System Point-of-view

Until now, we have been considering the effect of allocation strategies on individual jobs. Thus in our simulations we have not allowed jobs to effect their allocation decisions; we have only measured what would happen if they had. Furthermore, when we tuned these strategies, we chose parameters that were best for individual jobs.

In this section we modify our simulations to implement the proposed strategies and evaluate their effect on the performance of the system as a whole. We use two metrics of system performance: average turnaround time and utilization. We define utilization as the average of efficiency over time and processors, where efficiency is the ratio of speedup to cluster size, $S(n)/n$. The efficiency of an idle processor is defined to be 0. In our simulations, we can calculate efficiencies because we know the speedup curves for each job. In real systems this information is not usually available.

Table 2. Performance from the system's point-of-view.

	Average utilization (120 days)	Average turnaround time in minutes (30421 jobs)
AVG	.557	79.9
STUB	.523	113
HEUR	.526	109
PRED	.570	77.5
BIAS	.561	84.1

Table 2 shows the results for each allocation strategy, using the same workload as in the previous section. In the presence of self-interested users, the performance of AVG degrades severely. If users choose cluster sizes naively (STUB) the utilization of the system drops by 6% and turnaround times increase by 41%. The situation is only slightly better if users take steps to reduce long delays (HEUR).

PRED performs slightly better than AVG, which performs slightly better than BIAS. It may seem odd that PRED does better than BIAS, since BIAS is based on more accurate predictions. The reason is that PRED's predictions are consistently conservative, which has the effect of discouraging some borderline rebels. This conservativism reduces queue times and increases utilization. In practice, though, users might eventually notice that predicted queue times are too high and apply bias correction on their own behalf. Thus, in the presence of self-interested users, we expect PRED to yield performance similar to BIAS. Fortunately, this degradation is not nearly as severe as under AVG; the utilization of the system drops slightly (1.6%) and turnaround times increase by 8.5%.

One surprising result is that the predictive strategies yield higher utilization than AVG. Because these strategies often leave processors idle (which decreases utilization) and allocate larger clusters (which decreases efficiency), we expected these strategies to *decrease* overall utilization.

The reason they do not is that these strategies are better able to avoid L-shaped schedules. Figure 6 shows two schedules for the same pair of jobs. Under AVG, the second arrival would be forced to run immediately on the small cluster, which improves utilization in the short term by reducing the number of idle processors. But after the first job quits, many processors are left idle until the next arrival. Our predictive strategies allow the second job to wait for a larger cluster, which not only reduces the turnaround time of the second job; it also increases the average utilization of the system.

54

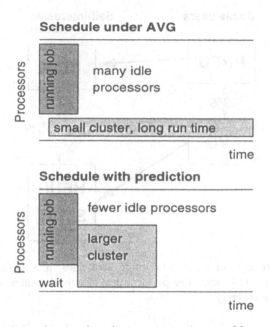

Fig. 6. Sample schedules showing how longer queue times and larger cluster sizes can, paradoxically, improve system utilization. Queue time prediction makes it possible to avoid L-shaped schedules and thereby reduce the number of idle processors.

7.1 Job-centric vs. System-centric

What, then, is the performance advantage of job-centric scheduling over system-centric scheduling? It depends on how aggressively users subvert the system. If users are docile, and do not interfere with the system, the difference is small: PRED saves about 3%, or 140 seconds per job, over AVG (95% confidence interval 1.7% to 4.4%).

But in the presence of self-interested users, the difference is much larger: compared to HEUR, BIAS saves 30%, or almost half an hour per job (95% confidence interval 29.1% to 30.6%).

8 Conclusions

We have proposed a job-centric allocation policy with the following properties:

- Because it is based on a FIFO queueing system, jobs never starve.
- Because it makes decisions on behalf of individual jobs, it does not create incentives for users to subvert the system. As a result, we show that it is robust in the presence of self-interested users.
- The overall performance of the system under this strategy is between 3% and 30% better than under a comparable system-centric policy.

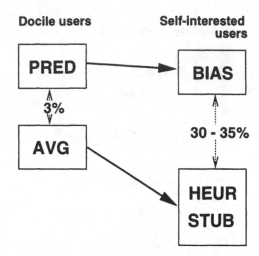

Fig. 7. The performance of many scheduling strategies, like AVG, degrades in the presence of self-interested users. The performance of our job-centric scheduler, PRED, does not degrade as severely.

Also, we show that the prediction techniques we propose are sufficiently accurate for making allocation decisions. From the point of view of individual jobs, our predictive strategy is within 3% of an optimal strategy (with perfect prediction).

8.1 Future Work

In this paper we have considered a single system size (128 processors), distribution of job characteristics (see Sect. 3), and load ($\rho = 0.75$). We would like to evaluate the effect of each of these parameters on our results.

Also, we have modeled an environment in which users provide no information to the system about the run times of their jobs. As a result, our queue time predictions are not very accurate. In the real systems we have examined, the information provided by users significantly improves the quality of the predictions [4]. We would like to investigate the effect of this improvement on our results.

As part of the DOCT project [11] we are in the process of implementing system agents that provide predicted queue times on space-sharing parallel machines. Users can take advantage of this information to choose what jobs to run, when to run them, and how many processors to allocate for each. We expect that this information will improve user satisfaction with these systems, and hope that, as in our simulations, it will lead to improvement in the overall performance of the system.

Acknowledgements

I would like to thank George Kremenek at SDSC and Steven Hotovy at CTC for providing workload data; Reagan Moore at SDSC, Jenny Schopf and Rich

Wolski at the University of California at San Diego, Ken Sevcik at the University of Toronto and the workshop reviewers for comments that greatly improved the quality and clarity of this paper.

References

1. Su-Hui Chiang, Rajesh K. Mansharamani, and Mary K. Vernon. Use of application characteristics and limited preemption for run-to-completion parallel processor scheduling policies. In *Proceedings of the 1994 ACM Sigmetrics Conference on Measurement and Modeling of Computer Systems*, 1994.
2. Allen B. Downey. A model for speedup of parallel programs. Technical Report CSD-97-933, University of California at Berkeley, 1997.
3. Allen B. Downey. A parallel workload model and its implications for processor allocation. In *The Sixth IEEE International Symposium on High Performance Distributed Computing (HPDC '97)*, 1997. To appear. Also available as University of California technical report number CSD-96-922.
4. Allen B. Downey. Predicting queue times on space-sharing parallel computers. In *Proceedings of the 11th International Parallel Processing Symposium*, April 1997.
5. Derek L. Eager, John Zahorjan, and Edward L. Lazowska. Speedup versus efficiency in parallel systems. *IEEE Transactions on Computers*, 38(3):408–423, March 1989.
6. Dror G. Feitelson and Bill Nitzberg. Job characteristics of a production parallel scientific workload on the NASA Ames iPSC/860. In *Job Scheduling Strategies for Parallel Processing, Springer-Verlag LNCS Vol 949*, pages 337–360, April 1995.
7. Dror G. Feitelson and Larry Rudolph. Evaluation of design choices for gang scheduling using distributed hierarchical control. *Journal of Parallel and Distributed Computing*, 35:18–34, 1996.
8. Dror G. Feitelson and Larry Rudolph. Towards convergence in job schedulers for parallel supercomputers. In *Job Scheduling Strategies for Parallel Processing, Springer-Verlag LNCS Vol 1162*, pages 1–26, April 1996.
9. Dipak Ghosal, Giuseppe Serazzi, and Satish K. Tripathi. The processor working set and its use in scheduling multiprocessor systems. *IEEE Transactions on Software Engineering*, 17(5):443–453, May 1991.
10. Shikharesh Majumdar, Derek L. Eager, and Richard B. Bunt. Scheduling in multiprogrammed parallel systems. In *Proceedings of the ACM Sigmetrics Conference on Measurement and Modeling of Computer Systems*, pages 104–113, 1988.
11. Reagan Moore and Richard Klobuchar. DOCT (distributed-object computation testbed) home page http://www.sdsc.edu/doct. San Diego Supercomputer Center, 1996.
12. Vijay K. Naik, Sanjeev K. Setia, and Mark S. Squillante. Performance analysis of job scheduling policies in parallel supercomputing environments. In *Supercomputing '93 Conference Proceedings*, pages 824–833, March 1993.
13. Eric W. Parsons and Kenneth C. Sevcik. Coordinated allocation of memory and processors in multiprocessors. In *Proceedings of the ACM Sigmetrics Conference on Measurement and Modeling of Computer Systems*, pages 57–67, May 1996.
14. Emilia Rosti, Evgenia Smirni, Lawrence W. Dowdy, Giuseppe Serazzi, and Brian M. Carlson. Robust partitioning policies of multiprocessor systems. *Performance Evaluation*, 19(2-3):141–165, Mar 1994.

15. Emilia Rosti, Evgenia Smirni, Giuseppe Serazzi, and Lawrence W. Dowdy. Analysis of non-work-conserving processor partitioning policies. In *Job Scheduling Strategies for Parallel Processing, Springer-Verlag LNCS Vol 949*, pages 165–181, April 1995.
16. Sanjeev K. Setia and Satish K. Tripathi. A comparative analysis of static processor partitioning policies for parallel computers. In *Proceedings of the Internationsal Workshop on Modeling and Simulation of Computer and Telecommunications Systems (MASCOTS)*, January 1993.
17. Kenneth C. Sevcik. Characterizations of parallelism in applications and their use in scheduling. *Performance Evaluation Review*, 17(1):171–180, May 1989.
18. Joseph Skovira, Waiman Chan, Honbo Zhou, and David Lifka. The EASY – LoadLeveler API project. In *Job Scheduling Strategies for Parallel Processing, Springer-Verlag LNCS Vol 1162*, pages 41–47, April 1996.
19. Evgenia Smirni, Emilia Rosti, Lawrence W. Dowdy, and Giuseppe Serazzi. Evaluation of multiprocessor allocation policies. Technical report, Vanderbilt University, 1993.
20. Kurt Windisch, Virginia Lo, Dror Feitelson, Bill Nitzberg, and Reagan Moore. A comparison of workload traces from two production parallel machines. In *6th Symposium on the Frontiers of Massively Parallel Computation*, 1996.

A Historical Application Profiler for Use by Parallel Schedulers

Richard Gibbons
gibbons@cs.ubc.ca

University of British Columbia
201-2366 Main Mall, Vancouver, B.C., Canada V6T 1Z4

Abstract. Scheduling algorithms that use application and system knowledge have been shown to be more effective at scheduling parallel jobs on a multiprocessor than algorithms that do not. This paper focuses on obtaining such information for use by a scheduler in a network of workstations environment.

The log files from three parallel systems are examined to determine both how to categorize parallel jobs for storage in a job database and what job information would be useful to a scheduler. A Historical Profiler is proposed that stores information about programs and users, and manipulates this information to provide schedulers with execution time predictions. Several preemptive and non-preemptive versions of the FCFS, EASY and Least Work First scheduling algorithms are compared to evaluate the utility of the profiler. It is found that both preemption and the use of application execution time predictions obtained from the Historical Profiler lead to improved performance.

1 Introduction

Many theoretical and modeling-based studies indicate that knowledge of the characteristics of parallel applications can improve the performance of scheduling algorithms [MEB90, PD89, GST91, MEB91, Wu93, PS95, AS97, BG96, PS96]. However, much less research has focused on practical ways of obtaining such application knowledge. Sevcik [Sev94] proposes simply having the user provide estimates of application characteristics. However, this is inconvenient for users and the accuracy of data is not assured. As a result, more technical solutions may be warranted.

Kumar [Kum88] proposes a tool that measures application parallelism by inserting statements into application code. However, the tool he proposes requires special versions of applications to be created and run to determine application characteristics. This is a great inconvenience for users.

Another approach is to measure application characteristics at run time. Dusseau, Arpaci and Culler [DAC96] use this method with their *implicit scheduling* technique for distributed time-shared workloads. Local schedulers use the communication and synchronization events implicit in parallel applications to estimate load imbalances. The local schedulers are able to determine from this data when to schedule parallel applications so that multiple processes of a job have a high probability of being scheduled simultaneously.

Nguyen, Vaswani and Zahorjan [NVZ96b, NVZ96a] use a combination of code instrumentation and hardware monitors to determine run time characteristics of iterative applications. By varying the processor allocations over several iterations of a loop, the scheduler can determine application characteristics. Although Nguyen, et. al. show the performance of schedulers using this method to be very good, thus far, this strategy requires that the application programmer instrument his code.

An alternative method of determining application characteristics is to keep a historical database containing data on every job that has been run on the system. The database could then deduce the resource usage of future jobs from the past usage. Despite results of workload characterization studies that seem to indicate that this approach holds some potential [PBK91, FN95, Hot96, HSO96], up to now, nobody has implemented this strategy. This paper addresses this issue by creating a Historical Profiler.

Through the examination of several production parallel systems, Section 2 justifies the use of and provides insight into an appropriate design of a Historical Profiler. Section 3 describes the features of the Historical Profiler, and discusses the issues associated with implementing such a profiler in a network of workstations (NOW) environment. Next, Section 4 proposes several scheduling algorithms and the workload to use to evaluate the performance of the Historical Profiler. Section 5 analyses the results of experiments discussed in the previous section. It notes that backfilling, preemption, and knowledge of application characteristics generally lead to reduced mean response times in the algorithms examined. Furthermore, it finds that in many cases, the performance of algorithms using the Historical Profiler is relatively close to the performance of the same algorithms using perfect information. Finally, Section 6 summarizes the findings and discusses future research.

2 Workload Characterization

Previous results [MEB90, Sev89, PD89, GST91, MEB91, Sev94] have indicated that knowledge of job characteristics can improve the performance of parallel schedulers. However, these results do not necessarily imply that such knowledge can be derived from the historical resource usage of applications, and they do not provide any indication of effective ways of classifying jobs to obtain this knowledge. To address these issues, it is necessary to examine the workload on production parallel systems. This analysis is used to guide the design of the Historical Profiler.

In order for the historical information to be of use in scheduling, it is necessary to first show that the duration of jobs can be predicted more accurately when historical information is used than when it is not. To determine if the job durations are predictable, we will use the coefficient of variation [1], or CV,

---

[1] The coefficient of variation is the ratio of the standard deviation to the mean.

of the service time distribution. Jobs can be classified into categories based on attributes such as the executable name or selected queue. It is desirable to find the attributes of jobs that lead to low runtime CVs for these categories. If the runtime CV of a given category is lower than the system-wide runtime CV, it implies that the historical knowledge may be used to provide more accurate estimates of runtimes than estimates that do not use historical knowledge. The lower the CV, the more accurate the estimates are likely to be. We will focus on choosing what attributes to use to classify jobs.

There have been only a few detailed workload characterization studies of parallel systems [CS85, PBK91]. Furthermore, the studies that do exist do not focus on different ways of classifying jobs, with the exception of Feitelson and Nitzberg's [FN95] analysis of the workload of the 128-node NASA Ames iPSC/860 hypercube. Feitelson and Nitzberg classify jobs by name, user, and number of processors, and discover that in the majority of cases where applications were run more than once, the coefficient of variation, or CV, of runtimes is less than one. Meanwhile, the overall systemwide CV is 3.56 during the day, and 2.11 during the night. This implies that in this system, historical knowledge could be used to predict future resource usage. Furthermore, it means that using name, user, and number of processors is a reasonable way of categorizing jobs.

To confirm that these results hold for other systems, we examine the Cornell Theory Center (CTC) IBM SP2 and network of workstations (NOW) sites at NASA Lewis and an anonymous university (which we shall refer to as University1).

Hotovy, et al. [Hot96, HSO96] have already done much analysis of the workload on the CTC IBM SP2. They have examined it in terms of utilization and user-node time. They find that the average utilization is only 60%[2]. They also find that half the jobs are serial, but these jobs account for only 8.6% of the user-node time. Hotovy, et. al. go on to examine the relationship between the number of processors and the job duration. They determine that sequential jobs have the longest job duration. The duration decreases for jobs using 2 to 16 processors, and then increases again for jobs of higher parallelism.

Hotovy, et. al. do not do analysis of the CVs of applications as was done by Feitelson and Nitzberg. However, they have made the log files available so that we can determine the CVs ourselves. Unfortunately, neither the job name nor the path name is available in these files. Nevertheless, it is still possible to calculate the system-wide CVs and the CVs when jobs are classified by user, degree of parallelism, and queue. The wall clock times and processor times are presented in Table 1. The CV for several categories is calculated using a weighted mean. Categories are only included in the mean CV if they include at least five jobs[3]. All other categories are given a weighting in proportion to the number of jobs in the category.

From the results in Table 1, it is evident that, in general, classifying jobs by

---

[2] Their definition of utilization is the percentage of processors allocated to active jobs.

[3] Categories have to include at least five jobs to be included in the results so that categories that include few jobs do not make the mean CV artificially low.

Table 1. Cornell Theory Center: Wall Clock and Processor Time Means and Coefficients of Variation

	Wall Clock Time		Processor Time	
	Mean	CV	Mean	CV
System-wide	6314	5.5	84603	4.3
By user	6315	3.9	84894	2.9
By parallelism	6202	4.6	76516	2.8
15 min queue	714	18.9	1870	3.7
3 hour queue	3690	10.0	25286	3.6
6 hour queue	5781	1.7	85880	3.0
12 hour queue	17935	3.8	280292	1.7
18 hour queue	30072	1.5	377261	1.7

user, parallelism, or queue leads to lower CVs than the system-wide CV. This is an expected result. For instance, it seems likely that a user would initiate jobs with similar characteristics, or that jobs with similar parallelism would run for similar amounts of time. The lower CV for the queues, too, is expected, since a user's selection of a queue to which to submit a job provides a prediction of the job's duration. Furthermore, in this system, jobs are killed when their duration exceeds the limit associated with the queue. This enforcement of a maximum duration can lead to lower CVs.

The only entries in Table 1 where the CV for a category is greater than the system-wide CV is for the wall-clock time for jobs in the short 15 minute and 3 hour queues. This could be because these are the primary queues used for development, testing, and debugging, while the longer queues are used for production jobs.

University1 (which shall remain anonymous) does parallel computing research using a network of workstations running LSF, the Load Sharing Facility distributed by Platform Computing. The system has 85 users using IBM RS/6000 and DEC Alpha workstations. There is a parallel queue for parallel jobs, but some parallel jobs are run in the short, regular, normal and long queues. For each job, these files contain information about the wall clock execution time, the job name, the user id, the number of processors used, and the queue used[4]. Unfortunately, although the log files cover 440 days and 16,000 jobs, only 90 of the jobs are parallel and all these jobs are submitted by only two users. Thus, it is unwise to make generalizations from these log files, but it is possible to identify trends.

The NASA Lewis network of workstations is used by 25 users for simulations, analysis and code development. It, like the University1 site, also runs LSF. The system consists of 60 SUN, HP, SGI, and IBM RS/6000 workstations running primarily over an Ethernet network, but also over FDDI and ATM networks. Most of the parallel jobs are submitted to the regular queue, although there are

---

[4] The next release of LSF is expected to contain additional information, including processor time and memory usage.

a few PVM jobs that are submitted to a separate PVM queue. The log files for NASA Lewis contain data for 3,682 jobs over a period of 152 days. Of these jobs, 395, or 11%, are parallel.

Table 2. University1 and NASA Lewis: Wall Clock Time Means and Coefficients of Variation

	University1		NASA Lewis	
	Mean	CV	Mean	CV
System-wide	242	4.1	35115	3.9
By user	232	4.1	35049	2.5
By queue	146	3.8	35839	2.8
By parallelism	209	3.6	35282	2.9
By executable	64	0.6	42124	2.0
By exec., user, parallel.	60	0.6	46490	1.5

Table 2 shows the wall clock mean times and CVs for the parallel jobs classified in different ways. In all the cases, the CVs for the various categories are lower than the CV of the entire system. The categories used by Feitelson and Nitzberg, executable, user, and degree of parallelism, proves to be the most effective categorization. In this case, the CVs for University1 and NASA Lewis are 0.6 and 1.5, versus system-wide CVs of 4.1 and 3.9 respectively.

This workload analysis not only supports the hypothesis that historical information may be used to provide accurate predictions of job duration. It also suggests how to categorize jobs to ensure that the predictions are accurate. Feitelson and Nitzberg's results and our results for the NOW systems suggest that classifying jobs by executable, user, and degree of parallelism leads to low CVs for the categories. Since the executable name was unavailable in the log files from CTC, these files cannot verify this result, although the lower CV when classifying by user or parallelism supports it. The CTC site files suggest an alternative classification might be by queue, but the NOW files show that a classification by executable, user, and degree of parallelism is more effective. Thus, the latter classification will be used.

3 The Historical Profiler

The first step in the design of the Historical Profiler is defining the information that the Historical Profiler should provide to the scheduler. In the literature [MEB90, Dow88, PD89, GST91, Wu93, Sev94, PS96] scheduling algorithms that use the execution time of jobs have been frequently examined. Therefore, the Historical Profiler will provide a method of obtaining an estimate of the time a job will take to execute, with an indication of the uncertainty in the estimate.

3.1 Environment

The experimental platform consists of a network of workstations environment, with 16 IBM RS/6000 UNIX workstations communicating over Ethernet, Fast Ethernet, and ATM networks. The Ethernet network will be the primary network used for all experimentation.

The development of a Historical Profiler and scheduling algorithms for parallel jobs in this environment requires system support in several areas such as job management, host management, and the remote execution of parallel jobs. The commercial Load Sharing Facility (LSF) [LSF96, ZZWD93] supports many of these requirements. LSF does job, host, and queue management, supports access to all the job information required, and allows an external scheduler to control jobs to specify when and on which processors each job will be started. It also allows access to system information through the LSF Application Programming Interface (API).

Unfortunately, every call to the LSF API requires crossing address spaces. For efficiency, another layer is required, the Job and System Information Cache (JSIC). The JSIC, developed by Parsons [Par97] with help from the author, stores the data required by the profiler and the scheduler in the same address space. The information in the JSIC is periodically updated by polling LSF.

The use of these two layers has several advantages. First, they reduce the development time required for a Historical Profiler. Second, LSF is commercial software for load balancing on a distributed system, so it is fault tolerant, and it helps to ensure that the profiler and schedulers are fault tolerant. Furthermore, since future versions of LSF are likely to include in the log files information about jobs' processor times and memory usage, it will be relatively easy to add these features to our software. Finally, and most importantly, LSF is used at many production sites on many different platforms. Since our software is developed on top of LSF, our software should be easy to install and test on production sites that use LSF.

3.2 Interface

The Historical Profiler is an object with a public method for estimating the execution time of a job. Both the inputs and outputs are shown in Figure 1. The inputs to the method indicate the desired accuracy of the estimate and the job for which the profiler is making the estimate. The outputs are the estimate and an indication of the uncertainty in the estimate.

Jobs are identified by five attributes. The first three are the executable name, the user who initiated the job, and the number of processors. The final two are the wall clock time used by the job so far and the maximum memory usage of the job so far. The attained wall clock time is used in the predictions so that the longer the job has run, the longer the total execution time will be predicted to be. If the job has already run for ten minutes, the prediction for the total job duration will exclude the data for jobs that ran less than ten minutes. The inclusion of the memory size metric is based on the premise that the problem

getEstimate()
Inputs:

string executionCommand	string user	int numProcs
float attainedWallClock	float memSize	float confidenceDesired

Outputs:

float confidenceIntervalSize	float estimate

Fig. 1. The Interface to the Profiler Class

size has a positive correlation to the execution time of an executable, and the maximum memory used gives an indication of the problem size. This feature is included for future versions of LSF that provide memory usage information.

The remaining input is the percentage confidence C in the estimate that is desired. The method returns a mean estimate and a confidence interval such that the actual mean execution time for the job is C percent likely to lie within the interval.

3.3 Design

The Historical Profiler obtains all of its information from the accounting files from LSF. However, searching all the data in the log files for all historical executions of a single executable whenever a scheduler requests information would be extremely costly. To deal with this difficulty, the Historical Profiler has its own permanent repository to store data in a more appropriate format.

Figure 2 shows the structure of the Historical Profiler. At the bottom is LSF, which obtains data about the jobs from the log files. The Job and System Information Cache calls functions in the LSF API to read this data. It then converts LSF's data structures into its own data structures, and stores the information in the Historical Profiler repository.

When the scheduler at the top of Figure 2 requests information from the Historical Profiler, the profiler first asks the JSIC to update the information in the Historical Profiler Repository. Then the Historical Profiler reads the information from the Historical Profiler Repository, and transforms the data into the format requested by the scheduler.

The Historical Profiler Repository The design of the Historical Profiler Repository is intended to support the desired functionality of the profiler without requiring excessive storage space. The schedulers request information based on executable and user names. Therefore, these criteria are used to index entries in the repository. Every time a particular user runs a particular executable, the resource usage for that job is included in the appropriate repository entry. (If

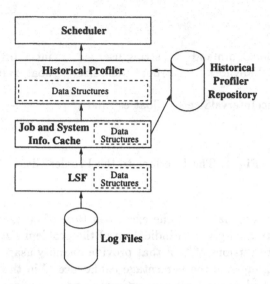

Fig. 2. High-level Design of the Historical Profiler

information about a particular executable-user pair is requested but is not in the repository, an entry that includes all the jobs ever run is used for the predictions instead.)

The next issue is determining what information is provided in each repository entry. Including complete detailed information for each job would be useful, but could lead to excessive use of storage space and either slow access times or complicated data structures. Therefore, each repository entry consists of several bins, each of which includes information for multiple jobs. Since the data for calculating mean execution times and confidences is required, the data stored in the bin includes the number of jobs included in the bin, the sum of the execution times, and the sum of the squares of the execution times [5].

It is also necessary to select an appropriate number of bins to use. In this case, a three-dimensional array of bins indexed by execution time, memory usage, and processor allocations is appropriate. The estimates of the execution time can vary based on the attained execution time, memory usage, and number of processors allocated. As a result, each repository entry must have bins containing data for multiple execution time, memory usage, and processor allocation ranges.

Calculating Execution Times The repository supplies the data required by the Historical Profiler, but the profiler is required to manipulate this information into an execution time estimate usable by a scheduler. To do this, the profiler uses well-known statistical methods for estimating means and confidence intervals based on a number of observations.

---

[5] Confidence intervals can be derived if data for the mean, number of entries, and standard deviation is available, and the standard deviation can be derived from the quantities recorded.

One complication arises when predicting the execution time of a job that is using a number of processors different from that the executable has used in the past. For instance, suppose a given executable has been run on two processors, four processors, and sixteen processors, but an estimate is desired for the executable running on eight processors.

This problem is dealt with by estimating the execution time function based on the available information. For any $p > 0$, the execution time function $T(p)$ represents the execution time of the job executing on p processors. Using weighted least squares [DS81], a standard method of approximating functions using several point estimates of varying accuracy, the Historical Profiler finds a quadratic approximation of $T(p)$. It then evaluates this function for the desired number of processors to find the appropriate execution time estimate [6].

4 Evaluation of the Historical Profiler

4.1 Algorithms

In order to evaluate the performance of the Historical Profiler, scheduling algorithms are required. Eight variants of three basic algorithms are used:

1. **First Come, First Serve (FCFS)**: Jobs are serviced in strict FCFS order.
2. **First Come, First Serve Fill (FCFS-fill)**: Jobs are generally serviced in FCFS order. However, if insufficient processors are available to service the next job in the queue, but a different job in the queue that requires fewer processors can run, that job will be run. Jobs are never preempted.
3. **EASY-kill**: Lifka's EASY algorithm [Lif95]. Estimates of each job's duration are used. If any job exceeds its estimate, it is killed. Jobs are serviced in FCFS order. However, if insufficient processors are available to service the next job in the queue, but a different job in the queue requiring fewer processors can run *and is guaranteed to finish without delaying any previously submitted job*, that job will be run. Jobs are never preempted.
4. **EASY-preemptive**: EASY-preemptive services jobs in the same order as EASY-kill. The only difference is that if a job exceeds its estimate, it is preempted and put at the end of the FCFS queue, just as if the job had been resubmitted. The estimate of the service time is unchanged.
5. **Least Estimated Work First (LEWF)**: Jobs are serviced is a strict least estimated work first order without preemption.
6. **Least Estimated Work First Fill (LEWF-fill)** : Jobs are serviced in a least estimated work first order without preemption. However, if insufficient processors are available to service the next job in the queue, but a different job in the queue requiring fewer processors can run, that job will be run.

---

[6] A more detailed description of the use of weighted least squares in this context is given discussed elsewhere [Gib97].

7. **Least Estimated Remaining Work First (LERWF)**: LEWF with the addition of preemption. Jobs are run in strict least estimated work first order. If a job is running, and another job arrives that is expected to complete in less time, the first job will be preempted to run the second.

8. **Least Estimated Remaining Work First Fill (LERWF-fill)**: LEWF-fill with the addition of preemption. Jobs run in least estimated work first order with preemption. Preemption occurs under the exact same conditions as LERWF: if a job is running, and another job arrives that is expected to complete in less time. Unlike LERWF, if insufficient processors are available to service the next job in the queue, but a different job in the queue requiring fewer processors can run, that job will be run.

Most of these algorithms require estimates of the execution times of jobs. For comparison purposes, the algorithms are tested using both the imperfect estimates provided by the profiler and perfectly accurate information obtained from the applications. The profiler estimate that is used is the greatest value in a 95% confidence interval for the mean execution time, a very conservative estimate typically much greater than the mean.

4.2 Workload

Thirteen synthetic applications are used to evaluate the performance of the algorithms. These applications execute for a period of time that depends on a pseudo-random total work parameter, W, Amdahl's fraction sequential parameter, D [Amd67], and the number of processors on which the application is running, p:

$$t = W(D + \frac{1-D}{p}) \tag{1}$$

For any job, p, W, and D are determined as follows. The number of processors p is selected randomly between 2 and 16 inclusive according to a Uniform distribution. The value D is a value that is constant for any application. The fraction sequential parameters, D, for the synthetic applications vary between 0.1 and 0.001. W is derived on the NASA Lewis workload as follows. The first twelve executables of the workload have mean work proportional to the product of the number of processors and the mean execution time for the twelve most frequently run parallel executables. The thirteenth job represents the aggregation of all the other parallel executables that were run in the system (approximately 35% of the jobs). Similarly, the coefficients of variation for the applications are chosen to be the same as the measured coefficients of variation for the corresponding executables in the NASA Lewis workload.

The actual work W required for a given job in Equation 1 is randomly determined based on the mean and variance associated with the corresponding executable. If the coefficient of variation is less than one, an Erlang distribution of work is assumed, if equal, an Exponential distribution, and if greater, a Hyperexponential distribution.

The test consists of 200 jobs submitted with interarrival times chosen from an exponential distribution with a mean of 150 seconds. The next executable to run is randomly determined. The probability of a given executable being the next job submitted is the proportion of the number of runs for this executable in the NASA Lewis workload.

The initial state of the Historical Profiler can affect the predictions significantly. In this case, the Historical Profiler is seeded with twenty-five random executions of each of the thirteen executables.

Table 3. Parameters Used in the Experiments

Number of Executables	13
Number of Jobs	200
Interarrival Time Distribution	Exponential
Interarrival Time Mean	150 s
Profiler estimate	greatest value in a 95% confidence interval
Number of Processors Distribution	Uniform
Minimum number of processors	2
Maximum number of processors	16
Initial Seeding of Profiler	25 random executions of each executable

In order to ensure a fair test of the algorithms, a single sequence of pseudo-random numbers is used. Thus, in a single experiment, every algorithm must handle the exact same jobs submitted at the exact same times, and the repository contains the exact same information.

5   Results

This section discusses the results of the experiments in which different schedulers are used to schedule a particular test workload. The primary criteria used to judge the performance of the algorithms is mean response times. The benefits of preemption, filling, and knowledge are examined. Table 4 classifies the algorithms based on these three criteria.

The results of the experiments are summarized in Table 5. In this table, the average response time is calculated as the average time from when a job is submitted until it finishes. The wait time is the average time from when a job is submitted until it first begins executing. The utilization is the average number of processors assigned to executing jobs during the test.

5.1   The Relative Performance of the Non-Preemptive Schedulers

To judge the relative performance of the algorithms, we compare the performance of the simplest non-preemptive versions of the algorithms using perfect service

Table 4. Classification of Algorithms

Accuracy of	Non-Preemptive		Preemptive	
Knowledge	Non-Filling	Filling	Non-Filling	Filling
None	FCFS	FCFS-fill		
Imperfect	EASY-kill-pro LEWF-pro	LEWF-fill-pro	EASY-pre-pro LERWF-pro	LERWF-fill-pro
Perfect	EASY-act[1] LEWF-act	LEWF-fill-act	LERWF-act	LERWF-fill-act

[1]Note: EASY-act is actually EASY-kill-act and EASY-pre-act. These two algorithms function in exactly the same way if the job durations are predicted accurately, since no jobs are killed or preempted.

Table 5. Performance of Scheduling Algorithms ("pro" means use of the profiler, "act" means use of actual service times)

Algorithm	Preempted (Killed)	Number Preemptions	Mean Response (s)	Mean Wait (s)	Elapsed Time (s)	Util. (%)
FCFS	0	0	6480	6251	43986	64.6
FCFS-fill	0	0	2284	2056	37609	75.0
EASY-act	0	0	2361	2138	36684	74.7
EASY-pre-pro	24	43	2429	1864	40130	69.9
LEWF-act	0	0	1031	804	41760	67.3
LEWF-pro	0	0	2965	2738	39116	71.6
LEWF-fill-act	0	0	926	697	39271	72.0
LEWF-fill-pro	0	0	1259	1031	38234	74.0
LERWF-act	31	124	908	469	44456	63.7
LERWF-pro	25	121	2404	1565	48017	61.5
LERWF-fill-act	34	135	855	267	42684	67.3
LERWF-fill-pro	38	163	1678	389	45441	65.8
EASY-kill-pro	(24)	0	∞^2	602	29781	58.9

[2]Note: This time is not given because 24 long-running jobs were killed. If this fact is ignored, the mean response time is 763.

time knowledge, FCFS, EASY-act and LEWF-act. Figure 3 shows the relative performance of these three algorithms. As would be expected, FCFS has the worst performance, EASY-act the middle, and LEWF-act the best. This is the expected result, since FCFS makes no attempts to change the ordering of jobs to decrease the mean response times. EASY-act does change the order somewhat, by the addition of filling, but not as much as LEWF.

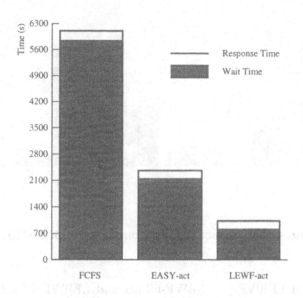

Fig. 3. The Non-Preemptive Schedulers' Mean Response Times

5.2 The Value of Filling

Filling is the first addition to the basic algorithms which will be examined. Figure 4 compares the mean response times for filling and non-filling algorithms. From these results, it is clear that in general, filling improves the mean response times. It is intuitive that FCFS would be improved by the addition of filling, so the results are not surprising. The average response time is reduced by almost two-thirds, while the total time required decreases by 17%. Filling means that jobs that could not be started if strict ordering were used can be started earlier. Thus, the wait times decrease, as is evident from the test.

Since the variants of LEWF order the queues in an attempt to minimize the mean response time, it was not clear that changing this ordering by using filling would lead to improved response times. Filling could result in a number of short jobs being delayed for a long time by a long job that was filled. However, the results indicate that this does not happen. In all cases, filling reduces the mean response times. The improvements in the wait times for jobs requiring few processors outweighs the effects of short jobs being delayed by long-running filled jobs. This is particularly true for the variants of LEWF that use the profiler.

5.3 The Value of Preemption

There are five pairs of algorithms that differ only in that one is preemptive and the other is not, EASY-kill-pro and EASY-pre-pro, LEWF-act and LERWF-act,

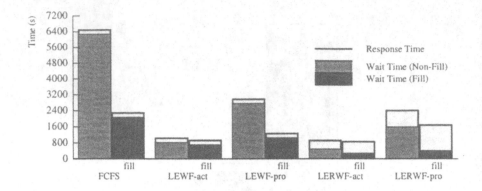

Fig. 4. The Impact of Filling on Mean Response Times

LEWF-pro and LERWF-pro, LEWF-fill-act and LERWF-fill-act, and LEWF-fill-pro and LERWF-fill-pro[7]. The relative performances of the final four pairs of algorithms are shown in Figure 5.

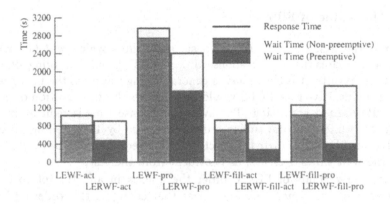

Fig. 5. The Impact of Preemption on Mean Response Times

Comparing the performance of the non-preemptive EASY scheduler using the profiler to the preemptive version of the same scheduler is meaningless. EASY-kill-pro disposes of all the jobs quickly, but only because it kills 24 of the longest

---

[7] Another comparison might be made between the preemptive version and non-preemptive versions of EASY that use perfect data. However, such a comparison is uninteresting because no jobs are preempted, and so the algorithms lead to the exact same schedule and have the exact same performance (that of EASY-act).

running jobs when they exceed the estimates. It is unlikely that users would prefer a scheduler that kills jobs in such as haphazard manner whenever the scheduler's estimates of the execution time are inaccurate.

For three of the four variants of the LEWF algorithm, preemption improves the mean response times. The improvements are greater than the additional overhead of preemption, and stem from the fact that long jobs that are running can be preempted in order to run shorter jobs. In the non-preemptive version, if a long job starts running, subsequently arriving shorter jobs must wait until that long job finishes if there are insufficient available processors. Because preempted jobs require more wall-clock time from when they are first started to when they finish, the difference in the average response time and the average wait time is higher for LERWF-act than for LEWF-act, but this increase is still less than the improvement in average wait time.

LEWF-fill-pro and LERWF-fill-pro are the only pair of algorithms in which the performance of the preemptive algorithm is worse than that of the non-preemptive algorithm. The poor response time is due to two factors. The first is the overhead of preemption. This by itself is not enough to make the preemptive algorithm worse, since the other variants of LEWF are able to overcome this overhead. The second factor is the limitations of the current heuristic for assigning processors in LERWF-fill. Whenever a job that begins execution has a choice of processors on which to run, the scheduler attempts to avoid assigning the processors of the next preempted job in the pending queue. This policy is an attempt to ensure that the processors required by the next preempted job will be available when it is ready to run. Unfortunately, this tends to lead to a scenario where all the jobs that require few processors are assigned the same processors, so that several jobs of this type cannot run concurrently. Jobs are started relatively quickly, but after they are suspended, it takes a long time before they are resumed. This hypothesis is supported by the large difference in the average response time and average wait time for LERWF-fill pro, relative to the other algorithms. Improving the heuristics for the LERWF-fill algorithms could reduce the mean response times.

5.4   The Value of Knowledge

Three different levels of knowledge will be compared: no knowledge, imperfect knowledge, and perfect knowledge. These levels will be represented by FCFS, the algorithms using the profiler, and the algorithms using the actual execution times, respectively. Figure 6 shows the performance of the algorithms. Each set of three algorithms consists of one algorithm using no knowledge of the application, one using imperfect knowledge, and one using perfect knowledge.

Comparing the use of no knowledge to the use of any knowledge, even imperfect knowledge, shows clearly that knowledge is highly beneficial. Both FCFS and FCFS-fill are much worse than the LEWF and LERWF algorithms that use the same type of filling. In the case of FCFS, the poorest comparable algorithm is LEWF-pro, which still has a mean response time less than half that of FCFS, while the other algorithms only improve on this performance. The results are

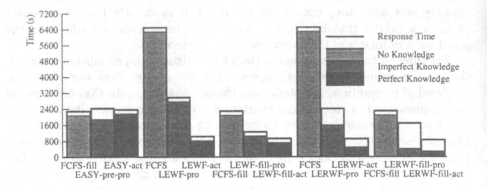

Fig. 6. The Improvements in Mean Response Time Due to Knowledge

similar for the filling variants. The only exceptions are the variants of EASY, where application knowledge does not improve performance. However, this is because EASY does not use application knowledge to ensure low mean response times, but rather only to make the schedule predictable. Both the perfect and imperfect knowledge variants of EASY have roughly the same mean response time.

Now we will examine the impact of the accuracy of knowledge by comparing the improvements in mean response times over FCFS and FCFS-fill that are attainable using imperfect knowledge to the improvements attainable using perfect knowledge. For the LEWF algorithm, LEWF-pro has mean response times 46% as long as FCFS, while LEWF-act has mean response times of only 16% as long. This difference is noticeable in Figure 6. For the filling version, the mean response time of LEWF-fill-act is approximately 41% of the mean response time of FCFS-fill, while the mean response time of LEWF-fill-pro is 55% of that of FCFS-fill. Thus, in the first case, the improvements due to knowledge are substantial, but not close to the results with perfect information. In the second, the difference is far less significant.

It is worthwhile examining the cause of this difference in performance between perfect and imperfect information. In general, the jobs are run in the "correct" executable order so that the executables with the least work are run before the ones with more. The problem arises in distinguishing between different jobs involving the same executable. In this case, the jobs requiring more processors are run first, since it is expected that the more processors available, the shorter the job[8] (a result that may not necessarily be true in a real workload[9]). As a result, when the profiler is used for scheduling, several jobs with short execution times but requiring few processors are delayed until the end of the test, after longer jobs with more processors have finished. This difference has less of an impact on the filling versions of the algorithm, since short jobs requiring few processors are likely to be filled regardless of how high the execution time estimates are.

Finally, there are the preemptive algorithms. As is evident in Figure 6, LERWF-pro has an average response time equal to 37% of the average response time for FCFS, while LERWF-act has an average response time of 14% of that of FCFS. LERWF-fill-pro has a mean response time equal to 73% of that of FCFS-fill, while LERWF-fill-act has a mean response time of 37% of that of FCFS-fill. In the former case, the scheduler using imperfect information attains most the benefits possible due to the use of knowledge. The latter has a much larger difference. As mentioned previously, the poor performance of the LERWF-fill-pro algorithm stem from the heuristic for assigning processors.

Thus, in every case, the use of knowledge is beneficial. In addition, for all but the LERWF-fill-pro algorithm, the algorithms using the profiler achieve 75% of the possible improvements in mean response times that are attainable using perfect information.

6 Conclusions

Through the analysis of the workload on parallel processing sites, it was evident that historical job information could be used to improve the performance of a scheduler. The execution times of jobs categorized by executable name, user, and number of processors were relatively predictable.

To take advantage of these results, a Historical Profiler that uses historical job information to calculate execution time estimates was designed and implemented. Experiments to evaluate this profiler with variants of the FCFS, EASY, and LEWF scheduling algorithms led to the following main results:

1. Out of the three basic, non-preemptive algorithms, FCFS is the worst, EASY-act is better, and LEWF-act is the best.
2. Filling reduces the mean response times attainable for all disciplines.
3. Preemption reduces the mean response times attainable for most disciplines.

---

[8] This is caused by the jobs that were used to seed the profiler's repository. For any job, the amount of work was selected according to the workload distribution, and the number of processors was selected from a uniform distribution. The run time of that job was then calculated to be approximately proportional to the ratio of the work to the number of processors, leading to a negative correlation between the run time and the number of processors.

[9] If instead, the reverse were true and jobs with more processors ran longer than jobs with fewer processors, the profiler's predictions of job length would still be relatively accurate. However, with such a workload, the importance of preemption might increase and the importance of filling might decrease.

4. The heuristic that the preemptive disciplines use for assigning processors to jobs has a large impact on the mean response times attainable using those disciplines.
5. Schedulers that use application knowledge can attain lower mean response times than those that do not.
6. In many cases, schedulers that use the imperfect knowledge from the profiler can attain most of the possible knowledge-related improvements to mean response times.

There are several possible areas of future work. First, the Historical Profiler could be installed at a production site. This would conclusively show the benefits possible from from a Historical Profiler. Second, this work only discussed non-adaptive space sharing scheduling algorithms that did not permit the migration of jobs. This is a small subset of all scheduling algorithms; future research could evaluate the performance of the profiler with other types of scheduling disciplines. Third, many of the performance problems of the LERWF algorithms were attributed to the methods of assigning processors. An examination of the performance improvements attainable using different heuristics for assigning processors would be interesting. Finally, the addition of more data to the repository, or the use of the existing data in the repository in different ways, could lead to interesting findings.

Future work is required to address these issues, but the most important issue has been resolved. The results indicate that it is feasible to use information about previously run parallel jobs to predict the characteristics of future jobs. Furthermore, these predictions can improve the performance of schedulers substantially.

7 Acknowledgements

Thanks to Kim Johnson for the NASA Lewis log files, Steve Hotovy for the Cornell Theory Center log files, and the University1 site for its log files. Thanks to Platform Computing for providing LSF. Also, thanks to Ken Sevcik, Eric Parsons, and Songnian Zhou for their help in writing this paper.

References

[Amd67]   G. Amdahl. Validity of the single-processor approach to achieving large-scale computing capabilities. In *Proceedings of the 1967 AFIPS Conference*, volume 30, AFIPS Press, pages 483–485, 1967.

[AS97]   S.V. Anastasiadis and K.C. Sevcik. Parallel application scheduling on networks of workstations. *To appear in: Journal of Parallel and Distributed Computing*, June 1997.

[BG96]   T.B. Brecht and K. Guha. Using parallel program characteristics in dynamic processor allocation policies. *Performance Evaluation*, 27(8):519–539, October 1996.

[CS85]   M. Calzarossa and G. Serazzi. A characterization of the variation in time of workload arrival patterns. *IEEE Transactions on Computers*, C-34(2):156–162, February 1985.

[DAC96]   A.C. Dusseau, R.H. Arpaci, and D.E. Culler. Effective distributed scheduling of parallel workloads. In *Proceedings of the 1996 ACM SIGMETRICS Conference on Measurement and Modeling of Computer Systems*, pages 25–36, 1996.

[Dow88]   L. W. Dowdy. On the partitioning of multiprocessor systems. Technical Report Technical Report 88-06, Vanderbilt University, March 1988.

[DS81]   N.R. Draper and H. Smith. *Applied Regression Analysis, 2nd ed.* John Wiley and Sons, Toronto, 1981.

[FN95]   D.G. Feitelson and B. Nitzberg. Job characteristics of a production parallel scientific workload on the NASA Ames iPSC/ 860. In *Proceedings of IPPS '95 Workshop on Job Scheduling Strategies for Parallel Processing*, pages 215–227, April 1995.

[Gib97]   R.B. Gibbons. A historical profiler for use by parallel schedulers. M. Sc. thesis, University of Toronto, Toronto, Ontario, Canada, 1997.

[GST91]   D. Ghosal, G. Serazzi, and S. K. Tripathi. The processor working set and its use in scheduling multiprocessor systems. *IEEE Transactions on Software Engineering*, 17(5):443–453, May 1991.

[Hot96]   S. Hotovy. Workload evolution on the Cornell Theory Center IBM SP2. In *Proceedings of IPPS '96 Workshop on Job Scheduling Strategies for Parallel Processing*, pages 15–22, April 1996.

[HSO96]   S. Hotovy, D. Scheider, and T. O'Donnell. Analysis of the early workload on the Cornell Theory Center IBM SP2. In *Proceedings of the 1996 ACM SIGMETRICS Conference on Measurement and Modeling of Computer Systems*, pages 272–273, May 1996.

[Kum88]   M. Kumar. Measuring parallelism in computation-intensive scientific/engineering applications. *IEEE Transactions on Computing*, 37(9):1088–1098, September 1988.

[Lif95]   D.A. Lifka. The ANL/IBM SP scheduling system. In *Proceedings of IPPS '95 Workshop on Job Scheduling Strategies for Parallel Processing*, pages 187–191, April 1995.

[LSF96]   *LSF Users's Guide*. Platform Computing Corporation, 5001 Yonge St, Suite 1401, North York, ONT, Canada M2N 6P6, 1996.

[MEB90]   S. Majumdar, D.L. Eager, and R.B. Bunt. Scheduling in multiprogrammed parallel systems. In *Proceedings of the 1988 ACM SIGMETRICS Conference on Measurement and Modelling of Computer Systems*, pages 104–113, May 1990.

[MEB91]   S. Majumdar, D.L. Eager, and R.B. Bunt. Characterization of programs for scheduling in multiprogrammed parallel systems. *Performance Evaluation*, 13(2):109–130, February 1991.

[NVZ96a] T.D. Nguyen, R. Vaswani, and J. Zahorjan. Parallel application characterization for multiprocessor scheduling policy design. In *Proceedings of IPPS '96 Workshop on Job Scheduling Strategies for Parallel Processing*, pages 105–118, April 1996.

[NVZ96b] T.D. Nguyen, R. Vaswani, and J. Zahorjan. Using runtime measured workload characteristics in parallel processor scheduling. In *Proceedings of IPPS '96 Workshop on Job Scheduling Strategies for Parallel Processing*, pages 93–104, April 1996.

[Par97]   E.W. Parsons. *Using Resource Requirements in Multiprogrammed Multipro-cessor Scheduling.* Ph. D. thesis, University of Toronto, Toronto, Ontario, Canada, 1997.

[PBK91]   J. Pasquale, B. Bittel, and D. Kraiman. A static and dynamic workload characterization study of the San Diego Supercomputer Center Cray X-MP. In *Proceedings of the 1991 ACM SIGMETRICS Conference on Measurement and Modeling of Computer Systems,* pages 218–219, 1991.

[PD89]   K.H. Park and L.W. Dowdy. Dynamic partitioning of multiprocessor sys-tems. *International Journal of Parallel Programming,* 18(2):91–120, Febru-ary 1989.

[PS95]   E.W. Parsons and K.C. Sevcik. Multiprocessor scheduling for high-variability service time distributions. In *Proceedings of IPPS '95 Work-shop on Job Scheduling Strategies for Parallel Processing,* pages 76–88, April 1995.

[PS96]   E.W. Parsons and K.C. Sevcik. Benefits of speedup knowledge in memory-constrained multiprocessor scheduling. *Performance Evaluation,* 27(8):253–272, October 1996.

[Sev89]   K.C. Sevcik. Characterizations of parallelism in applications and their use in scheduling. In *Proceedings of the 1989 ACM SIGMETRICS Conference on Measurement and Modeling of Computer Systems,* pages 171–180, May 1989.

[Sev94]   K. C. Sevcik. Application scheduling and processor allocation in multipro-grammed parallel processing systems. *Performance Evaluation,* 19:107–140, 1994.

[Wu93]   C.S. Wu. Processor scheduling in multiprogrammed shared memory numa multiprocessors. M. Sc. thesis, Department of Computer Science, University of Toronto, Toronto, Ontario, Canada, October 1993.

[ZZWD93] S. Zhou, X. Zheng, J. Wang, and P. Delisle. Utopia: a load sharing facility for large, heterogenous distributed computer systems. *Software: Practice And Experience,* 23(12):1305–1336, December 1993.

Memory Usage in the LANL CM-5 Workload

Dror G. Feitelson

Institute of Computer Science
The Hebrew University, 91904 Jerusalem, Israel
feit@cs.huji.ac.il or http://www.cs.huji.ac.il/~feit

Abstract. It is generally agreed that memory requirements should be taken into account in the scheduling of parallel jobs. However, so far the work on combined processor and memory scheduling has not been based on detailed information and measurements. To rectify this problem, we present an analysis of memory usage by a production workload on a large parallel machine, the 1024-node CM-5 installed at Los Alamos National Lab. Our main observations are

- The distribution of memory requests has strong discrete components, i.e. some sizes are much more popular than others.
- Many jobs use a relatively small fraction of the memory available on each node, so there is some room for time slicing among several memory-resident jobs.
- Larger jobs (using more nodes) tend to use more memory, but it is difficult to characterize the scaling of per-processor memory usage.

1 Introduction

Resource management includes a number of distinct topics, such as scheduling and memory management. However, in the context of parallel processing, scheduling is the single most important issue [9,6]. Memory management is hardly ever exercised, because of its performance implications and effect on synchronization [3,21]. Instead, jobs must be completely memory resident in order to execute.

Nevertheless, memory requirements may place severe constraints on scheduling, and therefore cannot be ignored. For example, in distributed memory machines processor allocation includes allocating part of the system's memory as well — the memory that is packaged with these processors. This memory must be large enough to fulfill the job's requirements. This consideration limits dynamic partitioning schemes and may prevent them from reducing the partition sizes when the load increases, thus undermining the whole idea of dynamic partitioning [16,17].

While there has been some research on the effect of memory requirements on job scheduling, this research has been hampered by the lack of concrete information about actual memory requirements that are experienced in practice. The unique contribution of this paper is to provide such information. We start with a brief overview of the system we analyzed, the LANL CM-5, in the next section. Section 3 contains the memory usage analysis, including such issues as the distribution of memory usage, the correlation of memory usage with degree of parallelism, the correlation of memory usage with runtime, and the relation between the memory requested and that actually used. Section 4 contains a discussion of the results and their implications, and Section 5 presents the conclusions.

2 The Analyzed System

The analysis presented in this paper is based on a detailed accounting log from the 1056-node Connection Machine CM-5 installed at Los Alamos National Lab. While such machines are no longer manufactured, this one is still in active use, and considered quite powerful — it ranked 21st in the world in the November '96 Top500 list, and came in first among Connection Machines [4].

The CM-5 is a distributed memory machine based on SPARC processors. 1024 of the 1056 nodes are used for parallel computation, with a total of 32 GB of memory (i.e. 32 MB per node). The machine is statically partitioned into partitions with power-of-two numbers of processors from 32 up to 512. Within each partition, jobs may be gang-scheduled, or they may request dedicated use of the partition [20]. While the fact that only 5 sizes are available is restrictive, other work on parallel workload characterization has shown conclusively that users prefer powers of two even if there are no architectural constraints [8,5].

The part of the log we worked on covers most of 1996 (from January 1 to September 23), and contains useful data on 36308 jobs (we ignore jobs that used 0 time etc.). The data includes a lot of information about the submittal process, but we mostly used the data on the number of processors used, the runtime, the requested memory, the memory actually used, and whether or not the nodes were dedicated. Runtimes are expressed in seconds (s), and memory usage in kilobytes (KB). The data was collected by DJM [14], the Distributed Job Manager used on CM-5 machines. Most jobs were indeed run using DJM, but 1492 of them were "foreign", i.e. launched directly by users. The log contains less information about foreign jobs, e.g. they do not have predefined resource requests.

Fig. 1 shows the histograms of job sizes and resource use during this period (there were also three 1024-node jobs, not shown). When counting jobs (left plot), 32-node jobs are the most common, followed by 128-node jobs. While there are less jobs that use 256 or 512 nodes, their numbers are still significant. If we weigh the number of jobs by the time they ran (middle plot), the variance is smaller: 32-node jobs occupied about twice as much time as each of the other sizes, which are all similar. If we also weigh the jobs by the number of nodes they use, and plot the total node-seconds for each size (right plot), then we find that the large jobs use more resources than smaller ones. The dashed lines across the columns denote the boundary between dedicated and non-dedicated use of the nodes: below are dedicated, and above are shared or foreign. Nearly all 256 and 512-node jobs ran in dedicated mode.

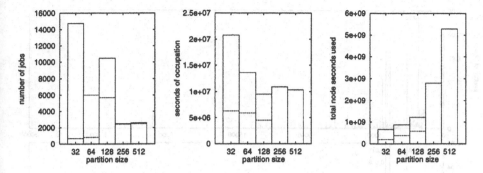

Fig. 1. *Histograms of job sizes in the analyzed log. In the left graph, all jobs have equal weights. In the middle, jobs are weighted by their runtime. At right, jobs are weighted by the product of runtime and parallelism, which is equivalent to counting node-seconds.*

3 Memory Usage Analysis

3.1 Memory Usage Distribution

Our goal is to characterize memory usage on parallel supercomputers. But memory by itself is not the resource in question: it is *the occupation of memory for a period of time*. A job that uses 1MB of memory for one second obviously requires less resources than one that uses the same 1MB for an hour. Therefore, the unit of resource use is not the KB, but the KB·s, or KiloByte Second.

On the other hand, a job using 1MB for one second also requires different resources from one that uses 10KB for 100 seconds, even though the total KB·s in both cases are equal. We therefore characterize memory usage by a weighted distribution, where the x axis denotes the *amount* of memory used (in KB), and the y axis reflects the *cummulative time* that this amount of memory was used. Using such a plot to characterize total memory usage by jobs is equivalent to creating a histogram where jobs are weighted by their runtime, rather than being given equal weights.

While characterizing the total memory usage by jobs is important, it is not enough. For parallel jobs, the memory used *per processor* is also important. Again, there are several ways to combine the requests of different jobs and create a single representation. The most meaningful seems to be to weigh the per-processor usage by *the product of runtime and number of processors*. Thus a job using 1MB across 10 processors for 10 seconds imposes a load of 100KB on each processor for 10 seconds, which is the same as 100 single-processor jobs using 100KB and running for 1 second each.

It should be stressed that choosing the right weights is extremely important, as typically a small fraction of the jobs account for a large fraction of the resource usage. The differences are shown graphically in Fig. 2 for the case of per-processor memory usage. If all jobs are given equal weights, it seems that most jobs only require less than 5MB of memory per processor (top plot). But if the more

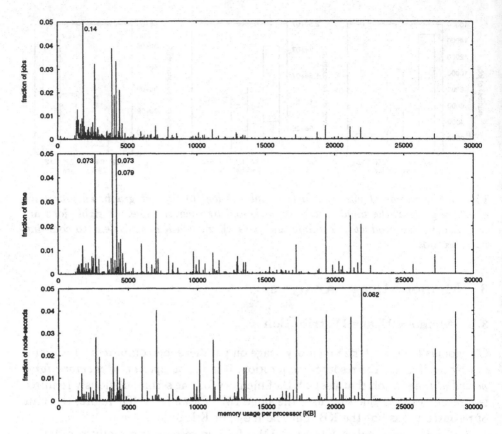

Fig. 2. *The distribution of per-processor memory usage, using a linear scale and buckets of 10 KB. In the top plot, all jobs have equal weight. In the middle, jobs are weighted according to their run time. The bottom plot shows the distribution for individual processors, which is equivalent to weighing the jobs according to the product of runtime and degree of parallelism.*

correct node-second weighting is used (bottom plot), it is evident that actually at any given monent a significant fraction of the processors are using a significant fraction of their memory (in the range of 20–30MB). In particular, the highest peak in the first plot, representing 14% of all the jobs, all but disappears in the other plots, because all these jobs were extremely short lived.

Characterization of discrete components A prominent feature of all these distributions is their discrete nature: they are composed of a number of very high discrete components, and very low "background noise". The question is what leads to this structure.

Table 1 contains information about all the discrete components that represent more than 1% of the total jobs or more than 1% of the total node-seconds. For each one, users that individually contributed more than 1% are identified. In

82

KB per proc	user	of	jobs		node sec	
			%	of	%	of
1400		14		1.27		0.42
1640	usr1	6	0.13	0.18	1.18	1.19
1830	usr2	6	1.15	1.33	0.00	0.02
1840	usr2	20	13.25	14.06	0.01	0.07
2650	usr3	10	2.00	3.01	1.96	2.71
2660	usr4	13	1.29	3.22	1.41	2.81
	usr3		1.12		0.88	
2900	usr5	7	0.26	0.40	1.37	1.93
3880	usr6	12	3.64	3.88	1.37	1.93
4040		20		1.89		0.22
4180	usr7	8	1.42	3.33	0.42	1.51
	usr3		1.17		0.46	
4190		4		1.21		0.46
4340		7		0.34		1.01
4430	usr8	17	1.21	2.11	0.01	0.28
5950	usr5	4	0.25	0.31	1.55	1.94
7010	usr3	2	0.57	0.57	4.02	4.02
10120	usr9	4	0.10	0.27	0.70	1.77
	usr5		0.17		1.07	
11150	usr9	4	0.16	0.40	1.08	2.68
	usr5		0.22		1.60	
11600	usr10	2	0.13	0.13	1.73	1.73
12950	usr2	2	0.19	0.20	1.11	1.12
13380	usr3	2	0.15	0.16	1.44	1.44
13530	usr11	2	0.13	0.14	1.43	1.44
17180	usr12	2	0.17	0.18	3.69	3.71
19330	usr5	3	0.41	0.55	2.81	3.81
	usr9		0.14		0.94	
19810	usr12	1	0.05	0.05	1.09	1.09
21120	usr5	3	0.40	0.52	2.85	3.70
21890	usr9	4	0.15	0.48	2.04	6.21
	usr5		0.31		4.08	
22550	usr10	2	0.06	0.06	1.02	1.02
25630	usr10	2	0.06	0.07	1.14	1.15
27220	usr13	2	0.17	0.21	1.76	2.28
28700	usr10	2	0.09	0.18	2.21	3.94
	usr1		0.09		1.73	

Table 1. *Single-user contributions to discrete components that are above 1% of the total. User names are replaced by numbers. Column 3 gives the total number of users contributing to this component. Columns 5 and 7 give the total fraction of jobs and node-seconds in this component, respectively, while columns 4 and 6 give the fraction contributed by the user specified in column 2.*

a few cases (1400, 4040, 4190, and 4340 KB per processor) the component is seen to be a combination of multiple users, who each contributed only less than 1%. But in the other 26 discrete components, most of the resource usage can be attributed to a single user (or sometimes two users). In particular, the hugh peak at 1840 KB per processor can be attributed to a single user who ran 13.25% of all the jobs in the log, and in fact did so in just over one week. It is thus risky to assign too much meaning to the discrete components themselves, but it is safe to assume that such a discrete structure is common, because some users are much more active than others.

Rendering with logarithmic scale Much information can be gleaned from the detailed distributions of memory usage such as those shown in Fig. 2. However, when investigating the distribution of an essentially continuous variable, one encounters the problem of choosing the granularity of observation. If the grain is too coarse, interesting details may be smoothed out. If it is too fine, the data will drown in a sea of noisy details.

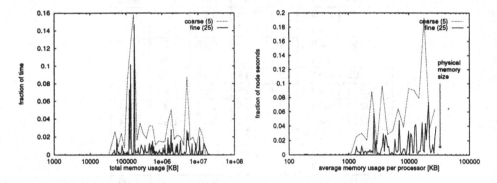

Fig. 3. *Distributions of memory usage using coarse and fine bucket sizes.*

When comparing jobs with different attributes, we shall use logarithmically-sized buckets and count how many jobs (with appropriate weights) fall into each such bucket. In order to reduce the granularity and observe finer details, we multiply the memory usage value by a scaling factor after taking the log. Thus the mapping from memory usage m to bucket b is

$$b = \lfloor f \cdot \log(m) \rfloor$$

The larger the scaling factor f, the more buckets that are used, with each one representing a smaller part of the spectrum. In most of what follows, we use a scaling factor of 5, which we feel is a good compromise. In Fig. 3 we compare the obtained distribution with one that would be obtained by using a scaling factor of 25 (in these figures the values for the different buckets are connected by a line; this is visually more convenient than drawing a bar chart with a bar for each bucket). This shows that the peaks in the coarse view of the distribution correspond to the larger narrow discrete components in the fine view of the distribution, or to regions where there are multiple peaks that are very close together. Taking this to the extreme, we note that the peaks in the fine distribution typically correspond to discrete peaks in the linear distribution of Fig. 2, where a linear scale and buckets of only 10 KB were used. The whole distribution is a combination of "background noise" with these strong discrete components.

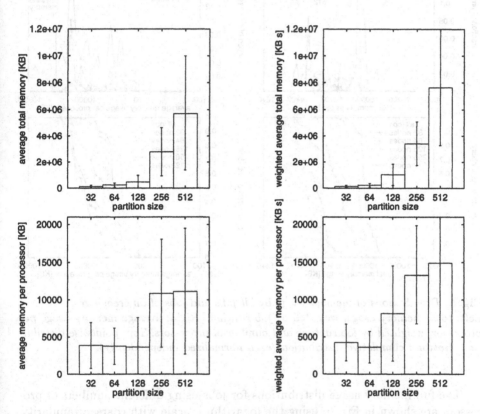

Fig. 4. *Average memory usage by jobs of different sizes. The top graphs are for total memory usage, and the bottom ones for per-processor usage. In each pair, the left graph is a simple average, while the right one is weighted by time. The error bars denote the standard deviation.*

3.2 Correlation of Memory Usage and Parallelism

The average memory usage by jobs of different sizes is shown in Fig. 4. Obviously, larger jobs require more memory, but the distribution is very wide. Interestingly, when the memory usage per processor is plotted, one sees that larger jobs also use more memory per-processor. The effect of larger memory use by larger jobs is even more pronounced when they are weighted by time. The standard deviation in most cases is somewhat smaller than the average, indicating that the coefficient of variation is less than 1 for each job size.

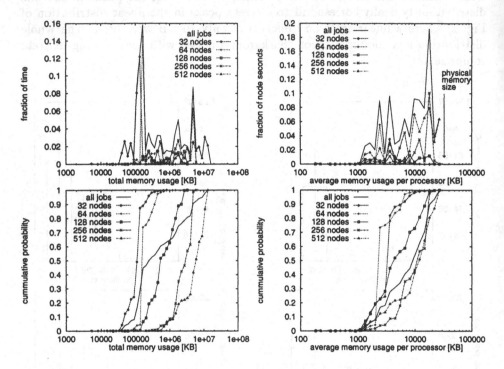

Fig. 5. *Distributions of memory usage by all jobs and jobs of different sizes. Left: total memory usage, weighted by job runtime. Right: average memory usage per processor, weighted by job runtime and number of processors. Top: pointwise distribution. Bottom: cumulative distribution (each normalized independently).*

The full memory usage distributions for jobs using different numbers of processors are shown in Fig. 5, using the logarithmic scale with coarse granularity. Both pointwise and cumulative distributions are shown for clarity, for both total and per-processor memory usage. Recall that peaks in these graphs actually correspond to very narrow discrete components in the distributions, and that weighing by time is used.

The distribution of memory usage for all jobs is rather wide, but the distributions for the different sizes are clearly distinguishable. This is especially clear in the cummulative plot of total memory usage, where the plots are neatly arranged in partition-size order, indicating that when more nodes are used, the weight of the distribution moves to higher memory usage values. The per-processor usage plots show again that this is not only a result of using memory on more nodes.

Interestingly, some of the discrete peaks in the distribution are dominated by a single partition size. This corresponds to the effects that the activity of single users sometimes have on the whole distribution, as described above.

3.3 Memory Usage in Dedicated and Shared Partitions

The same graphs are plotted again in Fig. 6, except that here the jobs are classified by their use of dedicated nodes rather than by size. About a third of the jobs ran in dedicated mode (12074 out of 36308), while the rest were gang-scheduled. However, it should be noted that nearly all jobs that ran on the large partition sizes did so in dedicated mode, so these jobs account for a very large fraction of the total node-seconds used (about 85.2%).

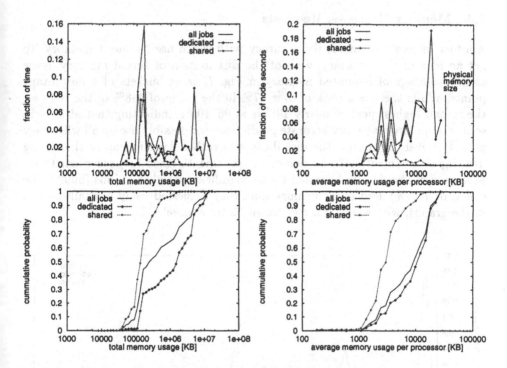

Fig. 6. *Distributions of memory usage by jobs using dedicated or shared nodes. Left: total memory usage, weighted by job runtime. Right: average memory usage per processor, weighted by job runtime and number of processors. Top: pointwise distribution. Bottom: cumulative distribution (each normalized independently).*

On average, dedicated jobs used more memory than jobs that shared their nodes with other jobs, as shown in Table 2. The distributions agree with this observation and show that actually the whole weight of the distributions is higher for dedicated jobs. Indeed, high memory usage values are completely dominated by dedicated jobs. This correlates with the fact that nearly all large jobs (on 256 and 512 processors) were dedicated.

job class	total memory		memory per proc	
	average	sd	average	sd
all	2029762	3299901	12187	8200
dedicated	3295679	3843629	13537	8049
shared	263188	334604	4444	3296

Table 2. *Average memory usage of different job classes. Numbers for total memory are wieghted by runtime, and those for memory per processor by node seconds.*

3.4 Memory Usage vs. Requests

Another interesting issue is the accuracy with which users request memory. To get an idea of this accuracy, we plot the distribution of actual memory usage as a percentage of requested memory in Fig. 7, using buckets of 4 percentage points. While there is a peak of over 17% in the range of 4-8% of the request, the second highest peak of nearly 10% is at 96-100%, indicating that at least in some cases users make very accurate predictions (or possibly use up all what they get). However, in general the distribution is rather flat, indicating that using user input as an estimate of memory requirements leads to poor predictions. Moreover, it should also be noted that a significant number of jobs (5992 to be exact, or 16.5%) used more memory than they requested (only partially shown in the graph), with a maximum factor of 32 time more!

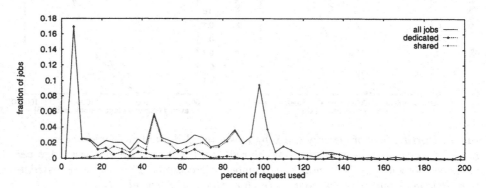

Fig. 7. *Distribution of actual memory usage as a fraction of requested memory.*

Some insight into the nature of user input is obtained by classifying the jobs into those that ran on dedicated nodes vs. those that shared their nodes with other jobs. It turns out that the peak at 4-8% can be attributed completely to dedicated jobs, whereas the peak at 96-100% is due to shared jobs. Furthermore, nearly all jobs that used more memory than requested ran on shared nodes (5887 out of 5992). This means that jobs that ran in dedicated mode typically did so for reasons other than their memory requirements. It also means that when users actually need to provide low memory estimates in order to run (as is the case on shared nodes) they sometimes make very accurate estimates, and sometimes they lie...

3.5 Correlation of Memory Usage and Runtime

Finally, we investigate the possible correlation between memory usage and runtime. The scatter plot on the left of Fig. 8 shows all pairs of runtime and total memory usage. The most striking features of this plot are the well-defined band of memory usage values, the horizontal stripes that indicate preferred memory usage values, and the sharp limits on runtime at the right-end side (probably due to NQS queue limits). But in addition, it is possible to discern a weak correlation: the weight at the left end is lower than at the right end.

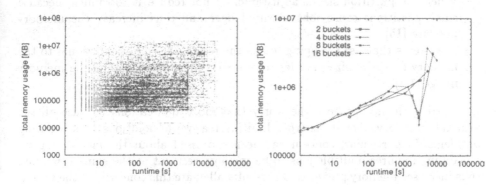

Fig. 8. *Scatter plot and functional relationship of memory usage and runtime.*

The graph on the right shows this correlation more clearly. Here the jobs are partitioned into a number of equal sized buckets according to their runtime (e.g. when using 4 buckets, the first bucket includes a quarter of the jobs, and specifically those with the shortest runtimes; the second bucket includes the next quadrant, and so on). One data point is drawn for each bucket, at the average runtime and average memory usage of the jobs in the bucket. When using 2 or 4 such buckets, the resulting graph is smooth and monotonically increasing. With 8 or 16 buckets, it is seen that some buckets with a high average runtime actually have a low average memory usage. Interestingly, the runtimes of these buckets correspond to the most prominent runtime limit from the scatter plot.

4 Discussion and Implications

The motivation for studying memory usage in parallel workloads is to provide data for the design and evaluation of scheduling algorithms that take memory requirements into account. This takes two forms. One is direct effects on scheduling algorithms and policies, for example the assertion that time slicing may be used because most jobs use a relatively small fraction of the available memory. The other is incorporation of memory requirements into workload models used to drive simulations or as inputs to analytical evaluations. For example, a model of how memory requirements change with the degree of parallelism facilitates the evaluation of scheduling policies for different machine configurations.

4.1 Time Slicing and Memory Pressure

Previous work about incorporating memory considerations into scheduling algorithms has been quite limited, and included ideas such as the following:

- In systems that use space slicing, place a lower bound on partition size so that enough memory will be available [16,17,13].
- When the partition size is adjustable, do not reduce it too much, because small partitions cause jobs to run longer and thus increase the memory pressure [15].
- In systems that use swapping, make the residence time proportional to the memory footprint size in order to amortize the cost of loading the memory image [1,7].

A recurring theme has been the worry that most applications will use all the available memory, thereby sharply limiting real-world solutions to scheduling problems. In particular, concern has been expressed about the fact that gang scheduling requires multiple jobs to be memory resident at the same time, and thus increases memory pressure. Our results alleviate this concern, as the weight of the distribution of per-processor memory usage is far below the actual memory available on each node, indicating that from a memory point of view there is room for sharing the nodes among a number of jobs (as indeed is done on the CM-5).

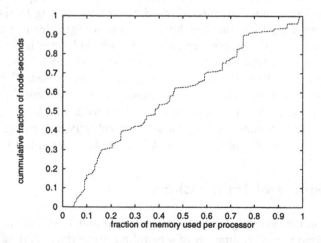

Fig. 9. *Cummulative distribution of per-processor memory usage, weighted by runtime and number of processors.*

To quantify this claim, we plot the cummulative distribution of the per-processor memory usage, weighted by runtime and number of processors (Fig. 9). This is actually the cummulative version of the distribution shown in the bottom plot of Fig. 2. The x axis shows the fraction of memory used on average on each processor, using the conservative estimate that 29.08 MB are available (rather than 32 MB; this was the highest value observed in the trace). The y axis shows cummulative node seconds. The way to read this graph is as follows: for each point (x, y) on the graph, y is the probability that up to x of the memory is being used. But more importatnly, it is also the probability that at least $1 - x$ is free.

Except for the extreme edges, the graph is above the diagonal, which indicates relatively low resource usage. For example, if we focus on the mid point of the x axis, where up to half the memory is used, we find that this happens 62.7% of the time on average. This means that there is a probability of 0.627 that a running job will leave at least half of the memory free for other jobs. Alternatively, if we focus on the midpoint of the y axis, we find that it corresponds to 38.3% memory usage. Thus half the time we will find that at least 61.7% of the memory is available.

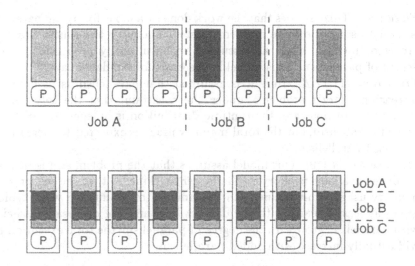

Fig. 10. *With space slicing, processor allocation dictates memory allocation due to the "vertical" partitioning (top). With gang scheduling, memory is partitioned "horizontally", so memory allocation is decoupled from processor allocation (bottom).*

The fact that nodes can be time-sliced without undue increase in memory pressure has far reaching implications. An important observation is that gang scheduling allows "horizontal" partitioning of memory, rather than the more rigid and inflexible "vertical" partitioning that happens when space slicing is used (Fig. 10). This added flexibility is expected to be instrumental in serving more jobs and reducing fragmentation. As a result, it allows more jobs to fit into the available memory, and delays the need to employ swapping.

The relatively unaggressive memory usage observed also has implications for space slicing policies, and particularly for adaptive and dynamic partitioning. One of the strengths of these policies is that the partition sizes are reduced under heavy load, leading to more efficient use of the resources (because most jobs display diminishing returns when more processors are added, and can use smaller numbers of processors more effectively than large numbers). Again, concern has been expressed that it would not be possible to reduce the partition sizes and exploit this feature, because of memory requirements [16]. Our results indicate that rather small partition sizes may suffice in many cases.

4.2 Modeling Memory Usage

A separate issue is the modeling of memory usage for use in simulations and analysis. Specifically, we would like to be able to model how resource requirements change when applications scale to larger systems. Three models have been proposed in the literature:

- *Fixed work*. This assumes that the work done by a job is fixed, and parallelism is used to solve the same problems faster. Therefore the runtime and per-processor memory usage are assumed to be inversely proportional to the degree of parallelism. This model is the basis for Amdahl's law [2].
- *Fixed time* [11,12,22]. Here it is assumed that parallelism is used to solve increasingly larger problems, under the constraint that the total runtime stays fixed. In this case, the runtime distribution is independent of the degree of parallelism, but the total memory usage is expected to increase with increased parallelism.
- *Memory bound* [19]. This model assumes that the problem size is increased to fill the available memory on the larger machine, so that the per-processor memory usage is maintained. As the amount of productive work typically grows at least linearly with the dataset size, and the overheads associated with parallelism grow with the degree of parallelism, the total execution time will actually increase with added parallelism.

We can get some speculative evidence concerning this question by comparing the resource requirements of jobs that actually ran on different size partitions.

Our preliminary results concerning memory usage, combined with our previous results regarding the correlation between runtime and parallelism [5], indicate that the truth probably lies between the fixed-time model and the memory bound model. In a nutshell, all three resources tend to scale up together: larger jobs use more processors, use more memory, and run longer. However, it seems that all these models are over-simplified to the point where it is hard to correlate them with measured results. In particular, users configure their applications according to their needs rather than according to the way resources happen to be packaged in the machine [18]. Thus users rarely use all the memory available, on any size partition. It is true, however, that they tend to use more on larger partitions.

Finally, we note that modeling the memory usage distribution itself is not easy, because it does not seem to be similar to commonly used "analytical" distributions. Instead, it has a number of large discrete components (Fig. 2). It is premature to draw too many conclusions about this distribution based on evidence from only one machine.

5 Conclusions

Scheduling is concerned with the allocation of scarce resources to competing jobs. Two of the most important resources are computing cycles and memory locations. The allocation of computing cycles allows for some tradeoff between the degree of parallelism and time — moldable and malleable jobs may use less processors for more time to accumulate the same overall number of cycles [10]. With memory, such a tradeoff is only possible if paging is used. As paging is typically considered to be too expensive due to its overhead and adverse effect on communication and synchronization, parallel jobs typically have to be memory resident throughout their execution. Memory requirements therefore impose a very rigid constraint on the scheduler and may severely limit its options.

In order to investigate the effect of memory requirements on scheduling, information about typical memory requirements is needed. We have studied the memory usage patterns of a production scientific workload on the LANL CM-5 parallel supercomputer for this purpose. Our main observations are

- The distribution of memory requests is rather wide, with strong discrete components (i.e. some sizes are much more popular than others). It is not similar to commonly used and mathematically tractable distributions.
- Many jobs use a relatively small fraction of the memory available on each node, e.g. less than half. Thus there is typically room for more than one job to be memory resident at the same time. However, it is advisable to pack the jobs according to their memory requirements, that is, to judiciously choose jobs with small requirements to fill in the space left by a job with large requirements. If this is done, time slicing among several memory-resident jobs is distinctly possible.
- Larger jobs (using more nodes) tend to use more memory than small jobs (using less nodes) in total, and also more memory per processor. However, it is difficult to characterize this scaling precisely, and further investigation (based on data from additional machines) is required.

Acknowledgement

Many thanks to Curt Canada of Los Alamos National Lab for providing the raw data used in this study.

References

1. G. Alverson, S. Kahan, R. Korry, C. McCann, and B. Smith, "*Scheduling on the Tera MTA*". In *Job Scheduling Strategies for Parallel Processing*, D. G. Feitelson and L. Rudolph (eds.), pp. 19–44, Springer-Verlag, 1995. Lecture Notes in Computer Science Vol. 949.
2. G. M. Amdahl, "*Validity of the single processor approach to achieving large scale computer capabilities*". In *AFIPS Spring Joint Comput. Conf.*, vol. 30, pp. 483–485, Apr 1967.
3. D. C. Burger, R. S. Hyder, B. P. Miller, and D. A. Wood, "*Paging tradeoffs in distributed-shared-memory multiprocessors*". *J. Supercomput.* **10(1)**, pp. 87–104, 1996.
4. J. J. Dongarra, H. W. Meuer, and E. Strohmaier, "*Top500 supercomputer sites*". http://www.netlib.org/benchmark/top500.html. (updated every 6 months).
5. D. G. Feitelson, "*Packing schemes for gang scheduling*". In *Job Scheduling Strategies for Parallel Processing*, D. G. Feitelson and L. Rudolph (eds.), pp. 89–110, Springer-Verlag, 1996. Lecture Notes in Computer Science Vol. 1162.
6. D. G. Feitelson, *A Survey of Scheduling in Multiprogrammed Parallel Systems*. Research Report RC 19790 (87657), IBM T. J. Watson Research Center, Oct 1994.
7. D. G. Feitelson and M. A. Jette, "*Improved utilization and responsiveness with gang scheduling*". In *Job Scheduling Strategies for Parallel Processing*, D. G. Feitelson and L. Rudolph (eds.), Springer Verlag, 1997. Lecture Notes in Computer Science (this volume).
8. D. G. Feitelson and B. Nitzberg, "*Job characteristics of a production parallel scientific workload on the NASA Ames iPSC/860*". In *Job Scheduling Strategies for Parallel Processing*, D. G. Feitelson and L. Rudolph (eds.), pp. 337–360, Springer-Verlag, 1995. Lecture Notes in Computer Science Vol. 949.
9. D. G. Feitelson and L. Rudolph, "*Parallel job scheduling: issues and approaches*". In *Job Scheduling Strategies for Parallel Processing*, D. G. Feitelson and L. Rudolph (eds.), pp. 1–18, Springer-Verlag, 1995. Lecture Notes in Computer Science Vol. 949.
10. D. G. Feitelson and L. Rudolph, "*Toward convergence in job schedulers for parallel supercomputers*". In *Job Scheduling Strategies for Parallel Processing*, D. G. Feitelson and L. Rudolph (eds.), pp. 1–26, Springer-Verlag, 1996. Lecture Notes in Computer Science Vol. 1162.
11. J. L. Gustafson, "*Reevaluating Amdahl's law*". *Comm. ACM* **31(5)**, pp. 532–533, May 1988. See also *Comm. ACM* **32(2)**, pp. 262–264, Feb 1989, and *Comm. ACM* **32(8)**, pp. 1014–1016, Aug 1989.
12. J. L. Gustafson, G. R. Montry, and R. E. Benner, "*Development of parallel methods for a 1024-processor hypercube*". *SIAM J. Sci. Statist. Comput.* **9(4)**, pp. 609–638, Jul 1988.
13. C. McCann and J. Zahorjan, "*Scheduling memory constrained jobs on distributed memory parallel computers*". In *SIGMETRICS Conf. Measurement & Modeling of Comput. Syst.*, pp. 208–219, May 1995.
14. Minnesota Supercomputer Center, Inc., *The Distributed Job Manager Administration Guide*. 1993. ftp://ec.msc.edu/pub/LIGHTNING/djm_1.0.0_src.tar.Z.
15. E. W. Parsons and K. C. Sevcik, "*Coordinated allocation of memory and processors in multiprocessors*". In *SIGMETRICS Conf. Measurement & Modeling of Comput. Syst.*, pp. 57–67, May 1996.

16. V. G. J. Peris, M. S. Squillante, and V. K. Naik, *"Analysis of the impact of memory in distributed parallel processing systems"*. In *SIGMETRICS Conf. Measurement & Modeling of Comput. Syst.*, pp. 5–18, May 1994.

17. S. K. Setia, *"The interaction between memory allocation and adaptive partitioning in message-passing multicomputers"*. In *Job Scheduling Strategies for Parallel Processing*, D. G. Feitelson and L. Rudolph (eds.), pp. 146–165, Springer-Verlag, 1995. Lecture Notes in Computer Science Vol. 949.

18. J. P. Singh, J. L. Hennessy, and A. Gupta, *"Scaling parallel programs for multiprocessors: methodology and examples"*. *Computer* **26**(7), pp. 42–50, Jul 1993.

19. X-H. Sun and L. M. Ni, *"Scalable problems and memory-bounded speedup"*. *J. Parallel & Distributed Comput.* **19**(1), pp. 27–37, Sep 1993.

20. Thinking Machines Corp., *Connection Machine CM-5 Technical Summary*. Nov 1992.

21. K. Y. Wang and D. C. Marinescu, *"Correlation of the paging activity of individual node programs in the SPMD execution model"*. In 28th *Hawaii Intl. Conf. System Sciences*, vol. I, pp. 61–71, Jan 1995.

22. P. H. Worley, *"The effect of time constraints on scaled speedup"*. *SIAM J. Sci. Statist. Comput.* **11**(5), pp. 838–858, Sep 1990.

Modeling of Workload in MPPs

Joefon Jann, Pratap Pattnaik, Hubertus Franke
IBM T. J. Watson Research Center, P. O. Box 218, Yorktown Heights, NY 10598

Fang Wang
Computer Science Department, Yale University, New Haven, CT 06520-8285

Joseph Skovira, Joseph Riordan
Cornell Theory Center, Cornell University, Ithaca, NY 14853-3801

email: joefon@watson.ibm.com

Abstract

In this paper we have characterized the inter-arrival time and service time distributions for jobs at a large MPP supercomputing center. Our findings show that the distributions are dispersive and complex enough that they require Hyper Erlang distributions to capture the first three moments of the observed workload. We also present the parameters from the characterization so that they can be easily used for both theoretical studies and the simulations of various scheduling algorithms.

1 Introduction

In recent years massively parallel processors (MPP) computers have made a significant presence. With this growth in MPPs, a number of researchers have developed and are continuing to develop various job scheduling subsystems for these MPPs [1, 2, 3, 4, 5, 6]. During the development of these schedulers and their related algorithms, it is important to have an accurate characterization of the workloads experienced by the MPPs. It is extremely advantageous to have these workloads characterized by a compact model that is representable by a few parameters, is suitable for theoretical queuing analysis of scheduling algorithms, and is reasonably straight-forward for the generation of synthetic workloads. In this paper we propose such a model, and demonstrate its efficacy by using it to fit the workload from the Cornell University Supercomputer.

The model we use for representing the inter-arrival time and the service time of jobs is a phase type distribution model, specifically, the Hyper Erlang Distribution of Common Order. Since we expect this model to be used by researchers with diverse background, we take a pedagogical approach in this paper, rather than simply refer the readers to the literature. In section 4, we describe the model parameter extraction procedure. In section 5, we present the parameters extracted from the workload of the SP2 at the Cornell Theory Center experienced during the period from June 25, 1996 to September 12, 1996. In section 6, we describe ways to generate synthetic workloads for simulation studies. In the appendix, we present a sample program to generate synthetic workloads.

2 Phase Type Distribution

The exponential distribution and the related Poisson process have been pervasively used in the stochastic modeling of computers and network workloads. The primary reason for the popularity of the exponential distribution is the ease with which it can be manipulated in theoretical studies, and not because of the presence of a large body of empirical data supporting it in a wide range of real life situations. The tractability of the exponential distribution in analytical work comes mainly from its memoryless property, leading to a simple form for the Laplace transform of the probability distribution function (pdf), namely,

$$f^*(s) = \left(\frac{\lambda}{s+\lambda}\right), \tag{1}$$

and to an underlying Markovian process. In this expression $1/\lambda$ is the first moment of the distribution and represents the average value of the random variable with the exponential distribution. In a Markovian process, the transition rate from a state to the next state depends only on the current state, and does not explicitly depend on past history. This property simplifies the steady state equations and enables one to represent all the needed information by a one dimensional vector of the current state, thus making the queuing analysis of the problem tractable. In 1947, Erlang generalized the exponential distribution to include more complex probability distributions, while preserving the analytic tractability. This generalized distribution is called the Erlang distribution and its Laplace transform is

$$f^*(s) = \left(\frac{\lambda}{s+\lambda}\right)^n. \tag{2}$$

Service time distributions that can be represented by the Erlang distribution can be thought of as originating from a system where the job goes through n phases or stages before completion. At each stage a job spends an exponentially distributed random amount of time, with the average time being $1/\lambda$. The distribution of the total service time of the jobs is then the convolution of n exponential distributions. The Laplace transform of this convolution is equation 2. The Erlang distribution, like the exponential distribution, has an underlying Markovian process, thus making it attractive for use in queuing theory. The Erlang distribution can represent more types of systems than the exponential distribution can. Finally in 1955, Cox, in a seminal paper [7], demonstrated that the key advantage of the Erlang and the exponential distributions for analytical work stems from the fact that their Laplace transforms are rational. He also developed a generalized distribution known as the Phase Type Distribution, which is capable of representing any stochastic process whose associated pdf's have Laplace transforms that are rational. Practically all the relevant systems one encounters in the stochastic modeling of workloads in computers can be modeled by the Phase Type Distribution.

In practice, one approximates only the first few moments of the probability distributions under study with Phase Type Distributions; and these Phase Type Distributions are characterized by a set of parameters m, p_0, p_i, n_i and $\lambda_{i,j}$ (where i,j=1,2,3,...), such that their Laplace transforms are of the form

$$f^*(s) = p_0 + \sum_{i=1}^{m} p_i \prod_{j=1}^{n_i} \left(\frac{\lambda_{i,j}}{s+\lambda_{i,j}}\right) \tag{3}$$

with

$$f^*(0) = 1. \tag{4}$$

Service time distributions representable by equation 3 can be thought of as coming from a system where jobs may reach completion using any of the m-possible paths. If a job goes through the ith path, then it will traverse through n_i phases or stages before completion; and like the Erlang distribution, the job spends an exponentially distributed random amount of time at each stage. These exponential distributions are characterized by the parameters $\lambda_{i,j}$.

The Phase Type Distribution, in addition to its ability to conveniently represent a wide class of stochastic processes, provides an underlying Markovian process, a great advantage for queuing studies [8], for the reasons described earlier. Recently they have also been used successfully in analyzing gang-scheduling in MPPs [5].

3 Hyper Erlang Distribution of Common Order

Oftentimes, in analytical modeling of a stochastic process, only the first few moments of the random variables are considered. For most stochastic processes, the first few moments represent attributes that tend to be relatively sample invariant. Here we consider the first three moments of the random variables for our modeling. They carry the information about the mean, the variance, and the skewness of the random variables respectively.

In this paper, we choose the simplest distribution with an underlying Markovian process, that can fit the the first three moments of the observed data. As mentioned in the previous section, the underlying Markovian process makes the distribution tractable in theoretical studies. The distribution we have chosen is the Hyper Erlang Distribution of Common Order, which is a Phase Type Distribution that can exactly fit the first three moments of the observed random distribution. The Hyper Erlang Distribution of Common Order is a generalization of the exponential, the hyper exponential, and the Erlang distribution. Our fitting procedure automatically selects the simplest of these 4 distributions that is commensurate with the first three moments of the observed data.

The Hyper Erlang Distribution of Common Order distribution has a Laplace transform of the form

$$f^*(s) = \sum_{i=1}^{2} p_i \left(\frac{\lambda_i}{s + \lambda_i} \right)^n \tag{5}$$

where n, a positive integer, is called the order of the distribution, and $0 \leq p_i \leq 1$ with $p_1 + p_2 = 1$. The Erlang distribution is a special case of the Hyper Erlang Distribution of Common Order with one of the p_is equal to 1, e.g. $p_1 = 1$. The hyper exponential distribution is a Hyper Erlang Distribution of Common Order with $n = 1$. The exponential distribution is also a special case with $p_1 = 1$ and $n = 1$.

An example of a server with service time distribution expressable by a Hyper Erlang Distribution of Common Order is a system where a job must pass through one and only one of two service paths to completion. In each path it has to pass through n stages (or phases), spending a random amount of service time at each of the n stages. The pdf of service time at each stage of path 1 is an exponential distribution with mean time $1/\lambda_1$, and that of path 2 is an exponential distribution with mean time $1/\lambda_2$. Let p_1 be the probability of the job selecting path 1, and $(1 - p_1)$ be that of selecting path 2. Pictorially, the stages of this system can be depicted by

The kth non-central moment of a distribution, for all integers $k \geq 1$, can be obtained from the Laplace transform of the distribution by,

$$\mu_k = E[t^k] = (-1)^k \left[\frac{d^k f^*(s)}{ds^k} \right]_{s=0} \tag{6}$$

which, for Hyper Erlang distribution of Common Order, is

$$\mu_k = \sum_{i=1}^{2} p_i \frac{n(n+1)...(n+k-1)}{\lambda_i^k} \tag{7}$$

The moments for the Erlang distribution are obtained by setting $p_1 = 1$ and $p_2 = 0$ in equation 7, yielding

$$\mu_k = \frac{n(n+1)...(n+k-1)}{\lambda^k}. \tag{8}$$

The moments for the hyper exponential distribution are obtained by setting $n = 1$ in equation 7, yielding

$$\mu_k = \sum_{i=1}^{2} p_i \frac{k!}{\lambda_i^k} \tag{9}$$

The moments for the exponential distribution is obtain by letting $n = 1$ in equation 8, giving

$$\mu_k = \frac{k!}{\lambda^k} \tag{10}$$

Examining the expressions for the first three moments of these distributions, and because physical situations imply non-negative p_is and λ_is, one finds a number of interrelationships among these moments. These interrelationships specify the constraints that must be satisfied by the moments of the observed data, for a particular model to represent the data. Without going into the proof (which is straight forward in most cases, but involves lengthy algebraic manipulations in the non-obvious cases), we state here the constraints on the first three moments of various distribution.

The constraints for the exponential distribution are:

$$\mu_2 = 2 * \mu_1^2 \tag{11}$$

and

$$\mu_3 = 6 * \mu_1^3 \tag{12}$$

Since the exponential distribution is a one parameter model, all higher moments are just functions of first moments. In the data we examined in this paper, none of the observed moments, either for inter-arrival time or the service time, fulfill this condition.

The constraints for the hyper exponential distribution are:

$$\mu_1\mu_3 > \frac{3}{2}\mu_2^2 \tag{13}$$

and

$$\mu_2 > 2\mu_1^2 \tag{14}$$

The constraints for the Erlang distribution are:

$$\mu_1\mu_3 = \frac{n+2}{n+1}\mu_2^2 \tag{15}$$

and

$$\mu_2 = \left(1+\frac{1}{n}\right)\mu_1^2 \tag{16}$$

The constraints for Hyper Erlang of Common Order are

$$\mu_1\mu_3 > \frac{n+2}{n+1}\mu_2^2 \tag{17}$$

and

$$\mu_2 > \frac{n+1}{n}\mu_1^2 \tag{18}$$

4 Our Modeling Procedure

Our procedure for modeling, selects the simplest model amongst exponential, hyper exponential, Erlang and Hyper Erlang Distribution of Common Order, as long as the first three moments of the data do not violate the constraints of the model under consideration. It also exactly matches the first three moments of the data to that of the model. In our procedure for modeling the data, we start with the three non-central moments of the data, namely the μs and fit them to the Hyper Erlang of Common Order distribution with the lowest value of n satisfying equations 17 and 18. The Hyper Erlang of Common Order distribution has four unknowns, namely λ_1, λ_2, n and p_1, p_2 where $p_1 + p_2 = 1$. For a given n, one can extract the remaining three parameters of this model by matching the expressions for μ_1, μ_2, and μ_3 obtained from equation 7,to the first three observed non-central moments. This involves solving 3 simultaneous equations with 3 unknowns. The analytical expression for the three parameters has been derived by Johnson and Taaffe [9]. In general, an infinite number of n's can fit the data, while satisfying equations 17 and 18. We select the smallest such n. Furthermore, after solving for the p_is, if one of the p_is is very close to zero, we set it to zero yielding an Erlang or exponential distribution as a model for the data.

For example, the first three moments of the distribution of inter-arrival times for jobs requiring just one processor in our Cornell SP2 data are $\mu_1 = 1.05 \times 10^3$, $\mu_2 = 8.86 \times 10^6$ and $\mu_3 = 1.78 \times 10^{11}$ (table 7). The unit of time used in these moments is one second. An examination of the above moments for inter-arrival time will show that they satisfy the constraints (equations 13, 14, 17 and 18) of the hyper exponential and the Hyper Erlang Distribution of Common Order, and do not satisfy those of the Erlang and the exponential distributions. Hence we choose the hyper exponential distribution (i.e. Hyper Erlang Distribution of Common Order, with $n = 1$, see line 2 of tables 1 and 2) to represent this data.

The moments for the service time distribution of these jobs requiring only one processor are: $\mu_1 = 1.54 \times 10^4$, $\mu_2 = 6.05 \times 10^8$ and $\mu_3 = 2.94 \times 10^{13}$. This set of data cannot be represented by exponential, hyper exponential or Erlang distributions, as the three moments do not satisfy the constraints of these distributions. A Hyper Erlang Distribution of Order 4 was needed to represent this data and this is reflected in the results section of this paper (see line 2 in tables 3, 4, 5 and 6, column n).

As the results section shows, none of the inter-arrival time and service time data examined in this paper is under-dispersive enough to satisfy equation 16, hence their second non-central moments are not representable by an Erlang or an exponential distribution. This over-dispersive data is sometimes referred to as longtail data.

Once the parameters of the model have been determined, it can be used either directly in theoretical studies, or in simulations by creating synthetic workloads. In the section following the results section, we outline a way to generate synthetic workloads from the model parameters presented in this paper. Also in the appendix section, we give a sample C program to illustrate the procedure for generating workloads.

5 Results

In our experimental workload, we have examined all the jobs for a 322 node SP2 at the Cornell Theory Center, for the period from June 25, 1996 to September 12, 1996. During this period, a total of 17440 jobs were serviced by the system. All these jobs required dedicated use of CPUs, and different jobs required different numbers of CPUs of the SP2. We have characterized the workload using Hyper Erlang Distribution of Common Order to model the inter-arrival time and the service time, the latter being the cumulative CPU time used by a job. For this, we have grouped the jobs into classes based on the number of CPUs they used. A job requesting p processors is assigned to a class, such that $p_{min} \leq p \leq p_{max}$, where p_{min} and p_{max} are the minimum and maximum number of processors of that class. The p_{min} and p_{max} values for classes considered in our study here are shown in tables 1 through 12. Tables 7 through 12 give the first three moments of the real workload, and these moments were used to extract the model parameters, shown in tables 1 through 6.

In order to provide models for different needs, we have done this classification in two different ways. In tables 1, 3 and 5, we have grouped jobs into classes by defining the upper boundary of the classes (p_{max}) at powers of two. In tables 2, 4 and 6, we have grouped jobs into classes by defining the upper class boundaries at multiples of five, except at the low end. Also when a class has less than 1% of the jobs, we have merged it with a neighboring class that has a smaller number of jobs; and we continue this process until the combined class contains at least 1% of the jobs. For completeness, we have included in the first row of each table information on the workload where we do not separate jobs into classes.

Columns 3 through 6 in tables 1, 2, 3, 4, 5 and 6, provide the parameters of the model. Column 7 gives E_4, which is the relative discrepancy (in percentage) between the non-central fourth moment of the data and that of the model. Since the model parameters are derived by fitting only the first three non-central moments, E_4 gives an estimate of the accuracy of the fit. The last column in these tables gives the percent of jobs in the workload that is modeled in this class.

A point to note is that the first three moments of the data and those of the model are identical, a consequence of our modeling procedure. Hence the numerical values of these moments, for any row of any of the tables in this paper, can be obtained by substituting the 4 parameter values (λ_1, λ_2, n, p_1) from the table into equation 7. For the convenience of the readers we have also included these first three moments from the workload data in tables 7 through 12. The rows in these tables are organized analogous to the rows of the corresponding table in tables 1 through 6.

Often in statistical modeling, one utilizes either the observed cumulative distribution function (cdf) or the moments of the random variables, as they do not depend on the quantization interval. To graphically illustrate the discrepancy between the observed cdf and the cdf obtained from the model, we show in Figure 1 the cdf's of the inter-arrival time of jobs requesting between 9 to 16 processors. Qualitatively the curves in this figure are typical in comparisons. Quantitatively this figure shows one of the workloads with high relative error between the fourth moment of the model and that of the observed data, namely 17% as shown in table 1, line 6, column E_4. We purposely chose this example so as to give an idea graphically of the accuracy of our modeling, even when the relative error in μ_4 is high. Even in this case, our model agrees quite well with the observed cdf for large values of inter-arrival time. This is a consequence of the ability of our model to handle long-tail (i.e. over-dispersive) distributions.

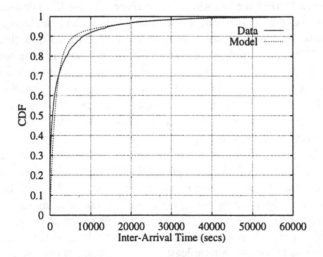

Fig. 1. Comparison of the observed cdf and that from the model for the inter-arrival time distribution for jobs requesting between 9 to 16 processors

Besides the inter-arrival time and CPU time, we have also characterized a derived quantity, which we call Scaled Wall-clock time. This is the amount of wall-clock time, in seconds, the job would need if it could use the maximum number of processors in its assigned class, while preserving its parallel efficiency. For example, if a job used 3 processors and 300 cumulative CPU seconds, i.e. running for 100 seconds concurrently on 3 processors, and we classify that job into a class having a maximum of 4 processors, then we define the Scaled Wall-clock time as 75 seconds, namely $100 * 3/4$ seconds.

Scaled Wall-clock time is often a theoretical quantity, as most of the time the parallel efficiencies are not invariant. We characterized this quantity because we feel that it is useful as an optimistic workload for various theoretical studies. The characterization of this Scaled Wall-clock time is presented in tables 5 and 6, in a format analogous to that in tables 3 and 4.

p_{min}	p_{max}	λ_1	λ_2	n	p_1	E_4	%of jobs
1	322	2.04e-04	3.80e-03	1	3.46e-02	11	100.00
1	1	1.43e-04	2.05e-03	1	8.56e-02	2	40.42
2	2	3.31e-05	9.94e-04	1	1.67e-01	5	7.17
3	4	5.58e-05	1.13e-03	1	1.55e-01	5	11.97
5	8	7.37e-05	1.88e-03	1	2.38e-01	9	11.64
9	16	6.87e-05	7.16e-04	1	1.30e-01	17	13.61
17	32	4.08e-05	4.98e-04	1	1.49e-01	12	7.89
33	64	5.67e-05	4.91e-03	1	4.79e-01	6	4.91
65	128	3.33e-05	6.07e-04	2	5.03e-01	3	1.32
129	256	4.48e-06	2.78e-04	1	2.78e-01	16	0.64
257	322	1.69e-06	1.99e-05	1	1.18e-01	17	0.37

Table 1. Hyper Erlang parameters for inter-arrival time. Unit of time is in seconds. The symbols are defined in Sections 3 and 5.

6 Synthetic Workload Generation

The first step in generating a synthetic workload from the models presented in this paper is to select the classes of jobs to be included in the synthetic workload, namely which rows or sets of p_{min} and p_{max} from table 1 or 2 are to be included. *In the program in the appendix, we denote the number of classes included in the workload generation by the variable* nmodels. Also we choose the size of the synthetic workload either in terms of the number of jobs to be generated in each of the chosen classes, or in terms of the total length of time for all arrivals to be generated. If one prefers to use the former criterion but only knows the total number of jobs for the synthetic workload, then the number of jobs in each of the chosen classes can be obtained by relative portioning of the total number of jobs amongst the chosen classes. These portions should be proportional to the % of jobs, i.e.the last column in the corresponding table. *In the sample program in*

p_{min}	p_{max}	λ_1	λ_2	n	p_1	E_4	%of jobs
1	322	2.04e-04	3.80e-03	1	3.46e-02	11	100.00
1	1	1.43e-04	2.05e-03	1	8.56e-02	2	40.42
2	2	3.31e-05	9.94e-04	1	1.67e-01	5	7.17
3	4	5.58e-05	1.13e-03	1	1.55e-01	5	11.97
5	10	8.48e-05	1.95e-03	1	2.06e-01	9	14.91
11	15	1.17e-05	1.58e-04	1	2.29e-01	2	1.71
16	20	6.57e-05	5.99e-04	1	1.81e-01	12	10.27
21	30	1.05e-05	5.72e-05	1	1.89e-01	5	1.30
31	35	3.78e-05	5.15e-04	1	2.00e-01	12	6.16
36	125	4.97e-05	1.23e-02	1	5.04e-01	8	4.13
126	322	3.43e-05	6.46e-04	2	3.43e-01	1	1.90

Table 2. Hyper Erlang parameters for inter-arrival time. Unit of time is in seconds. The symbols are defined in Sections 3 and 5.

p_{min}	p_{max}	λ_1	λ_2	n	p_1	E_4	%of jobs
1	322	3.40e-07	2.06e-05	1	1.48e-02	9	100.00
1	1	1.23e-04	4.72e-03	4	4.60e-01	7	40.43
2	2	8.04e-05	1.02e-01	7	3.94e-01	6	7.17
3	4	3.23e-05	1.61e-02	4	2.51e-01	9	11.97
5	8	1.17e-05	9.18e-03	1	3.76e-01	9	11.65
9	16	7.65e-06	6.40e-04	3	2.87e-01	9	13.62
17	32	2.80e-06	2.51e-04	1	3.75e-01	10	7.90
33	64	1.59e-06	7.99e-05	3	2.78e-01	9	4.92
65	128	1.19e-06	3.99e-04	6	2.07e-01	7	1.32
129	256	1.62e-05	3.15e-03	3	1.48e-01	9	0.65
257	322	5.18e-07	4.51e-04	6	1.65e-01	5	0.37

Table 3. Hyper Erlang parameters for CPU time used by the jobs. Unit of time is in seconds, and it is the cumulative CPU time used in all the processors on which the job is executing. The symbols are defined in Sections 3 and 5.

the appendix, we use the number of jobs to define the size of the workload, and comment on what needs to be modified to have the workload size based on total length of time for arrivals.

The model parameters for each of these classes are obtained from tables 1 through 6. With this information, for each job in each class to be included in the synthetic workload, one generates 3 random numbers: one for the inter-arrival time, one for the service time (i.e. CPU time used), and one for the number of CPUs needed for the job. The first of these 3 random numbers is from a Hyper Erlang distribution of Common Order (or a hyper exponential distribution, which is a special case of Hyper Erlang of Common Order), with appropriate model parameters for the particular class obtained from either

p_{min}	p_{max}	λ_1	λ_2	n	p_1	E_4	%of jobs
1	322	3.40e-07	2.06e-05	1	1.48e-02	9	100.00
1	1	1.23e-04	4.72e-03	4	4.60e-01	7	40.43
2	2	8.04e-05	1.02e-01	7	3.94e-01	6	7.17
3	4	3.23e-05	1.61e-02	4	2.51e-01	9	11.97
5	10	8.89e-06	3.21e-04	1	3.28e-01	8	14.91
11	15	1.34e-05	3.86e-03	5	1.68e-01	6	1.71
16	20	6.60e-06	1.29e-02	3	3.35e-01	10	10.28
21	30	3.66e-06	1.96e-04	2	2.10e-01	8	1.31
31	35	2.50e-06	6.90e-05	1	3.81e-01	11	6.17
36	125	1.45e-06	1.95e-04	3	2.86e-01	7	4.13
126	322	3.42e-07	1.99e-04	2	1.75e-01	3	1.91

Table 4. Hyper Erlang parameters for CPU time used by the jobs. Unit of time is in seconds, and it is the cumulative CPU time used in all the processors on which the job is executing. The symbols are defined in Sections 3 and 5.

p_{min}	p_{max}	λ_1	λ_2	n	p_1	E_4	%of jobs
1	322	6.80e-07	4.12e-05	1	1.48e-02	9	100.00
1	1	1.23e-04	4.72e-03	4	4.60e-01	7	40.43
2	2	1.61e-04	2.05e-01	7	3.94e-01	6	7.17
3	4	6.46e-05	3.23e-02	4	2.51e-01	9	11.97
5	8	2.33e-05	1.84e-02	1	3.76e-01	9	11.65
9	16	1.53e-05	1.28e-03	3	2.87e-01	9	13.62
17	32	5.60e-06	5.01e-04	1	3.75e-01	10	7.90
33	64	3.17e-06	1.60e-04	3	2.78e-01	9	4.92
65	128	2.39e-06	7.97e-04	6	2.07e-01	7	1.32
129	256	3.24e-05	6.29e-03	3	1.48e-01	9	0.65
257	322	1.04e-06	9.01e-04	6	1.65e-01	5	0.37

Table 5. Hyper Erlang parameters for Scaled Wall-clock time usedd by the jobs. Unit of time is in seconds. The symbols are defined in Sections 3 and 5.

table 1 or 2. Similarly, the second random number is also from a Hyper Erlang of Common Order (or hyper exponential) distribution, with appropriate model parameters for the particular class obtained from the corresponding table. The last random number, representing the number of CPUs needed, is a uniform random number that has been scaled to remain within the range of p_{min} and p_{max}. Once these 3 random numbers are obtained, one has the inter-arrival time, the service time, and the number of processors required by the job, which are commensurate with the workload model. This process continues for other jobs in the class until the desired amount of workload has been generated, and then the process is repeated for each of the other chosen classes in the synthetic workload.

p_{min}	p_{max}	λ_1	λ_2	n	p_1	E_4	%of jobs
1	322	6.80e-07	4.12e-05	1	1.48e-02	9	100.00
1	1	1.23e-04	4.72e-03	4	4.60e-01	7	40.43
2	2	1.61e-04	2.05e-01	7	3.94e-01	6	7.17
3	4	6.46e-05	3.23e-02	4	2.51e-01	9	11.97
5	10	1.78e-05	6.41e-04	1	3.28e-01	8	14.91
11	15	2.67e-05	7.71e-03	5	1.68e-01	6	1.71
16	20	1.32e-05	2.58e-02	3	3.35e-01	10	10.28
21	30	7.31e-06	3.92e-04	2	2.10e-01	8	1.31
31	35	5.00e-06	1.38e-04	1	3.81e-01	11	6.17
36	125	2.89e-06	3.91e-04	3	2.86e-01	7	4.13
126	322	6.84e-07	3.98e-04	2	1.75e-01	3	1.91

Table 6. Hyper Erlang parameters for Scaled Wall-clock time used by the jobs. Unit of time is in seconds. The symbols are defined in Sections 3 and 5.

p_{min}	p_{max}	μ_1	μ_2	μ_3	%of jobs
1	322	4.234e+02	1.794e+06	2.449e+10	99.99
1	1	1.046e+03	8.858e+06	1.778e+11	40.42
2	2	5.893e+03	3.070e+08	2.766e+13	7.17
3	4	3.529e+03	1.011e+08	5.371e+12	11.97
5	8	3.635e+03	8.808e+07	3.569e+12	11.64
9	16	3.107e+03	5.842e+07	2.416e+12	13.61
17	32	5.358e+03	1.858e+08	1.320e+13	7.89
33	64	8.544e+03	2.975e+08	1.573e+13	4.91
65	128	3.182e+04	2.727e+09	3.265e+14	1.32
129	256	6.471e+04	2.775e+10	1.857e+16	0.64
257	322	1.142e+05	8.698e+10	1.469e+17	0.37

Table 7. First three non-central moments of the of inter-arrival time distribution in the observed workload. Unit of time is in seconds. The symbols are defined in Sections 3 and 5. The model parameters extracted from these moments are given in table 1.

The only remaining algorithm that needs to be discussed here is a method to generate random numbers from a Hyper Erlang distribution of Common Order with appropriate model parameters for a particular class. A way to generate a sequence of random numbers, $\{x_j\}$, based on a non-uniform distribution, is to solve for x_j in

$$y_j = cdf(x_j) \tag{19}$$

where $\{y_j\}$, is a uniformly distributed sequence of random numbers, and $cdf(x_j)$ is the cumulative distribution function for the statistical model. For the Hyper Erlang distribution of Common Order, the cdf is obtained from equation 5 by inverse Laplace transform followed by a simple integral. After some straight-forward algebra, one ar-

p_{min}	p_{max}	μ_1	μ_2	μ_3	%of jobs
1	322	4.234e+02	1.794e+06	2.449e+10	99.99
1	1	1.046e+03	8.858e+06	1.778e+11	40.42
2	2	5.893e+03	3.070e+08	2.766e+13	7.17
3	4	3.529e+03	1.011e+08	5.371e+12	11.97
5	10	2.838e+03	5.774e+07	2.027e+12	14.91
11	15	2.447e+04	3.410e+09	8.593e+14	1.71
16	20	4.118e+03	8.825e+07	3.842e+12	10.27
21	30	3.207e+04	3.891e+09	9.927e+14	1.30
31	35	6.859e+03	2.869e+08	2.234e+13	6.16
36	125	1.019e+04	4.085e+08	2.467e+13	4.13
126	322	2.205e+04	1.759e+09	2.040e+14	1.90

Table 8. First three non-central moments of the of inter-arrival time distribution in the observed workload. Unit of time is in seconds. The symbols are defined in Sections 3 and 5. The model parameters extracted from these moments are given in table 2.

p_{min}	p_{max}	μ_1	μ_2	μ_3	%of jobs
1	322	9.126e+04	2.601e+11	2.255e+18	100.00
1	1	1.537e+04	6.051e+08	2.941e+13	40.43
2	2	3.432e+04	3.412e+09	3.821e+14	7.17
3	4	3.130e+04	4.814e+09	8.939e+14	11.97
5	8	3.230e+04	5.526e+09	1.421e+15	11.65
9	16	1.160e+05	5.895e+10	3.852e+16	13.62
17	32	1.365e+05	9.567e+10	1.024e+17	7.90
33	64	5.527e+05	1.328e+12	4.184e+18	4.92
65	128	1.052e+06	6.107e+12	4.097e+19	1.32
129	256	2.816e+04	6.754e+09	2.085e+15	0.65
257	322	1.928e+06	2.592e+13	4.005e+20	0.37

Table 9. First three non-central moments of the distribution of the CPU time used by the jobs in the observed workload. Unit of time is in seconds, and it is the cumulative CPU time used in all the processors on which the job is executing. The symbols are defined in Section 5. The model parameters extracted from these moments are given in table 3.

rives at an analytical expression for the cdf of the models used in this paper, namely

$$cdf(x_j) = 1 - \sum_{i=1}^{2} p_i e^{-\lambda_i x_j} \left(\sum_{k=0}^{n-1} \frac{(x_j \lambda_i)^k}{k!} \right) \tag{20}$$

From this expression of the *cdf* and a uniform random number generator, U[0,1], the random variables $\{x_j\}$ that are commensurate with equation 5 can be obtained by solving for x_j in equation 19. Since a *cdf(x)* is a monotonic function that is bounded by 0

p_{min}	p_{max}	μ_1	μ_2	μ_3	%of jobs
1	322	9.126e+04	2.601e+11	2.255e+18	100.00
1	1	1.537e+04	6.051e+08	2.941e+13	40.43
2	2	3.432e+04	3.412e+09	3.821e+14	7.17
3	4	3.130e+04	4.814e+09	8.939e+14	11.97
5	10	3.898e+04	8.313e+09	2.802e+15	14.91
11	15	6.409e+04	2.829e+10	1.482e+16	1.71
16	20	1.526e+05	9.239e+10	6.998e+16	10.28
21	30	1.230e+05	9.442e+10	1.032e+17	1.31
31	35	1.613e+05	1.223e+11	1.465e+17	6.17
36	125	6.043e+05	1.640e+12	5.665e+18	4.13
126	322	1.032e+06	8.971e+12	1.049e+20	1.91

Table 10. First three non-central moments of the distribution of the CPU time used by the jobs in the observed workload. Unit of time is in seconds, and it is the cumulative CPU time used in all the processors on which the job is executing. The symbols are defined in Sections 3 and 5. The model parameters extracted from these moments are given in table 4.

p_{min}	p_{max}	μ_1	μ_2	μ_3	%of jobs
1	322	4.563e+04	6.504e+10	2.819e+17	100.00
1	1	1.537e+04	6.051e+08	2.941e+13	40.43
2	2	1.716e+04	8.530e+08	4.776e+13	7.17
3	4	1.565e+04	1.204e+09	1.117e+14	11.97
5	8	1.615e+04	1.382e+09	1.777e+14	11.65
9	16	5.801e+04	1.474e+10	4.815e+15	13.62
17	32	6.824e+04	2.392e+10	1.280e+16	7.90
33	64	2.763e+05	3.319e+11	5.230e+17	4.92
65	128	5.262e+05	1.527e+12	5.121e+18	1.32
129	256	1.408e+04	1.688e+09	2.606e+14	0.65
257	322	9.641e+05	6.480e+12	5.006e+19	0.37

Table 11. First three non-central moments of the distribution of the Scaled Wall-clock time used by the jobs in the observed workload. Unit of time is in seconds, and it is the cumulative CPU time used in all the processors on which the job is executing. The symbols are defined in Sections 3 and 5. The model parameters extracted from these moments are given in table 5.

and 1, equation 19 can easily be solved by using any of the simple root finding techniques such as interval halving, etc.

Among the functions shown in the appendix,

- function **H_Er_cdf()** computes the $cdf(x_j)$ based on equation 20,
- function **solve_bisec()** finds the root of an equation by interval halving, and
- function **ur_to_HER_r()** solves equation 19 for a given y.

p_{min}	p_{max}	μ_1	μ_2	μ_3	%of jobs
1	322	4.563e+04	6.504e+10	2.819e+17	100.00
1	1	1.537e+04	6.051e+08	2.941e+13	40.43
2	2	1.716e+04	8.530e+08	4.776e+13	7.17
3	4	1.565e+04	1.204e+09	1.117e+14	11.97
5	10	1.949e+04	2.078e+09	3.502e+14	14.91
11	15	3.205e+04	7.073e+09	1.852e+15	1.71
16	20	7.631e+04	2.310e+10	8.748e+15	10.28
21	30	6.148e+04	2.361e+10	1.290e+16	1.31
31	35	8.067e+04	3.056e+10	1.832e+16	6.17
36	125	3.021e+05	4.100e+11	7.081e+17	4.13
126	322	5.158e+05	2.243e+12	1.311e+19	1.91

Table 12. First three non-central moments of the distribution of the Scaled Wall-clock time used by the jobs in the observed workload. Unit of time is in seconds, and it is the cumulative CPU time used in all the processors on which the job is executing. The symbols are defined in Sections 3 and 5. The model parameters extracted from these moments are given in table 6.

7 Conclusions

In this paper we have characterized in a compact model the workload of a large super-computing center. For this characterization we have chosen a phase type distribution, namely Hyper Erlang distribution of Common Order, that exactly fits the first three moments of the observed workload, and when appropriate, reduces to a simpler model such as exponential, hyper exponential or Erlang. The important findings of our study here are:

- The observed workload is quite dispersive, namely, the coefficient of variation is greater than one, and cannot be adequately represented by an Erlang or exponential distribution. A point to note is that, typically the number of users in these MPPs are relatively small, hence there is no a priori reason to expect an under-dispersive distribution to be able to represent the observed inter-arrival time or service time. Thus for theoretical studies and simulations dealing with scheduling of jobs in MPPs, it is more desirable, in our opinion, to use hyper exponential or Hyper Erlang distributions rather than simple exponential or Erlang distributions.

- Even though the inter-arrival time can often be modeled by hyper exponential distributions, the service time and the Scaled Wall-clock time often require Hyper Erlang distributions of order greater than one.

Another point to note is that, in light of the number of jobs we have sampled in each class, the relative errors in the fourth moment (shown as percentage in column 7 of the tables 1 through 6) are sometimes relatively high. However, as shown by Schassberger [10, 11, 12, 13], a number of steady state properties such as mean queue lengths, average waiting times, etc., depend only on the first few moments of the random distributions, and since we want a model that is simple enough to be tractable in theoretical studies of scheduling algorithms and parameters, we feel that our model for characterization of the workloads in MPPs is quite adequate.

8 Acknowledgments

Joseph Riordan's portion of this research was funded by the Cornell Theory Center, which receives major funding from NSF (the National Science Foundation) and New York State, with additional support from the National Center for Research Resources at the NIH (National Institute of Health), IBM Corporation, and other members of the center's Corporate Partnership Program.

9 Appendix

The program shown in this section can be used to generate synthetic workloads for model parameters given in the results section of this paper. The overall algorithm used in this program is described in section 6. Here we point out a few specifics relevant to the accurate generation of workloads.

- This program needs a uniform random number generator generating random numbers in the interval of 0 to 1. This is assumed to be obtained from a library function called **drand48()**. If this function is not available in your computer, or if you have a different favorite one, replace the call to **drand48()** with an appropriate call. The use of a good uniform random number generator is essential to the quality of the generated workloads. In our simulations, instead of **drand48()**, we used a very high quality, but machine dependent random number generator.

- A point to note is that, for each job we need 3 random numbers, drawn from independent uniform random number pools. We achieve this from a high quality, single uniform random number generator by creating 3 pools or streams of uniform random numbers. This is done in the function **str_rand()**.

- The tolerance for solution parameter, **tol**, in function **solve_bisec()** should be tight.

- At the end of the program we also compute the non-central moments μ_k for each of the classes, from the jobs generated in the synthetic workload. These should be close to the corresponding numbers from tables 7 through 12.

This program generates a workload based on one class with $p_{min} = 65$ and $p_{max} = 128$, and the CPU time is used as the service time. The parameters correspond to row 9 in tables 1 and 3. The μ_k should be compared with row 9 of tables 7 and 9.

```
/* This program generates a stream of jobs based on the
 *    models described in the main text of this paper.
 * To keep this program simple, we have elimated all
```

```
 *      the checkings of the input.  If you use the
 *      program often, we strongly recommend you to
 *      add code to catch the error conditions. This
 *      program is meant for illustration purposes only.
 */
#include <stdio.h>
#include <math.h>

#define min(a,b) (((a) < (b)) ? (a) : (b))
#define RANSTREAM 3
#define RANPOOLSIZE 10000

typedef struct
{ double p1,lambda1,lambda2,ur;
        int     order;
}   MODEL_DATA;

/* Global Variables: */
double ran_pool[RANSTREAM][RANPOOLSIZE];
int     ran_remain[RANSTREAM];

/* --------- Function prototypes: ------------------ */
double ur_to_HER_r( double ur, MODEL_DATA model);

double H_Er_cdf(double x, void *model);

void solve_bisec( double xleft_0,
                  double xright_0,
                  double tol,
                  double *x,
                  double *y,
                  void *model_data,
                  double (*f)(double, void *),
                  int *rc);

double fn_to_solve(double x, void *);

int     fac(int k);

double str_rand(int str);

/* ================================================== */
main(int argc, char **argv)
{ MODEL_DATA inter_arrival_model, cpu_model;
  double inter_arrival_mu1, inter_arrival_mu2,
```

```
inter_arrival_mu3;
 double cpu_mu1, cpu_mu2, cpu_mu3;
 double simtime, inter_arrival_time, cpu_time_used;
 double dtemp;

 int njobs,   pmin,pmax,p_needed;
 int ijob,    nmodels, imodel;
 int i,j;

 /* One needs to change the value of nmodels here to
  * reflect  the number of models (namely number of
  * lines from Tables 1 through 6 in the Results
  * section of this paper) concurrently used for
  *  generating the job stream.
  */
 nmodels=1;

for(imodel=0; imodel<nmodels; imodel++)
{ simtime=0;

   /* The following section describes the parameters
    * of model imodel, and should be modified to
    * correspond to your chosen model.
    */
   pmin = 65;
   pmax = 128;

   inter_arrival_model.lambda1 = 3.33e-05;
   inter_arrival_model.lambda2 = 6.07e-04;
   inter_arrival_model.order=2;
   inter_arrival_model.p1=5.03e-01;

   cpu_model.lambda1 = 1.19e-06;
   cpu_model.lambda2 = 3.99e-04;
   cpu_model.order=6;
   cpu_model.p1=2.07e-01;

   njobs=10000;
   /* End of the Input section */

   inter_arrival_mu1=0;
   inter_arrival_mu2=0;
   inter_arrival_mu3=0;

   cpu_mu1=0;
```

```
cpu_mu2=0;
cpu_mu3=0;

ijob=0;

/* Here we are using the number of jobs (njobs) as the
 * termination criterion.  One may choose to use
 * simtime (i.e. total length of time represented
 * in this workload) as a termination criterion.
 * In that case, use simtime in the following while
 * statement.
 */

while( ijob < njobs)
{   ijob++;

    dtemp=str_rand(0);
    inter_arrival_time =
            ur_to_HER_r(dtemp,inter_arrival_model);
    simtime += inter_arrival_time;
    inter_arrival_mu1 +=inter_arrival_time;
    inter_arrival_mu2 +=(inter_arrival_time *
                        inter_arrival_time);
    inter_arrival_mu3 +=(inter_arrival_time *
                        inter_arrival_time *
                        inter_arrival_time);


    dtemp=str_rand(1);
    cpu_time_used = ur_to_HER_r(dtemp,cpu_model);
    cpu_mu1 +=  cpu_time_used;
    cpu_mu2 += (cpu_time_used *
                cpu_time_used);
    cpu_mu3 += (cpu_time_used *
                cpu_time_used *
                cpu_time_used);


    dtemp=str_rand(2);
    dtemp *= (pmax-pmin+1);
    j=dtemp;
    if( ((double) j) < dtemp ) { p_needed = j + pmin; }
    else    { p_needed = j + pmin - 1; }

    /* One needs to replace the following section
```

```
 * (enclosed by #if and #endif) with appropriate
 * statements to  output the job stream information.
 * If multiple models are concurrently used, it
 * might be desirable to sort the final output by
 * job arrival time.
 */

#if 0
    if(ijob < 50 )
    { printf( "Job used %d CPUs and %e cummulative CPUtime",
               p_needed,   cpu_time_used);
      printf( " arrived at time %e \n", simtime);
    }
#endif
    } /* end of the while loop */

        printf(" For Model %d :\n",imodel);
        inter_arrival_mu1 /= (double)ijob;
        inter_arrival_mu2 /= (double)ijob;
        inter_arrival_mu3 /= (double)ijob;
        printf("Inter-arrival Time Moments of the jobs are \n");
        printf( " %d   mu1 = %e   "
                "       mu2 = %e   "
                "       mu3 = %e \n",
             ijob, inter_arrival_mu1,
                   inter_arrival_mu2,
                   inter_arrival_mu3 );

        cpu_mu1 /= (double)ijob;
        cpu_mu2 /= (double)ijob;
        cpu_mu3 /= (double)ijob;
        printf("CPU Time Moments of the jobs are \n");
        printf(" %d mu1 = %e   "
                 "mu2 = %e   "
                 "mu3 = %e\n",
              ijob, cpu_mu1, cpu_mu2, cpu_mu3 );

   } /* end of loop over models */
}    /* end of main program */

/* ================================================== */
double ur_to_HER_r(double ur, MODEL_DATA m)
{   double xleft, xright;
    double x,y;
    int rc;
```

```
    m.ur = ur;
    xleft = 1.e-20;    /* a small +ve number */
    xright = -log(1.0-ur) / min(m.lambda1,m.lambda2);
    xright *= 100;

    solve_bisec(xleft, xright,
                (double) 1.e-12,
                &x, &y, &m,
                fn_to_solve, &rc);
    if(rc !=0 )
    {  printf("Unable to find the Random Number for
                            ur = %e \n",m.ur);
    }
    return(x);
}
/* ===================================================== */
double fn_to_solve(double x, void *model_data)
{   MODEL_DATA *m;

    m = (MODEL_DATA *) model_data;
    return( H_Er_cdf(x, model_data)  - m->ur );
}
/* ===================================================== */
double H_Er_cdf(double x, void *model_data)
{   MODEL_DATA *p;
    double cdf, t1,t2, dtemp;
    int k;
    t1=0;
    t2=0;
    p = (MODEL_DATA *) model_data;

    for(k=0;  k< p->order;  k++)
    {  dtemp=fac(k);
       t1 += (pow(x*p->lambda1,k)/dtemp);
       t2 += (pow(x*p->lambda2,k)/dtemp);
    }
    cdf = 1.0 -   p->p1 *exp(-(p->lambda1*x))*t1
              - (1-p->p1)*exp(-(p->lambda2*x))*t2;
    return(cdf);
 }
/* ===================================================== */
void solve_bisec(double xleft_0,
                        xright_0,
                        double tol,
```

```
                          double *x,
                          double *y,
                          void *model_data,
                          double (*f)(double, void *),
                          int *rc)

{   double xleft, yleft,
           xright, yright,
           xnext,ynext;
    int    ic;

    xleft=xleft_0; xright=xright_0;
    yleft=(*f)(xleft, model_data);
    yright=(*f)(xright,model_data);
    *rc=1; ic=0;

    if( yleft*yright  > 0.0 ) { return; }
    /* No solution in this interval */

    while(ic < 100000 )
    {   ic++;
        xnext=(xleft+xright)/2.0;
        ynext=(*f)(xnext,model_data);
        if( ynext*yright >  0.0 )
        {    xright=xnext;
             yright=ynext;
        }
        else
        {    xleft=xnext;
             yleft=ynext;
        }
        if( fabs(ynext)  <  tol )
        {    *x=xnext; *y=ynext; *rc=0; return;}
    }
}
/* ================================================== */
int fac(int k)
{   int i,j;
    j=1;

    if(k==0) return (j);
    j=1;
    for(i=1;i<=k;i++) j*=i;
    return(j);
}
```

```
/* ===================================================== */
double str_rand(int strm)
{   int i;
    if( ran_remain[strm] <=  0 )
    {   for(i=0;i<RANPOOLSIZE;i++)
            ran_pool[strm][i]=drand48();
            ran_remain[strm]=RANPOOLSIZE;
    }
    ran_remain[strm]--;
    return( ran_pool[strm] [RANPOOLSIZE-ran_remain[strm]]) ;
}
```

References

1. A. Tucker and A. Gupta, "Process control and scheduling issues for multiprogrammed shared-memory multiprocessors," in *Proceedings of the 12th. ACM Symposium on Operating Systems Principle*, pp. 159–166, 1989.
2. D. Feitelson and L. Rudolph, "Mapping and scheduling in a shared parallel environment using distributed hierarchical control," in *Intl. Conf. Parallel Processing*, pp. 1–8, 1990.
3. D. G. Feitelson, "Packing schemes for gang scheduling," in *Job Scheduling Strategies for Parallel Processing Springer-Verlag, LNCS Vol. 1162, Apr 1996*, pp. 89–110, 1996.
4. F. Wang, H. Franke, M. Papaefthymiou, P. Pattnaik, L. Rudolph, and M. S. Squillante, "A gang scheduling design for multiprogrammed parallel computing environments," in *Job Scheduling Strategies for Parallel Processing Springer-Verlag, LNCS Vol. 1162, Apr 1996*, pp. 111–125, 1996.
5. M. S. Squillante, F. Wang, and M. Papaefthymiou, "An analysis of gang scheduling for multiprogrammed parallel computing environments," in *Proceedings of the Annual ACM Symposium on Parallel Algorithms and Architectures (SPAA)*, pp. 89–98, 1996.
6. H. Franke, P. Pattnaik, and L. Rudolph, "Gang scheduling for highly efficient distributed multiprocessor systems," in *Proceedings of the 6th Symposium on the Frontiers of Massively Parallel Computation, Annapolis, MD*, pp. 1–9, 1996.
7. D. R. Cox, "A use of complex probabilities in the theory of stochastic process," *Proc. Cambridge Philos. Soc*, 1955.
8. M. F. Neuts, *Matrix-Geometric Solutions in Stochastic Models*. The John Hopkins University Press, 1981.
9. M. A. Johnson and M. R. Taaffe, "Matching moments to phase distributions," *Commun. Stat. Stochastics Models*, vol. 5, pp. 711–743, 1989.
10. R. Schassberger, "Insensitivity of steady-state distributions of generalized semi-markov processes i," *Ann. Prob.*, pp. 87–99, 1977.
11. R. Schassberger, "Insensitivity of steady-state distributions of generalized semi-markov processes ii," *Ann. Prob.*, pp. 85–93, 1978.
12. R. Schassberger, "Insensitivity of steady-state distributions of generalized semi-markov processes with speeds," *Adv. Appl. Prob.*, pp. 836–851, 1978.
13. R. Schassberger, "The insensitivity of stationary probabilities in networks of queues," *Adv. Appl. Prob.*, pp. 906–912, 1978.

PScheD
Political Scheduling on the CRAY T3E

Richard N. Lagerstrom* and Stephan K. Gipp**

Cray Reasearch, a Silicon Graphics Company
655 Lone Oak Drive, Eagan MN 55121
URL http://www.cray.com

Abstract. *Large parallel processing environments present serious administrative challenges if high utilization of the available resources is a goal. In many cases there is also the need to support critical or time-dependent applications at the same time as development and routine production work is going on.*
This paper describes the components that help realize the Political Scheduling goals of the CRAY T3E system. The meaning of Political Scheduling is defined, we present a general overview of the Cray T3E hardware and operating system and describe the current implementation of the Political Scheduling feature of Unicos/mk.

1 Introduction

What do we mean by the term *Political Scheduling*? In a presentation one of us stated that it was "irrational" scheduling as opposed to "technical" scheduling. What we mean is that there are scheduling goals not easily described in terms of machine utilization or performance, but rather by organizational or economic requirements. This sort of requirement often cannot be well handled by classical scheduling mechanisms, especially if they try to support a very wide class of users and a complex environment at the same time.

A brief description of the CRAY T3E hardware and operating system will be followed by a discussion of the features of the Political Scheduler, configuration, and operational characteristics.

1.1 The CRAY T3E Hardware

Figure 1 shows a CRAY T3E with application, command and operating system processing elements. CRAY T3E scalable parallel systems use the DECchip 21164 (DEC Alpha EV5) from Digital Equipment Corporation. This reduced instruction set computing (RISC) microprocessor is cache-based, has pipelined functional units, issues multiple instructions per cycle, and supports IEEE standard 32-bit and 64-bit floating-point arithmetic. CRAY T3E processing elements

---

* E-mail rnl@cray.com
** E-mail skg@cray.com

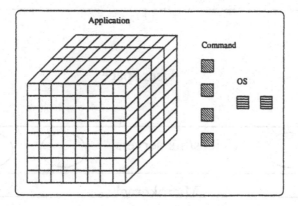

Fig. 1. A Small CRAY T3E

(PEs) include the DEC Alpha microprocessor, local memory, and performance-accelerating control logic.

Each PE has its own local DRAM memory with a capacity from 64 Mbytes to 2 Gbytes. A shared, high performance memory subsystem makes these memories accessible to every PE in a CRAY T3E system. PEs are connected by a bidirectional 3-D torus interconnect network. I/O channels are integrated into the 3-D torus and increase in number with system size.

CRAY T3E systems are available with from 16 to 2048 user[1] PEs. Air cooled models range in size from 16 to 128 user PEs, while liquid cooled models have 64 to 2048 user PEs.

1.2 The Unicos/mk Operating System

Unicos/mk is a scalable version of the CRAY UNICOS operating system and is distributed among the PEs, not replicated on each. Despite having the operating system distributed among the PEs, Unicos/mk provides a global view of the computing environment – a single-system image – that allows system administrators to manage a system wide suite of resources as a single entity.

Figure 2 shows the general organization of the operating system in each PE.

A number of *servers* provide the functionality needed to support the system. In this paper we will discuss only the Global Resource Manager (GRM), the operating system server that allocates applications to PEs and manages global resources such as barrier context register assignment, barrier network routing and Global Memory Segment register allocation. Features of the Political Scheduler work with GRM to accomplish the scheduling goals set by the administrator.

1.3 The Global Resource Manager

All user PEs have the capability of running single-PE processes, named *commands*, or multiple-PE entities, named *applications*. Command PEs run shells,

---

[1] Additional PEs may be present to support operating system needs.

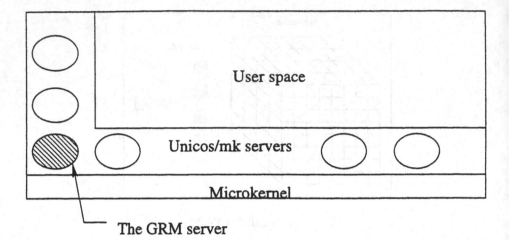

The GRM server

Fig. 2. Unicos/mk

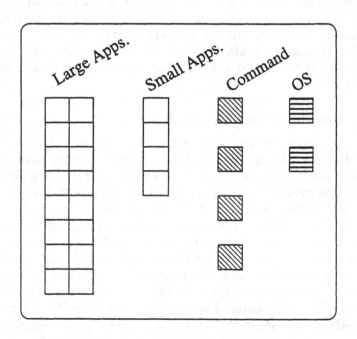

Fig. 3. An Example CRAY T3E GRM Configuration

daemons and other familiar Unix processes. All systems must have some number of Command and Operating System PEs [2] configured as the *Command and OS regions* while the remaining PEs are configured into one or more *application regions* in which applications execute.

Figure 3 shows a configuration with large and small application regions, a command region and some OS PEs. (Typically a recommend maximum of one or two application regions will be configured although special circumstances could make more regions useful.) Regions are made up of a number of PEs with consecutive *logical PE numbers*. These numbers (integers in the range $0 \cdots machinesize - 1$) are assigned when the machine is booted and are mapped to PE torus coordinates in a way to provide good physical proximity within the machine. Not every PE can be "next" to every other, so mapping is a compromise between the physical relationship of the PEs and their logical numbering. Each application *must* be assigned to a range of PEs having consecutive logical PE numbers.

In the command region GRM assigns each process to a PE having attributes compatible with those of the user[3] while at the same time attempting a degree of load balancing. A command will execute to completion in the same PE unless it is moved through a process known as *migration*[4].

Application regions may be configured to accept applications with only certain attributes. Some of the region attributes are User ID, Group ID, Account ID, Service Provider Type[5], size of the application, and some others.

It is the responsibility of GRM to match the attributes of an application requesting service with regions which will both allow it to run and have free resources with which to run it. GRM is not capable of very sophisticated scheduling since it is aware only of the running load and the immediate launch request backlog. Such information as batch queue backlog and the relative priorities of jobs waiting in the backlog are invisible to it. The Political Scheduler, however, does have access to that information and will direct GRM to do the "right" thing or take action to "fix" PE allocation problems as they arise.

The final major task of GRM is to manage the Barrier Context Registers, construct barrier routing trees and initialize the barrier routing registers when applications are started and manage the Global Memory Descriptors each application uses.

2 An Introduction to Political Scheduling

The term *feature* is used in this paper to generically include all of the different decision making components. Most features will be described separately.

---

[2] The number is determined by the size of the machine and the type of workload.
[3] Generally, the command region has no restrictive attributes.
[4] Migration is managed by the political scheduler.
[5] Batch and interactive job initiators, for example, have different service provider types.

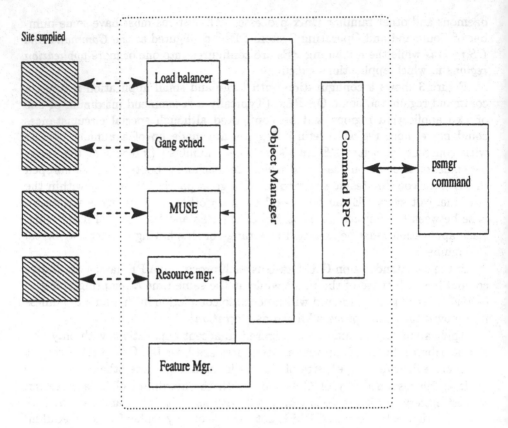

Fig. 4. The PScheD Daemon

High-level scheduling as defined in this paper is based on the concept of *scheduling domains*. Each scheduling domain represents a portion of the CRAY T3E that is managed by a common set of scheduling rules. Scheduling domains will be more fully described later in Section 2.2.

The Political Scheduler (PS) is implemented as a daemon which runs on one of the command PEs. There are a few special low-level system "hooks" to control such things as time slice width and to send special commands to GRM, but the remainder of the operating system interfaces are normal to Unicos/mk. An *information server* exists in the kernel for general use and this capability is heavily used by the various features of PS to collect system-wide information. As seen in Figure 4 PS is organized into the following major modules:

Object Manager Provides an information repository for configuration objects and other data. Communication among the components and with the outside world is centered here. Data objects consist of fundamental types such as integers and strings as well as more complex objects defined as needed. A hierarchical naming convention similar to names of directories and files in a file system is used. For example, an object used to specify the name of the global log file could be named /PScheD/logFile. This is a string object containing the name of the log file.

Command Interface This component implements an RPC interface used by administrative commands through which configuration, viewing and manipulation of the data controlled by the Object Manager. Other uses by various service daemons is also supported.

Feature Manager Each component registers itself so its *bind*, *verify*, *action* and *exception* functions are known to the feature manager. The meaning of these functions will be discussed below.

The remaining items are the features of PS that implement Political Scheduling.

Gang Scheduler Application CPU and memory residency control is provided by this feature.

Load Balancer Measurements of how well processes and applications are being serviced in each scheduling domain are made and acted upon by this feature. Moving commands and applications among eligible PEs in each domain is managed here.

MUSE A fair-share like capability is implemented by the Multilayered User-fair Scheduling Environment.

Resource Manager This is somewhat misnamed for historical reasons, but is the place where information about resource usage within the machine is collected, analyzed and formed for both internal and external uses. The Object Manager is used to make this information available in a uniform way to service providers such as NQS or NQE.
Unfortunately, the deadline makes a detailed description of this feature impossible.

Site Supplied Scheduling Features Each feature has an RPC interface allowing connection to a site-written program that can change the decisions made by the standard feature. To connect a feature to an external assistant, the RPC address of the assistant is made known to the feature through the configuration interface.

2.1 Scaling and Feature Design

The design of almost every feature of PScheD must deal with the scaling issue in some way. The same software is expected to run on machines of all sizes since special software configurations based on machine size will become a testing, maintenance and development nightmare if they are allowed to proliferate unchecked.

Another painfully discovered truth is that it is difficult to precisely control this class of machine with global controlling software. All of the features of PScheD are designed to guide the micro kernel toward delivering a desired global machine utilization goal. Since each micro kernel has a unique environment, the global managers must expect neither immediate nor full compliance with their requests in every case. This means that all management software must constantly analyze system information and adjust controlling parameters accordingly. Another issue arises since events at the PE level happen at much faster rates than the global controllers can monitor[6]. Often by the time information has traveled to a global manager and it takes some action, events have moved on and conditions are different.

All of these issues taught us that traditional kernel designs which expect to control every aspect of every event in a central place will not generally succeed. A different way of approaching these control requirements is needed, and some time must be spent simply to understand the environment and become comfortable with the range of control that it is reasonable to be able to maintain. A fairly strict expectation that the controllers will not consume a significant amount of network bandwidth and CPU resources is implicit.

2.2 Scheduling Domains

In earlier CRAY Parallel-Vector Processor (PVP) systems a high-level scheduler named the Unified Resource Manager (URM) analyzed system load information and resource usage. An interface to major service providers such as the Network Queuing System (NQS) existed to make the work backlog visible. Knowing the work backlog and with information about current machine activity acquired from the system, URM would compile recommendation lists from the backlog to suggest the order in which jobs should be initiated and send these lists to the registered service providers. The service providers perform the task of job initiation. Early design approaches to Unicos/mk recommended simply moving URM to Unicos/mk.

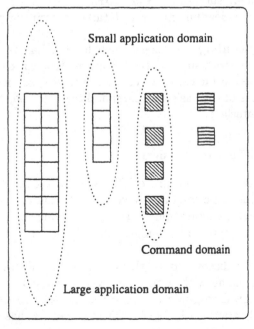

Fig. 5. Domains

---

[6] An early attempt to globally manage memory dramatically clarified this issue.

Deeper consideration of the implications of this recommendation led to the conclusion that the scheduling issues raised by the nature of the CRAY T3E were not similar enough to those of the PVP machines for URM to be useful. The fundamental flaw in the design of URM if simply made to work on the CRAY T3E is the idea that the machine is a uniform provider of computing resources. The CRAY T3E intrinsically divides into two very different domains. The command region can be looked upon as a number of separate single-CPU machines which must be managed so their workloads are fairly equal. The greater part[7] of the CRAY T3E is used to run multi-PE applications. The scheduling issues in this region involve making sure applications reside in memory and are given CPU resources at the same time, especially if they have fine-grain synchronization. It turns out that the URM on UNICOS can be considered a special, simplified case of Political Scheduling.

From a machine utilization point of view, the goals are to minimize fragmentation of PE allocation while reducing swapping and migration to a minimum. Even rough estimates result in very discouraging projected utilization levels if hundreds of large pieces of application memory must be transferred to and from swap space on a context switch.

Two regions[8] are present by default but user requirements often cause the administrator to divide the application region into two parts (see Figure 5), splitting it into a work region and a smaller region intended for development and testing. In the development region, test applications need few PEs and normally execute for short periods of time. Developers also may be using debugging tools so they want their applications to execute often, even if they are being gang scheduled. This behavior is different from that desired when running production work where long time slices improve system utilization.

To make these different scheduling approaches possible, the Political Scheduler is configured to have an instantiation of its scheduling features for each region. Each instantiation is independent of the others so time slices and PE loading can be tailored to the demands of each region. From the point of view of the administrator, the Political Scheduler behaves as though a number of separate schedulers were present. Appropriate scheduling rules are created, each with a separate *domain name*. The domains are bound to the scheduling features with a bind directive. Figure 4 shows a single instance of each feature, but imagine that there is a "depth" dimension to each feature where different instantiations can exist. Of course, some features may need no more than a global view of the entire machine. In these cases the depth is one.

---

[7] The design assumption is that the machine is to be used more for multi-PE applications than single-PE work.

[8] A command region and a single application region.

So why name them Domains? Each feature has some sanity-checking capability to help assure a reasonable relationship between the scheduling domains and the regions known to GRM. Early releases will not automatically keep the Political Scheduler and GRM synchronized, but future configuration tools are planned to integrate the configuration of both subsystems.

A PS domain and a GRM region must now, and probably always will, agree in size and location. During the design of PS it was thought important to recognize the difference between the GRM configuration and that of PS. In retrospect, it seems that having the two names results in more confusion than clarity. Save us from our cleverness!

3 The Feature Manager

The Feature Manager implements the internal execution control functions of the daemon. The daemon is single-threaded since at the time it was developed, multi-threading support for user-level processes was not available in Unicos/mk.

When execution begins, each feature registers its *bind* function with the Feature Manager. This function is called when a *bind* directive is received at the Command Interface. Binding associates a *node* in the Object Tree with the feature also named on the bind directive. The portion of the Object Tree below the named node typically contains the configuration parameters for this instance of the feature. The range of PEs making up the domain is generally a part of configuring a feature.

The specific binding function in the named feature instantiates an instance of the feature for this domain and will register an *action* function. The Feature Manager saves the pointer to the action function and an associated parameter pointer in a list of registered actions for the feature. An optional *exception* function may also be registered at this time. The same parameter pointer as that for the associated action function is assumed.

A *verify* function may also be registered. Verify is called by the feature manager when a *verify* directive is received. Verify is usually used by the administrator to make sure a changed or new configuration instance is acceptable to the feature.

On each cycle of the Feature Manager each of the registered action functions for each feature will be called with the indicated parameter pointer. The parameter is typically a *this* pointer to an instance of the feature *class* and establishes the environment of the feature for this specific domain. The cycle of calls to the action functions continues while the daemon is active.

Some features must perform cleanup or other transition activity when the daemon is terminated. The *exception* functions will be called when the daemon receives a shutdown directive or catches one of a set of registered signals. The daemon executes all of the exception functions before it terminates.

4 The Gang Scheduler

On the CRAY T3E Gang Scheduling is used to assure that in each PE assigned to an application, the execution thread of that application runs at the same time. Applications with fine-grain synchronization using the hardware barrier network require this service if they are to have reasonable performance. The Gang Scheduling feature of the Political Scheduler is designed to deliver the required scheduling behavior without imposing a high synchronization overhead cost. Achieving low overhead meant that methods requiring the CPU schedulers in each PE to have knowledge of each other were unacceptable.

Gang scheduling works in the CRAY T3E with a small amount of kernel support while the major part of the feature resides in the PScheD daemon. Kernel support consists of setting aside a range of priorities named *gang priorities*, making the thread scheduler and memory manager in each kernel aware of these priorities and enhancing an existing system call[9] to allow the Gang Scheduling feature of PScheD to communicate with the kernel. Briefly, the daemon picks an application and consequently the thread which will become the *gang thread* in each PE of its domain and broadcasts that information to the appropriate kernels. The kernels adjust their thread priorities as directed and schedule the threads as those priorities dictate. Since gang priorities are higher than any other user priority, the selected application executes as though it were dedicated.

The memory manager also knows the gang priorities so it takes the necessary action to make sure the memory segments belonging to that application remain resident in memory. When it becomes necessary to swap out memory belonging to an application, all of the PEs on which that application resides are informed to stop remote memory accesses from being issued. All remote memory accesses that are in progress at the time a memory swap begins will be completed.

A practical side-effect of this design is that, if the application which has gang priority for some reason gives up the CPU, the kernel will allow another thread to execute providing it can find one to run. When multiple applications are competing for the same CPU, the Gang Scheduler rotates them through the gang priorities on a configured time slice. Applications which have less than maximum gang priority still enjoy an enhanced priority so they will execute in priority order if the CPU becomes free.

In Figure 6 four applications share a domain of 12 PEs. The slots are intervals of time specified by the configuration of the domain. In Slot 1 Application A occupying PEs 0-5 and Application B occupying PEs 6-11 run, in Slot 2 Application C occupying PEs 3-8 runs and in Slot 3 Application A and Application D occupying PEs 6-11 run. Application A runs twice in three slot periods while the other applications run once.

Application placement greatly influences how often each application runs, so the Gang Scheduler and the Application Load Balancer (see Section 5.2 and Figure 9) cooperate to reduce the *depth* of the gangs. A smaller depth means each application runs more often.

---

[9] The policy() system call.

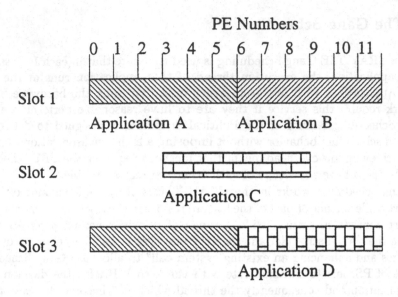

Fig. 6. A Domain With Four Applications

Each domain of Gang Scheduling is configured separately making it possible to provide long slot periods for domains running large batch applications and short slot periods for domains running smaller interactive applications. Thus, the amount of overhead needed to manage the gangs and their time slices can be controlled by the administrator to suite the needs of the users. Domains which are configured to allow only one application to be assigned to a PE at once have no need for supervision by the Gang Scheduler. In these domains the Gang Scheduler feature is simply not bound and so does not execute.

4.1 Controlling a Gang Scheduling Domain

Each domain has these configuration attributes.

Heartbeat: The gang time slice center point in seconds.
Partial: If true, applications not currently assigned to the prime gang will execute; if false, non-prime gangs will not consume CPU time even if the prime gang is idle.
Variation: A floating point number n, $n \geq 1.0$, that **Heartbeat** is multiplied or divided by to effect the MUSE factor when MUSE is active in the domain.

5 The Load Balancer

Load balancing is done in order to maximize overall system utilization. The three steps to load balancing are:

- Filter the processes into eligible and ineligible groups,
- classify the eligible processes, and
- balance the processes by migrating them.

The balancing process is identical for both application and command domains, but the details of how candidates are picked and the evaluation of the cost of migration are different. Command balancing will be described first to lay the basis for the additional work needed to properly balance the application domain.

5.1 Load Balancing a Command Domain

The classification stage involves comparing the candidates[10] in the domain. This is done by generating a *Classification Score*, C, of each candidate, p. In order to properly compare resource consumption levels among the candidates, each is assigned a normalized entitlement[11], (E), memory, (M), and CPU, (U), classification score component. The administrator will have configured each domain with the desired evaluation weights for these factors. The factors are entitlement weight, W_e, memory weight, W_m, and usage weight, W_u. The W factors are assigned[12] by the administrator through the configuration interface and the

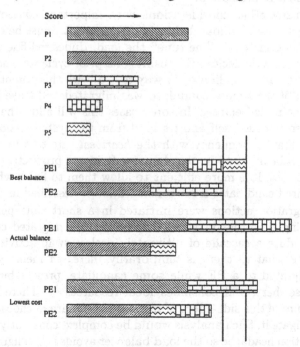

Fig. 7. Load Balancing the Command Region

---

[10] See Section 5.1

[11] See MUSE, Section 6

[12] The three factors are quite different so typically only one of them has a dominant weight.

values are assumed to range between zero and one. The classification score of each candidate, C_p, is determined by evaluating

$$C_p = W_e E_p + W_m M_p + W_u U_p \tag{1}$$

The list of candidates is ordered by decreasing numerical value of C_p as shown in the top portion of Figure 7, *P1 ... P5*. This list is then used to create an ideal balance given the weights and the number of PEs available. This is shown in the same Figure labeled *Best balance*. If the cost of migrating the candidates was not a consideration, this would be the end of the evaluation process. In reality, though, the ideal balance is usually a poor choice since many of the candidates would have to be moved and the overhead to do this could be unacceptably high. As a compromise to lower migration cost, only candidates which would most effectively improve overall load balance will be moved. This is shown in Figure 7 next to the label *Lowest cost*.

In this example, candidate P4 was the only one migrated while the ideal balance would have migrated both P3 and P4. Of course, in actual systems, the number of candidates would be much greater and the number of choices increase dramatically. Poor choices can result in high overhead cost, perhaps without much improvement in utilization.

There are many other considerations with important consequences to an effective solution to domain load balancing. Constraints must be established to prevent trying continually to "fine tune" the load. Undesired fine tuning occurs when an evaluation cycle decides the results of a prior cycle were not "best" and so proceeds to rearrange candidates. A way to deal with this potential instability is to keep track of the time a candidate was migrated and leave it alone until a configured time period elapses. In some cases this will allow the candidate to terminate and so remove itself and its load from the system. Another strategy is to set the evaluation frequency with the *heartbeat* rate to a value suitable to the type of work being done in the domain. It is not productive to deal with short-lived processes. It is more efficient to allow them to finish where they are. Filtering undesired candidates from consideration is described in Section 5.1.

If many migration actions were initiated in a short time period, a nasty problem involving the order in which candidates are migrated could arise. It is possible to induce a cascade of ultimately useless swap activity as PEs try to accommodate what to them is temporarily *increased* memory usage when a process is migrated to a PE while some candidate, present but destined to be migrated elsewhere, still consumes local resources [13]. There is no way to completely eliminate this side-effect of migration but care in choosing migration order could mitigate it. Such analysis would be complex, constantly controversial and a configuration headache so the load balancer avoids it by migrating no more than one candidate per cycle.

The command domain load balancer has the configuration controls listed below. Recall that an instance of the load balancer sees only its own domain.

---

[13] This could have devastating consequences with large multi-PE applications

- Minimum candidate CPU usage
- Minimum time before a migrated candidate will be reconsidered
- Frequency of evaluation
- Minimum candidate memory size
- Lower bound of candidate User IDs (This can be used to exempt system or maintenance processes from consideration.)
- Entitlement weight
- CPU usage weight
- Memory usage weight

It is possible that other controls will be necessary as experience with the actual environments in which the evaluator must be effective grows.

Filtering Evaluation Candidates The measurement of consumption rates, especially in the command region, can be very noisy since short-lived processes and the uneven resource consumption of many processes can lead to misleading evaluation scores. The filters are configured with the minimum CPU usage and minimum memory size to help moderate the effects of short-term process behavior on the evaluation of migration candidates. The minimum UID factor is intended to exempt system processes and other special users from consideration.

5.2 Load Balancing an Application Domain

Balancing an application domain is a somewhat more complex issue than that of a command domain. The objectives of application load balancing are to

- minimize swapping,
- minimize migration cost,
- do expensive migrations only when needed,
- minimize the number of *gangs*, and
- maximize contiguously allocated PEs per *gang*.

Unicos/mk imposes the requirement that all PEs allocated to an application have contiguous logical PE numbers. The location of an application is specified by its base PE number and its size (in number of PEs). This can lead to situations where occupied PEs are scattered throughout a region in such a way that no application waiting to be allocated can be fit into any contiguous span of available PEs. Fragmentation of this kind lowers the utilization of the machine by leaving portions of it effectively unavailable.

In Figure 8 a fragmented domain of PEs has developed. The load balancer will have recognized this, but will take no action unless the fragmentation is causing some application to wait for initiation. Further, the load balancer must be able to make space available in sufficient quantity to allow at least one of the waiting applications to be accommodated before it will initiate migration.

Assuming that the cost considerations have been satisfied, migration will increase the size of contiguous free space by pushing applications right or left

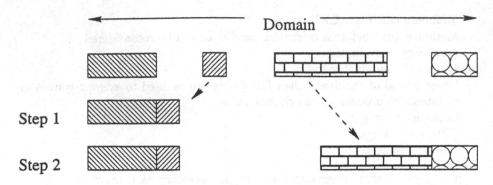

Fig. 8. Migrating Parallel Applications

in the domain to squeeze out allocation holes, starting with the lowest cost migration that increases the span of available PEs. As with command balancing, this is done one application at a time. Figure 8 shows the migration steps (Step 1 and Step 2) as the applications are moved into contiguous ranges. At the same time this is going on, GRM will be reevaluating its waiting applications. As soon as space becomes available, GRM will initiate whatever it can. Because of this competition between GRM and the Load Balancer, it is necessary to completely reevaluate the domain on every cycle.

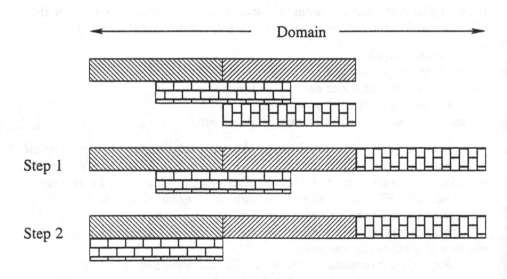

Fig. 9. Balancing Gangs of Applications

The gang balancing goals apply only when a domain is configured to allow more than one application to be assigned at once to the PEs. This decision is made by the administrator based on typical application sizes and behavior and the performance demands of the computing environment. From the standpoint of throughput of an application, sharing PEs simply means it will take longer for each application to complete. Gangs are more fully described in Section 4.

Two of the load balancing goals deal with the number of gangs in a domain. This refers to how many applications share the same PEs in a domain. Reducing this number improves the performance of each application and makes better use of the resources of each PE. Figure 9 shows the steps needed to fully utilize a domain and reduce the number of gangs.

6 MUSE

The Multi layered User-fair Scheduling Environment (MUSE) feature implements a scheduling strategy similar to the well known Fair-Share Scheduler as implemented on systems such as UNICOS. In contrast to those implementations, MUSE and its integration with the concept of scheduling domains allows for better scaling to large CRAY T3E environments. The CRAY T3E presents many challenges to a useful implementation of fair-share scheduling strategies. The first challenge is of scaling, the second of determining exactly what an entitlement means under these circumstances.

6.1 MUSE Entitlement

Every user or account is assigned an *entitlement* by the administrator. A user's entitlement is the proportion of the machine resource (in this implementation, CPU time) that user should be given in competition with other active users. MUSE determines, based on the load and usage history, what priority each user should be given in order to reach the entitlement goal.

6.2 An Outline of MUSE

As in UNICOS, a global representation of the entitlement tree is maintained in the User Database (UDB). Because of this, a global instantiation of MUSE exists to collect resource consumption information delivered by each of the MUSE domains into the global domain, the UDB. The administrator's view is that of a single-system image even though there may be many domains controlling resources being consumed at vastly differing rates.

When the MUSE UDB domain is bound, a global entitlement representation is created as the source of the information needed by the controlling MUSE domains. The UDB domain neither adjusts PE parameters nor collects usage information from the PEs. The controlling domains do that work. Usage information filters up to the global UDB domain from the controlling domains and from there is generally distributed.

In the typical minimum case two controlling domains are bound. The first domain is that of the command PEs which run ordinary Unicos/mk processes, while the second domain is responsible for multi-PE applications. Each controlling domain maintains a virtual entitlement tree private to the domain, having the same structure as that of the global tree. The virtual tree, however, includes only the resource consumers that populate that domain. Domain usage is propagated to the global domain at a configured rate, and the global domain distributes new consumption information to interested controlling domains.

Every PE has a Process Manager (PM) responsible for handling work assigned to the PE. When a process is assigned to a PE, the responsible controlling domain creates a controlling node within the PM for the user[14]. PM uses the nodes to adjust local priorities based on effective entitlement and collects usage information in the nodes for harvesting by the controlling domain for global dissemination.

A PM has no global view of a user's activity, working only with resources locally consumed. The controlling domain periodically assesses both global usage and overall domain usage and, when necessary, adjusts PE entitlements.

6.3 MUSE Domain Configuration

The configuration parameters provide a good view of the MUSE feature. Each domain (including the global domain) has its own set of configuration parameters. A certain degree of configuration consistency among the domains must be assumed since each domain should be working toward more or less uniform goals. Certain domains may intentionally be excluded from some of the general rules to provide for dedicated applications or other special needs. Sanity checking software examines individual domain configurations and reports unexpected or contradictory rules. Such mistakes as configuring more than one domain to include the same PE are strictly prohibited, but many seemingly inconsistent rules may be intentional and necessary. The administrator must act, based on this analysis and the established performance goals, to make any needed configuration adjustments.

Heartbeat: How often (in seconds) the MUSE scheduling feature is executed for the domain.

Decay: The decay rate (in seconds) of accumulated usage. This discards historical usage over time.

IdleThreshold: The percentage of entitled usage below which a resource consumer is considered idle. Being considered idle means
  - the priority of the associated process is set to the non-MUSE priority of 100 and
  - the entitlement and usage of the resource consumer are no longer considered in any global calculation. Thus, the scheduler behaves as if the idle resource consumer is not active in this domain. This effectively controls redistribution of usage.

---

[14] Either share-by-UID or share-by-account may be selected. Share-by-UID is assumed here.

ShareByACID: If true, the domain is controlled by the user's account ID; if false, the domain is controlled by the user's UID.

NodeDecay: How long (in seconds) resource consumer usage information is kept on the same levels of the system as information about active resource consumers.

UdbHeartbeat: How often (in seconds) the domain synchronizes its usage information with the global UDB domain. This makes usage information visible to other domains and controls how often usage accumulated in other domains becomes visible to this domain.

OsHeartbeat: The frequency (in seconds) that the operating system should accumulate usage and adjust the priorities of running processes or applications.

OsActive: If true, the system actively enforces assigned entitlements by adjusting priorities; if false, the system accumulates usage but does not adjust priorities.

6.4 The MUSE Factor

Service providers such as NQS/NQE need information from a system to help order the backlog and initiate jobs which are most likely to run. It is harmful to system performance when many jobs belonging to users with little effective entitlement are brought into the system and compete for resources with users of high entitlement. These jobs generally end up swapped after some small initial activity and stay inactive until system workload drops to a point where the job is eligible for system resources. Users and administrators would also like to have a simple way to determine how well a given user might have jobs serviced at a certain time.

In UNICOS systems, NQS had an elaborate entitlement analysis capability that mimicked that of the fair-share component in the kernel. The result of this analysis was a rank that had meaning when compared with the ranks of other users. This helped NQS decide which jobs to initiate. Although this analysis worked well, it was complex and required tinkering as the underlying operating system evolved. The influence of small analysis errors can be subtle and not at all apparent in every environment. Thus, it was not always obvious whether the entitlement assessment conformed with that of the host system.

When PScheD was in its early design stages, the NQS/NQE developers lobbied strenuously for an interface to the system which would provide an externally useful entitlement assessment upon request. It was becoming clear that writing an external analyzer similar to that used with UNICOS would be a difficult job for Unicos/mk because of its much more complex organization and non-uniform service regions. The *MUSE factor* was created to fill this need.

The MUSE factor is a machine-independent measure of a user's effective entitlement. This means a service provider can compare the MUSE factors of competing users and decide how to rank them for a single machine as well as determine which of a number of machines able to process the job would offer the best service[15].

Figure 10 demonstrates the MUSE factor for a particular user and shows how it represents a user's effective entitlement. A MUSE factor of 1.0 means the user could consume all the resources of the machine for some period. A MUSE factor of 0.0 means the user has consumed at least all the entitled resources and the system will give other users with non-zero MUSE factors a higher priority. The numeric value of a MUSE factor is meaningful with respect to the MUSE factors of other users on either the same or different machines.

In Figure 10 the line labeled **Usage** shows the cumulative resources consumed by fictitious user r. This is shown only to describe the way the user consumed resources over time. The line labeled **Decayed usage** is calculated by MUSE and is the effective usage, modified by the decay factor, that characterizes this user with respect to the user's entitlement. The MUSE factor M for user r (labeled **MUSE factor** in Figure 10) is

$$M_r = \frac{e_r^2}{u_r} \tag{2}$$

where e_r is the user's normalized entitlement and u_r is the user's normalized decayed usage. The MUSE factor is clipped at 1.0 since values higher than that decay very rapidly with small amounts of usage.

A PScheD interface is provided which takes as input a list of one or more space separated UID,ACID or user name,account name pairs and returns the associated muse factors. Both user and account ID are needed since MUSE may be configured for either UID or ACID usage monitoring but the caller probably does not know which mode is configured. For example, if a service provider wanted to know the current MUSE factors for users (user rnl, account Sdev), user skg, account 9657) and (UID 6789, account LibDev) it would compose a MUSE factor request with the string "rnl,Sdev skg,9657 6789,LibDev" and MUSE running in UID mode could respond "rnl=0.0022 skg=0.1577 6789=0.0399". Only one ID of the configured type of each pair will be returned. The values change over time so the service provider must refresh its notion of the MUSE factors of active IDs from time to time.

Other features within PScheD also acquire the MUSE factors to order gang scheduling and load balancing candidates in cases where entitlement is a factor in their decision.

7 Does Migration Improve Performance?

The requirement that applications occupy consecutive logical PEs has often been mentioned as a factor which could limit the utilization of the CRAY T3E. This is certainly intuitive and has been seen to occur, especially on small machines, with some frequency.

---

[15] Not necessarily fastest turn-around, though, since the MUSE factor does not indicate the performance capability of a machine.

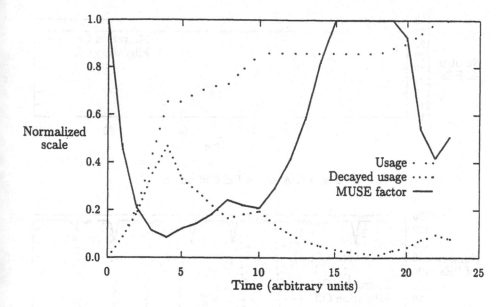

Fig. 10. The MUSE Factor

The Load Balancer attempts to reduce fragmentation by removing unoccupied gaps between applications. The result of this process is to make larger contiguous spaces in which to allocate new work. To test whether migration was an effective way to improve PE utilization in the CRAY T3E, we developed a workload for a machine with 128 application PEs that we could run both on the Load Balancing Simulator and the hardware. The results reported below are from the Load Balancing simulator. The configuration was set to run one application per PE.

A workload consisting of an unlimited source of applications is introduce into the system. About 100 of them are either active or queued for initiation at one time. We wanted a large backlog in order to give GRM sufficient choice in its ability to fill the machine. The parameters of each application are taken in turn from a list of seven sizes ranging from 25 to 128 PEs and another list of 19 execution times ranging from 180 to 1260 seconds. The test is run until the average PE utilization value stabilizes.

Figure 11 shows that with this workload, the average PE utilization with migration active stabilizes at about 122 PEs while without migration the stable level of utilization is about 115 PEs. This means that migration delivered about seven more PEs to the users or about five percent more machine power. Figure 12 shows PE usage at each measurement interval. This graph is quite busy but it does show that without migration the number of PEs in use varies over the range 90 to 122 while with migration utilization varies only between 115 and 123. In both figures the time scale is the percentage of the run period.

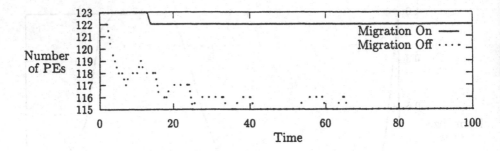

Fig. 11. Average PE Utilization

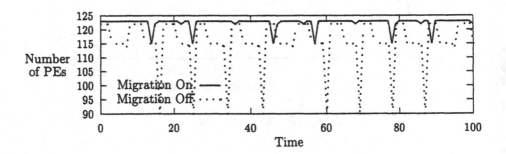

Fig. 12. PE Utilization

8 Summary

PScheD has been conceived to support solutions for the general administrative needs of large CRAY T3E systems and future machines. As of this writing, the feature is powerful enough to support the requirements of system scheduling. Special system enhancements to support political scheduling are minimal. This was a primary goal since we did not want to require complex kernel assistance as this makes future system development more difficult to design, implement and test. Unicos/mk will run without PScheD, but not with the same degree of hardware utilization and administrative control as when it is present.

It has not been feasible to describe all of the features of PScheD in detail, especially those capabilities intended to provide insight into what decisions are being made, within the scope of this paper, but we trust enough detail has been provided to communicate the flavor of our design.

PScheD is an evolving tool intended to support current as well as anticipated future hardware and system advances. The flexibility of feature management and configuration means additional capabilities can be added without the need to rewrite the existing features. It is also easy to remove unwanted feature bindings when PScheD is configured so only the features needed to handle the present needs of an installation are active. For example, if only Gang Scheduling is needed, other features such as MUSE or Load Balancing can remain unbound and inactive. Features which are initially unbound may at any time be bound if their configuration information has been set up.

CRAY T3E and UNICOS are trademarks of Cray Research. DECchip is a trademark of Digital Equipment Corporation.
We wish to acknowledge the many people who helped to review and critique this work. Comments from the referees were very helpful. Even with the best scrutiny, errors will creep into any work. The authors assume responsibility for all misleading or incorrect content.

An Experimental Evaluation of Processor Pool-Based Scheduling for Shared-Memory NUMA Multiprocessors

Timothy B. Brecht

Department of Computer Science, York University
4700 Keele Street, North York, Ontario, CANADA M3J 1P3
URL: http://www.cs.yorku.ca/~brecht
email: brecht@cs.yorku.ca

Abstract. In this paper we describe the design, implementation and experimental evaluation of a technique for operating system schedulers called *processor pool-based scheduling* [51]. Our technique is designed to assign processes (or kernel threads) of parallel applications to processors in multiprogrammed, shared-memory NUMA multiprocessors. The results of the experiments conducted in this research demonstrate that: 1) Pool-based scheduling is an effective method for localizing application execution and reducing mean response times. 2) Although application parallelism should be considered, the optimal pool size is a function of the the system architecture. 3) The strategies of placing new applications in a pool with the largest potential for in-pool growth (*i.e.*, the pool containing the fewest jobs) and of isolating applications from each other are desirable properties of algorithms for operating system schedulers executing on NUMA architectures. The "Worst-Fit" policy we examine incorporates both of these properties.

1 Introduction

The number of bus-based shared-memory multiprocessors being manufactured and sold continues to increase at a rapid rate. In fact, the success of these systems has lead several major computer manufacturers to develop and offer a complete product line of shared-memory multiprocessors, from single bused systems containing a small number of processors to larger more scalable systems that contain tens or hundreds of processors.

The design of larger more scalable shared-memory multiprocessors has necessitated the need for a departure from single bus-based systems because of the inherent limits on the bandwidth of the bus. Recent efforts in designing shared-memory multiprocessors (for even small systems) have focused on more scalable architectures. Scalable multiprocessor architectures typically distribute memory modules throughout the system in order to optimize access times to some memory locations. This approach leads to a class of shared-memory architectures in which memory access latencies depend on the relative distance between the processor requesting the access and the location of the memory module being addressed. Such systems, called NUMA (Non-Uniform Memory Access) multiprocessors, are a departure from the more common single bus-based UMA (Uniform Memory Access) multiprocessors. Some examples of NUMA multiprocessors include the University of Toronto's Hector [48], MIT's Alewife [1], Stanford's DASH and FLASH [23][21], Kendall Square Research's KSR1 [9], SUN Microsystem's S3.mp [31], the Convex Exemplar SPP1000/1200 [13] and the Sequent STiNG [25].

The proliferation of more scalable, shared-memory multiprocessors presents new opportunities for the users and new challenges for the designers of such systems. Users are granted opportunities to solve much larger problems than previously possible, with applications that use more processors and more memory, as well as the opportunity to solve several problems concurrently, by simultaneously executing parallel applications. One of the challenges that these opportunities present to the operating system designer, which is the focus of this paper, is the implementation of scheduling algorithms designed to effectively utilize the processors while enabling the efficient execution of multiple applications. This multiprogramming of parallel applications is essential for the effective utilization of all of the processors because in larger systems not all applications will be capable of efficiently executing on all processors. [49].

A critical difference between processor scheduling in UMA and NUMA multiprocessors is that scheduling decisions in NUMA systems must also consider the time it takes to access different memory locations from different processors. Thus, NUMA scheduling policies must consider the latency incurred during remote communication (in some systems determined by the number of levels in the memory access hierarchy) and to the extent possible preserve the locality of data references inherent in parallel applications. Therefore, an important aspect of scheduling in shared-memory NUMA multiprocessors is application placement. That is, how should the parallel processes of an application be placed in a NUMA multiprocessor?

In this paper we experimentally evaluate a technique, called processor pool-based scheduling, specifically designed for scheduling kernel threads onto processors in NUMA multiprocessors. (We use the terms thread and process interchangeably and intend both to refer to schedulable kernel entities, in our case a kernel thread.) We examine two central issues related to processor pools. First, how should processor pools be formed? For example, what influences which processors should belong to which pool and how closely should pools match the architecture of the system? Second, how are processor pools used? That is, once we have formed the processor pools what algorithms should be used in assigning processes of parallel applications to pools?

The results of our experimental evaluation of this technique show that pools should be chosen to reflect the architecture of the systems (the clusters inherent in scalable shared-memory systems) and that the properties of co-locating processes of the same application and isolating separate parallel applications are keys to obtaining good performance. We found that the "Worst-Fit" policy we consider for assigning processes to pools incorporates both of these properties and that the benefits of using this approach can reduce mean job execution times significantly. Moreover, our results demonstrate that the benefits obtained from using processor pools increase as the gap between processor and memory speeds continues to widen.

The remainder of this paper is organized as follows: Section 2 describes the issues addressed by and the approach used in implementing processor pool-based scheduling. Section 3 describes the environment in which we experimentally evaluate our techniques and compare the performance of our algorithms. The applications and the workload used in our evaluation are described in Section 4. In Section 5 we discuss and experimentally evaluate a number of issues related to the formation of processor pools (that is deciding which processors belong to each pool). In Section 6 we outline and compare the performance of algorithms related to the use of processor pools (i.e., the assignment of threads of parallel applications to pools). In Section 7 we discuss related work and we conclude the paper with a summary of our results in Section 8.

2 Processor Pools

We believe that the requirements of an operating system scheduler for NUMA multiprocessors are essentially different from the requirements of processor schedulers for small-scale UMA multiprocessors. The requirements that we believe to be critical to the design and implementation of schedulers for multiprogrammed parallel application workloads executing on NUMA multiprocessors are:

- **Localization**: Parallel threads of the same application need to be placed close to each other in order to minimize overhead due to remote communication.

- **Isolation**: When possible, different applications should be placed in different portions of the system in order to reduce contention for shared resources such as buses, memory modules and interconnection networks.

- **Adaptability**: The system should be able to adapt to varied and changing demands. A scalable multiprocessor should support the execution of a single highly parallel application that is capable of utilizing all of the processors, as well as a number of applications each executing on a smaller number of processors.

- **Scalability**: A pervasive requirement of all software designed for scalable architectures is that the software also scales.

A *processor pool* is a software construct for organizing and managing a large number of processors by dividing them into groups called pools. Since the goal of localization is to place parallel threads of the same application in a manner in which the costs of memory references are minimized. This implies that the architectural clusters inherent in NUMA multiprocessors must be considered when forming pools. The locality of applications is preserved by choosing pools to match the clusters of the system and executing the parallel processes of an application within a single pool (and thus a cluster), unless there are performance advantages for it to span multiple pools. Isolation is enforced by allocating different applications to different pools, thus executing applications within separate sub-systems and keeping unnecessary traffic off of higher levels of the interconnection network. Note that it is possible for several applications to share one pool.

In very large systems (with 100 or more processors), processor pools can be grouped together to form "pools of pools". These "pools of pools" are chosen and managed in the same way as the original smaller pools except that they are constructed and managed in a hierarchical fashion. Hierarchical structuring techniques have been proposed and studied by other researchers [17][45][15]. In particular, Unrau, Stumm, and Krieger have used a technique called Hierarchical Symmetric Multiprocessing to structure operating systems for scalability [45][44]. They have demonstrated significant performance improvements in applications executing on the Hector NUMA multiprocessor whose operating system, Hurricane, is structured using this approach. We use Hector and Hurricane for our experimental platform. Hierarchical structuring is therefore not a focus of our study.

Although the concept of a processor pool is driven by the size and NUMA characteristics of scalable multiprocessors it is not tied to any particular architecture. In actually implementing processor pools on a specific system, the NUMA characteristics of that architecture should be identified and fully exploited. In most architectures, there are clusters of processors that are good candidates for pools. For example, in a large-scale KSR1 system [9] containing a number of RING:0 subsystems connected together with a RING:1 at the higher level, pools may be formed by grouping together the processors in each of the RING:0's. In the case of the University of Toronto's Hector system [48] as well as in Stanford's DASH [23] and FLASH systems [21], pools may be formed by grouping the processors of an individual station or cluster. In the MIT Alewife multiprocessor [1], pools might be chosen to consist of the four processors forming the smallest component of the mesh interconnect or a slightly larger set of nearest neighbour processors.

Since the concept of processor pools is proposed to help simplify the placement problem, processors are grouped together so that the main location decision to be made is which pool to place the process in. The decision of which processor within the pool to use, the *in-pool* scheduling decision, is one that can be made by another level of software that handles scheduling within the pool. In our implementation we consider processors within a pool to be indistinguishable, thus simplifying the task of in-pool scheduling. Once the scheduling server determines which processor to assign to the thread, the kernel is only responsible for creating it on that processor and for the subsequent dispatching of threads. Therefore, we focus our attention on the problem of determining which of the pools to place a process in.

Processor pool-based scheduling algorithms involve making scheduling decisions based on pools rather than individual processors. In modern multiprocessors scheduling decisions must be made at each of the following points during a job's execution (the issues related to these decision points are discussed more more detail in Section 6):

1. **Arrival**: A kernel thread is created and must be assigned to a processor (pool). The essential problem is which pool to assign the first thread of a new job to when it is not know how many (if any) children that thread will create. This decision is referred to as *initial placement*.

2. **Expansion**: A job creates a new thread for parallel execution. We call this decision point *job expansion*.

3. **Contraction**: When a thread of a parallel program completes, a processor becomes available which could be assigned to execute a new thread.

Contraction can be performed by permitting the scheduler to initiate expansion by contacting one of the executing jobs. Expansion of this type requires coordination between the scheduler and the user-level thread package's run-time system. Alternatively, the scheduler could also contact and coordinate with a job to reduce the number of threads currently executing in order to reallocate processors to another job (e.g., a newly arriving job). This this type of dynamic reallocation of processors is referred to as *dynamic repartitioning*.

In fact some parallel jobs involve multiple phases of expansion and contraction and dynamic repartitioning several algorithms have been designed in order to reallocate processors fairly and/or in order to minimize mean response time [43][50][8]. This previous work has been conducted under the assumption that memory access latencies are uniform. Unfortunately, the problem of repartitioning becomes considerably more complex on clustered, NUMA architectures. We leave this important and interesting problem as a topic for future research (see [7] for a more detailed discussion of the problem). In this paper we do not consider the dynamic repartitioning of processors because of the issues related cache affinity in the assignment of user-level threads to kernel-level threads [27][28]. This ensures that the only differences in execution times are due to job scheduling decisions rather than trying to account for possible differences in execution times due to user-level thread scheduling decisions.

3 Experimental Environment

The system used to conduct the experiments presented in this paper is a prototype shared-memory NUMA multiprocessor called Hector, developed at the University of Toronto [48]. The prototype used contains a total of 16 processors grouped into four clusters, called stations. Stations are connected with a bit-parallel slotted ring and each station consists of four processor modules connected with a bus. Each processor module contains a Motorola MC81000 processor, separate instruction and data caches and 4 Mbytes of memory for a total of 64 Mbytes of globally addressable memory. Cache coherence is enforced in software by the HURRICANE operating system's memory manager at a 4 Kbyte page level of granularity, by permitting only unshared and read-shared pages to be cacheable [45][44]. Enforcing cache coherence in software simplifies the hardware design and has permitted a simple and elegant design that has relatively mild NUMA characteristics.

Although the prototype Hector system used to conduct the experiments is configured with sixteen processors, we dedicate one station (the four processors in Station 0) to the execution of system processes, including the shell scripts used to generate the workload. This ensures that differences in execution times are due solely to differences in scheduler placements of application processes.

The *NUMAness* of a shared-memory multiprocessor can be thought of as the degree to which memory access latencies are affected by the distance between the requesting processor and the desired memory location. The degree of NUMAness of a multiprocessor is affected by: 1) The differences in memory access times between each of the levels in the memory access hierarchy. 2) The amount of memory (and number of processors) that are co-located within each level. 3) The number of levels in the NUMA hierarchy.

The Hector prototype features a set of "delay switches" that add additional delays to off-station memory requests. Packets destined for a memory module not located on the same station are held up at the requesting processor for the number of specified cycles. The range of possible settings are: 0, 1, 2, 4, 8, 16, 32, and 64 processor cycles. The delay switches are used to emulate and gain insight into the performance of: 1) Systems with faster processors — because processor speeds continue to increase at a faster rate than memory and interconnection networks, thus increasing remote memory access latencies. 2) Systems of different designs — because some systems have larger memory latencies due to the complexity of the interconnection network or hardware cache coherence techniques. 3) Systems with more processors — since increases in the number of processors will require larger and possibly more complex interconnection networks, resulting in increased remote memory access latencies.

Table 1 shows latencies for local, on-station, and off-station (or ring) memory accesses in units of 60 nano-second cycles. Off-station requests, or those requiring the use of the ring are shown for 0, 4, 8, 16, 32 and 64 cycle delays. Note that the delay switches have no affect on local or on-station requests and that with the delay switches set to 16 cycles, the off-station access times for Hector are still below those of other systems that contain faster processors, more processors or mechanisms for hardware cache-coherence [6]. Off station latencies in DASH and remote node latencies on the KSR1 are 100 or more processors cycles and latencies to memory on a remote ring in the KSR1 are about a factor of six times slower [38]. For more detailed descriptions of Hector see [48][18][41].

Table 1. Memory reference times, in processor cycles, on the 16 processor Hector system

	32bit load	32bit store	cache load	cache writeback	Delay
local	10	10	19	19	—
station	19	9	29	62	—
ring	27	17	37	42	0
	35	21	49	58	4
	43	25	61	74	8
	59	33	85	106	16
	91	49	133	170	32
	155	81	229	298	64

In the experiments conducted in this paper we consider systems with relatively mild NUMA characteristics by using a maximum delay setting of 16. The affect that larger delays have on application performance and on the importance of application placement is explored more fully in [6]. The results of our experiments show that even for such systems the proper placement of the parallel threads of an application can significantly affect the execution time of the application.

The HURRICANE operating system also supports page migration and replication, but these features were disabled while conducting our experiments in order to ensure that difference in mean response times (and parallel application execution times) are due only to difference in scheduling algorithms. For the purposes of this study we simplify the larger problem of scheduling in a NUMA environment by not considering thread migration. Our scheduler implements a space-partitioning [43][50] of processors with strong affinity of processes to processors [42][39][19]. In fact the operating system kernel contains separate ready queues for each processor. The migration of processes is discouraged because of the cache and memory contexts that can be associated with each process (recall that besides data and instruction caches, each processor module also contains local memory).

We also assume that the parallelism of the application and the number of processors it is allocated are not known *a priori*. In our implementation, when an application wishes to create a thread and thus gain access to another processor, the library call to create a thread first contacts the scheduling server, which executes outside of the kernel's address space. The scheduling server determines if the calling application should be allocated another processor and if so, which processor it should be allocated. If the scheduler decides to allocate another processor to the application, the system call is then passed on to the kernel, which creates the thread on the processor specified by the scheduler. When a thread finishes executing or is killed by an exception, the scheduler is notified and updates its internal state. The kernel is only responsible for dispatching threads. The scheduler, therefore, sees requests for processors one at a time and assigns them to applications until all processors have been allocated, at which point requests to create additional processes fail. All of our applications and workloads have been written to execute in this fashion. We believe this to be a more realistic approach to scheduling than assuming that the number of processors required will be known when the application starts. Note that if the number of processors required by each application is fixed and know at the time of the job arrival, the problem of determining which processors to allocate is similar to a bin packing problem with multiple bins.

The use of the Hector multiprocessor and the HURRICANE operating system provides us with the opportunity to examine the affects that increased memory access latencies are likely to have on our results. Since we have access to the complete source code for the HURRICANE operating system, scheduling server, run-time system and applications, we have the ability to modify the system to support our experiments. Because this system uses processors with relatively slow clock rates and contains only 16 processors, remote memory accesses latencies are quite low relative to systems with newer processors with higher clock rates and systems with larger and more complex interconnection networks (that support more processors and cache coherence). Therefore, we believe that our results and conclusions are somewhat conservative and that the importance of application placement and the decreases in execution times observed from using processor pool-based scheduling will only increase as the gap between processor speeds and memory speeds continues to increase and as the size of scalable NUMA multiprocessors continues to grow.

4 Parallel Applications

The applications comprising the workloads used in our experiments are listed in Table 2 along with the problem size, precision used, the number of lines of C source code, and the speedup measured using four processors of one station, S(4). For the single processor execution time, we use the time required to execute the parallel application on one processor because we did not have access to a serial version of each application. More detailed descriptions of each application and how their execution can be affected by poor processor placement decisions can be found in [6][7].

Table 2. Summary of the applications used

Name	Application / Problem Size	Precision	Lines of C	S(4)
FFT	2D Fast fourier transform 256x256	Single	1300	2.9
HOUGH	Hough transformation 192x192, density of 90%	Double	600	3.4
MM	Matrix multiplication 192x192	Double	500	3.4
NEURAL	Neural network backpropagation 3 layers of 511 units, 4 iterations	Single	1100	3.8
PDE	Partial differential equation solver using successive over-relaxation 96x96	Double	700	3.7
SIMPLEX	Simplex Method for Linear Programming 256 constraints, 512 variables	Double	1000	2.4

Although the size of the data sets may appear to be relatively small, they were chosen for a number of reasons: 1) They should execute on four processors in a reasonable amount of time since multiple executions of each workload are used to compute means and confidence intervals. 2) The size of the data cache on each processor is relatively small (16 Kbytes). Consequently cache misses and memory accesses will occur, even with a relatively small sized problem. 3) The amount of memory configured per processor is relatively small (4 Mbytes). If problem sizes are too large, data structures that are designed to be allocated to the local processor may have to be allocated to a remote processor, resulting in remote memory references where the application programmer had not intended.

Some of the applications may appear not to execute very efficiently on four processors. This is due to the relatively small data sets used. Most of the applications were designed to be used with larger data sets on more processors (i.e., the parallelism is relatively coarse-grained). However, we believe that these applications represent a reasonable mix of efficiencies and should provide an adequate workload for the purposes of our experiments.

5 Forming Processor Pools

The question of how to choose the groupings of processors that form processor pools (i.e., how many processors should belong to each pool) is one that is potentially influenced by two main factors, the parallelism of the applications and the architecture of the system.

Issues related to the specific policies for assigning processors to pools are considered in detail Section 6. For now we assign newly arriving jobs to the pool with the largest number of available processors. Other processes of the job are placed within the same pool if possible. If there are no available processors in that pool then the pool with the largest number of available processors is chosen. This algorithm was devised using observations made while conducting experiments for a previous study [6] and is designed to isolate the execution of different jobs and to allow them "room to grow". This strategy corresponds to the "Worst-Fit" algorithm that is described in Section 6.

We now conduct a series of experiments designed to further explore the influences on the choice of processor pools. Although we do not exclude the possibility of choosing processor pools of different sizes, this work only considers pools of equal sizes. The goal in this paper is to gain insight into the forming of pools, the design of policies for their use, and the benefits of processor pool-based scheduling.

5.1 Determining Processor Pool Sizes

The first experiment is designed to determine if processor pool-based scheduling improves performance and, if it does, to examine appropriate pool sizes. This is done by varying the pool size while executing the same workload. Using 12 processors we compare the mean execution times of applications when executing under a scheduler that uses: 1 pool of 12, 2 pools of 6, 3 pools of 4, and 6 pools of 2 processors. We also consider 12 pools each containing one processor. Note that one pool of size 12 is comparable to not using processor pools and is equivalent to using a central ready queue from which idle processors grab processes. Because no grouping of pools is done to form "pools of pools", 12 pools of one processor is also equivalent to not using pools, with the exception of the overheads required to manage 12 pools. These overheads, although not significant, are present. Recall that although applications are permitted to span more than one pool and multiple jobs may execute within a single pool, our implementation of pool-based scheduling avoids these situations whenever possible.

When possible, pools are chosen to correspond to the hardware stations in Hector. Therefore, when pools of size two are used, each of the three stations used contains two pools, and when pools of size four are used, they exactly correspond to hardware stations. When two pools of size six are used, Pool 1 contains four processors from Station 1 and two from Station 2, while Pool 2 contains four processors from Station 3 and two from Station 2.

5.2 Workload and Results

The workload used for this experiment is comprised of five of the parallel application kernels FFT, HOUGH, MM, NEURAL, and PDE. The SIMPLEX application is not used in all of the experiments conducted in this paper because in order to obtain a reasonably efficient execution, the data set had to be large enough that it significantly increased the execution time of the entire workload, making multiple executions in order to obtain confidence intervals difficult.

The workload consists of a number of "streams" of parallel jobs. A stream is formed by repeatedly executing the five applications, one after another. Since each stream is implemented using a shell script, there are unpredictable but small delays between the completion of one application and the start of the next. The delays are small enough that they do not significantly affect the results. Each stream contains a different ordering of the five applications and all streams are started at the same time (recall that one station is dedicated to the execution of system and sequential processes, including the workload generator). The number of streams is adjusted to determine the multiprogramming level. The number of streams used is determined by dividing the number of processors used for the execution of parallel applications (12) by the parallelism of the applications (in this experiment 4). In the first experiment, each stream consists of 15 repetitions of the five applications for a total of 75 jobs per stream. The applications are each allocated four processors, so three streams are used and the entire workload consists of 225 jobs.

Because the system is relatively small, has very mild NUMA characteristics and because we are interested in how increases in NUMAness affect the results, we also run each set of experiments with delay settings of 0, 8, and 16 cycles. The results of these experiments can be seen in Figure 1. Each line in a graph plots the mean response time versus the pool size. Graphs are shown for each of the different applications with the graph labelled "COMBINED" representing the mean response times over all jobs. The vertical bars represent 90 percent confidence intervals.

We first note that, as expected in a small system with only mild NUMA characteristics, represented by the lines in the graphs labelled Delay=0, the mean response times are not significantly improved by using processor pools. However, as the NUMAness of the system increases, the performance improvements due to pool-based scheduling increase and are substantial when using a delay of 16 cycles. Also note that these improvements increase with the NUMAness of the system. The improvements can be seen by comparing the execution times of the applications using a pool of size of 12 (the no pool case), with those using other pool sizes. The closer the pool size is to 4 the better the performance. The exception is the NEURAL application which, as described in detail in previous work [6], suffers from an excessive number of system calls which overshadow the locality in the application.

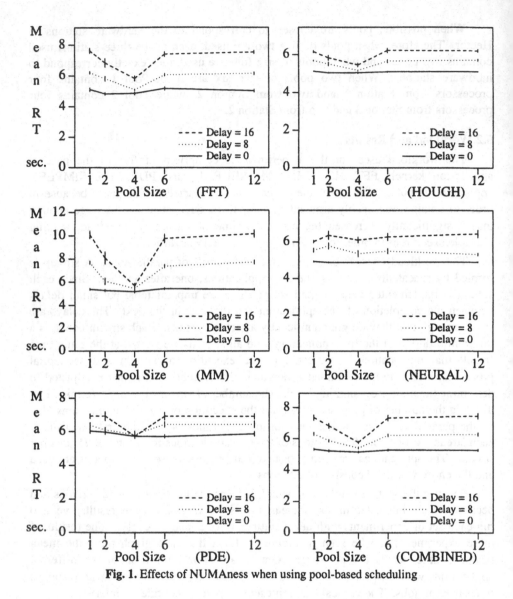

Fig. 1. Effects of NUMAness when using pool-based scheduling

Although two pools of six processors may not seem appropriate for the current workload, it is included for completeness, since it will play a central role in a future experiment. It also permits us to determine if a small enforcement of localization improves performance. The results show that even though there is a trend toward improved performance when using two pools compared with using no pools, those improvements are not large enough to be considered significant. The degree to which performance is improved varies from application to application and depends on the number and frequency of remote memory references. However, the mean response time over all jobs is improved by using pools, as shown in the graph labelled "COMBINED" in Figure 1.

The graphs in Figure 1 also show that for this set of experiments a pool size of four yields the best performance. However: 1) The parallelism of each application is four. 2) Each station in the Hector system contains four processors. Consequently, we next explore the relative influence of these two factors, application parallelism and system architecture, on the choice of pool sizes.

5.3 Application Influences on Pool Size

In order to examine the importance of application parallelism in determining an appropriate pool size, we now vary the parallelism of the applications and perform the same experiments conducted in the previous section. A delay of 16 cycles is used and the number of streams is adjusted with the parallelism of the applications (when possible keeping all processors busy). Figure 2 shows the results obtained when executing each application with two, four, and eight processes. In the case when the application parallelism is two, six streams are used, each consisting of 10 repetitions, for a total of 300 jobs. When the application parallelism is four, three streams are used, each consisting of 15 repetitions, for a total of 225 jobs. In the case when the application parallelism is eight, one stream with 25 repetitions is used for a total of 125 jobs. In this case applications are not multiprogrammed because we can not space-share two applications each using eight processors on 12 processors. The three lines plotted in each graph represent the mean response times of the applications obtained with application parallelism of two, four, and eight, versus different pool sizes. The vertical bars at each data point represent 90 percent confidence intervals.

We first observe that when eight processes are used for each application, performance is not significantly affected by the pool size. This is because the placement of eight processes within a 12-processor system does not afford as much room for localization as applications which use a smaller number of processors. Next, we observe that when applications are allocated two processors, pools of size two and four yield the best performance, again with the exception of the NEURAL application (due to excessive system calls). When the applications each require two processors, there is no significant difference in performance between using pools of size two or four because in either case each application is able to execute within one hardware station. Finally, we observe that when the application parallelism is four, the mean response time is minimized when pools of size four are used. These results might suggest that the appropriate choice of pool size might be related to the parallelism of the jobs (this is explored in the next sub-section).

An interesting outcome of the experiments shown in Figure 2 is that for some applications, most notably MM, increasing the number of processors the application uses does not necessarily improve response time. This can be seen in the case of MM by observing that the mean response time obtained using eight processors is equal to or higher than the mean response time obtained using four processors, no matter what pool size is used. These graphs demonstrate that an application's execution time can be dramatically affected by the NUMA environment and that in some cases a localized execution using fewer processors will outperform a necessarily less localized execution using more processors. Thus, there is a relationship between the allocation problem (how many processors to allocate to each application) and the

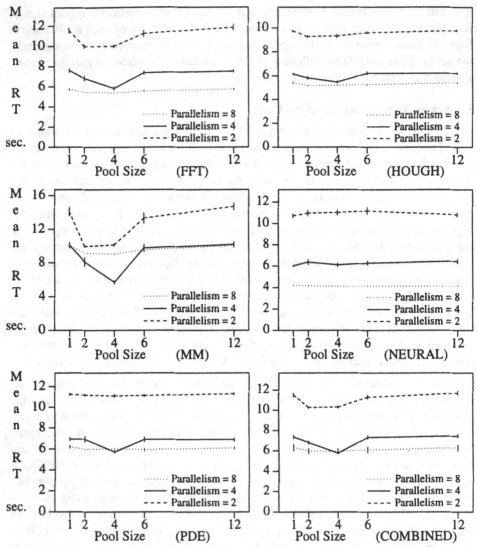

Fig. 2. Various pool sizes with application parallelism of 2, 4 and 8, delay = 16

placement problem (which processors to allocate to each application), since the number of processors to allocate to a job may depend on which processors are available. In this paper we concentrate on obtaining a first-order understanding of the issues involved in making placement decisions and in the performance benefits that can result from making good placement decisions. The relationship between these problems is discussed in more detail in [7] and is an interesting topic of future research.

152

5.4 Architectural Influences on Pool Size

While the experiments shown in Figure 2 suggest that there is a relationship between pool size and application parallelism, these experiments do not fully explore the relationship between pool size and the system architecture. To determine the strength of the connection between pool size and system architecture, we conduct another experiment in which each application executes using six processors. In this experiment the HOUGH, MM and SIMPLEX applications were used. The other applications (FFT, NEURAL, and PDE) are not used because, unfortunately, they are written in such a way that executing them on six processors is not possible. In these experiments, we use two streams, each of which executes the three applications 15 times, for 45 jobs per stream and a total of 90 jobs.

The graphs in Figure 3 plot the mean response times for each of the applications versus different pool sizes. The mean response times over all of the applications is shown in the graph labelled "COMBINED". The number above each of the bars gives the percentage improvement when compared with one pool of size 12. A negative value indicates that the mean response time was increased.

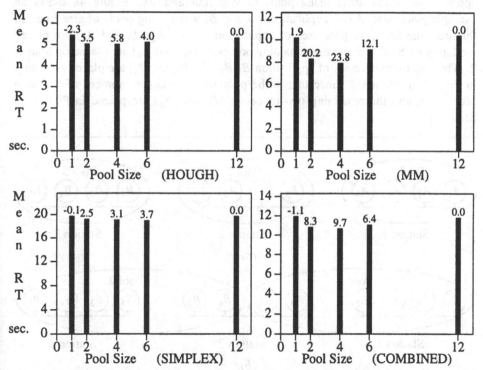

Fig. 3. Various pool sizes with application parallelism of 6, delay = 16

The main data points of interest in these experiments are the pools of size four, because this matches the size of a Hector station, and pools of size six, because this matches the application parallelism. For the HOUGH and SIMPLEX applications, although we observe slight differences in mean response times when pools of size four and six are used, the differences are not statistically significant. A pronounced difference is observed for the MM application. This is somewhat surprising since exactly the same set of processors is assigned to each application in each case. The differences in mean response times are, however, due to the placement of processes within the pools.

First, we briefly review the pool placement policy in order to understand why the placements are different. Then we explain why the resulting execution times are different. The first process of each job is placed in the pool with the largest number of available processors. Subsequent processes of that job are placed in the same pool as the first process until all of the processors in the pool are used. If more processors are required, the next pool with the most available processors is chosen. One of the goals in the design of processor pools is to form groups of processors that can be managed easily and uniformly within the pool. Therefore, we place processes randomly within pools and point out that if placement within processor pools affects performance significantly, the pools have not been chosen to appropriately reflect the architecture.

Figure 4 illustrates a scenario in which the response times of the same applications would differ using pools of size four and six. Figure 4a shows an example placement of two applications, A and B, when using pools of size four. In this case the first four processes of application A (A_1, A_2, A_3 and A_4) are placed randomly on Station 1 and the remaining processes (A_5 and A_6) are placed on Station 2. The first four processes of application B (B_1, B_2, B_3 and B_4) are placed randomly in Pool 3 on Station 3, since that is the pool with the largest number of available processors, and the remaining two processes (B_5 and B_6) are placed in Pool 2 on Station 2.

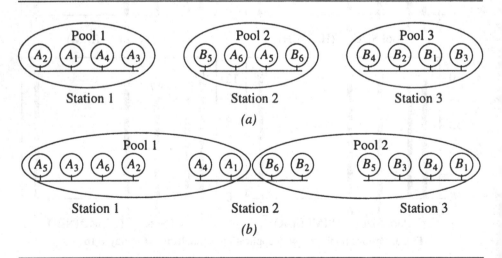

Fig. 4. Individual process placement using processor pools of size 4 and 6

Figure 4b shows an example placement when pools of size six are used. In this case each application fits entirely within a single pool. Application A is placed and executed in Pool 1 and application B is placed and executed in Pool 2. In previous work [6] we observed that if the first process of an application (the parent) is located on a station that is different from the rest of the processes of the application, the response time can be affected significantly because of the substantial memory context often associated with the first process of an application. Note that in the case when pools of size four are used, as many children as possible will be placed in the same pool as the parent. However, under closer inspection we determined in that the same is not always true when the pool size is six.

The results of this experiment, the details of which can be found in [7], show that there is a difference between using three pools of size four and two pools of size six when allocating six processors to each application. Three pools of size four yield better performance, indicating that in this case it is more important to choose pool sizes to reflect the architecture of the system than the parallelism of the applications. Also, matching pools to the architecture is likely to be relatively straightforward while, in general, a workload will consist of a number of applications with different (and possibly changing) degrees of parallelism, making it difficult to match pool sizes with application parallelism.

6 Using Processor Pools

One motivation for processor pool-based scheduling is to ease placement decisions by reducing the number and types of considerations required to make good placement decisions. This is accomplished by making placement decisions that consider pools rather than individual processors when scheduling parallel applications. An important aspect of pool-based scheduling is the strategy used for making placement decisions. We first outline the types of placement decisions that are made during the lifetime of an application and briefly point out how these decisions may influence placement strategies before examining actual strategies.

- **Initial Placement**: Before an application begins execution it must be assigned to a processor. The decision of where to place the first process of an application is an important one that can influence not only the placement of the remaining processes of the application but also the placement of other applications.

- **Expansion**: Once a parallel application begins execution, it will, at some point, create and execute a number of processes. We call this creation of new processes *expansion*. How to properly place these processes is a key consideration in preserving the locality of an application. As a result, it is essential to consider where the existing processes of the application are located. As noted in the previous section, the first (parent) process of an application may contain significant cache and memory context thus making it desirable to place as many of the child processes of that application as close as possible to the parent.

- **Repartitioning with Pools**: A change in the number of processors allocated to each application may require a dynamic repartitioning of the processors [43][24][50][29]. An important and difficult problem is how to repartition the processors while maintaining the locality of the executing applications.

The topic of repartitioning with pools is discussed in more detail in [7] and is an interesting topic for further research. In this paper we examine the first two decision points more carefully, present algorithms for making these decisions and, when possible, evaluate their performance. We begin by examining the problem of application expansion.

6.1 Expansion

Processor pool-based scheduling strategies for supporting application expansion are relatively straightforward. The desirable properties of an expansion policy are:

1. Place new processes as close to existing processes of the application as possible. This is accomplished by placing new processes in pools that are already occupied by the application. In so doing, processes are placed close to the shared data being accessed.

2. If there are no available processors in the pools already occupied by the application, choose new pools so there is as much room for future expansion as possible and interference with other applications is minimized.

Property one above is quite easy to satisfy by keeping track of where the job is already executing and assigning new processes only to pools that are already occupied by that job (using the pool containing the fewest processes). Since property two has similar requirements to the problem of initial placement, this phase of expansion can use the same algorithms as those used for initial placement. All of our experiments use the same strategy for this phase of expansion as that used for initial placement.

6.2 Initial Placement

The main considerations for making an initial placement decision (for the first process of an application) are:

1. Give the new application as much room as possible for the future creation of processes. That is, provide as much room for expansion as possible.

2. Try to isolate the execution of each application to the extent possible. That is, try to reduce the possibility of interfering with the execution of other applications by placing each application in its own portion of the system.

The problem of placing applications into pools has similarities to the problem of allocating memory in non-paged systems. An especially notable similarity is the desire to avoid fragmentation, since fragmenting processes of an application across different pools will hurt localization. Because of these similarities, we briefly consider a number of possible strategies for initial placement adapted from well known placement policies for non-paged memory systems [37].

- **First-Fit**: Pools are listed in a predetermined order by simply numbering each pool. The first process of an application is then placed in the first pool with an available processor.

- **Best-Fit**: The first process of an application is placed in a pool with the smallest, non-zero number of available processors.

- **Worst-Fit:** The first process of an application is placed in a pool with the largest number of available processors.

Of these techniques the Best-Fit and the First-Fit policies do not isolate applications from each other and may not provide room for the expansion of applications within a pool. For example, if three applications arrive in an empty system, all three may be initially placed within the same pool, thus leaving little room for the localized placement of subsequently created parallel processes of each application (recall that the number of processors an application will use is not known *a priori*). However, the Worst-Fit policy would place each of these three applications into different pools, thus permitting each to execute in their own portion of the system.

A comparison of the performance of the First-Fit and Worst-Fit policies is shown in Figure 5. A workload of three streams of applications of parallelism four is used, with each of the five applications FFT, HOUGH, MM, NEURAL and PDE being repeated in different orders within each stream. Each stream consists of 15 repetitions of the five applications for a total of 75 jobs per stream and a grand total of 225 jobs. Pools of size four are chosen to correspond to the hardware stations and a delay of 16 cycles is used to emulate systems that have stronger NUMA characteristics than our small, mildly NUMA prototype. The normalized mean response times of each of the five applications and the overall mean response time (the bars labelled COMBINED) are shown. The mean response times obtained using the Worst-Fit policy are normalized with respect to the mean response times obtained using the First-Fit policy.

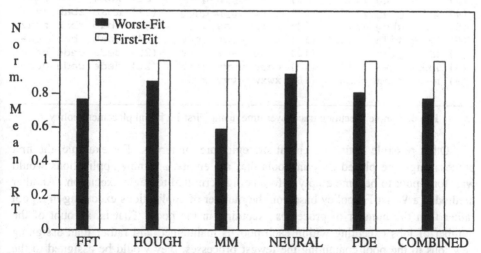

Fig. 5. Comparing Worst-Fit with First-Fit placement strategies, pool size = 4, delay = 16

As expected the Worst-Fit policy performs significantly better than the First-Fit policy and in fact it reduces the mean response times of three of the five applications by 20% or more. By examining the execution traces obtained when using the First-Fit policy (shown in Figure 6), we observe that the different applications are not always placed within one pool (and therefore one station). Figure 6 shows a number of snapshots of the allocation of processes of an application to pools and thus to stations. The numbers in parentheses to the left of each column represent, and are used to refer to, specific snapshots taken over regular time intervals. Threads within an application are labelled with the same letter of the alphabet and an unallocated processor is represented with a dash. Processors within a pool (and thus station) are grouped together by by leaving a space between pools. For example, line (1) shows that all processors are unallocated and line (16) shows that four processes of the same application (represented by "u") are allocated to the first four processors (the first pool corresponding to Station 1), the next four processors (the second pool corresponding to Station 2) are idle and the last four processors (the third pool corresponding to Station 3) are all allocated to the same application (represented by "t"). From the trace in Figure 6, we can see a period of execution where each of the applications is executing within a separate station, in lines (12) through (17). Each application is therefore localized and isolated from the others. Lines (22) and (23) show an example of how all three applications can each have one process executing in the same station ("a", "b" and "z" each have a processes on Station 2). These snapshots and the results of the previous experiment demonstrate that although placements using the First-Fit policy are not always bad placements, the mean response time is significantly improved by using the Worst-Fit policy.

	Stn1	Stn2	Stn3		Stn1	Stn2	Stn3		Stn1	Stn2	Stn3
(1)	----	----	----	(10)	mooo	mnmm	nnno	(19)	xwxw	yyyy	wxxw
(2)	----	----	f---	(11)	-ooo	p---	---o	(20)	xwxw	yyyy	wxxw
(3)	ghhh	ghgg	ffff	(12)	----	pppp	q---	(21)	xwxw	----	wx--
(4)	ghhh	ghgg	ffff	(13)	rrrr	pppp	qqqq	(22)	abab	zbab	zzaz
(5)	ghhh	ghgg	iiii	(14)	rrrr	ssss	q---	(23)	abab	zbab	zzaz
(6)	k---	jjjj	iiii	(15)	uuuu	ssss	tttt	(24)	abab	-bab	cca-
(7)	kkkk	jjjj	l---	(16)	uuuu	----	tttt	(25)	dede	cede	ccdc
(8)	kkk-	----	llll	(17)	uuuu	vvvv	tttt	(26)	dede	cede	ccdc
(9)	m---	mnmm	nnno	(18)	xwxw	vvvv	wxxw				

Fig. 6. Sample execution trace, over time, using First-Fit initial placement policy

Other possible initial placement strategies are numerous. For example, the first process might be placed only in pools that are empty, and new applications would wait for a pool to become empty before being permitted to begin execution. Another method is a Worst-Fit policy based on the number of applications executing in a pool rather than the number of processes executing in the pool. That is, a count of the number of jobs executing within each pool is maintained and rather than assigning new jobs to the pool containing the fewest processes, they would be assigned to the pool containing the fewest jobs. This policy may be more suited to isolating applications and providing room for expansion under certain types of workloads. We believe that this last approach is likely be an improvement over our existing Worst-Fit policy. However, both algorithms behaved similarly under our current workloads.

7 Related Work

The notion of grouping processors to enhance scalability has also been proposed by other researchers [4][17][16][2][15]. Feitelson and Rudolph's distributed hierarchical technique is designed to also gang-schedule and load balance multiple applications in large multiprocessor systems [17][16][15]. Their evaluation of this technique does not take into account NUMA multiprocessors. They do point out that this technique could be used in NUMA systems. However, they do not describe how to map their tree structured distributed hierarchy onto NUMA architectures, although in a symmetric tree structured architecture the mapping is direct and should preserve locality. One advantage offered by processor pools is that they are explicitly designed to preserve the locality of parallel applications in a fashion that is not tied to a particular architecture. Furthermore, they are also designed to isolate the execution of multiple applications from one another. The combination of these two properties is intended to reduce the cost of remote references to shared data and to reduce the likelihood of contention for the interconnection network. Other work has also used the concept of clustering for different purposes. For example, Chapin *et al.* [12] use their notion of clusters (called cells) to prevent faults that occur in one cell from propagating to other cells, thus containing or localizing hardware and software faults.

Recent work has recognized that applications can build considerable cache context, or footprints [42] and that it may be more efficient to execute a process or thread on a processor that already contains relevant data in the processor's cache. Much of this work is concerned with the design and evaluation of techniques that attempt to track where processes or threads may have established cache context and to use this information to try reuse this context [39][46][19][27][28][40][26][3][35]. Our work in this paper is complementary to processor-cache affinity and lightweight thread scheduling techniques for improving locality of data references. While these previous studies investigate the importance of scheduling techniques for reducing the number of memory accesses by co-locating processes with processor caches that contain the data being accessed, our work investigates the importance of scheduling techniques for reducing the cost of required memory accesses (i.e., those references that are not cached).

Another area of work concerned with reducing remote memory access latencies concentrates on virtual memory management techniques for migrating and/or replicating pages of virtual memory. The goal of this research is to place the data being frequently referenced close to the processor or processors requesting the data [20][14][22][5][11][47]. Again, we view our work as complementary to these techniques, since it is our goal to locate the kernel threads of an application as close to each other as possible. A localized placement of processes of an application and the isolation of different applications from each other by placing them in different portions (clusters) of the system will reduce, but not eliminate, the need for migration and replication. More importantly, it will reduce the costs of migration and replication operations because of the already close proximity of processes to the data being accessed and because contention for shared resources, such as the interconnection network, will be reduced.

Several scheduling studies have recognized that that the execution time of parallel applications are affected not only by how many processors they are allocated but also by how much memory they are allocated and require. New techniques for determining how many processors to allocate are considering the memory requirements of such applications [34][30][36][33]. The techniques we present and evaluate in this paper are not concerned with the problem of how many processors to allocate but rather which processors to allocate to a job. Although we've previously discussed the relationship between the problems of allocation (how many processor to allocate) and placement (which processor to allocate) [7], the work in this paper concentrates on first gaining an understanding of the issues related to the placement problem before concerning ourselves with the interplay between the allocation and placement problems.

Chandra et al. [10] add cache-affinity and cluster-affinity to a UNIX scheduler by modifying the traditional priority mechanisms. Using a sixteen processor DASH system they found that while a sequential workload benefited significantly from the improved locality, this approach did not improve execution times when compared with the baseline UNIX scheduler for parallel workloads. They also compare the use of gang scheduling [32], processor sets [4], and process control [43] scheduling policies for executing parallel workloads. While they exploit cluster level locality in their implementations of each of these policies, they do not fully explore the strategies used in exploiting locality for parallel workloads nor how effective these strategies are at localization. In this paper we focus on developing guidelines and algorithms designed specifically to enforce localized placements and on evaluating the benefits of such algorithms.

In previous work Zhou and Brecht [51] present the initial concept of processor pools and conduct a simulation study which demonstrates the potential benefits obtained from using processor pools for scheduling in NUMA multiprocessors. Since then [6] we have implemented and executed a number of parallel applications on a sixteen node multiprocessor to demonstrate the significant decreases in execution times that can be obtained by considering the architecture of NUMA systems when making application placement decisions. Motivated by both of these previous studies the work in this paper undertakes an operating system level implementation and an experimental performance evaluation of processor pool-based scheduling. This work differs from the simulation study in that it focuses on the relationships between the choice of processor pool sizes and architectural clusters and pool sizes and the parallelism of the jobs being executed. While the concept of processor pools has not changed significantly from the previous paper, the algorithms, system and workload assumptions are different in several key ways:

- In the simulation model, arriving jobs request a predetermined number of threads and the scheduler permits the creation of possibly fewer threads (proportional to the number requested). In this paper the number of threads desired by a job is not known *a priori* (as is the case in most multiprogrammed multiprocessors). Also, we limit the number of threads in the system to be equal to the number of processors. This avoids unnecessary overheads due to context switching and improves processor affinity.

- The simulation model used a single ready queue per processor pool and scheduled threads within each pool in a round-robin fashion. Our implementation uses one ready queue per processor, thus providing strong processor affinity and eliminating contention for a shared pool-based queue.

- We've eliminated the "tunable parameters" present in the algorithms used in the simulation and concentrated on algorithmic decisions that are relatively easy to implement. For example, the degree of pool-spanning which is a control on the extent to which threads of the same job are permitted to be assigned to different pools is not present in the implementation. Instead the number of pools a job is permitted to span is tempered only by the parallelism of the job and the number of available processors.

- Obviously the system model and most components of the workload model used in this paper are more realistic than those used in the simulation.

8 Summary

In this paper we have proposed algorithms for scheduling in NUMA multiprocessors based on the concept of processor pools. A processor pool is a software construct for organizing and managing processors by dividing them into groups called pools. The main reasons for using processor pools are to preserve the locality of an application's execution and to isolate the execution of multiple applications from each other. The locality of applications is preserved by executing them within a pool when possible, but permitting them to span pools if it is beneficial to their execution. Isolation is enforced by executing multiple applications in separate pools (to the extent possible). This reduces execution times by reducing the cost of remote memory accesses. We also expect that processor pools reduce contention for the interconnection network, although we were not able to observe this on our small-scale, mildly NUMA multiprocessor. (Reducing the distance required to obtain remote memory references should reduce the use of the interconnection network.) It is expected that the scalability of the system will also be enhanced because processors within a pool can be treated equally.

We have conducted a series of experiments that explore desirable attributes of processor pool-based scheduling. In particular, we have found:

- Pool-based scheduling is an effective method for localizing application execution and reducing mean response time.

- Optimal pool size is a function of the parallelism of the applications and the system architecture. However, we believe that it is more important to choose pools to reflect the architectural clusters in the system than the parallelism of the applications, especially since the parallelism of an application may not be known and may change during execution.

- The strategies of placing new applications in a pool with the largest potential for in-pool growth (*i.e.*, the pool containing the fewest jobs) and of isolating applications from each other seem to be desirable properties of algorithms for using pools. The Worst-Fit policy incorporates both of these properties.

An observation made in [6] that is also apparent when analyzing the experiments conducted in this work is that the proper placement of processes of an application is critical and localized placements are essential for the efficient execution of parallel applications. As well, the importance of placement decisions and the improvements resulting from proper decisions increase as the size of NUMA multiprocessors increase and as the gap between processor and remote memory access speeds continues to widen.

9 Acknowledgments

This work was conducted while at the University of Toronto. I would like to thank the members of the Hector and HURRICANE projects there for their dedication and hard work in implementing, debugging and tuning the system hardware and software, most notably: Ron White, Michael Stumm, Ron Unrau, Orran Krieger, Ben Gamsa, and Jonathan Hanna. I wish to also thank Songnian Zhou, Ken Sevcik, and the other members of the scheduling discussion group for many discussions related to scheduling in multiprocessors. James Pang, Deepinder Gill, Thomas Wong and Ron Unrau contributed some of the parallel applications. I am also grateful to the Natural Sciences and Engineering Research Council for the support they provided during the course of this work.

10 References

[1] A. Agarwal, D. Chaiken, K. Johnson, D. Kranz, J. Kubiatowicz, K. Kurihara, B. Lim, G. Maa, and D. Nussbaum, "The MIT Alewife Machine: A Large-Scale Distributed-Memory Multiprocessor", **Scalable Shared Memory Multiprocessors**, ed. M. Dubois and S. S. Thakkar, Kluwer Academic Publishers, Norwell, Massachusetts, pp. 239-261, 1991.

[2] I. Ahmad and A. Ghafoor, "Semi-Distributed Load Balancing for Massively Parallel Multicomputer Systems", *IEEE Transactions on Software Engineering*, *Vol.* 17, *No.* 10, pp. 987-1004, October, 1991.

[3] F. Bellosa, "Locality-Information-Based Scheduling in Shared-Memory Multiprocessors", **Job Scheduling Strategies for Parallel Processing**, ed. D. G. Feitelson and L. Rudolph, *Vol.* 1162, Springer-Verlag, Lecture Notes in Computer Science, pp. 271-289, April, 1996.

[4] D. L. Black, "Scheduling Support for Concurrency and Parallelism in the Mach Operating System", *IEEE Computer*, pp. 35-43, May, 1990.

[5] W. Bolosky, M. Scott, R. Fitzgerald, and A. Cox, "NUMA Policies and their Relationship to Memory Architecture", *Proceedings of the International Conference on Architectural Support for Programming Languages and Operating Systems*, pp. 212-221, April, 1991.

[6] T. Brecht, "On the Importance of Parallel Application Placement in NUMA Multiprocessors", *Proceedings of the Fourth Symposium on Experiences with Distributed and Multiprocessor Systems (SEDMS IV)*, San Diego, CA, pp. 1-18, September, 1993.

[7] T. Brecht, "Multiprogrammed Parallel Application Scheduling in NUMA Multiprocessors", Ph.D. Thesis, University of Toronto, Toronto, Ontario, Technical Report CSRI-303, June, 1994.

[8] T. Brecht and K. Guha, "Using Parallel Program Characteristics in Dynamic Processor Allocation Policies", *Performance Evaluation*, *Vol*. 27 & 28, pp. 519-539, October, 1996.

[9] H. Burkhardt, S. Frank, B. Knobe, and J. Rothnie, "Overview of the KSR1 Computer System", Kendall Square Research, Boston, Technical Report KSR-TR-9202001, February, 1992.

[10] R. Chandra, S. Devine, B. Verghese, A. Gupta, and M. Rosenblum, "Scheduling and Page Migration for Multiprocessor Compute Servers", *Proceedings of the International Conference on Architectural Support for Programming Languages and Operating Systems*, San Jose, CA, pp. 12-24, October, 1994.

[11] J. Chapin, S. Herrod, M. Rosenblum, and A. Gupta, "Memory System Performance of UNIX on CC-NUMA Multiprocessors", *Proceedings of the 1995 ACM SIGMETRICS Joint International Conference on Measurement and Modeling of Computer Systems*, Ottawa, ON, May, 1995.

[12] J. Chapin, M. Rosenblum, S. Devine, T. Lahiri, D. Teodosiu, and A. Gupta, "Hive: Fault Containment for Shared-Memory Multiprocessors", *Proceedings of the Fifteenth ACM Symposium on Operating Systems Principles*, pp. 12-25, December, 1995.

[13] Convex, **Convex: Exemplar SPP1000/1200 Architecture**, Convex Press, 1995.

[14] A. Cox and R. Fowler, "The Implementation of a Coherent Memory Abstraction on a NUMA Multiprocessor: Experiences with Platinum", *Proceedings of the Twelfth ACM Symposium on Operating Systems Principles*, pp. 32-43, December, 1989.

[15] D. Feitelson and L. Rudolph, "Evaluation of Design Choices for Gang Scheduling using Distributed Hierarchical Control", *Journal of Parallel and Distributed Computing*, *Vol*. 35, *No*. 1, pp. 18-34, May, 1996.

[16] D. G. Feitelson and L. Rudolph, "Mapping and Scheduling in a Shared Parallel Environment Using Distributed Hierarchical Control", *1990 International Conference on Parallel Processing*, pp. I1-I8, 1990.

[17] D. G. Feitelson and L. Rudolph, "Distributed Hierarchical Control for Parallel Processing", *IEEE Computer*, pp. 65-77, May, 1990.

[18] B. Gamsa, "Region-Oriented Main Memory Management in Shared-Memory NUMA Multiprocessors", M.Sc. Thesis, University of Toronto, Toronto, Ontario, September, 1992.

[19] A. Gupta, A. Tucker, and S. Urushibara, "The Impact of Operating System Scheduling Policies and Synchronization Methods on the Performance of Parallel Applications", *Proceedings of the 1991 ACM SIGMETRICS Conference on Measurement and Modeling of Computer Systems*, San Diego, CA, pp. 120-132, May, 1991.

[20] M. Holliday, "Reference History, Page Size, and Migration Daemons in Local/Remote Architectures", *Proceedings of the International Conference on Architectural Support for Programming Languages and Operating Systems*, pp. 104-112, April, 1989.

[21] J. Kuskin, D. Ofelt, M. Heinrich, J. Heinlein, R. Simoni, K. Gharachorloo, J. Chapin, D. Nakahira, J. Baxter, M. Horowitz, A. Gupta, M. Rosenblum, and J. Hennessy, "The Stanford FLASH Multiprocessor", *Proceedings of the 21st Annual International Symposium on Computer Architecture*, pp. 302-313, April, 1994.

[22] R. LaRowe Jr., C. Ellis, and L. Kaplan, "The Robustness of NUMA Memory Management", *Proceedings of the Thirteenth ACM Symposium on Operating Systems Principles*, Pacific Grove, CA, pp. 137-151, October, 1991.

[23] D. Lenoski, J. Laudon, T. Joe, D. Nakahari, L. Stevens, A. Gupta, and J. Hennessy, "The DASH Prototype: Implementation and Performance", *The Proceedings of the 19th Annual International Symposium on Computer Architecture*, pp. 92-103, May, 1992.

[24] S. T. Leutenegger and M. K. Vernon, "The Performance of Multiprogrammed Multiprocessor Scheduling Policies", *Proceedings of the 1990 ACM SIGMETRICS Conference on Measurement and Modeling of Computer Systems*, Boulder, CO, pp. 226-236, May, 1990.

[25] T. Lovett and R. Clapp, "STiNG: A CC-NUMA Computer System for the Commercial Marketplace", *Proceedings of the 23rd Annual International Symposium on Computer Architecture*, pp. 308-317, May, 1996.

[26] E. P. Markatos, "Scheduling for Locality in Shared-Memory Multiprocessors", Ph.D. Thesis, Department of Computer Science, University of Rochester, Rochester, New York, May, 1993.

[27] E. P. Markatos and T. J. LeBlanc, "Load Balancing vs. Locality Management in Shared-Memory Multiprocessors", *1992 International Conference on Parallel Processing*, pp. 258-267, August, 1992.

[28] E. P. Markatos and T. J. LeBlanc, "Using Processor Affinity in Loop Scheduling on Shared-Memory Multiprocessors", *Proceedings of Supercomputing '92*, Minneapolis, MN, pp. 104-113, November, 1992.

[29] C. McCann, R. Vaswani, and J. Zahorjan, "A Dynamic Processor Allocation Policy for Multiprogrammed, Shared Memory Multiprocessors", *ACM Transactions on Computer Systems*, Vol. 11, *No.* 2, pp. 146-178, May, 1993.

[30] C. McCann and J. Zahorjan, "Scheduling Memory Constrained Jobs on Distributed Memory Parallel Computers", *Proceedings of the 1995 ACM SIGMETRICS Joint International Conference on Measurement and Modeling of Computer Systems*, Ottawa, ON, pp. 208-219, May, 1995.

[31] A. Nowatzyk, G. Aybay, M. Browne, E. Kelly, M. Parkin, B. Radke, and S. Vishin, "The S3.mp Scalable Shared Memory Multiprocessor", *Proceedings of the International Conference on Parallel Processing*, 1995.

[32] J. K. Ousterhout, "Scheduling Techniques for Concurrent Systems", *Proceedings of the 3rd International Conference on Distributed Computing Systems*, pp. 22-30, October, 1982.

[33] E. Parsons and K. Sevcik, "Coordinated Allocation of Memory and Processors in Multiprocessors", *Proceedings of the 1996 ACM SIGMETRICS Conference on Measurement and Modeling of Computer Systems*, Philadelphia, PA, pp. 57-67, May, 1996.

[34] V. Peris, M. Squillante, and V. Naik, "Analysis of the Impact of Memory in Distributed Parallel Processing Systems", *Proceedings of the 1994 ACM SIGMETRICS Conference on Measurement and Modeling of Computer Systems*, Nashville, TN, pp. 5-18, May, 1994.

[35] J. Philbin, J. Edler, O. Anshus, C. Douglas, and K. Li, "Thread Scheduling for Cache Locality", *Proceedings of the International Conference on Architectural Support for Programming Languages and Operating Systems*, Cambridge, MA, pp. 60-71, October, 1996.

[36] S. Setia, "The Interaction Between Memory Allocations and Adaptive Partitioning in Message-Passing Multiprocessors", **Job Scheduling Strategies for Parallel Processing**, ed. D. G. Feitelson and L. Rudolph, *Vol.* 949, Springer-Verlag, Lecture Notes in Computer Science, pp. 146-164, April, 1995.

[37] A. Silberschatz and P. Galvin, **Operating System Concepts**, Addison-Wesley, Reading, Massachusetts, 1994.

[38] J. P. Singh, T. Joe, A. Gupta, and J. Hennessy, "An Empirical Comparison of the Kendall Square Research KSR-1 and Stanford Dash Multiprocessors", *Proceedings of Supercomputing '93*, Portland, OR, pp. 214-225, November, 1993.

[39] M. S. Squillante, "Issues in Shared-Memory Multiprocessor Scheduling: A Performance Evaluation", Ph.D. Thesis, Department of Computer Science and Engineering, University of Washington, Seattle, Washington, Technical Report 90-10-04, October, 1990.

[40] M. S. Squillante and E. D. Lazowska, "Using Processor Cache Affinity Information in Shared-Memory Multiprocessor Scheduling", *IEEE Transactions on Parallel and Distributed Systems*, *Vol.* 4, *No.* 2, pp. 131-143, February, 1993.

[41] M. Stumm, Z. Vranesic, R. White, R. Unrau, and K. Farkas, "Experiences with the Hector Multiprocessor", *Proceedings of the International Parallel Processing Symposium Parallel Processing Fair*, pp. 9-16, April, 1993.

[42] D. Thiebaut and H. S. Stone, "Footprints in the Cache", *ACM Transactions on Computer Systems*, *Vol.* 5, *No.* 4, pp. 305-329, November, 1987.

[43] A. Tucker and A. Gupta, "Process Control and Scheduling Issues for Multiprogrammed Shared-Memory Multiprocessors", *Proceedings of the Twelfth ACM Symposium on Operating Systems Principles*, pp. 159-166, December, 1989.

[44] R. Unrau, "Scalable Memory Management through Hierarchical Symmetric Multiprocessing", Ph.D. Thesis, University of Toronto, Toronto, Ontario, January, 1993.

[45] R. Unrau, M. Stumm, and O. Krieger, "Hierarchical Clustering: A Structure for Scalable Multiprocessor Operating System Design", *Proceedings of the USENIX Workshop on Micro-Kernels and Other Kernel Architectures*, Seattle, WA, pp. 285-303, April, 1992.

[46] R. Vaswani and J. Zahorjan, "The Implications of Cache Affinity on Processor Scheduling for Multiprogrammed, Shared Memory Multiprocessors", *Proceedings of the Thirteenth ACM Symposium on Operating Systems Principles*, Pacific Grove, CA, pp. 26-40, October, 1991.

[47] B. Verghese, S. Devine, A. Gupta, and M. Rosenblum, "Operating System Support for Improving Data Locality on CC-NUMA Compute Servers", *Proceedings of the International Conference on Architectural Support for Programming Languages and Operating Systems*, Cambridge, MA, pp. 279-289, October, 1996.

[48] Z. Vranesic, M. Stumm, D. Lewis, and R. White, "Hector: A Hierarchically Structured Shared-Memory Multiprocessor", *IEEE Computer, Vol. 24, No. 1*, pp. 72-79, January, 1991.

[49] S. Woo, M. Ohara, E. Torrie, J.P. Singh, and A. Gupta, "The SPLASH-2 Programs: Characterization and Methodological Considerations", *Proceedings of the 22nd Annual International Symposium on Computer Architecture*, pp. 24-36, 1995.

[50] J. Zahorjan and C. McCann, "Processor Scheduling in Shared Memory Multiprocessors", *Proceedings of the 1990 ACM SIGMETRICS Conference on Measurement and Modeling of Computer Systems*, Boulder, CO, pp. 214-225, May, 1990.

[51] S. Zhou and T. Brecht, "Processor Pool-Based Scheduling for Large-Scale NUMA Multiprocessors", *Proceedings of the 1991 ACM SIGMETRICS Conference on Measurement and Modeling of Computer Systems*, San Diego, CA, pp. 133-142, May, 1991.

Implementing Multiprocessor Scheduling Disciplines

Eric W. Parsons and Kenneth C. Sevcik

Computer Systems Research Institute
University of Toronto

{eparsons,kcs}@cs.toronto.edu

Abstract. An important issue in multiprogrammed multiprocessor systems is the scheduling of parallel jobs. Consequently, there has been a considerable amount of analytic research in this area recently. A frequent criticism, however, is that proposed disciplines that are studied analytically are rarely ever implemented and even more rarely incorporated into commercial scheduling software. In this paper, we seek to bridge this gap by describing how at least one commercial scheduling system, namely Platform Computing's Load Sharing Facility, can be extended to support a wide variety of new scheduling disciplines.

We then describe the design and implementation of a number of multiprocessor scheduling disciplines, each differing considerably in terms of the type of preemption that is assumed to be available and in terms of the flexibility allowed in allocating processors. In evaluating the performance of these disciplines, we find that preemption can significantly reduce overall response times, but that the performance of disciplines that must commit to allocations when a job is first activated can be significantly affected by transient loads.

1 Introduction

As large-scale multiprocessor systems become available to a growing user population, mechanisms to share such systems among users are becoming increasingly necessary. Users of these systems run applications that range from computationally-intensive scientific modeling to I/O-intensive databases, for the purpose of obtaining computational results, measuring application performance, or simply debugging new parallel codes. While in the past, systems may have been acquired exclusively for use by a small number of individuals, they are now being installed for the benefit of large user communities, making the efficient scheduling of these systems an important problem.

Although much analytic research has been done in this area, one of the frequent criticisms made is that proposed disciplines are rarely implemented and even more rarely ever become part of commercial scheduling systems. The commercial scheduling systems presently available, for the most part, only support run-to-completion (RTC) disciplines and have very little flexibility in adjusting processor allocations. These constraints can lead to both high response times and low system utilizations. On the other hand, most research results support the need for both preemption and mechanisms for adjusting processor allocations of jobs.

Given that a number of high-performance computing centers have begun to develop their own scheduling software [Hen95,Lif95,SCZL96,WMKS96], it is clear that existing commercial scheduling software is often inadequate. To support these centers, however, mechanisms to extend existing systems with external (customer-provided) policies are starting to become available in commercial software [SCZL96]. This allows new scheduling policies to be easily implemented, without having to re-implement much of the base functionality typically found in this type of software.

The primary objective of this paper is to help bridge the gap between some of the analytic research and practical implementations of scheduling disciplines. As such, we describe the implementation of a number of scheduling disciplines, involving various types of job preemption and processor allocation flexibility. Furthermore, we describe how different types of knowledge (e.g., amount of computational work or speedup characteristics) can be included in the design of these disciplines. A secondary objective of our work is to briefly examine the benefits preemption and knowledge may have on the performance of parallel scheduling disciplines.

The remainder of the paper is organized as follows. In the next section, we present motivation for the types of scheduling disciplines that we chose to implement. In Sect. 3, we describe Load Sharing Facility (LSF), the commercial software scheduling software on which we based our implementation. In Sects. 4 and 5, we describe an extension library we have developed to facilitate the development of multiprocessor scheduling disciplines, followed by the set of disciplines we have implemented. Finally, we present our experimental results in Sect. 6 and our conclusions in Sect. 7.

2 Background

There have been many analytic studies done on parallel-job scheduling since it was first examined in the late eighties. Much of this work has led to three basic observations.

First, the performance of a system can be significantly degraded if a job is not given exclusive use of the processors on which it is running. Otherwise, the threads of a job may have to wait for significant amounts of time at synchronization points. This can either result in large context-switch overheads or wasted processor cycles. In general, a single thread is associated with each processor, an approach which is known as *coordinated* or *gang* scheduling [Ous82,FR92]. Sometimes, however, it is possible to multiplex threads of the same job on a reduced number of processors and still achieve good performance [MZ94]. (In the latter case, it is still assumed that only threads from a single job are simultaneously active on any given processor.)

Second, jobs generally make more efficient use of the processing resources given smaller processors allocations. As a result, providing the scheduler with some flexibility in allocating processors can significantly improve overall performance [GST91,Sev94,NSS93,RSD+94]. In most systems, users specify precisely the number of processors which should be allocated to each job, a practice that is known as *rigid* scheduling. In *adaptive* scheduling disciplines, the user specifies a minimum processor allocation, usually resulting from constraints due to memory, and a maximum, corresponding to the point after which no further processors are likely to be beneficial. In some cases, it may also be necessary to specify additional constraints on the allocation, such as being a power of two. If available, specific knowledge about jobs, such as amount of work or speedup characteristics, can further aid the scheduler in allocating processors in excess of minimum allocations.

In adaptive disciplines, jobs can be allocated a large number of processors at light loads, giving them good response times. As the load increases, however, allocation sizes can be decreased so as to improve the efficiency with which the processors are utilized, and hence allowing a higher load to be sustained (i.e., a higher *sustainable throughput*). Also, adaptive disciplines can better utilize processors than rigid ones because, with the latter, processors are often left idle due to packing inefficiencies, while adaptive disciplines can adjust allocations to make use of all available processors.

The third observation is that workloads found in practice tend to have a very high degree of variability in the amount of computational work (also known as *service demand*) [CMV94,FN95,Gib96]. In other words, most jobs have very small service demands but a few jobs can run for a very long time. Run-to-completion (RTC) disciplines exhibit very high response times because once a long-running job is dispatched, short jobs must wait a considerable amount of time before processors become available. Preemption can significantly reduce the mean response times of these workloads relative to run-to-completion disciplines [PS95].

Unlike the sequential case, preemption of parallel jobs can be quite expensive and complex to support. Fortunately, results indicate that preemption does not need to be invoked frequently to be useful, since only long-running jobs ever need to be preempted. In this paper, we consider three distinct types of preemption, in increasing order of implementation complexity.

Simple In simple preemption, a job may be preempted but its threads may not be migrated to another processor. This type of preemption is the easiest to support (as threads need only be stopped), and may be the only type available on message-passing systems.

Migratable In migratable preemption, a job may be preempted and its threads migrated. Normally, this type of preemption can be easily supported in shared-memory systems, but ensuring that data accessed by each thread is also migrated appropriately can be difficult. In message-passing systems, operating-system support for migration is not usually provided, but checkpointing can often be employed instead.[1] For example, the Condor system provides a transparent checkpointing facility for parallel applications that use either MPI or PVM [PL96]. When a checkpoint is requested, the run-time library flushes any network communications and I/O and saves the images of each process involved in the computation to disk; when the job is restarted, the run-time library re-establishes the necessary network connections and resumes the computation from the point at which the last checkpoint was taken. As such, using checkpointing to preempt a job is similar in cost to swapping, except that all kernel resources are relinquished.

Malleable In malleable preemption, the size of a job's processor allocation may be changed after it has begun execution, a feature that normally requires explicit support within the application.[2] In the *process control* approach, the application must be designed to to adapt dynamically to changes in processor allocation while it is running [TG89,GTS91,NVZ96]. As this type of support is uncommon, a simpler strategy may be to rely on application-level checkpointing, often used by long-running jobs to tolerate system failures. For these cases, it might be possible to modify the application so as to store checkpoints in a format that is independent of allocated processors, thus allowing the job to be subsequently restarted on a different number of processors.

A representative sample of coordinated scheduling disciplines that have been previously studied is presented in Fig. 1, classified according to the type of preemption available and the flexibility in processor allocation (i.e., rigid versus adaptive). Adaptive disciplines are further categorized by the type of information they assume to be available, which can include service demand, speedup characteristics, and memory requirements.[3] All types of preemption (simple, migratable, malleable) can be applied to all adaptive disciplines, but only simple and migratable preemption are meaningful for rigid disciplines. The disciplines proposed in this paper are highlighted in italics. (A more complete version of this table can be found elsewhere [Par97].)

LoadLeveler is a commercial scheduling system designed primarily for the IBM SP-2 system. A recent extension to LoadLeveler that has become popular is EASY [Lif95,SCZL96]. This is a rigid RTC scheduler that uses execution-time information provided by the user to offer both greater predictability and better system utilization. When a user submits a job, the scheduler indicates immediately a time by which that job will be run; jobs that are subsequently submitted may be run before this job only if they do not delay the start of any

---

[1] Although the costs of this approach may appear to be large, we have found that significant reductions in mean response times can be achieved with minimal impact on throughput, even with large checkpointing overheads.

[2] Malleable preemption is often termed dynamic partitioning in the literature, but we find it more convenient to treat it as a type of preemption.

[3] Some rigid schedulers do use service-demand information if available, but this distinction is not shown in this table.

Table 1. Representative set of disciplines that have been proposed and evaluated in the literature. Disciplines presented in this paper are italicized and have the prefix "LSF-"; for the adaptive ones, a regular and a "SUBSET" version are provided.

	RIGID	ADAPTIVE	Work	Speedup	Mem.
RTC	RTC [ZM90]	A+,A+&mM [Sev89]	yes	min/max	no
	PPJ [RSD+94]	ASP [ST93]	no	pws	no
	NQS	PWS [GST91]	no	no	no
	LSF	Equal,IP [RSD+94]	no	no	no
	LoadLeveler	SDF [CMV94]	yes	no	no
	EASY [Lif95]	AVG,Adapt-AVG [CMV94]	no	avg	no
	LSF-RTC	*LSF-RTC-AD(SUBSET)*	either	either	either
Preemption simple	Cosched (matrix) [Ous82]				
	LSF-PREEMPT	*LSF-PREEMPT-AD(SUBSET)*	either	either	either
migratable	Cosched (other) [Ous82]	Round-Robin [ZM90]	no	no	no
	RRJob [MVZ93]	FB-ASP,FB-PWS	no	pws	no
	LSF-MIG	*LSF-MIG-AD(SUBSET)*	either	either	either
malleable		Equi/Dynamic Partition [TG89,MVZ93]	no	no	no
		FOLD,EQUI [MZ94]	no	no	no
	(not applicable)	W&E [BG96]	yes	yes	no
		BUDDY,EPOCH [MZ95]	no	no	yes
		MPA [PS96b,PS96a]	no	yes	yes
		LSF-MALL-AD(SUBSET)	either	either	either

previously-scheduled job's execution (i.e., a gap exists in the schedule containing enough processors for sufficient time).

The disciplines that we present in this paper have been implemented as extensions to another commercial scheduling system, called Load Sharing Facility (LSF). By building on top of LSF, we found that we could make direct use of LSF for many aspects of job management, including the user interfaces for submitting and monitoring jobs, as well as the low-level mechanisms for starting, stopping, and resuming jobs. LSF runs on a large number of platforms, including the SP-2, SGI Challenge, SGI Origin, and HP Exemplar, making it an attractive vehicle for this type of scheduling research. Our work is based on LSF version 2.2a.

3 Load Sharing Facility

Although originally designed for load balancing in workstation clusters, LSF is now becoming popular for parallel job scheduling on multiprocessor systems. Of greatest relevance to this work is the batch subsystem.

Queues provide the basis for much of the control over the scheduling of jobs. Each queue is associated with a set of processors, a priority, and many other parameters not described here. By default, jobs are selected in FCFS order from the highest-priority non-empty queue and run until completion, but it is possible to configure queues so that higher-priority jobs preempt lower priority ones (a feature that is currently available only for the sequential-job case). The priority of a job is defined by the queue to which the job has been submitted.

To illustrate the use of queues, consider a policy where shorter jobs have higher priority than longer jobs (see Fig. 1). An administrator could define several queues, each in turn corresponding to increasing service demand and having decreasing priority. If jobs are submitted to the correct queue, short jobs will be executed before long ones. Moreover, LSF can be configured to preempt lower priority jobs if higher priority ones arrive, giving short jobs still better responsiveness. To permit enforcement of the policy, LSF can be configured to terminate any job that exceeds the execution-time threshold defined for the queue.

The current version of LSF provides only limited support for parallel jobs. As part of submitting a job, a user can specify the number of processors required. When LSF finds a sufficient number of processors satisfying the resource constraints for the job, it spawns an application "master" process on one of the processors, passing to this process a list of processors. The master process can then use this list of processors to spawn a number of "slave" processes to perform the parallel computation. The slave processes are completely under the control of the master process, and as such, are not known to the LSF batch scheduling system. LSF does provide, however, a library that simplifies several distributed programming activities, such as spawning remote processes, propagating Unix signals, and managing terminal output.

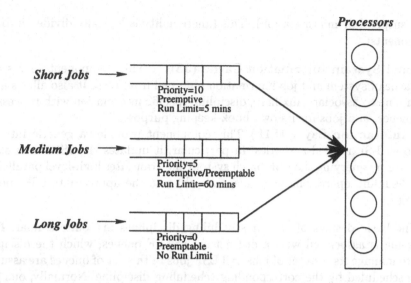

Fig. 1. Example of a possible sequential-job queue configuration in LSF to favour short-running jobs. Jobs submitted to the short-job queue have the highest priority, followed by medium- and long-job queues. The queues are configured to be preemptable (allowing jobs in the queue to be preempted by higher-priority jobs) and preemptive (allowing jobs in the queue to preempt lower-priority jobs). Execution-time limits associated with each queue enforce the intended policy.

4 Scheduling Extension Library

The ideal approach to developing new scheduling disciplines is one that does not require any LSF source code modifications, as this allows any existing users of LSF to experiment with the new disciplines. For this purpose, LSF provides an extensive application-programmer interface (API), allowing many aspects of job scheduling to be controlled. Our scheduling disciplines are implemented within a process distinct from LSF, and are thus called *scheduling extensions*.

The LSF API, however, is designed to implement LSF-related commands rather than scheduling extensions. As a result, the interfaces are very low level and can be quite complex to use. For example, to determine the accumulated run time for a job—information commonly required by a scheduler—the programmer must use a set of LSF routines to open the LSF event-logging file, process each log item in turn, and compute the time between each pair of suspend/resume events for the job. Since the event-logging file is typically several megabytes in size, requiring several seconds to process in its entirety, it is necessary to cache information whenever possible. Clearly, it is difficult for a scheduling extension to take care of such details and to obtain the information efficiently.

One of our goals was thus to design a scheduling extension library that would provide simple and efficient access to information about jobs (e.g., processors currently used by a job), as well as to manipulate the state of jobs in the system (e.g., suspend or migrate a job). This functionality is logically divided into two components:

Job and System Information Cache (JSIC) This component serves as a cache of system and job information obtained from LSF. It also allows a discipline to associate auxiliary, discipline-specific information with processors, queues, and jobs for its own book-keeping purposes.[4]

LSF Interaction Layer (LIL) This component provides a generic interface to all LSF-related activities. In particular, it updates the JSIC data structures by querying the LSF batch system and translates high-level parallel-job scheduling operations (e.g., suspend job) into the appropriate LSF-specific ones.

The basic designs of all our scheduling disciplines are quite similar. Each discipline is associated with a distinct set of LSF queues, which the discipline uses to manage its own set of jobs. All LSF jobs in this set of queues are assumed to be scheduled by the corresponding scheduling discipline. Normally, one LSF queue is designated as the submit queue, and other queues are used by the scheduling discipline as a function of a job's state. For example, pending jobs may be placed in one LSF queue, stopped jobs in another, and running jobs in a third. A scheduling discipline never explicitly dispatches or manipulates the processes of a job directly; rather, it implicitly requests LSF to perform such actions by switching jobs from one LSF queue to another. Continuing the same example, a pending queue would be configured so that it accepts jobs but never dispatches them, and a running queue would be configured so that LSF immediately dispatches any job in this queue on the processors specified for the job. In this way, a user submits a job to be scheduled by a particular discipline simply by specifying the appropriate LSF queue, and can track the progress of the job using all the standard LSF utilities.

Although it is possible for a scheduling discipline to contain internal job queues and data structures, we have found that this is rarely necessary because any state information that needs to be persistent can be encoded by the queue in which each job resides. This approach greatly simplifies the re-initialization of the scheduling extension in the event that the extension fails at some point, an important property of any production scheduling system.

Given our design, it is possible for several scheduling disciplines to coexist within the same extension process, a feature that is most useful in reducing overheads if different disciplines are being used in different partitions of the system. (For example, one partition could be used for production workloads while another could be used to experiment with a new scheduling discipline.) Retrieving system and job information from LSF can place significant load on the master processor,[5] imposing a limit on the number of extension processes that can be run concurrently. Since each scheduling discipline is associated with a

---

[4] In future versions of LSF, it will be possible for information associated with jobs to be saved in log files so that it will not be lost in the event that the scheduler fails.

[5] LSF runs its batch scheduler on a single, centralized processor.

different set of LSF queues, the set of processors associated with each discipline can be defined by assigning processors to the corresponding queues using the LSF queue administration tools. (Normally, each discipline uses a single queue for processor information.)

The extension library described here has also been used by Gibbons in studying a number of rigid scheduling disciplines, including two variants of EASY [Lif95,SCZL96,Gib96,Gib97]. One of the goals of Gibbons' work was to determine whether historical information about a job could be exploited in scheduling. He found that, for many workloads, historical information could provide up to 75% of the benefits of having perfect information. For the purpose of his work, Gibbons added an additional component to the extension library to gather, store, and analyze historical information about jobs. He then adapted the original EASY discipline to take into account this knowledge and showed how performance could be improved. The historical database and details of the scheduling disciplines studied by Gibbons are described elsewhere [Gib96,Gib97].

The high-level organization of the scheduling extension library (not including the historical database) is shown in Fig. 2. The extension process contains the extension library and each of the disciplines configured for the system. The extension process mainline essentially sleeps until a scheduling event or a timeout (corresponding to the scheduling quantum) occurs. The mainline then prompts the LIL to update the JSIC and calls a designated method for each of the configured disciplines. Next, we describe each component of the extension library in detail.

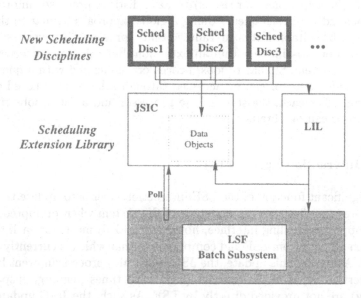

Fig. 2. High-level design of scheduling extension extension library. As shown, the extension library supports multiple scheduling disciplines running concurrently within the same process.

4.1 Job and System Information Cache

The Job and System Information Cache (JSIC) contains all the information about jobs, queues, and processors that are relevant to the scheduling disciplines that are part of the extension. Our data structures were designed taking into consideration the types of operations that we found to be most critical to the design of our scheduling disciplines:

- A scheduler must be able to scan sequentially through the jobs associated with a particular LSF queue. For each job, it must then be able to access in a simple manner any job-related information obtained from LSF (e.g., run times, processors on which a job is running, LSF job state).
- It must be able to scan the processors associated with any LSF queue and determine the state of each one of these (e.g., available or unavailable).
- Finally, a scheduler must be able to associate book-keeping information with either jobs or processors (e.g., the set of jobs running on a given processor).

In our library, information about each active job is stored in a JobInfo object. Pointers to instances of these objects are stored in a job hash table keyed by LSF job identifiers (jobId), allowing efficient lookup of individual jobs. Also, a list of job identifiers is maintained for each queue, permitting efficient scanning of jobs in any given queue (in the order submitted to LSF).

The information associated with a job is global, in that a single JobInfo object instance exists for each job. For processors, on the other hand, we found it convenient (for experimental reasons) to have distinct processor information objects associated with each queue. Using a global approach similar to that for jobs would also be suitable if it is guaranteed that a processor is never associated with more than one discipline within an extension, but this was not necessarily the case on our system. Similar to jobs, processors associated with a queue can be scanned sequentially, or can be accessed through a hash table keyed on the processor name. For each, the state of the processor and a list of jobs running on the processor can be obtained.

4.2 LSF Interaction Layer (LIL)

The most significant function of the LSF interaction layer is to update the JSIC data structures to reflect the current state of the system when prompted. Since LSF only supports a polling interface, however, the LIL must, for each update request, fetch all data from LSF and compare it to that which is currently stored in the JSIC. As part of this update, the JSIC must also process an event logging file, since certain types of information (e.g., total times pending, suspended, and running) are not provided directly by LSF. As such, the JSIC update code represents a large fraction of the total extension library code. (The extension library is approximately 1.5 KLOC.)

To update the JSIC, the LIL performs the following three actions:

- It obtains the list of all active jobs in the system from LSF. Each job record returned by LSF contains some static information, such as the submit time, start time, resource requirements, as well as some dynamic information, such as the job status (e.g., running, stopped), processor set, and queue. All this information about each job is recorded in the JSIC.
- It opens the event-logging file, reads any new events that have occurred since the last update, and re-computes the pending time, aggregate processor run time, and wall-clock run time for each job. As well, aggregate processor and wall-clock run times since the job was last resumed (termed residual run times) are computed.
- It obtains the list of processors associated with each queue and queries LSF for the status of each of these processors.

LSF provides a mechanism by which the resources, such as physical memory, licenses, or swap space, required by the job can be specified upon submission. In our extensions, we do not use the default set of resources to avoid having LSF make any scheduling decisions, but rather add a new set of pseudo-resources that are used to pass parameters or information about a job, such as minimum and maximum processor allocations or service demand, directly to the scheduling extension. As part of the first action performed by the LIL update routine, this information is extracted from the pseudo-resource specifications and stored in the JobInfo structure.

The remaining LIL functions, illustrated in Table 2, basically translate high-level scheduling operations into low-level LSF calls.

Table 2. High-level scheduling functions provided by LSF Interaction Layer.

OPERATION	DESCRIPTION
switch	This operation moves a job from one queue to another.
setProcessors	This operation defines the list of processors to be allocated to a job. LSF dispatches the job by creating a master process on the first processor in the list; as described before, the master process uses the list to spawn its slave processes.
suspend	This operation suspends a job. The processes of the job hold onto virtual resources they possess, but normally release any physical resources (e.g., physical memory).
resume	This operation resumes a job that has previously been suspended.
migrate	This operation initiates the migration procedure for a job. It does not actually migrate the job, but rather places the job in a pending state, allowing it to be subsequently restarted on a different set of processors.

Preemption Considerations The LSF interaction layer makes certain assumptions about the way in which jobs can be preempted. For simple preemption, a job can be suspended by sending it a SIGTSTP signal, which is delivered to the master process; this process must then propagate the signal to its slaves (which is automated in the distributed programming library provided by LSF) to ensure that all processes belonging to the job are stopped. Similarly, a job can be resumed by sending it a SIGCONT signal.

In contrast, we assume that migratable and malleable preemption are implemented via a checkpointing facility, as described in Sect. 2. As a result, preempted jobs do not occupy any kernel resources, allowing any number of jobs to be in this state (assuming disk space for checkpointing is abundant).

To identify migratable jobs, we set an LSF flag in the submission request indicating that the job is re-runnable. To migrate such a job, we first send it a checkpoint signal (in our case, the SIGUSR2 signal), and then send LSF a migrate request for the job. This would normally cause LSF to terminate the job (with a SIGTERM signal) and restart it on the set of processors specified (using the setProcessors interface). In most cases, however, we switch such a job to a queue that has been configured to not dispatch jobs prior to submitting the migration request, causing the job to be simply terminated and requeued as a pending job.

The interface for changing the processor allocation of a malleable job is identical to that for migrating a job, the only difference being the way it is used. In the migratable case, the scheduling discipline always restarts a job using the same number of processors as in the initial allocation, while in the malleable case, any number of processors can be specified.

4.3 A Simple Example

To illustrate how the extension library can be used to implement a discipline, consider a sequential-job, multi-level feedback discipline that degrades the priority of jobs as they acquire processing time. If the workload has a high degree of variability in service demands, as is typically the case even for batch sequential workloads, this approach will greatly improve response times without requiring users to specify the service demands of jobs in advance. For this discipline, we can use the same queue configuration as shown in Fig. 1; we eliminate the run-time limits, however, as the scheduling discipline will automatically move jobs from higher-priority queues to lower-priority ones as they acquire processing time.

Users initially submit their jobs to the high-priority queue (labeled short jobs in Fig. 1); when the job has acquired a certain amount of processing time, the scheduling extension switches the job to the medium-priority queue, and after some more processing time, to the low-priority queue. In this way, the extension relies on the LSF batch system to dispatch, suspend, and resume jobs as a function of the jobs in each queue. Users can track the progress of jobs simply by examining the jobs in each of the three queues.

5 Parallel-Job Scheduling Disciplines

We now turn our attention to the parallel-job scheduling disciplines that we have implemented as LSF extensions. Important to the design of these disciplines are the costs associated with using LSF on our platform. It can take up to thirty seconds to dispatch a job once it is ready to run. Migratable or malleable preemption typically requires more than a minute to release the processors associated with a job; these processors are considered to be unavailable during this time. Finally, scheduling decisions are made at most once every five seconds to keep the load on the master (scheduling) processor to an acceptable level.

The disciplines described in this section all share a common job queue configuration. A pending queue is defined and configured to allow jobs to be submitted (i.e., *open*) but preventing any of these jobs from being dispatched automatically by LSF (i.e., *inactive*). A second queue, called the run queue, is used by the scheduler to start jobs. This queue is open, active, and possesses absolutely no load constraints. A scheduling extension uses this queue by first specifying the processors associated with a job (i.e., **setProcessors**) and then moving the job to this queue; given the queue configuration, LSF immediately dispatches jobs in this queue. Finally, a third queue, called the stopped queue, is defined to assist in migrating jobs. It too is configured to be open but inactive. When LSF is prompted to migrate a job in this queue, it terminates and requeues the job, preserving its job identifier. In all our disciplines, preempted jobs are left in this queue to distinguish them from jobs that have not had a chance to run yet (in the pending queue).

Each job in our system is associated with a minimum, desired, and maximum processor allocation, the desired value lying between the minimum and maximum. Rigid disciplines use the desired value while adaptive disciplines are free to choose any allocation between the minimum and the maximum values.

If provided to the scheduler, service demand information is specified in terms of the amount of computation required on a single processor and speedup characteristics are specified in terms of the fraction of work that is sequential. Basically, service-demand information is used to run jobs having the least remaining processing time (to minimize mean response times) and speedup information is used to favour efficient jobs in allocating processors. Since jobs can vary considerably in terms of their speedup characteristics, computing the remaining processing time will only be accurate if speedup information is available.

5.1 Run-to-Completion Disciplines

Next, we describe the run-to-completion disciplines. All three variants listed in Table 1 (i.e., LSF-RTC, LSF-RTC-AD, and LSF-RTC-ADSUBSET) are quite similar and, as such, are implemented in a single module of the scheduling extension. The LSF-RTC discipline is defined as follows:

LSF-RTC Whenever a job arrives or departs, the scheduler repeatedly scans the pending queue until it finds the first job for which enough processors are available. It assigns processors to the job and switches the job to the run queue.

The LSF system, and hence the JSIC, maintains jobs in order of arrival, so the default RTC discipline is FCFS (skipping any jobs at the head of the queue for which not enough processors are available). If service-demand information is provided to the scheduler, then jobs are scanned in order of increasing service demand, resulting in a shortest processing time (SPT) discipline (again with skipping).

The LSF-RTC-AD discipline is very similar to the ASP discipline proposed by Setia *et al.* [ST93], except that jobs are selected for execution differently because the LSF-based disciplines take into account memory requirements of jobs (and hence cannot be called ASP).

LSF-RTC-AD Whenever a job arrives or departs, the scheduler scans the pending queue, selecting the first job for which enough processors remain to satisfy the job's minimum processor requirements. When no more jobs fit, leftover processors are used to equalize processor allocations among selected jobs (i.e., giving processors to jobs having the smallest allocation). The scheduler then assigns processors to the selected jobs and switches these jobs to the run queue.

If speedup information is available, the scheduler allocates each leftover processor, in turn, to the job whose efficiency will be highest *after* the allocation. This approach minimizes both the processor and memory occupancy in a distributed-memory environment, leading to the highest possible sustainable throughput [PS96a].

The SUBSET variant seeks to improve the efficiency with which processors are utilized by applying an algorithm known as a subset-sum algorithm [MT90]. The basic principle is to try to minimize the number of processors allocated to jobs in excess to each of the job's minimum processor allocation (termed *surplus* processors). Since we assume that a job utilizes processors more efficiently as its allocation size decreases (down to the minimum allocation size), then this principle allows the system to run at a higher overall efficiency.

LSF-RTC-ADSUBSET Let L be the number of jobs in the system and N_{ff} be the number of jobs selected by the first-fit algorithm used in LSF-RTC-AD. The scheduler only commits to running the first N' of these jobs, where

$$N' = \left\lfloor N_{ff} * \max(1 - \frac{L}{\delta N_{ff}}, 0) \right\rfloor$$

(δ is a tunable parameter that determines how aggressively the scheduler seeks to minimize surplus processors as the load increases; for our experiments, we chose $\delta = 5$.) Using any leftover processors and leftover jobs, the scheduler applies the subset-sum algorithm to select the set of jobs that minimizes the number of surplus processors. The jobs chosen by the subset-sum algorithm are added to the list of jobs selected to run, and any surplus processors are allocated as in LSF-RTC-AD.

Simple Preemptive Disciplines In simple preemptive disciplines, jobs may be suspended but their processes may not be migrated. Since the resources used by jobs are not released when they are in a preempted state, however, one must be careful to not over-commit system resources. In our disciplines, this is achieved by ensuring that no more than a certain number of processes ever exist on any given processor. In a more sophisticated implementation, we might instead ensure that the swap space associated with each processor would never be overcommitted.

The two variants of the preemptive disciplines are quite different. In the rigid discipline, we allow a job to preempt another only if it possesses the same desired processor allocation. This is to minimize the possibility of packing losses that might occur if jobs were not aligned in this way.[6] In the adaptive discipline, we found this approach to be problematic. Consider a long-running job, either arriving during an idle period or having a large minimum processor requirement, that is dispatched by the scheduler. Any subsequent jobs preempting this first one would be configured for a large allocation size, causing them, and hence the entire system, to run inefficiently. As a result, we do not attempt to reduce packing losses with the adaptive, simple preemptive discipline.

LSF-PREEMPT Whenever a job arrives or departs or when a quantum expires, the scheduler re-evaluates the selection of jobs currently running. Available processors are first allocated in the same way as in LSF-RTC. Then, the scheduler determines if any running job should be preempted by a pending or stopped job, according to the following criteria:

1. A stopped job can only preempt a job running on the same set of processors as those for which it is configured. A pending job can preempt any running job that has a same desired processor allocation value.
2. If no service-demand information is available, the aggregate cumulative processor time of the pending or stopped job must be some fraction less than that of the running job (in our case, we use the value of 50%); otherwise, the service demand of the preempting job must be a (different) fraction less than that of the running job (in our case, we use the value of 10%).
3. The running job must have been running for at least a certain specified amount of time (one minute in our case, since suspension and resumption only consist of sending a Unix signal to all processes of the job).
4. The number of processes present on any processor cannot exceed a prespecified number (in our case, five processes).

If several jobs can preempt a given running job, the one which has the least acquired aggregate processing time is chosen first if no service-demand knowledge is available, or the one with the shortest remaining service demand if service-demand knowledge is available.

Our adaptive, simple preemptive discipline uses a matrix approach to scheduling jobs, where each row of the matrix represents a different set of jobs to run

---

[6] Packing losses occur when processors are left idle, either because there are an insufficient number to meet the minimum processor requirements of pending jobs or if only some of the processors required by stopped jobs are available.

and the columns the processors in the system. In Ousterhout's co-scheduling discipline, an incoming job is placed in the first row of the matrix that has enough free processors for the job; if no such row exists, then a new one is created. In our approach, we use a more dynamic approach.

LSF-PREEMPT-AD Whenever the scheduler is awakened (due either to an arrival or departure or to a quantum expiry), the set of jobs currently running or stopped (i.e., preempted) is organized into the matrix just described, using the first row for those jobs that are running. Each row is then examined in turn. For each, the scheduler populates the uncommitted processors with the best pending, stopped, or running jobs. (If service-demand information is available, currently-stopped or running jobs may be preferable to a pending job; these jobs can switch rows if all processors being used by the job are uncommitted in the row currently being examined.) The scheduler also ensures that jobs that are currently running, but which have run for less than the minimum time since last being started or resumed, continue to run. If such jobs cannot be accommodated in the row being examined, then the scheduler skips to the next row.

Once the set of jobs that might be run in each row has been determined, the scheduler chooses the row that has the job having the least acquired processing time or, if service-demand information is available, the job having the shortest remaining service demand. Processors in the selected row available for pending jobs are distributed as before (i.e., equi-allocation if no speedup knowledge is available, or favouring efficient jobs if it is).

Migratable and Malleable Preemptive Disciplines In contrast to the simple preemptive disciplines, the migratable and malleable ones assume that a job can be checkpointed and restarted at a later point in time. The primary difference between the two types is that, in the migratable case, jobs are always resumed with the same number of processors allocated when the job first started, whereas in the malleable case, a job can be restarted with a different number of processors.

LSF-MIG Whenever a job arrives or departs or when a quantum expires, the scheduler re-evaluates the selection of jobs currently running. First, currently-running jobs which have not run for at least a certain configurable amount of time (in our case, ten minutes, since migration and processor reconfiguration are relatively expensive) are allowed to continue running. Processors not used by these jobs are considered to be available for reassignment. The scheduler then uses a first-fit algorithm to select the jobs from those remaining to run next, using a job's desired processor allocation. As before, if service-demand information is available, jobs are selected in order of least remaining service demand.

LSF-MIG-AD and LSF-MALL-AD Apart from their adaptiveness, these two disciplines are very similar to the LSF-MIG discipline. In the malleable version, the scheduler uses the same first-fit algorithm as in LSF-MIG to select jobs, except that it always uses a job's minimum processor allocation to determine if a job fits. Any leftover processors are then allocated as before, using an equi-allocation approach if no speedup information is available, and favouring efficient jobs otherwise. In the migratable version, the scheduler uses the size of a job's current processor allocation instead of its minimum if the job has already run (i.e., has been preempted) in the first-fit algorithm, and does not change the size of such a job's processor allocation if selected to run.

Similar to the run-to-completion case, SUBSET-variants of the adaptive disciplines have also been implemented.

6 Performance Results

The evaluation of the disciplines described in the previous section is primarily qualitative in nature. There are two reasons for this. First, experiments must be performed in real time rather than in simulated time, requiring a considerable amount of time to execute a relatively small number of jobs. Moreover, failures that can (and do) occur during the experiments can significantly influence the results, although such failures can be tolerated by the disciplines. Second, we intend our implementations to demonstrate the practicality of a discipline and to observe its performance in a real context, rather than to analyze its performance under a wide variety of conditions (for which a simulation would be more suitable).

The experimental platform for the implementation is a network of workstations (NOW), consisting of sixteen IBM 43P (133MHz, PowerPC 604) systems, connected by three independent networks (155 Mbps ATM, 100 Mbps Ethernet, 10 Mbps Ethernet).

To exercise the scheduling software, we use a parameterizable synthetic application designed to represent real applications. The basic reason for using a synthetic application is that it could be designed to not use any processing resources, yet behave in other respects (e.g., execution time, preemption) as a real parallel application. This is important in the context of our network of workstations, because the system is being actively used by a number of other researchers. Using real (compute-intensive) applications would have prevented the system from being used by others during the tests, or would have caused the tests to be inconclusive if jobs were run at low priority.

Each of our scheduling disciplines ensures that only a single one of its jobs is ever running on a given processor and that all processes associated with the job are running simultaneously. As such, the behaviour of our disciplines, when used in conjunction with our synthetic application, is identical to that of a dedicated system running compute-intensive applications. In fact, by associating a different set of queues with each discipline, each one configured to use all processors, it was possible to conduct several experiments concurrently. (The jobs submitted to each submit queue for the different disciplines were generated independently.)

The synthetic application possesses three important features. First, it can be easily parameterized with respect to speedup and service demand, allowing it to model a wide range of real applications. Second, it supports adaptive processor allocations using the standard mechanism provided by LSF. Finally, it can be checkpointed and restarted, to model both migratable and malleable jobs.

An experiment consists of submitting a sequence of jobs to the scheduler according to a Poisson arrival process, using an arrival rate that reflects a moderately-heavy load. A small initial number of these jobs (e.g., 200) are tagged for mean response time and makespan measurements. (The makespan is the maximum completion time of any job in the set of jobs under consideration, assuming that the first job arrives at time zero.) Each experiment terminates only when all jobs in this initial set have left the system. To make the experiment more representative of large systems, we assume that each processor corresponds to eight processors in reality. Thus, all processor allocations are multiples of eight, and the minimum allocation is eight processors. Scaling the number of processors in this way affects the synthetic application in determining the amount of time it should execute and the scheduling disciplines in determining the expected remaining service demand for a job.

6.1 Workload Model

Service demands for jobs are drawn from a hyper-exponential distribution, with mean of 8000 seconds (2.2 hours) and coefficient of variation (CV) of 4, a distribution whose median is 2985 seconds.[7] The parameters are consistent with measurements made over the past year at the Cornell Theory Center (scaled to 128 processors) [Hot96b,Hot96a]. The most significant difference is that the mean is about a quarter of that actually observed, which should not unduly affect results as it only magnifies scheduling overheads. (Recall that in the migratable and malleable preemption cases, we only preempt a job if it has run at least 10 minutes, since preemption requires at least one minute.) All disciplines received exactly the same sequence of jobs in any particular experiment, and in general, individual experiments required anywhere from 24 to 48 hours to complete.

Minimum processor allocation sizes are uniformly chosen from one to sixteen processors, and maximum sizes are set at sixteen.[8] This distribution is similar to those used in previous studies in this area [PS96a,MZ95,Set95]. The processor allocation size used for rigid disciplines is chosen from a uniform distribution between the minimum and the maximum processor allocations for the job.

It has been shown previously that performance benefits of knowing speedup information can only be obtained if a large fraction of the total work in the workload has good speedup, and moreover, if larger-sized jobs tend to have better speedup than smaller-sized ones [PS96a]. As such, we let 75% of the jobs have

---

[7] The 25%, 50%, and 75% quantiles are 1230, 2985, and 6100 seconds, respectively.
[8] Note that maximum processor allocation information is only useful at lighter loads, since at heavy loads, jobs seldom receive many more processors than their minimum allocation.

good speedup, where 99.9% of the work is perfectly parallelizable (corresponding to a speedup of 114 on 128 processors). Poor speedup jobs have a speedup of 6.4 on 8 processors and a speedup of 9.3 on 128 processors.[9]

6.2 Results and Lessons Learned

The performance results of all disciplines under the four knowledge cases (no knowledge, service-demand knowledge, speedup knowledge, or both) are given in Table 3 and summarized in Figs. 3 and 4. As can be seen, the response times for the run-to-completion disciplines are much higher (by up to an order of magnitude) than the migratable or malleable preemptive disciplines. The simple preemptive, rigid discipline does not offer any advantages over the corresponding run-to-completion version. The reason is that there is insufficient flexibility in allowing a job to only preempt another that has the same desired processor requirement. The adaptive preemptive discipline is considerably better in this regard.

Adaptability appears to have the most positive effect for run-to-completion and malleable disciplines (see Fig. 4). In the former case, makespans decreased by nearly 50% from the rigid to the adaptive variant using the subset-sum algorithm. To achieve this improvement, however, the mean response times generally increased because processor allocations tended to be smaller (leading to longer average run times). In the malleable case, adaptability resulted in smaller but noticeable decreases in makespans (5–10%). It should be noted that the opportunity for improvement is much lower than in the RTC case because the minimum makespan is 65412 seconds for this experiment (compared to actual observed makespans of approximately 78000 seconds).

Service-demand and speedup knowledge appeared to be most effective when either the mean response time (for the former) or the makespan (for the latter) were large, but may not be as significant as one might expect. Service-demand knowledge had limited benefit in the run-to-completion disciplines because the high response times result from long-running jobs being activated, which the scheduler must do at some point. In the migratable and malleable preemptive disciplines, the multilevel feedback approach achieved the majority of the benefits of having service demand information. Highlighting this difference, we often found queue lengths for run-to-completion disciplines to grow as high as 60 jobs, while for migratable or malleable disciplines, they were rarely larger than five.

Given our workload, we found speedup knowledge to be of limited benefit because poor-speedup jobs can rarely run efficiently. (To utilize processors efficiently, such a job must have a low minimum processor requirement, and must be started at the same time as a high-efficiency job; even in the best case, the maximum efficiency of a poor-speedup job will only be 58% given a minimum processor allocation of eight after scaling.) From the results, one can observe that

---

[9] Such a two-speedup-class workload appears to be supported by data from the Cornell Theory Center if we examine the amount of CPU time consumed by each job relative to its elapsed time [Par97].

Table 3. Performance of LSF-based scheduling disciplines. In some trials, the discipline did not terminate within a reasonable amount of time; in these cases, a minimum bound on the mean response times is reported (indicated by a >) and the number of unfinished jobs is given in parenthesis.

DISCIPLINE	NO KNOWLEDGE		SERVICE-DEMAND		SPEEDUP		BOTH	
	MRT	MAKESPAN	MRT	MAKESPAN	MRT	MAKESPAN	MRT	MAKESPAN
LSF-RTC	5853	147951	4040	140342	5279	130361	5627	143507
LSF-RTC-AD	10611	129093	8713	126531	8034	91003	8946	126917
LSF-RTC-ADSUBSET	8264	76637	8410	81767	8039	73324	8074	75340
LSF-PREEMPT	5793	145440	5039	143686	5280	130314	5028	143631
LSF-PREEMPT-AD	> 2293	> 219105(2)	1078	127204	2207	172768	821	111489
LSF-MIG	678	83985	662	81836	690	82214	660	82708
LSF-MIG-AD	769	88488	858	103876	784	86080	> 1342	> 192031(1)
LSF-MIG-ADSUBSET	770	90789	854	106065	769	85828	> 1347	> 193772(1)
LSF-MALL-AD	667	77534	632	78760	666	78215	650	78840
LSF-MALL-ADSUBSET	681	78537	680	79191	680	76481	644	78065

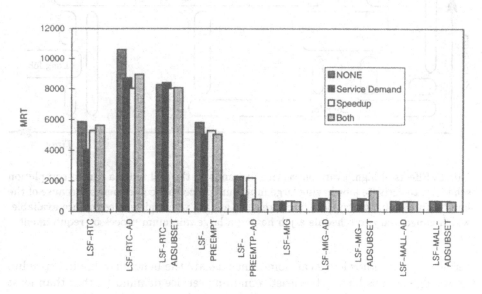

Fig. 3. Observed mean response times for each discipline.

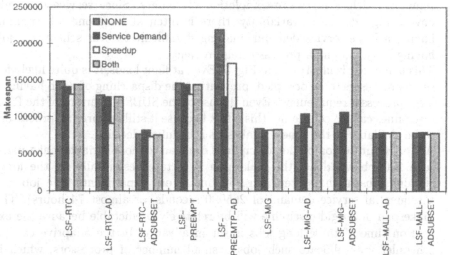

Fig. 4. Observed makespans for each discipline.

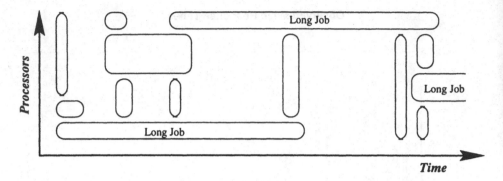

Fig. 5. Effects of highly variable service demands on the ability for a run-to-completion scheduler to activate jobs having large minimum processor requirements. Because of the long-running jobs, the system rarely reaches a state where all processors are available, which is necessary to schedule a job having a large minimum processor requirement.

service-demand knowledge can sometimes negate the benefits of having speedup knowledge as jobs having the least remaining service demand (rather than least acquired processing time) are given higher priority.

While performing the our experiments, we monitored the behaviour of each of our schedulers, in order to further understand the performance results. Our observations can be summarized as follows:

– Jobs having large minimum processor requirements can often experience significant delays in run-to-completion disciplines. Since service demands have a high degree of variability, there is often at least one job running having a large service demand, making it difficult to ever schedule a job having large minimum processor requirement.
  This behaviour is illustrated in Fig. 5. Even at light loads, it is quite likely for some processors to be occupied, preventing the dispatching of a job having a large processor requirement. Even the use of the SUBSET variant of the RTC disciplines cannot counteract this effect because it still requires all processors to be available at the time it makes its scheduling decision.
– Adaptive run-to-completion disciplines can lead to more variable makespans. In a 200-job workload, the makespan is dictated essentially by the long-running jobs in the system (e.g., in one of our experiments, one job had a sequential service demand of 265000 seconds, or almost 74 hours). The makespan of a rigid discipline will be relatively predictable because the execution time of these long jobs is set in advance. In the adaptive case, a scheduler may allocate such jobs a small number of processors, which is good from an efficiency standpoint, but can lead to much longer makespans. Also, if long jobs are allocated few processors, which tends to occur in most adaptive disciplines as the load increases, these long jobs will occupy processors for longer periods of time (relative to the rigid case). This can make it even more difficult for jobs with large minimum processor requirements to ever find enough available processors.

The conclusion is that run-to-completion disciplines are even more problematic than originally indicated. It has previously been shown how high variability in service demands can lead to poor response times if memory is abundant; these observations show that highly variable service demands can also lead to starvation for jobs having large minimum processor requirements.

- Migratable disciplines can significantly reduce response times relative to RTC ones. However, adaptive versions of migratable disciplines can exhibit unpredictable completion times for long-running jobs, as a scheduler must commit to an allocation when a job is first activated. In some cases, the scheduler allocates a small number of processors to long-running jobs, only to have other processors subsequently become available. In a production environment, this may encourage users submitting high service-demand jobs to specify a large minimum processor allocation simply to ensure that their jobs complete within a more desirable amount of time, but having a negative effect on the sustainable throughput.

  In other cases, long-running jobs were allocated a large number of processors, leading to potential starvation problems. (This was the cause of the large makespans in the full-knowledge LSF-MIGRATE-AD and LSF-MIGRATE-ADSUBSET experiments.) In order to resume such a job once stopped, the scheduler must be capable of preempting a sufficient number of running jobs to satisfy the stopped job's processor requirement. This can be difficult at high loads where jobs with small processor allocations are continuously being started, suspended, and resumed, since we only preempt jobs that have run at least ten minutes. In a real workload, we believe this problem will become less important as the ratio of the migration overhead to the mean service demand becomes smaller.

- From a user's perspective, malleable disciplines are most attractive. During periods of heavy load, the system allocates jobs a small number of processors, and as the load becomes lighter, long-running jobs receive more processors. Unused processors arising from imperfect packing are never a problem, allowing a high level of utilization to be achieved. Also, jobs rarely experience starvation because the scheduler does not commit itself to a processor allocation upon activating a job for the first time. As a result, adaptive malleable disciplines consistently performed best and have the highest potential for low response times and high throughputs (even given a 10% re-allocation overhead).

7 Conclusions

In this paper, we present the design of parallel-job scheduling implementations, based on Platform Computing's Load Sharing Facility (LSF). We consider a wide range of disciplines, from run-to-completion to malleable preemptive ones, each with varying degrees of knowledge of job characteristics. Although these disciplines were implemented on a network of workstations, they can be used on any distributed-memory multiprocessor system supporting LSF.

The primary objective of this work was to demonstrate the practicality of implementing parallel-job scheduling disciplines. By building on top of an existing commercial software package, we found that implementing new disciplines was relatively straightforward. Given the lack of maturity of parallel-job scheduling, the approach taken in extending commercial scheduling software is a good one. Future work in this area, however, would be aided by the inclusion of the Job and System Information Cache (JSIC) and the corresponding update routines directly into the base scheduling software.

The secondary objective of this work was to study the behaviour of these disciplines in a more realistic environment and to illustrate the benefits of different types of preemption and knowledge. We found that preemption is crucial to obtaining good response times. We believe that the most attractive discipline for today is a hybrid migratable/malleable discipline. Many long-running jobs in production environments already perform checkpointing to tolerate failures, and as mentioned before, technology exists to perform automatic checkpointing of many parallel jobs. Given that only long-running jobs ever need to be migrated or "malleated", disciplines that expect either of these two types of preemption are practical today. Although the majority of applications used today may support only migratable preemption, it is relatively simple to modify our adaptive migratable/malleable scheduling module to support both kinds of jobs. Using such a hybrid scheduling discipline would greatly benefit jobs that already support malleable preemption, and would further encourage application writers to support this kind of preemption in new applications.

Our observations suggest that further work could be done to better choose processor allocations given approximate speedup and service-demand knowledge about jobs in order to reduce the variability in completion times for any given job. In particular, better decisions may be made by taking into consideration average load over some period of time rather than instantaneous load. Such improvements would be most relevant for simple and migratable preemption, since in this case, the scheduler must commit to a processor allocation for a job when the job is first started.

Acknowledgements

The network of workstations used for this study is part of a cooperative project between the University of Toronto and the Centre for Advanced Studies at the IBM Toronto Development Lab. The research in this paper was supported by the Information Technology Research Centre of Ontario, the Natural Sciences and Engineering Council of Canada, and Northern Telecom.

References

[BG96]   Timothy B. Brecht and Kaushik Guha. Using parallel program characteristics in dynamic processor allocation policies. *Performance Evaluation*, 27&28:519–539, 1996.

[CMV94] Su-Hui Chiang, Rajesh K. Mansharamani, and Mary K. Vernon. Use of application characteristics and limited preemption for run-to-completion parallel processor scheduling policies. In *Proceedings of the 1994 ACM SIGMETRICS Conference on Measurement and Modelling of Computer Systems*, pages 33–44, 1994.

[FN95] Dror G. Feitelson and Bill Nitzberg. Job characteristics of a production parallel scientific workload on the NASA Ames iPSC/860. In Dror G. Feitelson and Larry Rudolph, editors, *Job Scheduling Strategies for Parallel Processing*, Lecture Notes in Computer Science Vol. 949, pages 337–360. Springer-Verlag, 1995.

[FR92] Dror G. Feitelson and Larry Rudolph. Gang scheduling performance benefits for fine-grain synchronization. *Journal of Parallel and Distributed Computing*, 16:306–318, 1992.

[Gib96] Richard Gibbons. A historical application profiler for use by parallel schedulers. Master's thesis, Department of Computer Science, University of Toronto, 1996.

[Gib97] Richard Gibbons. A historical application profiler for use by parallel schedulers. In Dror G. Feitelson and Larry Rudolph, editors, *Proceedings of the Third Workshop on Job Scheduling Strategies for Parallel Processing*, 1997. To appear.

[GST91] Dipak Ghosal, Guiseppe Serazzi, and Satish K. Tripathi. The processor working set and its use in scheduling multiprocessor systems. *IEEE Transactions on Software Engineering*, 17(5):443–453, May 1991.

[GTS91] Anoop Gupta, Andrew Tucker, and Luis Stevens. Making effective use of shared-memory multiprocessors: The process control approach. Technical Report CSL-TR-91-475A, Computer Systems Laboratory, Stanford University, July 1991.

[Hen95] Robert L. Henderson. Job scheduling under the portable batch system. In Dror G. Feitelson and Larry Rudolph, editors, *Job Scheduling Strategies for Parallel Processing*, Lecture Notes in Computer Science Vol. 949, pages 279–294. Springer-Verlag, 1995.

[Hot96a] Steven Hotovy. Private communication, November 1996.

[Hot96b] Steven Hotovy. Workload evolution on the Cornell Theory Center IBM SP-2. In Dror G. Feitelson and Larry Rudolph, editors, *Job Scheduling Strategies for Parallel Processing*, Lecture Notes in Computer Science Vol. 1162, pages 27–40. Springer-Verlag, 1996.

[Lif95] David A. Lifka. The ANL/IBM SP scheduling system. In Dror G. Feitelson and Larry Rudolph, editors, *Job Scheduling Strategies for Parallel Processing*, Lecture Notes in Computer Science Vol. 949, pages 295–303. Springer-Verlag, 1995.

[MT90] Silvano Martello and Paolo Toth. *Knapsack Problems: Algorithms and Computer Implementations*. Wiley & Sons, 1990.

[MVZ93] Cathy McCann, Raj Vaswani, and John Zahorjan. A dynamic processor allocation policy for multiprogrammed shared-memory multiprocessors. *ACM Transactions on Computer Systems*, 11(2):146–178, May 1993.

[MZ94] Cathy McCann and John Zahorjan. Processor allocation policies for message-passing parallel computers. In *Proceedings of the 1994 ACM SIGMETRICS Conference on Measurement and Modeling of Computer Systems*, pages 19–32, 1994.

[MZ95]   Cathy McCann and John Zahorjan. Scheduling memory constrained jobs on distributed memory parallel computers. In *Proceedings of the 1995 ACM SIGMETRICS Joint International Conference on Measurement and Modelling of Computer Systems*, pages 208–219, 1995.

[NSS93]   Vijay K. Naik, Sanjeev K. Setia, and Mark S. Squillante. Performance analysis of job scheduling policies in parallel supercomputing environments. In *Proceedings of Supercomputing '93*, pages 824–833, 1993.

[NVZ96]   Thu D. Nguyen, Raj Vaswani, and John Zahorjan. Using runtime measured workload characteristics in parallel processor scheduling. In Dror G. Feitelson and Larry Rudolph, editors, *Job Scheduling Strategies for Parallel Processing*, Lecture Notes in Computer Science Vol. 1162, pages 175–199. Springer-Verlag, 1996.

[Ous82]   John K. Ousterhout. Scheduling techniques for concurrent systems. In *Proceedings of the 3rd International Conference on Distributed Computing (ICDCS)*, pages 22–30, October 1982.

[Par97]   Eric W. Parsons. *Using Knowledge of Job Characteristics in Multiprogrammed Multiprocessor Scheduling*. PhD thesis, Department of Computer Science, University of Toronto, 1997.

[PL96]   Jim Pruyne and Miron Livny. Managing checkpoints for parallel programs. In Dror G. Feitelson and Larry Rudolph, editors, *Job Scheduling Strategies for Parallel Processing*, Lecture Notes in Computer Science Vol. 1162, pages 140–154. Springer-Verlag, 1996.

[PS95]   Eric W. Parsons and Kenneth C. Sevcik. Multiprocessor scheduling for high-variability service time distributions. In Dror G. Feitelson and Larry Rudolph, editors, *Job Scheduling Strategies for Parallel Processing*, Lecture Notes in Computer Science Vol. 949, pages 127–145. Springer-Verlag, 1995.

[PS96a]   Eric W. Parsons and Kenneth C. Sevcik. Benefits of speedup knowledge in memory-constrained multiprocessor scheduling. *Performance Evaluation*, 27&28:253–272, 1996.

[PS96b]   Eric W. Parsons and Kenneth C. Sevcik. Coordinated allocation of memory and processors in multiprocessors. In *Proceedings of the 1996 ACM SIGMETRICS Conference on Measurement and Modelling of Computer Systems*, pages 57–67, 1996.

[RSD+94]   E. Rosti, E. Smirni, L. W. Dowdy, G. Serazzi, and B. M. Carlson. Robust partitioning policies of multiprocessor systems. *Performance Evaluation*, 19:141–165, 1994.

[SCZL96]   Joseph Skovira, Waiman Chan, Honbo Zhou, and David Lifka. The EASY-LoadLeveler API project. In Dror G. Feitelson and Larry Rudolph, editors, *Job Scheduling Strategies for Parallel Processing*, Lecture Notes in Computer Science Vol. 1162, pages 41–47. Springer-Verlag, 1996.

[Set95]   Sanjeev K. Setia. The interaction between memory allocations and adaptive partitioning in message-passing multiprocessors. In Dror G. Feitelson and Larry Rudolph, editors, *Job Scheduling Strategies for Parallel Processing*, Lecture Notes in Computer Science Vol. 949, pages 146–164. Springer-Verlag, 1995.

[Sev89]   Kenneth C. Sevcik. Characterizations of parallelism in applications and their use in scheduling. In *Proceedings of the 1989 ACM SIGMETRICS International Conference on Measurement and Modeling of Computer Systems*, pages 171–180, May 1989.

[Sev94]   K. C. Sevcik. Application scheduling and processor allocation in multipro-
            grammed parallel processing systems. *Performance Evaluation*, 19:107–140,
            1994.
[ST93]   Sanjeev Setia and Satish Tripathi. A comparative analysis of static proces-
            sor partitioning policies for parallel computers. In *Proceedings of the Inter-
            national Workshop on Modeling and Simulation of Computer and Telecom-
            munication Systems (MASCOTS)*, pages 283–286, January 1993.
[TG89]   Andrew Tucker and Anoop Gupta. Process control and scheduling issues
            for multiprogrammed shared-memory multiprocessors. In *Proceedings of
            the 12th ACM Symposium on Operating Systems Principles*, pages 159–
            166, 1989.
[WMKS96] Michael Wan, Regan Moore, George Kremenek, and Ken Steube. A batch
            scheduler for the Intel Paragon with a non-contiguous node allocation al-
            gorithm. In Dror G. Feitelson and Larry Rudolph, editors, *Job Schedul-
            ing Strategies for Parallel Processing*, Lecture Notes in Computer Science
            Vol. 1162, pages 48–64. Springer-Verlag, 1996.
[ZM90]   John Zahorjan and Cathy McCann. Processor scheduling in shared memory
            multiprocessors. In *Proceedings of the 1990 ACM SIGMETRICS Confer-
            ence on Measurement and Modelling of Computer Systems*, pages 214–225,
            1990.

Objective-Oriented Algorithm for Job Scheduling in Parallel Heterogeneous Systems

Pham Hong Hanh * and Valery Simonenko **

Department of Computer Science
National Technical University of Ukraine
KPI-20-20, Pr. Pobedy 37, Kiev-252056,Ukraine.

* Hanh@pham.kiev.ua
** V.Simonenko@p47.f360.n463.z2.fidonet.org

Abstract. This paper presents a new approach to solve the problem of job scheduling for parallel processing in *heterogeneous* systems. The optimization goals are: (i) minimum total execution time including communication costs and (ii) shortest response time for all jobs. We introduce a classification for the given scheduling problem by the heterogeneity of the systems, from the view of the schedulers' eyes. Then, according to this analysis, a new scheduling strategy for so-called "Strictly-Heterogeneous" systems is proposed. The key idea of the new approach is the use of the Hungarian method, which provides a quick and objective-oriented search for the best schedule by the given optimization criteria. In addition, by modifying this method into so-called Objective-Oriented Algorithm (OOA), the time complexity for scheduling is decreased to $O(n(E+nlogn))$. The simulation results show us that OOA provides better solution quality while scheduling time is less than the existing methods.

1 Introduction

For the last few years, a number of job scheduling algorithms for uniform systems have been published. However, in heterogeneous systems, where not only jobs (tasks) belong to different classes but also, resources (computing nodes) can be heterogeneous, scheduling problems are *more complex* than the ones in uniform systems. Besides, a lot of algorithms for uniform systems are specialized on a particular uniform type of the system architecture [4],[15],[2]. Therefore, applications of these algorithms for heterogeneous systems are limited.

In the uniform systems, because of the homogeneity of the jobs and the resources, the optimization for job scheduling is carried out at high level where the jobs (and the resources) are considered not alone but in some groups (batches or gangs). Meanwhile, in the heterogeneous systems, the optimization for job scheduling must be carried out at *both* high and low levels. At the low level, where every single job is assigned to a single resource, because of the *heterogeneity* of the jobs and the resources, there is a *problem of choosing the best job-resource assignment* among the different and possible ones. The solution of this problem has big influence on the utilization of the hardware: not only on the fraction of the used resources to the available ones, but also on the efficiency with which these resources are used.

Therefore, while keeping on solving other common problems as in uniform systems, job scheduling strategies in heterogeneous systems must *focus* on the problem which is mentioned above and which derives from the *heterogeneity* of the computing systems.

In this paper we study the job scheduling problem for parallel processing in heterogeneous systems by this way. We provide a heuristic algorithm (named Objective-Oriented Algorithm) based on a strategy that has not yet been used before in job scheduling.

The paper is organized as follows: In section 2 we provide a classification for the given job scheduling problem by the heterogeneity of the computing systems; Then, in order to make the scheduling algorithm comparable with the others and available for its application in the real systems, we give section 3 for a detailed description of the computing model and the problem statement; In section 4, a quick review of related work and the key ideas of the new strategy are provided; The algorithm itself is described in section 5; Simulation results are analyzed in section 6; And finally, the conclusions are stated in section 7.

2 Influence of Systems' Heterogeneity on Job Scheduling

Before moving on to describing the computing model, we would like to make a preliminary classification of the types of the systems' heterogeneity in parallel processing (from the view of schedulers' eyes).

Suppose that at a moment in time, in a parallel heterogeneous system, there are M jobs ready to be executed and there are N resources available. The requirement of the job scheduling problem is to assign these M jobs to N resources so that the received schedule is satisfied by the following: First, the *processing requirements* of the system (e.g. the resource must have enough memory and communication capacity, which are required by the job that is assigned to this resource etc.); Second, the *optimization requirements* (e.g. minimum parallel executing time, high resource utilization etc.).

We assume that the scheduling process can be divided into two smaller ones:

- *Checking* processing requirements: from Ri all possible and different variants of schedules, we have to pick out the set of Rp variants which are satisfied by the processing requirements, but not yet the optimization requirements (OR);
- *Optimizing* by satisfying OR: from Rp variants we have to choose Ro optimum schedules (in most cases $Ro=1$) which are satisfied by the optimization requirements.

Obviously, the numbers Ri and Rp determine the scale and the complexity of the Checking and the Optimizing steps.

In the case, when there are two OR: (i) shortest response time for all jobs and (ii) minimum total executing time, one of the ways to achieve these two goals at the same time is to distribute the jobs to the maximal number of resources (suppose that there are Rmm such variants) and then choose from Rmm variants the best one with minimum total execution time. Now, we see how the heterogeneity of a system (how different the jobs and the resources are) can have influence on Ri and Rp, which show us the *scale* and the *complexity* of job scheduling problem.

- In so-called *"Half-Heterogeneous"* systems, where there is no processing requirement (i.e. any assignment of a job to a resource is possible), the resources are the same (uniform) but the jobs are different [3] or vice versa. In this case, we have $Ri = Rp$, which means that the job scheduling problem leads straightforward to the second step: the optimization step without dealing with processing requirements. The scale of the problem is $Rp = \dfrac{M!}{(M-N)!}$,

- In so-called *"Completely-Heterogeneous"* systems, there is no processing requirement but either the resources and the jobs are different [8,16]. In this case, the complexity of the job scheduling problem is the same as the previous one, but the scale is different with $Ri = Rp = \dfrac{M!}{(M-N)!} \times N!$,

- In so-called *" Strictly-Heterogeneous "* systems, the resources and also the jobs can be different. Moreover, in this case there are processing requirements (i.e. not all assignments of jobs to resources are possible) [15]. Therefore, job scheduling problem is more complicated. It now contains two steps: checking processing requirements and optimizing the schedule. The scale is almost the same as in the previous case with $Ri = \dfrac{M!}{(M-N)!} \times N!$ and $Rp = Rmm$, where

Rmm is the number of the variants of maximum matching for the bipartite graph of M and N nodes. Theoretically, $Rmm \in [0, Ri]$ but usually in practice $Rmm \ll Ri$. Besides, it is possible that $Rmm = 0$, which means that there is no schedule with N size (i.e. for N resources). This also means that some resources are strongly unrelated to such a kind of M given jobs.

Note that the scheduling strategies, which are for commonly-called uniform systems, belong to the first class: *"Half-Heterogeneous"* systems, where the resources are the same (uniform) but the jobs are different (even just by the amount of execution time for each job). The scheduling strategies, which are for commonly-called heterogeneous systems, actually belong to the second class: *"Completely-Heterogeneous"* systems. The third class: *" Strictly-Heterogeneous "* systems, has received the least attention because of the following reason: The parallel computing systems in this class are characterized with having not only *jobs and resources of different classes* but also some strict *processing requirements*. This kind of parallel systems (e.g. PVM) became available for common use in the real world only several years ago. One more fact is that any algorithm that works for the systems of the third class will also work for the systems of the second one, although with a little less efficiency than in its own class.

In this paper we will focus on the third class of scheduling, for *" Strictly-Heterogeneous "* systems.

3 Heterogeneous Computing Model

3. 1 Description of System's Model

The computing model for a *"Strictly-Heterogeneous"* systems, in which our scheduling algorithm works, has derived from a large parallel and distributed system (Fig. 1.) and has been studied before in [13].

In the real world, this system consists of : First, *different resources,* they are heterogeneous nodes-users U_i (e.g. different computers or processors) and the common resources CRj (e.g. the severs) ; Second, *tasks of different kinds* T_i, which come from users-nodes or from outside (e.g. from other systems). As in any parallel systems, these so-called mother-tasks have to be maximally parallelized. They are divided into son-tasks (small computing modules) which we will call jobs. These *jobs are different* as well because they come from different tasks.

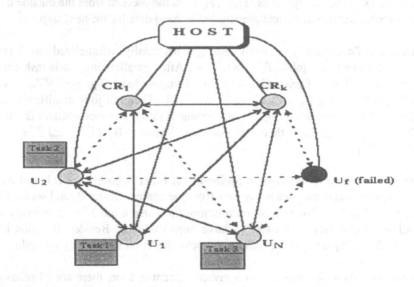

- Tasks in the system.
- Available resources in the system. (● Broken down resource)
- Communication Channels between Resources.
        (▪ ▪ ▪ Failed channels)
- Channels for Management.

Fig. 1. *Tasks and Resources in a Parallel Heterogeneous System.*

Therefore, the given system can be represented by:

- a data set about Q *tasks* ST={T_1, ...,T_Q} with their heterogeneous processing *requirements*.

- a data set about N *resources* SR={R_1, ...,R_N} with their heterogeneous processing *capacities*;
- a data matrix about the *communication channels between the resources* MCR[1..N,1..N], where MCR[i,j] is the rate of the cost for communicating between R_i and R_j , and MCR[i,j] $\in \Re^+$. We say there is "no connection" between R_i and R_j when MCR[i,j] > Ω_0 (some given number).

3. 2 General Scheduling Scheme

In order to make explicit how much and what kind of work the job scheduling problem does and where it takes place in the general scheduling process, we provide here a quick review of the general scheduling scheme. Usually, it contains the following steps:

(1) Input Tasks: First, accept tasks T_1, ...,T_Q from the users or from the outside of the system; Second, analyze tasks and prepare beforehand data for the next step.

(2) Parallelize Tasks into Jobs: Each task T_i is maximally parallelized (without the resource constraint) into jobs J^i_k , k=1,..,K_i . After parallelizing, each task can be represented by a DAG of job-nodes (Fig.2.a). Thus, we have Q graphs: VT_1, ...,VT_Q, where VT_1={J^1_1, .., J^1_{K1}} , ..., VT_Q={J^Q_1 , .., J^Q_{KQ}}. Then, all jobs of different tasks (i.e. of different classes) are grouped (and renamed) into S common clusters B_1, B_2, .., B_S (Fig.2.b) considering their precedence, where B_1={$J^{1,1}$, ..,$J^{1,M1}$}, .. , B_S={$J^{S,1}$,..,$J^{S,MS}$}.

(3) Prepare and send Ready Jobs to Buffer-in: A Filter, whose work is based on the rule of job precedence, chooses ready jobs from the nearest cluster B_1 and sends it into the Buffer-in (Fig.2.b). The rule of job relationship is that a job $J^{i,t} \in B_i$ is ready only when all its predecessor in cluster B_{i-1} have been executed. Besides, the jobs in all clusters B_1,B_2, .., B_S are also moved into the next cluster all the time by this rule.

(4) Schedule Jobs to Resources: At a given moment in time, there are M ready and independent jobs in the Buffer-in and N available resources in the system. The scheduler has to assign these jobs onto the resources so that the received schedule is optimum by one or some given optimization criteria.

(5) Reschedule Failed Jobs: In the case, when a resource fails during executing the job that has been assigned on it, the ID of this job has to appear in the Buffer-in again, as a ready job for the next scheduling cycle (this step may be executed by the system monitor but not by the scheduler).

(6) Output Executed Tasks: This is the reverse process of step (2). After the execution, each job is put to Buffer-out (Fig. 2.b). Then, they are collected back to their mother-tasks. A task is completely executed and removed from the scheduling system when all its son-jobs have been executed.

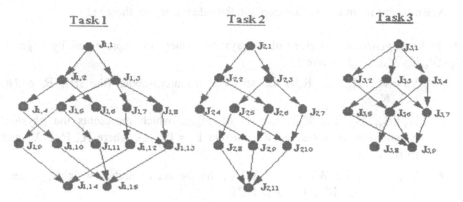

Fig. 2. a *Parallelizing Tasks into Jobs.*

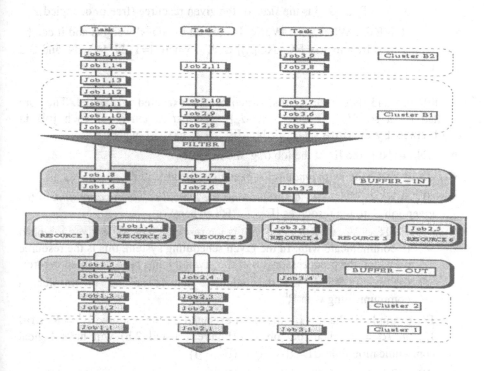

Fig. 2.b *Jobs in clusters during the scheduling process.*

3. 3   Statement for Job Scheduling Problem

As is discussed above, the scheduling process is a complex of procedure-steps. In this paper we will focus on the most important step (4) - step of scheduling jobs to resources. In more detail, it can be stated as follows:

At a moment in time, after the step 3 in the scheme above, there are:

■ N *heterogeneous resources* of the system, which are represented by a graph $G_R=(V_R,E_R,W_{VR},W_{ER})$, where:

* $V_R =\{R_1, R_2, ..., R_N\}$ is the set of N resources-nodes (the ID), $R_i \in N|$, i=1..N.

* $E_R=\{E_1, E_2, ..., E_d\}$ is the set of edges, which represents the *physical communication link between resources* $E_i = \{R_i,R_j\}$, where $R_i, R_j \in V_R$ and $0 \leq d \leq N^2$.

* $W_{VR}=\{ WVR_1, WVR_2, ..., WVR_N \}$ is the set of nodes' weights, where $WVR_i =\{RE_i, RT_i\}$. For $\forall$ i=1..N :
    (i) $RE_i \in \Re^+$ is the ratio that characterizes the *capacity* (e.g. the speedup, local memory) of the given resource R_i ;
    (ii) $RT_i \in \{0,1\}$ is the *state* of the given resource (free or occupied).

* $W_{ER}=\{ WER_1, WER_2, ..., WER_p \}$ is the set of edges' weights and it can be represented by a matrix $RC=RC[i,j] \in \Re^+$, where i=1..N, j=1..N, and $0 \leq p \leq N*N$.

■ M different and independent jobs, which can be executed in parallel. They are represented by a set $V_J =\{J_1, J_2, ..., J_M\}$. The *heterogeneity* of each job is characterized by the data set $J_i =\{JN_i, JE_i, JL_i\}$, i=1..M, where:

* $JN_i \in N|$ is the ID of the job (e.g. the number).

* $JE_i \in \Re^+$ is the *work amount* for executing the given job.

* $JL_i =\{(R^1, \varphi_1), ..., (R^q, \varphi_q)\}$ represents the *logical communication link* of the given job J_i to the resources $\{R^1, ..., R^q\}$, where:
    (i) $R^t \in V_R$ (t=1..q , q $\in$ N|) is the resource which the given job need to communicate with. In the given scheduling system, this is the resource on which the predecessor-job of the given job has been executed before;
    (ii) $\varphi_t \in \Re^+$ is the data amount that is needed to transfer in communicating with R^t.

For example, if the job $J_{1,2}$ has been executed on the resource $R^1 = R_1$ and $J_{1,6}$ on $R^2 = R_3$ then the job $J_{1,6}$ (Figure 2.a and 2.b) will have logical communication link $JL= \{(R^1, \varphi_1), (R^2, \varphi_2)\}$.

* $JP_i \in \Re^+$ is the *priority* of the job J_i if the priority system for jobs exists.

■ The *requirement* of the given problem is to find out a schedule for assigning M jobs onto N resources so that we can achieve two following optimization goals:

* minimum total actual execution time (and)
* shortest response time for all jobs.

4. Solution Basis

4.1 Related work

It has been shown in [10] that the given problem (with the name "Assignment Problem") comes from the "Traveling Salesman Problem", which is NP-complete [9]. Moreover, the given problem, indeed, is listed in the form of the problem N43 in section A2.5. of the List of NP-complete problems in [9]. Therefore, most algorithms for solving it use heuristic or genetic approaches [7],[16],[5],[3],[19].

In solving any scheduling problem, there are two important issues that we should consider. They are: *solution quality* (how the received schedule is near to the optimum one) and *solving time* (for how long it takes to find the schedule).

In dealing with solution quality: Solution quality depends on the optimization criteria and the scale of the optimization area. Usually, there are three main kinds of optimization criteria :
- Focus on the executing time of jobs and not consider communication costs (as in most of balancing algorithms) [8].
- Focus on the minimization of communication costs [7] (e.g. using "critical path" in clustering algorithms[20]).
- Focus on other parameters (e.g. response time or other time constraints in the Real-time systems[15]).

After choosing criteria, the optimization can be carried out in two ways:
- Through local minimization [15],[6]. This is simpler than the next way and it requires less information (in local scale). However, because it is local, it has to be carried out several times during a scheduling cycle.
- Through global minimization [7],[8]. This is more complex than the first way and it requires more information about jobs, resources, system performance (in global scale). Therefore, in practice, the algorithms usually are simplified in order to decrease the scheduling time.

To achieve the desired results with more than one optimization criterion, the scheduling is sometimes carried out by a combination of the above discussed ways.

In dealing with solving time: The requirement of the solving time depends on the scheduling type. Static scheduling algorithms can have a long solving time while the Dynamic ones always have a short solving time.

As is said above, because of the complexity of the problem, most of the scheduling algorithms are heuristic or genetic. In the algorithms that have been published recently, a genetic method called Simulated Annealing (SA) is used very popularly [7],[16],[11],[18]. This method is good because of its flexibility. By resetting the values of the parameters for the simulation (the initial and freezing temperatures, the ratio for decreasing temperatures) we can have many kinds of schedulers, which are different by the correlation between solution time and solution quality as follows:
- From the fastest scheduler, which gives a schedule with a random quality for the minimum solution time;

- To the slowest one, which checks all possible variants of schedules and gives us the exact solution (real optimum schedule).

Usually, the simulation parameters are set so that the result is in the middle between these two extremists. However, the solution time for achieving an acceptable-optimum schedule is too long, especially when the problem size (M,N) is large, and also at the same time, the solution quality is unpredictable.

4. 2 New Approach with Hungarian Method

As it has been reviewed above, in order to achieve two conflicting goals: short scheduling time and good quality of the schedule, we always have a trade-off between solving time and solution quality. The point is how to achieve the "golden mean".

Scheduling strategy for dealing with solving time: For the system that is described above, our aim is to develop a balanced algorithm, which gives us a schedule of good quality for an acceptable solving time.

In order to see explicitly the difference of our approach from the existing ones, let us analyze again (but now from the view of the strategists' eyes) the above approach of scheduling by using simulated annealing (SA). Suppose that all possible variants (Ri) of the schedules can be set as the "balls" in a "box". The variants-balls are located in chaos. Among them, there is a real optimum one that has to be found. Now, see how it is found by SA and by our algorithm using Hungarian method, which is described in [10],[12],[1].

In SA, all the variants are put in the Markovian chain as if all the balls are connected each to another with a visual "thread" (this is not shown in Fig.3.a). The search is started with a random variant-ball Vs (which is put in the "pocket") and is guided by this thread. Continuing the search, the next ball is compared with the one in the pocket. If the next one is better than the one in the pocket then it will occupy the pocket, and so on. After a given number of steps with the last-checked ball Vf, the variant-ball in the pocket is regarded as the optimum one of all the balls in the box. Usually, the Markovian chain is built so that the "thread" is spread over all the box in order to avoid local minimum. However, still, if the real optimum variant-ball was not in the searched area (the red line in Fig. 3.a) then the received variant, obviously, is not optimum.

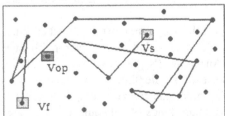
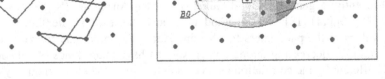

Fig. 3.a *Scheduling strategy in SA*   Fig. 3.b *New scheduling strategy.*

The key idea of the new approach is to detach from all possible variants (the box) a zone, which contains exactly the real optimum variant *Vop* (for the given optimization criteria) and is much smaller than the box (Fig.3.b). Then, the search is carried out *only* in this area until it reaches the real optimal variant *Vop*. Therefore, we will receive the exact solution while the solving time is much less than it is in SA for finding a solution of the same quality.

Moreover, using the Hungarian method (which will be described in detail later) for such an approach allows us to carry out not a random search (as it is in SA) but a so-called *"objective-oriented search"* in the chosen area, where the objective is the real optimum variant *Vop*. That is why we name the algorithm "Objective-Oriented" (OOA). The selection of the Hungarian method is not by chance but is based on a careful investigation which is studied in [14].

Scheduling Strategy for dealing with solution quality: Now we have to determine the optimization criterion and the scale of optimization area.

■ Heterogeneous systems usually are distributed. Therefore, we think that it is necessary to consider communication costs in scheduling for such systems. To escape the conflicting goals: (i) minimizing execution time (by choosing separately the most fitting job-resource pairs); (ii) minimizing response time of jobs (by maximally parallelizing them on the maximum number of resources); (iii) minimizing communication costs (by decreasing the number of the used resources), we use the following balanced optimization scheme. The optimization is carried out by two steps:

(1) maximize the number of resources for executing the given jobs as far as possible (for achieving minimum response time);

(2) choose the best schedule with the minimum total weight that is determined by an estimating function (which characterizes the execution time of jobs including communication costs).

■ Because the Hungarian method works very efficiently when the problem size is 20-100, we propose two variants of optimization:

- First variant; when M>100 , the jobs are randomly gathered into a group of N jobs. Then the local optimization is carried out for N jobs and N resources. The size of the optimization zone n = N.
- Second variant; when M<100, all the jobs are in a global optimization with K groups of N resources, where $K \in N|$ and $K>[M/N]$. The size of the optimization area n = M.

4. 3 Algorithm Basis

With the chosen strategies for scheduling, which are mentioned above, there are three important steps which now will be studied in detail:

- Forming the "box".
- Determining the searching zone.
- Building a rule-guide for the objective-oriented search.

A. Box Forming

This means the way to represent the data for scheduling. For the initial data (which is described in 3.3.), we have: a set of M independent jobs with their heterogeneous processing requirements; a graph of N resource-nodes with their heterogeneous processing capacities.

Now, in order to form the box, we have to reform these two separate data sets into a form that represents directly the relationship between jobs and resources: a matrix of size M*N and which we will call Job-Resource matrix (JR). Each element JR[i,j] of this matrix is the weight of the assignment of the job i onto the resource j. These weights are determined by an optimization function $\Delta(i,j)$. The formation of this function is based on the optimization criteria that is determined in 3.3.

Suppose that the jobs and the resources are identified respectively by two sets $V_J=\{J_1, J_2, ..., J_M\}$, $V_R=\{R_1, R_2, ..., R_N\}$. In general, the optimization function can be determined as the following:

$$\Delta(J_i, R_j) = \delta_{i,j} = \prod_{k=1}^{K} P_k^{i,j} \times \prod_{x=1}^{H} C_x^{i,j} \times \sum_{y=1}^{G} L_y O_y^{i,j} \qquad (1)$$

Where,

- $\prod_{k=1}^{K} P_k^{i,j}$ is called absolute *priority* of assignment (J_i, R_j). It is calculated by multiplication all K relative priorities $P_k^{i,j} \in \Re^+$ which are derived from different factors (e.g. the permitted waiting time of the given job, the desirable usage frequency of the given resource).

- $\prod_{x=1}^{H} C_x^{i,j}$ is the final result of analyzing all H *processing requirements* (e.g. the requirements about memory, speedup...), where $C_x^{i,j}$ is the degree of satisfying the processing requirement x ($x = 1..H$) for the assignment (J_i, R_j), $C_x^{i,j} \in \{0,1\}$: $C_x^{i,j} = 1$ if the resource R_j is satisfied by a requirement x of the job J_i, otherwise, $C_x^{i,j} = 0$.

- $\sum_{y=1}^{G} L_y O_y^{i,j}$ is the final result of analyzing all G *optimization requirements*, where $O_y^{i,j} \in \Re^+$ is the degree of satisfying the optimization requirement y for the assignment (J_i, R_j); $L_y \in \Re^+$ is the weights assigned to the optimization criterion y.

For the given computing system with the given optimization criteria and according to the scheduling strategy for dealing with solution quality in section 4.2., the estimating function (which calculates the weight of the assignment of a job J_i onto a resource R_j, $R_j \in V_R$ and $J_i \in V_J$) should be determined as follows:

■ To reduce the complexity of the problem, we suppose that $\prod_{k=1}^{K} P_k^{i,j} = \rho_i$ (2),

where $\rho_i = JP_i$ is the priority of the job J_i (e.g. it can be formed by the time Tw_i , for which the job J_i has been waited in the system).

■ For simplicity, we suppose that there is only one *processing requirement* (H=1):

$\prod_{x=1}^{H} C_x^{i,j} = C^{i,j}$ which is determined by comparing the physical communication

links of the resource R_j: $E_R = \{E_1, E_2, .., E_d\}$ in the resource graph with the logical communication links of the job J_i: $JL_i = \{(R^1, \varphi_1), ..., (R^q, \varphi_q)\}$. Recall that $R^t \in V_R$ (t=1..q) is the resource which the given job needs to communicate with.

The rule for determining them is: $\quad C^{i,j} = \prod_{t=1}^{q} CC_l^{i,j}$ (3)

where, $\forall$ t=1..q : $\quad CC_l^{i,j} = 1$, if $(R_j , R^t) \in E_R$;

$\qquad\qquad\qquad CC_l^{i,j} = 0$, if $(R_j , R^t) \notin E_R$;

■ The third part of (1) is determined as the follows:

$\sum_{y=1}^{G} L , O_y^{i,j} = 1/Te_{i,j} + 1/ Tc_{i,j}$, where

• $Te_{i,j}$ is the *executing time* for the job Ji on the resource Rj. If the *amount of work for executing the given job* $JE_i = \varepsilon_i$; the *realization ratio of the resource* $RE_j = k_j$, then it can be determined by the following: $Te_{i,j} = \varepsilon_i * k_j$;

• $Tc_{i,j}$ is the communication costs for the assignment (J_i, R_j). If the list of the resources which the job requires to communicate with is $JL_i = \{(R^1, \varphi_1), ..., (R^q, \varphi_q)\}$, and the communication ratio between the resources R_j and R_l (l=1..N) is $RC[j,l] = \beta_{j,l}$; then we have $Tc_{i,j} = \sum_{l=1}^{q} (\varphi_l * \beta_{j,l})$

Therefore, $\sum_{y=1}^{G} L , O_y^{i,j} = 1 + (\varepsilon_i \times k_j) + 1 + \sum_{l=1}^{q} (\varphi_l * \beta_{j,l})$ (4)

From (1),(2),(3), and (4) we have:

$$\Delta(J_i, R_j)= \delta_{i,j} = \rho_i \times C^{i,j} \times [1 \div (\varepsilon_i \times k_j)+1 \div \sum_{l=1}^{q} (\varphi_l * \beta_{j,l})]$$ (5)

Obviously, $\delta_{i,j} \geq 0 \ \forall$ i=1..N , j=1..M . Therefore:

$\qquad inf (\Delta(J_i, R_j)) = 0$.

We will assume that there is no physical communication link between resources R_j and R_l when $Tc_{i,j} = \sum_{l=p}^{q} (\varphi_l * \beta_{j,l}) > \lambda_0$, where λ_0 is some given number. This is the threshold for determining if the communication between two resources is possible or not. According to this value, we have some value δ_{exist} which determines if the discussed assignment is possible or not.

The executing time $Te_{i,j}$ must have some lower limit T^o, then the highest limit for $\Delta(J_i,R_j)=\delta_{ij}$ can be determined as the following:

$$sup\ (\Delta(J_i,\ R_j)) = (\mu_{0j} \times \rho_{0j}) \times [1 / T^0 + 1 / \lambda_0] = \delta_{max}.$$

For applying the Hungarian method in the next step, we have to rebuild a new optimization function:

$$\Psi(J_i,\ R_j) = \delta_{max} - \Delta(J_i,\ R_j) = \psi_{i,j} \qquad (6)$$

Therefore, finally, for all elements of the matrix $JR[i,j]=\psi_{i,j}$, i=1..M, j=1..N, we have : $0 \leq \psi_{i,j} \leq \delta_{max}$ and the value $\psi_{exist} = \delta_{max} - \delta_{exist}$ as the threshold for determining if the assignment(J_i,R_j) is possible or not. The size of the box n is determined as in section 2 (based on the value of M and N) and according to the optimization area, which is determined in section 4.2.

For the example that is given in Fig. 2.b., the "box" or the Job-Resource matrix JR will have the size M=5 and N=3 as in Figure 4. The values of matrix elements are supposed to be the results of the calculation by the formulas (5) and (6) with some data which are given in section 3.3 for the jobs $J_{1,6}$, $J_{1,8}$, $J_{2,7}$, $J_{2,8}$, $J_{3,2}$ and for the resources R_1, R_3, R_5 .

RESOURCES

J		$J_{1,6}$	$J_{1,8}$	$J_{2,7}$	$J_{2,6}$	$J_{3,2}$
O	R_1	18	45	7	47	6
B	R_3	6	3	39	61	4
S	R_5	75	9	3	6	58

Fig. 4. *BOX with Matrix JR (* $\delta_{max} = 80;\ \psi_{exist} = 20;$ *)*

However, for a good explanation in the next sections, we suggest to study the searching technique with such a "box" (the Job-Resource matrix JR) as in Fig.5.a, where M=N=n=6.

B. Determining searching zone

After determining the job-resource matrix JR as the "box" (suppose that it is in   Fig. 5.a), the next and important step is to determine the zone for searching the real optimum variant of possible schedules. For further study, we provide some definitions about the assignments and the schedules as follows:

Definition 1: There are two given sets: $V_J=\{J_1,\ J_2,\ ...,\ J_n\}$ and $V_R=\{R_1,\ R_2,\ ...,\ R_n\}$. The pair $a=(J_i,R_j)$ is called *Assignment* of the job $J_i \in V_J$ onto the resource $R_j \in V_R$. Each assignment has its *weight*, which is determined as $\Psi(a)=\Psi(J_i,R_j)$, where Ψ is the function determined by (6).

Definition 2: For two given sets: $V_J=\{J_1,\ J_2,\ ...,\ J_n\}$ and $V_R=\{R_1,\ R_2,\ ...,\ R_n\}$, a set $A=\{a_1,a_2,\ ...,\ a_{n^*}\}= \{(J^1,\ R^1),\ (J^2,\ R^2),\ ...,\ (J^{n^*},\ R^{n^*})\}$ is called *Maximum matching* for such jobs and resources if:

- $\forall\ i=1..\ n^*,\ \Psi(a_i)=\Psi(J^i,R^i)<\psi_{exist}$.
- $\forall\ i=1..n^*,\ R^i\notin AR\backslash R^i\,,\ J^i\in AJ\backslash J^i$, where $AR=\{R^1,\ R^2,\ ...,\ R^{n^*}\}$, $AJ=\{J^1,\ J^2,\ ...,\ J^{n^*}\}$.
- n^* is maximized as far as it can be.

Definition 3: A maximum matching A* with the size n* for two given sets: $V_J=\{J_1, J_2,..., J_n\}$ and $V_R=\{R_1,\ R_2,\ ...,\ R_n\}$ is a possible *Schedule* for such jobs and resources if $n^* = n$. The weight of the schedule then is determined by: $D(A^*) = \sum\limits_{i=1}^{n}\Psi(a_i^*)\cdot$

Definition 4: Suppose that $Xp=\{A_1,\ A_2,\ ...,\ A_p\}$, $p\in N|$ is the set of all possible schedules. A schedule A* is the *real optimum variant* of possible schedules if :

$$D(A^*) = \sum\limits_{i=1}^{n}\Psi(a_i^*) = min\,(D(A_1),D(A_2),....,D(A_p)) = \overset{p}{\underset{j=1}{min}}\,(D(A_j))$$

According to the Hungarian method, the searching zone SZ is limited by so-called minimum assignments $a^*=(J^*,R^*)$ which have the minimum weights $\Psi(J^*,R^*)$ in comparison with other assignments in the same rows or in the same columns of the matrix JR with size n. These minimum assignments create the first bound for SZ (we call it B0), which can be found in the following way:
For i=1.. n, j=1..n, *if* :

- $(\Psi(a^*)=\Psi(J^*,R^*)<\psi_{exist}$) and
- $(\Psi(a^*)=\overset{n}{\underset{i=1}{min}}\Psi(J_i,R_j)$ or $\Psi(a^*)=\overset{n}{\underset{j=1}{min}}\Psi(J_i,R_j)$)
  then $a^*=(J^*,R^*)\in B0$.

Therefore, the bound B0 of the searching zone SZ is determined by a set of minimum assignments $A_b = \{a_1^*,a_2^*,..a_{b0}^*\}$, $b0\in N|$.

In the Hungarian method, the bound is marked by making the minimum assignments A_{b0}, which are on it, become the so-called zero assignments. It is obvious that if we subtract the same number S from all elements of a row (or of a column) in the matrix JR then the minimum assignments still remain as the minimum ones. In other words, if we subtract the weight of the minimum assignment from all elements, for each row and each column, we will still have the same bound B0 with the same minimum assignments $A_b = \{a_1^*,a_2^*,..a_{b0}^*\}$. The only difference is that these assignments will have zero weights.

In summery, the first bound B0 of the searching zone is a set of the zero assignments $A_b=\{a_1^*,a_2^*,..a_{b0}^*\}$ as in Fig.5.b. (for the "box" in Fig.5.a).

RESOURCES

		1	2	3	4	5	6
J	1	8	5	71	7	6	9
O	2	6	3	9	1	47	7
B	3	5	59	3	6	8	8
S	4	9	1	8	95	5	4
	5	1	2	1	80	2	3
	6	69	70	3	5	3	10

RESOURCES

		1	2	3	4	5	6
J	1	3	0		2	0	2
O	2	5	2	8	0		4
B	3	2		0	3	4	3
S	4	8	0	7		3	1
	5	0	1	0		0	0
	6			1	3	0	6

Fig.5.a *BOX with Matrix JR*

Fig.5.b *B0 of "0"s in Matrix JR*
(n=6; $\delta_{max.}=100$; $\psi_{exist}=30$;)

C. Objective-Oriented Search

After determining the bound of the searching zone, we have to carry out the last and the most important step - to search the optimum variant of the schedules in the determined searching zone. The search starts from the found bound B0, which is marked by zero assignments, and goes to the so-called current "Searching Line" (SL) by the following steps:

(1) First, check if the optimum variant Vop is on SL or not (for the first time, SL is the bound B0). That means to check if there is a schedule among the minimum assignments $A_{b0}=\{a_1{*},a_2{*},..a_{b0}{*}\}$ on B0. If so, go to (2). If not, go to (3).

According to definition 3, we have a schedule on SL if there are such n minimum assignments $A{*}=\{a_1{*},a_2{*},...a_n{*}\} \subseteq A_{b0}$ that A* is the maximum matching for the given jobs $V_J=\{J_1, J_2, ..., J_n\}$ and the given resources $V_R = \{R_1, R_2, ..., R_n\}$.

Suppose that (for these two sets), we have $A{*}=\{(J^1, R^1), (J^2, R^2), ..., (J^n, R^n)\}$ and $AR=\{R^1, R^2, ..., R^n\}$, $AJ=\{J^1, J^2, ..., J^n\}$. By definition 2, A* is the maximum matching if:

- $\forall\ i=1..\ n,\ \Psi(a_i{*})=\Psi(J^i,R^i)< \psi_{exist}$.
- $\forall\ i=1..n,\ R^i \notin AR\backslash R^i,\ J^i \notin AJ \backslash J^i$.

In the given example in Fig.5.b, the maximum matching for the minimum assignments (the zeros) on B0 is $\{(5,1),(1,2),(3,3),(2,4),(6,5)\}$ in Fig.6.a. It has the size 5 which is less than the matrix size n=6. Therefore, in this case there is not any schedule in the bound B0. We go to (3).

(2) If any schedule is found, it is the real optimum variant Vop. The search has to be stopped.

(3) If we can not find any schedule from the first-minimum assignments $A_{b0}=\{a_1{*},a_2{*},..,a_{b0}{*}\}$, this means there is no real optimum variant Vop on SL. Therefore, the search must be continued in the searching zone. The new SL inside the search zone SZ is found from the current SL by the procedure of Making New Zeros in the Hungarian method [10] as the set of second-minimum assignments (Fig.7.a). Then, go to (1) and repeat the same procedures for the new SL as for the current ones.

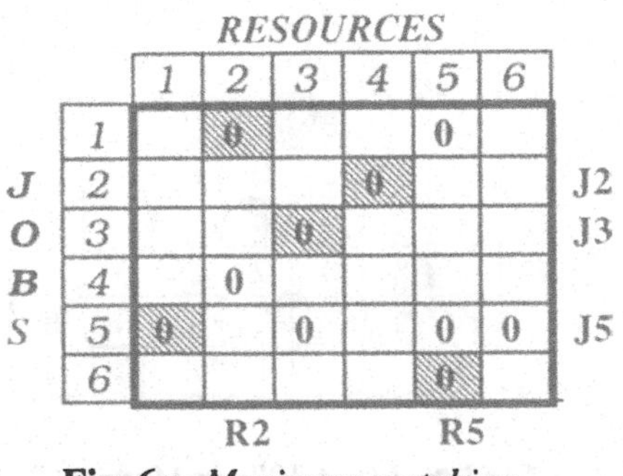

RESOURCES

	1	2	3	4	5	6	
1		0			0		
J 2				0			J2
O 3			0				J3
B 4		0					
S 5	0		0		0	0	J5
6					0		

R2   R5

RESOURCES

	1	2	3	4	5	6	
1	3	0		2	6	2	
J 2	5	2	8	0		4	#
O 3	2		0	3	8	3	#
B 4	8	0	7		5	1	
S 5	0	1	0		0	0	#
6			1	3	0	6	
	#		#	#		#	

Fig. 6.a *Maximum matching and Zero Lines for B0 of "0"s*

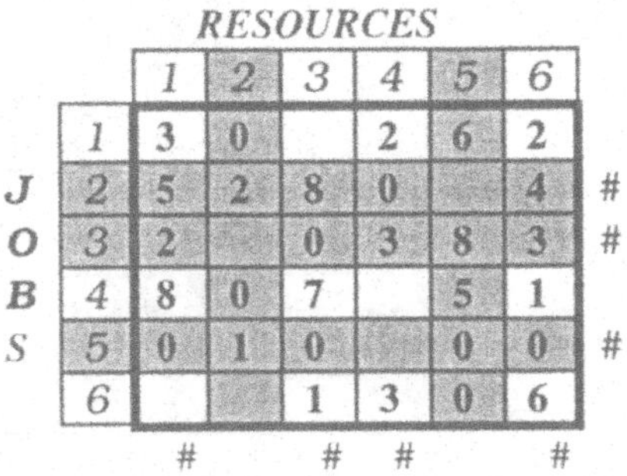

Fig.6.b *Marked Columns and Rows in JR*

The procedure of Making New Zeros contains the following steps:

1. Find the Zero Lines. This is the minimum set of lines that cover all the current zeros. For the given example, the Zeros Lines are J2,J3,J5, R2, and R5 (Fig. 6.a).

2. Find the minimum value of the elements which are not on the Zeros Lines. For the given example, these elements are the clear cells in Fig. 6.b: (1,1), (1,3), (1,4), (1,6), (4,1), (4,3), (4,4), (4,6), (6,1), (6,3), (6,4), (6,6), and the minimum value of them is 1.

3. Subtract this minimum value from all the elements of the columns that are not the Zeros Lines (R1,R3,R4,R6). Then add this minimum value to all the elements of the rows that are the Zeros Lines (J2,J3,J5). In the given example, these columns and rows are marked with # (Fig.6.b).

After doing so we receive the new set of zero elements (Fig.7.a), which indeed is the set of second-minimum assignments. In this way, the new SL for further searching is found. In the given example, the new SL are the set of the new zero elements in Fig.7.b. According to the procedure of searching, which is described above, we go to (1). In checking SL, we find the maximum matching A*={(1,2), (2,4), (3,3), (4,6), (5,1), (6,5)} with size 6 (equal to the size of the matrix JR) for the new zero assignments in Fig.7.b. Therefore, we go to (2) and finish the search.

RESOURCES

		1	2	3	4	5	6
J	1	2	0		1	0	1
	2	5	3	8	0		4
O	3	2		0	3	5	3
B	4	7	0	6		3	0
S	5	0	2	0		1	0
	6			0	2	0	6

RESOURCES

		1	2	3	4	5	6
J	1		0			0	
	2				0		
O	3			0			
B	4		0				0
S	5	0		0			0
	6			0		0	

Fig.7.a *New SL of "0"s in Matrix JR*   **Fig.7.b** *Vop on SL is found in Matrix JR*

In this way, by applying the Hungarian method, we receive the schedule A*. This is the optimum schedule for the given jobs $V_J=\{1,2,3,4,5,6\}$ and given resources $V_R = \{1,2,3,4,5,6\}$, whose relationship has been estimated by the formulas (5) and (6), and is given in the matrix form in Fig.5.a.

The found schedule A* is optimum because: (i) the response time is 0 for each job (only one job is assigned to one resource and therefore no job has to wait); (ii) the total processing time (including execution time and communication time) for all jobs is minimum: $D(A^*) = \Psi(1,2)+ \Psi(2,4)+ \Psi(3,3)+ \Psi(4,6)+ \Psi(5,1)+ \Psi(6,5) = 5+1+3+4+1+3 =17$ (from Fig.5.a)

Note that there are two conditions for finding Vop: First, there is a set of the minimum assignments; Second, there is a schedule (a maximum matching) in this set. In the steps described above, the search is continued not randomly inside the whole area of SZ but only with the assignments on the line SL which characterizes the first condition for having Vop. Therefore, *the search is oriented to Vop* all the time, unlike the random search in the simulated annealing method. And that is why we call the algorithm objective-oriented (OOA).

5 Objective-Oriented Algorithm

5. 1 Description of Data Input and Data Output

The input data for OOA is the needed data for forming matrix JR. The input data comes from:

■ *Buffer-in:* For characterizing the *states of M jobs*, which are in the buffer-in at the given moment in time, there are 3 data sets. According to sections 3.3. and 4.3., they are:
  - BIN.E[i]= ε_i (execution time),
  - BIN.LR[i]={Rp, .. , Rq}, BIN.LC[i]={ϕ_p , .. , ϕ_q} (communication requirements about the communicating resources and data transfer amounts),
  - BIN.P[i]=ρ_i (priority).
  For all: i=1..M.

■ *Monitor:* For characterizing the *states of R resources* in the system, there are 2 data sets (according to sections 3.3. and 4.3.) :
  - SIR.TR[i]=0(if resource is free) or 1(if otherwise),
  - SIR.J[i]=J_i (the ID number of the job that is executing on i resource),
  (Suppose that there are N free resources at the given moment in time).
  For all: i=1..R.

■ *System archive:* For characterizing the *capacity of the resources* and the *physical links* between them, according to sections 3.3. and 4.3., there are 2 data sets:
  - RC[j,h]=$\beta_{j,h}$, where j=1..R, h=1..R (ratios of resource connection),
  - RE[j]=k_j , where j=1..R (ratio of resource performance for job execution).

The output data from OOA is a schedule for M jobs and N resources, which has the following form: SCH.J[i]=J_i and SCH.R[j]=R_j where i=1..M, j=1..N.

The input data above is considered for the general case, when the schedulers try to use all *possible knowledge* about the system. They are the knowledge about the jobs (work amount), the resources (capacities and resources' network), and also the historical profile (with which resources the latest jobs have been executed).

5. 2 Algorithm Description

The steps of OOA are executed in the following order (Fig.8): The needed data for OOA is inputted from the buffer-in (Fig.2.b), the monitor and the system archive as is described above. The first step of OOA is to determine the number N of the free resources and the number M of the ready jobs. Then, the optimization scale *n* is determined by the rule in 3.3. The second step is to form the matrix JR of size n by the formulas (5) and (6) in 4.3.A. The third step is to determine the bound B0 of the searching zone SZ as is described in 4.3.B, the bound B0 is marked as the current searching line SL. Then, in the fourth step, the search for the real optimal variant of schedules Vop is carried out on this SL. If Vop is found, the search is stopped and we output the found optimal schedule Vop. Otherwise, do the fifth step, which determines a new searching line SL (as is described in 4.3.C) and then go back to the fourth step and so on, until Vop is reached. Finally, when the optimal schedule Vop is found the search is finished.

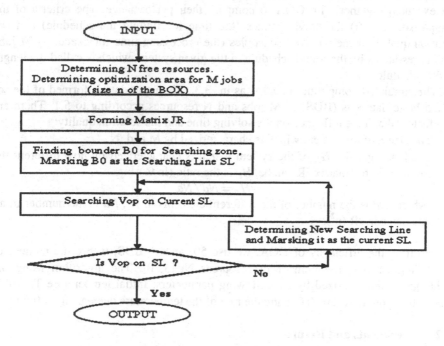

Fig.8. *Objective-Oriented Algorithm.*

The time complexity for the Hungarian method is $O(n^3)$, plus the time complexity for forming matrix JR, which is n^2. Therefore the time complexity for OOA is $O(n^3+n^2)$. However, if we use algorithm AMA which is described in [14] for searching Vop on SL the time complexity for OOA will be $O(n(E+n\log n)+n^2)$, where E is the maximum number of zero assignments on SL in the matrix JR, therefore $n \leq E \leq n^2$. Since the time complexity for forming the initial data usually is not taken into account, and the matrix JR is only the initial data for the job scheduling problem. Therefore, actually the time complexity of OOA is $O(n(E+n\log n))$.

In addition to this theoretical estimation that is considered for the *worst case*. We note that the scheduling algorithm OOA is dealing with the data in the matrix form all the time. Therefore this algorithm can be *parallelized* as well. The time complexity of the parallelized OOA then might be around $O(E+n\log n)$.

6 Analysis of Simulation Results

Besides the theoretical analysis, the practical analysis that is based on the simulation results is another way to show the advantage of a new algorithm and to examine its performance in comparison with the existing ones.

6. 1 Simulation Issues

An algorithm with the random scheduling and an algorithm using SA technique [16] are executed together with OOA to compare their performance. The criteria of the comparison are: (i) the solving times (the time for finding the schedule) and (ii) solution quality of the received schedules (the processing time for executing M jobs with N resources by the found schedule in the given system, which is called the length of the schedule).

The simulated computing model is as in 3.3.. The input data is formed of the so-called basic data sets (BDS) of M jobs and N resources according to 5.1. There are two factors that have influence on the solving time and the solution quality:

- The size n of the system which is characterized by M and N.
- The heterogeneity H_{et} of the system which is characterized by how different the elements in the matrix JR can be. H_{et} is the ratio (in %):
$$H_{et} = Nd / Na$$
where, Nd is the number of the different elements in JR; Na is the number of all elements in JR (n^2).

To illustrate the efficiency of OOA, we use 50 random BDS, where the number of jobs $M \in [20,120]$; the number of resources $N \in [3,30]$. The algorithm using SA technique is characterized by the following parameters: Initial temperature Ti=1000; Freezing temperature Tfr=0.01; and the rate of the temperature decreasing λ=0.999.

6. 2 Experiments and Results

First, the problem size n is changed from 3 to 30 while the heterogeneity is fixed. For each given value n, we investigate the solving times and the solution quality of Random, SA, and OOA. The simulation results are shown in Fig. 9.a and Fig. 9.b. They show us that the quality of the received schedule by OOA is much better than the ones by SA and, of course, by Random scheduling (Fig. 9.b.). Although the solving time of OOA is more than the one of Random scheduling, it is much less than the solving time of SA (Fig. 9.a.). We will have similar graphics if the problem size is increasing to more than 30. We do not provide the graphics of comparing with larger size than 30 because of the long solving time of SA. Indeed, the larger the problem size (n) is, the better OOA is, in both scheduling issues: solution quality and solving time.

Second, while the problem size is fixed, in our case $n = 30$, but the heterogeneity is changed and $H_{et} \in [10\%,90\%]$, we study the solving times and the solution quality of Random, SA, and OOA. The simulation results show us that the solving time of all algorithms (Random,SA, and OOA) do not depend on system heterogeneity.

Therefore we do not provide this graphic in the paper. However, the heterogeneity of the systems has influence on the solution quality. The graphics in Fig. 10. shows us that the more heterogeneous the systems are, the more efficiently OOA works, compared with SA and Random.

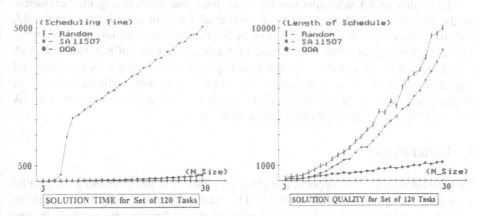

Fig.9.a *Investigation of Solving Time*   **Fig.9.b** *Investigation of Solution Quality*

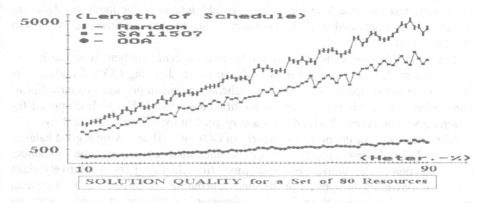

Fig.10. *Investigating the Dependency of Solution Quality on the Heterogeneity of the System.*

6.3 Analysis

The simulation results have proved our theoretical analysis which is discussed in the sections 4 and 5. In comparing with the existing methods, the scheduling quality of OOA is much better, and the scheduling time of OOA is decreased extensively. That is because the search area in OOA is reduced substantially. This efficiency of OOA is shown while both factors: the problem size and the heterogeneous of the systems are changing.

In Fig.9.b, the results show us that SA does not do much better than the random one in terms of schedule quality. That is because of the chosen parameters for the simulated annealing. With the given parameters above, we have a SA scheduler that gives us the "best" schedule after $11507 \approx 10^4$ times of changing the temperature (Tct). In the meantime, the real best schedule can be found, theoretically, only after 120!*30!/(120-30)! Tct, which is more than 10^{120} Tct (!). That is why the result of SA does not look very good.

The quality of SA scheduler can easily be improved by changing the parameters for the simulated annealing so that the number of Tct is increased, for example SA with 10^{10}. However, the scheduling time of SA then is increased too. And when the scheduling time of SA is too long it makes the scheduling times of Random and OOA (which are much less than the SA's one as in Fig.9.a.) become closer each to other and also closer to 0. Since such a picture of relationship between scheduling times of Random and OOA are not real, we think that it is better to show the results of SA with 11507 Tct than the results of SA with more Tct .

7. Conclusions

We have presented a new approach to solve the problem of job scheduling for parallel processing in *heterogeneous* systems. The new approach, using the Hungarian method, provides a quick and objective-oriented search for the best schedule by two optimization goals: (i) minimum total execution time including communication costs and (ii) shortest response time for all jobs. In addition, using the modified algorithm (which has been provided in [14]) for this method, the solving time is decreased to $O(n(E+nlogn))$.

Note that this time complexity is for finding the *real* optimum schedule by the given optimization criteria and can be *reduced* by parallelizing OOA. Besides, as is shown in the simulation results, the actual scheduling time in practice is almost linear. The explanation of this fact is that the modified algorithm [14] which is applied for searching Vop on current SL (in 4.3.) is a very good fit for this kind of searching.

The advantages of the proposed algorithm OOA are: (i) achieving a good balance of several conflicting optimization goals: minimum execution time, minimum communication costs, shortest response time; (ii) scheduling for a relatively short time; (iii) flexibility in application because scheduling is carried out in a general computing model, where there is no requirement for the system architecture; and finally, (iv) especially efficient for so-called Strictly-Heterogeneous systems, where either the jobs and the resources can be very different, even unrelated.

In future work, there are two ways by which we can decrease the solving time or increase the solution quality of the proposed algorithm OOA: (i) combine OOA with SA technique for creating a new algorithm that has less solving time while keeping the control of the solution quality so that it is acceptable; (ii) simplify the local optimization in OOA and add a simple optimization function for global optimization (e.g. by considering workload balance at the high level).

Acknowledgment

We would like to thank the anonymous reviewers for their very helpful comments that improved both the content and the presentation of this paper.

References

[1]   C. Berge, *Theorie des graphes et ses application*, Dunod, Paris, 1958.
[2]   J. Blazevicz, M. Drozdowski, G. Schmidt, and D. De Werra, "Scheduling independent multiprocessor tasks on a uniform k-processor system", *Journal of Parallel Computer* 20, pp. 15-28, 1994.
[3]   T. Bultan and C. Aykanat, "A new mapping heuristic based on mean field annealing", *Journal of Parallel and Distributed Computing*, Vol. 16, N4, December 1992.
[4]   T.L. Casavant and J.G. Kuhl, "A taxonomy of scheduling in general-purpose distributed computing systems", *IEEE Trans. Softw.Eng.14*, pp. 141-154, 1988.
[5]   K. Efe, "Heuristic models for task assignment scheduling in distributed systems", *IEEE Computer*, June 1982.
[6]   H. El-Rewini and T.G. Lewis, "Scheduling Parallel tasks onto Arbitrary Target Machines", *Journal of Par. and Distr. Com.*, Vol.9, pp. 138-153, 1990.
[7]   A. A. Elsadek and B.E Wells, "Heuristic model for task allocation in a heterogeneous distributed systems", *Proceeding of PDPTA'96*, California USA, Vol.2, pp. 659-671, August 1996.
[8]   R. F Freund, B.R.Carter, Daniel Watson, et al., "Generational Scheduling for Heterogeneous Computing Systems", *Proceeding of PDPTA'96*, California-USA, Vol.2, pp769-778, August 1996.
[9]   M.R. Garey and D.S. Johnson, *Computer and Intractability-A guide to the Theory of NP- completeness*, Freeman New York , 1979.
[10]   A. Kaufmann, *Introduction a la combinatorique en vue des aplications*, Dunod, Paris, 1968.
[11]   S. Kirkpatrick, C.D. Gelatt, and M.P. Vecchi, "Optimization by simulated annealing", *Journal of Science*, Vol.220, N.4589, May 1983.
[12]   X. Papadimitry, K. Stayglitsh, *Combinatory optimization, algorithm and complexity*, Moscow- Mir, 1985.
[13]   Hanh H. Pham and Valery Simonenko, "A new algorithm and simulation for task assignment in parallel distributed systems", *Proceeding of the 11th European Simulation Multiconference '96*, Budapest- Hungary, pp. 95-99, June 1996.
[14]   Hanh H. Pham and Valery Simonenko, "Adaptation of algorithms for Job-Resource Assignment in Heterogeneous Distributed Systems", *Proceeding of PDPTA'96*, California-USA, Vol.2, pp. 835-845, August 1996.
[15]   Riedl Reinhard and Richter Lutz, "Classification of Load Distribution Algorithms", *Proceeding of IEEE PDP'96*, pp. 404-413, 1996.
[16]   P.Shroff, D.W Watson, N.F. Flann, and R.F. Freund, "Genetic simulated annealing for scheduling data-dependent tasks in heterogeneous environments", *Proceeding of Heterogeneous Computing Workshop '96*, pp.98-104, April 1996.
[17]   M. Tan, J.K Antonio, et. al. , "Scheduling and data relocation for sequentially executed subtasks in a heterogeneous computing system", *Proceeding of Heterogeneous Computing Workshop '95*, pp109-120, 1995.
[18]   Salleh Shaharuddin et. al., "A Mean-field Annealing Model For Task Scheduling in Multi-processor Systems", *Proceedings of PDPTA'96*, California-USA, Vol.2, pp. 189-198, August 1996.
[19]   Shen S. Wu and David Sweeting, "Heuristic algorithms for task assignment and scheduling in a processor network", *Journal of Parallel Computing* 20, pp. 1-14, 1994.
[20]   Honbo Zhou, Scheduling DAGs on a Bounded number of Processors, *Proceedings of PDPTA'96*, Vol.2, pp. 823-834, August 1996.

Implications of I/O for Gang Scheduled Workloads

Walter Lee, Matthew Frank, Victor Lee, Kenneth Mackenzie, and Larry
Rudolph *

M.I.T. Laboratory for Computer Science
Cambridge, MA 02139, U.S.A.
{walt, mfrank, wklee, kenmac, rudolph}@lcs.mit.edu

Abstract. The job workloads of general-purpose multiprocessors usually include both compute-bound parallel jobs, which often require gang scheduling, as well as I/O-bound jobs, which require high CPU priority for the individual gang members of the job in order to achieve interactive response times. Our results indicate that an effective interactive multiprocessor scheduler must be *flexible* and tailor the priority, time quantum, and extent of gang scheduling to the individual needs of each job.

Flexible gang scheduling is required because of several weaknesses of traditional gang scheduling. In particular, we show that the response time of I/O-bound jobs suffers under traditional gang scheduling. In addition, we show that not all applications benefit equally from gang scheduling; most real applications can tolerate at least a small amount of scheduling skew without major performance degradation. Finally, we show that messaging statistics contain information about whether applications require gang scheduling. Taken together these results provide evidence that flexible gang scheduling is both necessary and feasible.

1 Introduction

While gang scheduling provides better performance than uncoordinated scheduling for compute-bound parallel jobs with frequent synchronization, it leads to poor performance of I/O-bound jobs that require short, high-priority bursts of processing. Rather than religiously following the gang scheduling paradigm, a scheduler for a parallel computer should be *flexible*, capable of delivering acceptable performance for both compute and I/O-bound jobs.

Uniprocessor schedulers assign I/O-bound jobs higher priority than compute-bound jobs in the hope of reducing the average response time and without decreasing the machine utilization. It is well known that scheduling shortest job first minimizes the average response time. Traditional multiprocessor gang schedulers, on the other hand, schedule jobs in a strict round-robin fashion and ensure

* This research is funded in part by ARPA contract # N00014-94-1-0985, in part by NSF Experimental Systems grant # MIP-9504399, in part by a NSF Presidential Young Investigator Award.

that each member of a gang be allocated a processor at the same time. The CPUs allocated to gang members that perform I/O often sit idle. The disks allocated to gang members I/O requests often sit idle until the member gets a chance to execute again.

In effect, the presence of I/O-bound jobs complicates scheduling decisions by exerting pressure on the system not to gang schedule. The pressure comes in two forms. The first comes from the opportunity to improve response time by interrupting gang scheduled, compute-bound jobs in order to execute a I/O-bound job. The second comes from the need to schedule fragmented cpu resources. These features of flexible gang scheduling motivate the need to find out how compute-bound jobs benefit from gang scheduling. We study this issue and show that many applications can in fact tolerate the nearly gang environments provided by a flexible gang scheduler.

The studies of both I/O-bound jobs and compute-bound jobs demonstrate that flexible gang scheduling can be an improvement over traditional gang scheduling. Central to the realization of a flexible gang scheduler is the ability to determine dynamically the level to which individual applications benefit from gang scheduling. We show how one can extract such information from raw messaging statistics.

Although gang scheduling improves the performance of many workloads, it conflicts with the goal of providing good response time for workloads containing I/O-bound applications. The results in this paper motivate the need to analyze the costs and benefits of gang scheduling each job by showing that gang scheduling jobs increase the response time of I/O-bound applications and by showing that some jobs benefit only marginally from a dedicated machine abstraction. In addition, we show that a scheduler can collect the necessary information for a cost-benefit analysis from raw messaging statistics.

The rest of the paper is organized as follows. Section 2 describes our experimental environment. Section 3 studies the impact of gang scheduling on I/O-bound applications. Section 4 studies the performance of compute-bound applications in near-gang scheduled environments. Section 5 explores the use of messaging statistics to aid scheduling decisions. Finally, Section 6 and Section 7 present related work and conclude, respectively.

2 Experimental Setup

In this section, we describe the experimental environment used in Sections 4 and 5. The environment also provides the basis for the more abstract simulation models used in Section 3. We provide information about the Fugu multiprocessor, the scheduler, and the multiprocessor simulator used by the experiments.

Fugu is an experimental, distributed-memory multiprocessor supporting both cache-coherent shared memory and fine-grain message passing communication mechanisms [13]. The applications studied in this paper use only the message-passing mechanism. Messages in Fugu have extremely low overhead, costing roughly 10 cycles to send and roughly 100 cycles to process a null active message via an interrupt. The Fugu operating system, Glaze, supports virtual memory, preemptive multiprogramming and user-level threads. The message system is novel in that messages received when a process is not scheduled are buffered by the operating system at an extra cost.

The Fugu scheduler is a distributed application organized as a two-level hierarchy with a global component and local, per-processor components. The cost of the global communication and computation is amortized by pre-computing a *round* of several time-slices of work which is then distributed to the local schedulers. Results for this paper employ a four-processor configuration running small workloads, so the cost of the global work is small and the round size is kept minimal. The scheduler uses an Ousterhout-style matrix coscheduling algorithm to assign work to processors. Jobs have fixed processor needs and are assigned to processors statically, one process per processor, at the time the jobs begin. Each job is marked with a *gang* bit that indicates to the scheduler whether constituent processes may independently yield their time-slices when they have no work to do.

Experiments are run on an instruction-level simulator of the Fugu multiprocessor. The simulator counts instructions, not strictly cycles. Since the scheduling issues we are interested in are orthogonal to any memory hierarchy issues, we believe instruction counts will give us the same qualitative results as cycle counts.

3   Gang Scheduling and I/O Jobs

In this section we study the implications of gang scheduling in the presence of I/O-bound jobs. We find that the requirements of gang scheduling lead to a tradeoff between disk utilization and cpu utilization. Traditional uniprocessor schedulers, based on multilevel feedback queues, manipulate job priorities to effectively overlap disk requests with processing. Because gang schedulers ignore information about job behavior, they make suboptimal choices which lead to slowdowns for both I/O-bound and compute-bound jobs.

Section 3.1 discusses a variety of ways in which gang scheduling can lead to poor I/O and cpu utilization. Section 3.2 demonstrates the tradeoffs that gang scheduling must make between I/O and compute-bound jobs. Our results suggest that gang schedulers require considerable information to make good decisions. Along with the priority information collected by traditional uniprocessor schedulers, a gang scheduler can benefit from knowledge about the coscheduling requirements of compute-bound jobs.

3.1   Costs of Gang Scheduling

The costs of gang scheduling can be divided into two categories, under-utilization of disk resources, which we call *priority inversion*, and under-utilization of cpu resources, which we call *cpu fragmentation*. Disk resources can best be utilized if processes of I/O-bound jobs are given priority to use the cpu whenever they

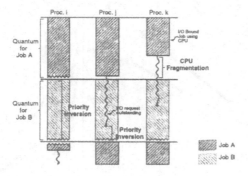

Fig. 1. Adverse effects of gang scheduling in the presence of I/O. In processor i (left), the process for job A reaches the end of its quantum before it is able to issue an I/O. The disk is left idle for the entire duration of the quantum for job B. In processor j (middle), an I/O request from job A finishes before the end of quantum B. The higher priority, I/O-bound process must wait till the end of job B's quantum. When job A makes a request before the end of its quantum (processor k, right), it leaves behind fragmented CPU resources.

are ready to run. This policy ensures that a process's next I/O request will come as soon as possible after the previous one finishes. Note that it is the thread or process, not the job, that makes an I/O request. When a job consists of multiple threads or processes, it is likely that only a subset of them will block on an I/O operation. Since gang schedulers schedule whole jobs, they cause priority inversion problems whenever they permit a compute-bound job to use the cpu while processes of an I/O-bound job is ready to run.

There are two different causes of priority inversion. Either the scheduling quantum length for an I/O-bound job can be set too short, or the scheduling quantum length for a compute-bound job can be set too long. The left hand side of Figure 1 demonstrates the first of these problems. Here, the quantum for job A, an I/O-bound job, ends shortly before process i of job A is ready to make an I/O request. The disk sits idle for the entirety of quantum B before job A is permitted to resume. If quantum A had been slightly longer, a disk access could have been overlapped with job B's computation.

A second form of priority inversion occurs when the scheduler sets the quantum length for a compute-bound job too long. This problem is shown in the middle part of Figure 1. In this case, process j of job A makes an I/O request. Shortly afterward, job A's quantum expires and the scheduler switches to running job B. When the I/O request finishes, the scheduler does not return to job A because job B's quantum has not yet finished. The time remaining in the quantum is devoted to the compute-bound job, which unnecessarily delays the occurrence of the next I/O operation from job A.

In contrast, the right hand side of Figure 1 demonstrates the cpu fragmentation problem that occurs when the quantum for an I/O-bound is too long. In this case process k of job A makes an I/O request considerably before the end

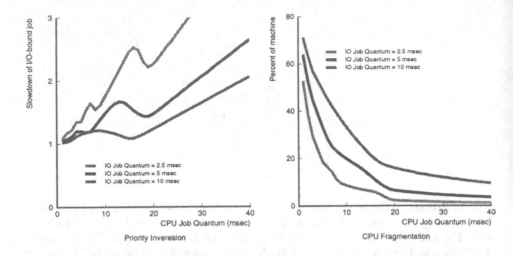

Fig. 2. Increasing the cpu-bound job's quantum length increases priority inversion but reduces cpu fragmentation. An I/O-bound job and a compute-bound job are scheduled against each other on a 32-processor, gang-scheduled machine. Each process of the I/O job uses the CPU for an average of 5 msec between making 20-msec I/O requests. Three experiments are shown, with the scheduler quanta for the I/O-bound job set to 2.5, 10, and 20 msec. The scheduler quanta for the compute-bound job is varied on the X axis for both graphs. The left graph plots the level of priority inversion, represented as a slowdown factor of the I/O-bound job as compared to running the job on a dedicated machine. The right graph plots the amount of cpu fragmentation as a percentage of the total available cpu resources.

of quantum A. Because job B requires gang scheduling, it is unable to make progress because the rest of the processors are still running processes of job A. Processor **k** remains idle until the beginning of quantum B.

The next subsection examines these issues quantitatively and finds that dealing with priority inversion requires that the quanta be allocated dynamically to suit the I/O requirements of the workload. A more flexible scheduling scheme can deal with the problems of priority inversion and resource fragmentation by allowing the characteristics of each job to drive the schedule.

3.2 I/O-CPU Utilization Tradeoffs

By varying the quantum length for different jobs, the effects discussed above can be observed. In particular, priority inversion, which causes poor disk utilization, occurs when either the quantum length for an I/O-bound job is too short or when the quantum length for a compute-bound job is too long. Cpu fragmentation, which causes poor cpu utilization, occurs when the quantum length of the I/O-bound job is too long.

Because a variable quantum policy requires considerably more flexibility than

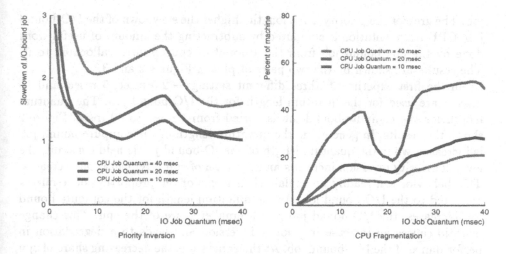

Fig. 3. Increasing the I/O-bound job's quantum length generally reduces priority inversion but increases cpu fragmentation. The workload parameters are identical to those in the last figure. Three experiments are shown, with the scheduler quanta for the compute-bound job set to 10, 20 and 40 msec. For both graphs, the scheduler quanta for the I/O-bound job is varied on the X axis. The left graph plots the slowdown of the I/O-bound job, which reflects the level of priority inversion; the right graph plots the amount of cpu fragmentation.

is traditionally available in gang schedulers, the experiments reported in this section were run on a simple event-driven simulator. The experiments consist of gang scheduling a synthetic I/O-bound job against a synthetic compute-bound job. Like a traditional gang scheduler, the scheduler in the experiments switches back and forth between the two jobs in a round-robin fashion; however, the quantum lengths for the two jobs are not required to be the same, and in fact they are varied across different runs of the experiment. When a process for the I/O-bound job is blocked on an I/O operation, its remaining time quantum is donated to the process of the cpu-bound job.

The I/O-bound job alternates between short bursts where it requires the cpu and I/O requests where it simply waits for a disk request to finish. Its cpu time is modeled by an Erlang-5 distribution, which resembles a normal distribution, with a mean of 5 msec. The latency of I/O requests is fixed at 20 msec. The compute-bound job makes no I/O requests, and it represents a job with heavy synchronization so that it makes progress only when all its processes are scheduled simultaneously.

We vary the gang scheduler quantum allocated to each of the two jobs, and we infer the level of priority inversion and cpu fragmentation by observing the slowdown for each job, defined to be the ratio of the run times of the job when it is run in the experimental environment versus when it is run in a dedicated machine. Priority inversion relates directly to the slowdown of the I/O-bound job. The greater the priority inversion, the higher the slowdown of the I/O-bound job. CPU fragmentation is computed by subtracting the amount of useful work done by the cpu-bound job from the amount of cpu resources allocated to it. The results are shown by the two pairs of plot in Figures 2 and 3.

In the first experiment, three different settings – 2.5 msec, 5 msec, and 10 msec – are used for the quantum length for the I/O-bound job. The quantum length for the compute-bound job is varied from 1 msec to 40 msec. Figure 2 shows the results. In general, as the quantum length of the compute-bound job is increased while the quantum length of the IO-bound job is held constant, the level of priority inversion increases and the level of cpu fragmentation decreases. This behavior can readily be explained in terms of the proportion of resources allocated to the I/O-bound job. As the quantum length for the compute-bound job increases, the I/O-bound job gets a smaller share of the cpu. This change in ratio causes an increase in priority inversion and leads to a degradation in performance of the I/O-bound job. At the same time, the decreasing share of cpu allocated to I/O-bound job reduces cpu fragmentation because fragmentation only occurs during the scheduling of I/O-bound jobs.

Most of the curves for both graphs in Figure 2 follow the monotonic trend expected from the explanation in the previous paragraph. The "waviness" in the priority inversion plot, as well as the bumps in the cpu fragmentation plot, are a result of the harmonics between the periodicity of the I/O-bound job (at a frequency of about 25 msec) and the scheduling quanta.

Figure 3 presents the result of the second experiment, where the quantum length of the I/O-bound job is varied from 1 msec to 40 msec while the quantum length for the compute-bound job is fixed at either 10 msec, 20 msec, or 40 msec. The general results can be explained as before. Increasing the quantum length for the I/O-bound job increases the share of cpu allocated to the I/O-bound job, which generally reduces priority inversion but increases cpu fragmentation. The deviation from this expectation, more prominent in this figure than in the previous one, comes from the harmonics between the periodicity of the I/O-bound job and the scheduling quanta.

Note that Figure 3 illustrates clearly the inherent tradeoff between the level of priority inversion and the amount of cpu fragmentation. In the regions where the level of priority inversion is low (namely, the 10 msec curve and the 20 msec curve with IO-job quantum length between 10-15 ms and 25-40 ms), the amount of cpu fragmentation is high.

3.3 Summary

Two lessons follow from these experiments. First, CPU fragmentation can be a significant effect, especially when one optimizes for the response time of IO-bound jobs. Second, proper quantum lengths depend on the characteristics of each job as well as the workload. In order to provide interactive response time, a multiprocessor scheduler needs to carefully monitor the requirements of each of its jobs and react accordingly. Today's gang schedulers lack this reactive capability, making them unsuitable for workloads containing I/O-bound jobs.

Even an adaptive quantum length is not sufficient to deal completely with the problems of priority inversion and cpu fragmentation. A more flexible scheduling policy is called for, where higher priority jobs can interrupt lower priority jobs in order to keep disk utilization high. In addition, the cpu fragmentation problem can be partially alleviated if compute-bound jobs can be scheduled into the fragmented slots.

Interrupting processes of a low priority job and scheduling them in fragmented slots will only be beneficial, however, if that job is amenable to scheduling skew. If a compute-bound parallel job synchronizes frequently, interrupting one of its processes may improve disk utilization only at the cost of a large drop in cpu utilization. The next section explores the issue of skew in more depth.

4 Application Performance in Near-Gang Scheduled Environments

The presence of I/O-bound jobs exerts pressure against perfectly gang scheduling compute-bound jobs. This pressure appears in two forms. The first comes from the opportunity to reduce priority inversion by interrupting gang scheduled, compute-bound jobs to run I/O-bound jobs. The second comes from the need to schedule fragmented cpu resources. Together, they motivate the desire to flexibly gang schedule, and they lead to two questions about compute-bound jobs which relate to the cost of flexible gang scheduling. The first question concerns how well parallel jobs tolerate interruptions. The second question considers how fragmented resources can be utilized by parallel jobs.

This section explores the degree to which compute-bound applications benefit from gang scheduling. The more a job benefits from gang scheduling, the less it can tolerate interruptions, and the less efficiently it can utilize non-gang, fragmented resources. Our goal is to identify characteristics of an application which relate to its degree of benefit from gang scheduling.

Many studies have measured the benefits of gang scheduling relative to un-coordinated scheduling [1, 3, 9, 17]. Our study differs in that we are interested in the *marginal* benefit of a pure gang scheduled environment when compared to a gang scheduled environment with disruptions.

In order to get a quantification tool, we measure the performance of applications under various near-gang scheduled environments on a four-processor machine. These environments are produced by introducing perturbations [2] to a fully ganged environment. We set up four environments, each with a different set of perturbation characteristics.

In two of the environments, Sub_{FX} and Sub_{RR}, each perturbation removes a quantum of processing time from a single processor. In Sub_{FX}, the processor

---

[2] We use the term *perturbation* to refer to both positive deviations (granting of additional resources) and negative deviations (revocation of originally allocated resources)

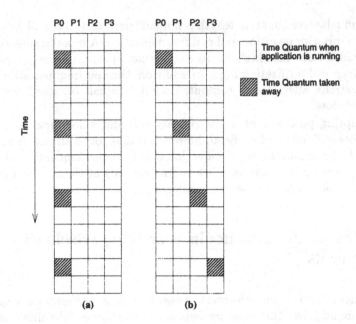

Fig. 4. Experimental setup for (a) fixed-processor takeaway and (b) round-robin take-away

is fixed. We call this experiment fixed-processor takeaway. In Sub_{RR}, the processor is selected in a round-robin fashion. We call this experiment round-robin takeaway. See Figure 4.

In environments Add_{FX} and Add_{RR}, each perturbation gives an extra time quantum of processing time to a single processor. In Add_{FX}, called fixed-processor giveaway, the processor is fixed. In Add_{RR}, called round-robin giveaway, the processor is selected by round-robin.

The exact times of the perturbations are randomly distributed across the run time of the application in batches of four. Within a batch of four, the time of the first perturbation determines the times for the other perturbations. A fixed interval of three time quanta separate perturbations within a batch. Perturbations are batched in closely spaced groups of fours so that round-robin perturbations maintain coarse-grain load balance.

Quantum size is fixed at 500,000 instructions across the runs.

The motivations for the setup of these environments are as follows. The takeaway experiments indicates how compute-bound jobs behave when some of their processes are interrupted by I/O-bound jobs. The giveaway experiments indicates whether compute-bound jobs can utilize fragmented cpu resources. The results of the fixed-processor experiments are compared with the results of the round-robin experiments to examine the issue of load balance.

We run each application under the four scheduling environments, and we compare the run time of each to the run time under perfect gang scheduling. The results are presented in two sections below, one for a set of synthetic ap-

Type	Num	Description	Parameter
Emp	1	Constituent processes work independently without communication.	—
Barrier	1	Consists entirely of synchronizing barriers.	—
Workpile	4	Consists of a fixed amount of global work broken into independent units of work. The units of work is distributed dynamically to maintain load balance under arbitrary scheduling conditions.	Granularity of work unit (14%-2400% of a quantum)
Msg	4	Phases of request/reply communication are separated by barriers. Requests are asynchronous, but all replies must be received before a process proceeds to the next phase.	Communication pattern

Table 1. Information on the synthetic applications used in the giveaway/takeaway experiments. Applications are grouped into four types. Each entry gives the name of the type of application, the number of applications in that type, a description of the type of applications, and the parameter whose value differs between different members of that type.

plications and one for a set of real applications, which includes three applications from the SPLASH benchmark suite. As expected, we find that for load balanced applications with fine grain synchronization, the perturbations effect applications significantly. Real applications, however, exhibit internal algorithmic load-imbalance and are often somewhat latency tolerant. Because of these factors, the effects of perturbations on these applications are between a factor two and four smaller on a four-processor machine.

4.1 Synthetic Applications

Table 1 describes the set of synthetic applications used in this experiment. Based on the experimental results, each application can be classified as one of three types. Figure 5 presents the characteristic plots of the three types of applications. Each line on the graph plots the number of perturbations versus the change in run time for an environment. We have plotted the lines for all four experiments on the same graph. The three types of applications are:

i. **Synchronization intensive** This type of applications makes little progress unless it is being gang scheduled. When time quanta are taken away from a processor, all other processors stall as well. The entire application slows by the amount of time taken away. When time quanta are given to a processor, the processor stalls also, so the application receives no benefit from the extra time at all. *Barrier* and all of the *Msg* applications fall into this category.

ii. **Embarrassingly parallel** This type of applications exhibits the same poor behavior as synchronization intensive applications when time is given to or taken away from a single processor. However, the behavior is caused not

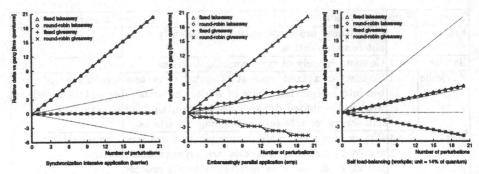

Fig. 5. Characteristic plots from giveaway-takeaway experiment for three types of applications. The actual application from which each plot is taken is listed in parenthesis below the plot. The four dotted lines are reference lines representing total cpu time taken away (worst case slowdown), 1/4 (1/P) of time taken away (best case slowdown), zero (worst case speedup), and -1/4 of time given away (best case speedup).

by synchronization but by load imbalance. In the round-robin experiments, where load balance is maintained, application of this type performs much better. When time quanta are taken away round-robin, run time degrades by 1/P quantum (here, P=4) per quantum taken away. The factor of 1/P arises because the single quantum of lost processing time is jointly recovered by the P processors. Similarly, when extra quanta are given to the job round-robin, run time improves by 1/P. *Emp* and coarse-grain *Workpile* (work unit = 24 time quanta) belong in this category.

iii. **Self load-balancing** This type of applications performs optimally under all scheduling conditions, because it suffers from neither synchronization nor load imbalances. Performance degrades by 1/P quantum per quantum taken away, and it improves by 1/P quantum per quantum given away. Three of the four *Workpile* applications fall into this category. Their granularity of work unit ranges from 14% of a time quantum to 240%.

Each class of applications above may also be identified by their minimum scheduling requirements. Synchronization intensive applications require gang scheduling. Embarrassingly parallel applications require fair scheduling of the constituent processes. We call this scheduling criteria *interprocess fairness*. Self load-balancing applications can utilize any processor resource; they have no requirement at all.

Of course, applications from real life will not fit cleanly into one of the above classes. An application with a moderate but nontrivial synchronization rate, for example, will have behavior which falls somewhere between that of a synchronization intensive application and an embarrassingly parallel application. Similarly, workpile-like applications with limited load-balancing mechanism will have behavior which falls somewhere between that of an embarrassingly parallel application and a self-scheduling application. We can indeed run the experi-

App.	Quanta/Barrier	Type Msgs	Msgs/Proc/Quantum
Enum	50	Non-blocking	254
Water	10	Blocking	12
LU	10	Blocking	3
Barnes	50	Blocking	28

Table 2. Characteristics of the real applications

ments with more exhaustive sets of parameter values to quantify some of these effects, but such studies have been done before before [6, 9, 18], and here we are more interested in the qualitative difference in behavior at extreme ends of the application spectrum.

4.2 Real Applications

The takeaway/giveaway experiments are applied to four real applications as well. One, *Enum*, finds the total number of solutions to the triangle puzzle (a simple board game) by enumerating all possibilities breadth-first. The other three, *Barnes*, *Water*, and *LU*, are scientific applications from the Splash benchmark suite implemented using CRL, an all-software shared-memory system [12]. See Table 2 for statistics describing the applications. Because the applications are non-homogeneous in time, we obtain each data point by taking the average result from 20 runs, each with a different set of time quanta given or taken away. Because the applications are also non-homogeneous across processors, we run the fixed processor takeaway experiment on processors 0, 1, and 3.

Figures 6-9 show the results of the experiments. To better understand the applications for the purpose of explaining the results, we obtain a trace for each application run under gang scheduling, and we plot the progress made on each processor versus time. These traces are presented next to the experimental results. Because the progress plot for *Water* follows such a regular pattern, only a magnified subsection is presented.

Enum Of the four sets of results, *Enum* stands out by itself. Its experimental plot closely resembles that of an embarrassingly parallel application. In reality, *Enum* has three characteristics which make it embarrassingly parallel:

- It is load balanced, as suggested by its progress plot.
- It has infrequent barrier synchronization (compared to the length of a time quantum).
- It communicates with non-blocking messages.

The results for *Enum* are actually consistently worse than that of a perfect embarrassingly parallel application for three reasons. First, even in the absence of synchronization, failure to gang schedule incurs overhead in the form buffering

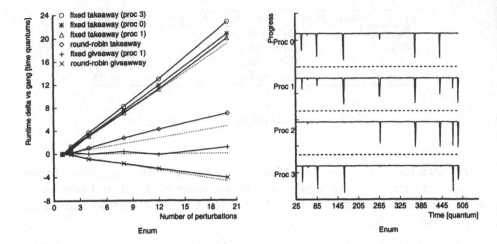

Fig. 6. Experimental plot (left) and progress plot under gang scheduling (right) for *Enum*. Note that in the experimental plot, each line starts at perturbation = 1. The four dotted lines are reference lines representing time taken away (worst case slowdown), 1/4 of time taken away (best case slowdown), zero (worst case speedup), and -1/4 of time given away (best case speedup).

cost in our system. At about 250 instructions per buffered message, this overhead can be up to three quanta when 20 quanta are taken away. Note that this cost is smaller for the quantum giveaway experiments because the buffer overhead is spread over P-1 processors.

Second, as load balanced as any real application can expect to be, *Enum* still has some load imbalances. The effect of imbalances on run time is evident by comparing the run time of the takeaway experiment from processor 3 with the run time of the takeaway experiments from processors 0 and 1. Processor 3 is the bottleneck processor for over 60% of the application (as evident by the lack of valleys in much of the progress graph). As a result, taking away time from processor 3 results in a slower run time than taking away time from processor 0 or 1.

Finally, for the round-robin experiments, the benefit from maintaining interprocess fairness is lost if a barrier interrupts a set of round-robin perturbations. Consequently, the slowdown is noticeably higher than the expected 25% of the time taken away.

Water, LU, and Barnes The results for *Water*, *LU*, and *Barnes* are similar. Because these applications exhibit significant load imbalances (as seen by the deep and long valleys in their progress plots), their results do not directly resemble that of any of the synthetic applications. In fact, load imbalance and blocking messages are two common features which explain most of the results for these applications.

In the fixed-processor quantum takeaway experiments, the amount by which

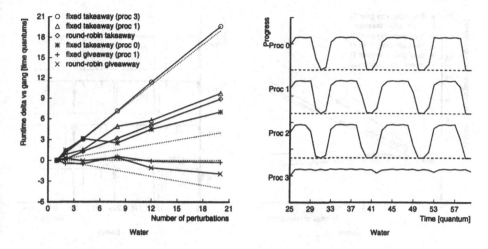

Fig. 7. Experimental plot (left) and progress plot under gang scheduling (right) for *Water*.

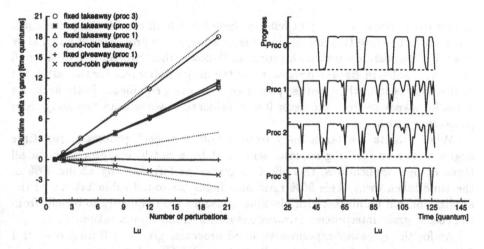

Fig. 8. Experimental plot (left) and progress plot under gang scheduling (right) for *LU*.

the application slows down depends largely on the degree to which the processor taken away is a bottleneck. In the progress plot, a processor bottleneck is marked by full progress (absence of a valley) at a time when one or more processors are not making progress (valleys). For *Water*, processor 3 is the clear bottleneck, so taking away cpu time from processor 3 slows down the application by 100% of the time taken away. For *LU*, processors 0 and 3 alternate as bottlenecks. However, when processor 0 is the bottleneck, it is only slightly behind the other processors. So any other processor with time taken away readily overtakes processor 0's role

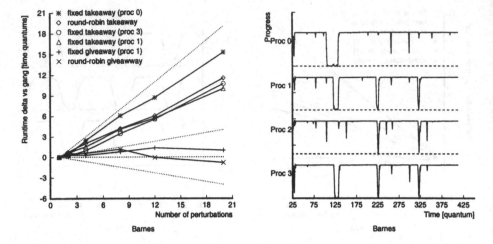

Fig. 9. Experimental plot (left) and progress plot under gang scheduling (right) for *Barnes*.

as half the bottleneck. The plot reflects these bottleneck conditions: processor 3 slows down by close to 100% of time taken away, while processors 0 and 1 slow down by considerably less, with processor 0 slower than processor 1 by a small amount. Finally, in *Barnes*, processor 0 is the major bottleneck for the latter 2/3 of the application, while neither processor 1 or 3 is a significant bottleneck. As a result, takeaway from processor 0 is considerably worse than takeaway from processors 1 or 3.

When quanta are taken away from a non-bottleneck processor, run time degrades due to blocking requests sent to it by a bottleneck processor. In all three of our applications, this effect degrades performance by about 50% of the time taken away. This 50% ratio also holds for round-robin takeaway: the application communicates with blocking messages too frequently to benefit from the coarse grain interprocess fairness ensured by round-robin takeaway.

As for the giveaway experiments, fixed processor giveaway from processor 1 fails to improve performance for all three applications because processor 1 is not the bottleneck processor. Round-robin giveaway improves performance of *Water* and *LU* because time is given to the bottleneck processor and the rate of blocking request is low. On the other hand, round-robin giveaway fails to improve performance of *Barnes* due to the application's high rate of blocking requests.

4.3 Summary

We summarize the results of the experiments with several observations and conclusions.

Synchronization intensive applications reap full benefits from gang scheduling and in fact require it for good performance. Embarrassingly parallel applications and self load-balancing applications, on the other hand, do not benefit from gang scheduling. Note that the volume of communication is an orthogonal issue. *Enum* is an example of a real embarrassingly parallel application, even though it communicates a lot.

Load imbalance is a common application characteristic in practice. Enforcing gang scheduling on applications with this characteristic hurts machine utilization.

Many real applications can tolerate at least a small amount of perturbations in a gang scheduling environment. Load imbalanced applications are tolerant of perturbations if they are not occurring at the bottleneck processors. And all applications that we studied are tolerant to round-robin perturbations. Even the inherently load-imbalanced CRL applications slow down by only 50-60% of the time taken away by the round-robin disturbances. This is because round-robin perturbations do not introduce severe artificial load imbalances.

For applications without self load-balancing, two characteristics primarily determine how they behave under various scheduling conditions. The characteristics are the level of load imbalances and the volume of blocking communication. Total volume of communication is a second order effect.

To avoid scheduler-induced load imbalances, interprocess fairness is a good criteria to keep in mind when a gang scheduler does alternate scheduling. The failure to do so could be a reason why research has found that random alternate scheduling provides little gain to system throughput [17].

To first order, there are two types of blocking communication. One is the barrier-like communication used to check that processes have all reached a checkpoint. The other type is the request/reply-type message, where one process is trying to obtain information which can be readily provided by another.[3]

The two types of communication have different scheduling characteristics. Wait time for barrier is affected by load imbalances. To minimize this wait time, it is more important to minimize the load imbalances than it is to gang schedule. Wait time for request/reply, on the other hand, depends on whether the sender and receiver are scheduled simultaneously. This wait time can only be minimized by gang scheduling the sender/receiver pair.

5 Runtime Identification of Gangedness

Section 3 illustrates the benefits of flexible gang scheduling derived from not being required to gang schedule compute-bound jobs. Section 4 shows that the costs of relaxing gang scheduling varies between applications. Together, they suggest that a scheduler can benefit from identifying the *gangedness* of each application, defined to be the level to which the application benefits from gang scheduling. Jobs with high gangedness indicate both a low tolerance of interruptions and

---

[3] We can also have blocking communication where the receiver is blocked instead of the sender. A processor blocks waiting for an incoming message containing the information it requires. But there is no fundamental difference between that and request/reply: it's like request/reply done with "polling."

the inability to utilize fragmented cpu resources, while jobs with low gangedness can be scheduled much more flexibly to improve overall system performance.

In this section, we consider how gangedness can be determined from coarse-grain messaging statistics.

5.1 Information Content of Message Arrival Times

To relate messaging statistics to gangedness, we look at the high level information contained in message arrival times, and we try to find a relationship between that information and gangedness.

First, messages contain information about synchronization, because they are the medium through which synchronization is implemented. And synchronization relates directly to gangedness. Unfortunately, messages don't necessarily synchronize, and there is no way of distinguishing synchronizing messages from non-synchronizing ones.

Alternatively, message arrival times contain information about the state of a process. A process can send a message only if it is not blocked, or in other words, if the process is making forward progress. To relate gangedness to progress, a high gangedness means that an application must be gang scheduled in order to make forward progress.

5.2 Experiment

We test our intuition on the relationship between message counts and gangedness with the following experiment. For each of the real applications described in Subsection 4.2, we run it in the fixed-processor takeaway environment described in Section 4. The environment is suitable because it contains both gang scheduled quanta and non-gang scheduled quanta. Any of the four environments in Section 4 could have been used for this purpose, and we do not expect the choice of environment to effect the conclusions we draw.

For every processor-quantum unit, we collect the number of messages received and the amount of progress made. These statistics are used to generate four pairs of values per quantum, one pair for each processor. In the pair of values, we associate the number of messages received by a processor to the amount of progress made by all *other* processors. This association corresponds to the intuition that the number of messages received should correlate with the amount of progress made by the senders of the messages.

Within this scheduling environment, we distinguish between three sets of data values. *Gang-all* is the set of values collected on ganged, undisturbed quanta. *Non-Gang-running* is the set of values collected on the running processors in non-ganged, disturbed quanta. Finally, *Non-Gang-non-running* is the set of values collected on the non-running processors in non-ganged, disturbed quanta.

To collect enough data values for all three sets, we run the experiment five times. Table 3 summarizes the results. Each row gives the average and standard deviation of message count per quantum as well as the average and standard deviation of progress per quantum.

Description	Msg Avg	Msg SD	Prog Avg	Prog SD
Enum				
Gang-all	247.73	47.51	1483678	209519
Non-Gang-running	162.29	60.21	882735	307236
Non-Gang-non-running	242.30	88.57	1324103	459779
Water				
Gang-all	15.41	19.63	1127732	485835
Non-Gang-running	2.54	3.40	479135	387983
Non-Gang-non-running	1.17	0.70	718703	554749
LU				
Gang-all	2.85	3.19	1242051	397927
Non-Gang-running	1.40	1.82	740624	313568
Non-Gang-non-running	0.89	0.73	1110937	421677
Barnes				
Gang-all	28.44	56.99	1436370	282763
Non-Gang-running	2.53	3.00	507318	300674
Non-Gang-non-running	1.80	0.78	760978	389349

Table 3. Aggregate statistics for correlation experiment in non-gang environment. Each row gives the average and standard deviation of message count, and the average and standard deviation of sender progress.

The progress data are consistent with the characteristics of the applications. *Enum* uses infrequent barriers and non-blocking messages, so it can make progress without gang scheduling. As expected, the experiment shows that sender progress for *gang-all* and *non-gang-running* are roughly within 10% of each other (1483678 vs. 1324103). The sender progress for *non-gang-non-running* is lower than that of *gang-all* and *non-gang-running*, but that only reflects the fact it has one less sender than the other data values; normalizing these values with the number of senders would yield the expected nearly identical values.

Water, *LU*, and *Barnes* all have infrequent barriers, but they use blocking messages. The rate of messages then determines how much progress an application can make in a non-gang time quantum. [4] *LU* has the lowest message rate, so low that it in fact runs quite well in non-gang quanta. *Barnes* and *Water*, on the other hand, have message rates which are high enough to cause their performance to degrade in non-gang quanta, with *Barnes*'s higher rate yielding a more severe degradation.

Figure 10 plots the range of number of messages received for each application in both gang quanta and non-gang quanta. To obviate the need to normalize all the values by the number of sender processors, for the non-gang quanta we

---

[4] As Section 4 shows, the issue of load balance is an important consideration as well. Frequency of barriers and blocking messages determines the level of progress that can be made in non-gang environments. Level of load balance determines whether such progress is ultimately *useful*, *i.e.*, whether it reduces the run time of the application.

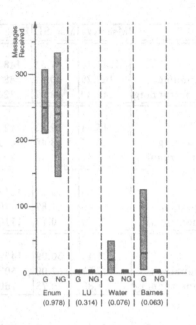

Fig. 10. Number of messages received per quantum per processor for each application in gang quanta (G) and non-gang quanta (NG). Each bar represents the 90% confidence interval; the thick line within the bar marks the average message count. Each number in parenthesis below the application name shows the ratio of the average message counts between the non-gang and the gang quanta.

use data from *non-gang-non-running*, which has the same number of sender processors as *gang-all*.

The results confirm our intuition. *Enum* is the only application which uses non-blocking messages. Therefore, it is the only application which can sustain a high volume of communication in non-gang quanta. As stated in Subsection 5.1, this run-time observation allows one to conclude that the application has low gangedness and does not require gang scheduling. On the other hand, *Water*, *LU*, and *Barnes* all use blocking messages, so their volume of communication during non-gang quanta is low. One cannot, however, draw any conclusion about gangedness from this lack of communication: applications can be making progress without sending any message.

Rather than using message count of non-gang quanta, a more robust way to determine the gangedness of an application is to use its ratio of message counts between non-gang and gang quanta. A high ratio corresponds to low gangedness, while a low ratio corresponds to high gangedness. As shown in Figure 10, ordering the applications by ratio corresponds exactly to reverse-ordering the applications by gangedness. Moreover, the ratios for applications with low gangedness (*Enum* and *LU*) are at least a factor of five larger than the ratios for applications with high gangedness (*Water* and *Barnes*). This sizable difference makes it easy to accurately categorize the applications into a high gangedness class and a low gangedness class simply based on their message ratios.

5.3 Summary

We summarize what we learn about the relationships between message count, progress, and gangedness. Message count relates to progress in the following way. High message count always implies progress. Low message count, on the other hand, can arise because the application is not sending any message, so it does not necessarily imply a lack of progress.

As for the relationship between message count and gangedness, a high message count while an application is not gang scheduled shows that an application can make progress without gang scheduling. It thus indicates a low gangedness. More generally, one can compare the average message counts between non-gang and gang environments to determine the gangedness of the application. A high ratio of non-gang message count to gang message count corresponds to low gangedness, while a low ratio corresponds to high gangedness.

Note that our conclusion is somewhat counterintuitive to conventional thinking. Conventional thinking has the notion that the more an application makes use of communication resources, the greater the need for the application to be gang scheduled. In fact, Sobalvarro [17] bases his dynamic coscheduling scheme directly on this principle, as he achieves coscheduling behavior by taking each incoming message as a cue to schedule the addressed process. We argue that if a processor continues to receive messages for an unscheduled process, the sending processes must be making progress under the status quo, and no scheduler intervention is necessary.

6 Related Work

Multiprocessors can be shared by partitioning in space, in time, or both. Much work has been done to explore and compare the various options [7]. Space-sharing can be very efficient for compute-bound applications and is desirable when permitted by the programming model and application characteristics [3, 11]. Time-sharing remains desirable for flexibility in debugging and in interleaving I/O with computation. These considerations become more important as multiprocessors become more mainstream.

Ousterhout introduced the idea of coscheduling or gang scheduling to improve the performance of parallel applications under timesharing [15]. There are two benefits to gang scheduling. First, from a programmability standpoint, gang scheduling is attractive because it is compatible with conventional programming models, where processes of a parallel application are assumed to be scheduled simultaneously. This feature simplifies reasoning about performance issues as well as correctness issues like deadlock and livelock. Second, from a performance standpoint, gang scheduling is absolutely necessary for applications that synchronize frequently.

Several studies have quantified the benefits of gang scheduling [1, 3, 9]. Feitelson and Rudolph [9] demonstrate that gang scheduling benefits applications that perform fine-grain synchronization. Arpaci *et al* [1] and Mraz [14] observe that the disruption of system daemons in a network of workstation is potentially intolerable without some efforts to synchronize gangs across processors. Our study confirms these observations and draws detailed conclusions about the causes of slowdown for specific applications.

There are costs to gang scheduling as well. Much literature focuses on its cost of implementation [2, 8, 17, 19]. This cost comes about because gang scheduling requires global coordination and centralized scheduling. The implementation of our scheduler uses a two level distributed hierarchical control structure for efficiency similar to Distributed Hierarchical Control [8, 19]. But even in a system where these features come for free, gang scheduling still has costs which make its universal use undesirable. Our study shows the degradation of response time due to a form of priority inversion. Other effects degrade utilization, for instance by losses due to constraints on the packing of jobs into the global schedule and by the inability to recover wasted time in a job with load imbalance. An ideal scheduler would perform a cost-benefit analysis which gives proper weights to all the issues above.

Studies have pointed out that parallel scientific applications may consist of a significant amount of I/O activities due to reading and writing of results [4, 5]. I/O activities may also come from paging activities, and Wang [20] notices that even for programs written with a SPMD programming model, there is little coordination of I/O across processing nodes because of data dependencies. This behavior is consistent with our assumption in the experiments that I/O activities across the processing nodes are independent.

In our work, we assume that the members of the job are known *a priori* and concentrate on the problem of deciding whether to gang schedule based on indirect measurements. A fully dynamic solution to gang scheduling includes the identification of gang members at run-time. Sobalvarro [17] uses individual message arrivals as cues to the identification of a gang, while Feitelson and Rudolph [10] monitor the rate at which shared communication objects are being accessed to determine whether and which processes need to be ganged.

Given the processes that make up each job, our system monitors communication rate between job members to identify those jobs that require coscheduling versus those jobs that can tolerate having their processes individually scheduled. In this respect our scheduler differs from both the Meiko CS-2 [16], and SGI IRIX [2] schedulers.

7 Conclusion

We summarize the results presented in this paper. First, traditional gang scheduling hurts workloads containing I/O. Second, interrupting ganged, compute-bound jobs can benefit workloads. Third, one needs to schedule fragmented cpu resources intelligently, by selecting jobs with low gangedness to run in those spaces, and by preserving interprocess fairness. Finally, message statistics can identify the gangedness of applications.

We envision a scheduling strategy flexible enough to accommodate all jobs. I/O-bound jobs can have either coordinated I/O or uncoordinated I/O. Compute bound jobs may either be perturbation-friendly or perturbation-sensitive. Scheduling would be done in two sets of rounds. Uncoordinated I/O-bound jobs and perturbation-friendly compute-bound jobs are scheduled in rounds with loose coordination. Coordinated I/O-bound jobs and perturbation-sensitive compute-bound jobs can be scheduled in rounds with strict coordination.

At the very high level, we demonstrate that a flexible gang scheduler is both necessary and possible.

References

1. R. Arpaci, A. Dusseau, A. Vahdat, L. Liu, T. Anderson, and D. Patterson. The Interaction of Parallel and Sequential Workloads on a Network of Workstations. In *Proceedings of Sigmetrics/Performance '95*, pages 267–278, May 1995.

2. J. M. Barton and N. Bitar. A Scalable Multi-Discipline, Multiple-Processor Scheduling Framework for IRIX. In *Lecture Notes in Computer Science, 949*, pages 45–69, Santa Barbara, 1995. Springer Verlag. Workshop on Parallel Job Scheduling, IPPS '95.

3. M. Crovella, P. Das, C. Dubnicki, T. LeBlanc, and E. Markatos. Multiprogramming on Multiprocessors. In *Proceedings of the third IEEE Symposium on Parallel and Distributed Processing*, 1991.

4. R. Cypher, S. Konstantinidou, A. Ho, and P. Messina. A Quantitative Study of Parallel Scientific Applications with Explicit Communication. In *The Journal of Supercomputing*, pages 5–24, January 1996.

5. J. M. del Rosario and A. Choudhary. High Performance I/O for Parallel Computers: Problems and Prospects. In *IEEE Computers, vol. 27, no. 3*, pages 59–68, 1994.

6. A. Dusseau, R. Arpaci, , and D. Culler. Effective Distributed Scheduling of Parallel Workloads. In *Proceedings of ACM SIGMETRICS 1996*, Philadelphia, May 1996. ACM.

7. D. G. Feitelson. A Survey of Scheduling in Multiprogrammed Parallel Systems. Technical Report IBM/RC 19790(87657), IBM, October 1994.

8. D. G. Feitelson and L. Rudolph. Distributed Hierarchical Control for Parallel Processing. In *Computer*. IEEE, May 1990.

9. D. G. Feitelson and L. Rudolph. Gang Scheduling Performance Benefits for Fine-Grain Synchronization. In *Journal of Parallel and Distributed Computing*, pages 306–318, December 1992.

10. D. G. Feitelson and L. Rudolph. Coscheduling Based on Runtime Identification of Activity Working Sets. In *International Journal of Parallel Programming*, pages 135–160, April 1995.

11. A. Gupta, A. Tucker, and L. Stevens. The Impact of Operating System Scheduling Policies and Synchronization Methods of the Performance of Parallel Applications. In *Proceedings of 1991 ACM Sigmetrics Conference*, 1991.

12. K. L. Johnson, M. F. Kaashoek, and D. A. Wallach. CRL: High-Performance All-Software Distributed Shared Memory. In *Proceedings of the 15th ACM Symposium on Operating Systems Principles*, December 1995.
13. K. Mackenzie, J. Kubiatowicz, M. Frank, W. Lee, V. Lee, A. Agarwal, and M. F. Kaashoek. UDM: User Direct Messaging for General-Purpose Multiprocessing. Technical Memo MIT/LCS/TM-556, March 1996.
14. R. Mraz. Reducing the Variance of Point-to-Point Transfers for Parallel Real-Time Programs. In *IEEE Parallel & Distributed Technology*, 1994.
15. J. K. Ousterhout. Scheduling Techniques for Concurrent Systems. In *3rd International Conference on Distributed Computing Systems*, pages 22–30, 1982.
16. K. E. Schauser and C. J. Scheiman. Experience with Active Messages on the Meiko CS-2. In *Proceedings of the 9th International Symposium on Parallel Processing*, 1995.
17. P. G. Sobalvarro and W. E. Weihl. Demand-based Coscheduling of Parallel Jobs on Multiprogrammed Multiprocessors. In *Lecture Notes in Computer Science, 949*, pages 106–126, Santa Barbara, 1995. Springer Verlag. Workshop on Parallel Job Scheduling, IPPS '95.
18. A. Tucker and A. Gupta. Process Control and Scheduling Issues for Multiprogrammed Shared-Memory Multiprocessors. In *Proceedings of the 12th ACM Symposium on Operating System Principles (SOSP-12)*, pages 159–166, December 1989.
19. F. Wang, H. Franke, M. Papaefthymiou, P. Pattnaik, L. Rudolph, and M. S. Squillante. A Gang Scheduling Design for Multiprogrammed Parallel Computing Environments. In *Lecture Notes in Computer Science, 1162*, pages 111–125, Honolulu,Hawaii, 1996. Springer Verlag. Workshop on Parallel Job Scheduling, IPPS '96.
20. K. Y. Wang and D. C. Marinescu. Correlation of the Paging Activity of the Individual Node Programs in the SPMD Execution Mode. In *Proceedings of the Hawaii International Conference on System Sciences*, 1995.

Improved Utilization and Responsiveness with Gang Scheduling

Dror G. Feitelson[1] and Morris A. Jette[2]

[1] Institute of Computer Science
The Hebrew University of Jerusalem
91904 Jerusalem, Israel
feit@cs.huji.ac.il
[2] Livermore Computing
Lawrence Livermore National Laboratory
Livermore, CA 94550
jette@llnl.gov

Abstract. Most commercial multicomputers use space-slicing schemes in which each scheduling decision has an unknown impact on the future: should a job be scheduled, risking that it will block other larger jobs later, or should the processors be left idle for now in anticipation of future arrivals? This dilemma is solved by using gang scheduling, because then the impact of each decision is limited to its time slice, and future arrivals can be accommodated in other time slices. This added flexibility is shown to improve overall system utilization and responsiveness. Empirical evidence from using gang scheduling on a Cray T3D installed at Lawrence Livermore National Lab corroborates these results, and shows conclusively that gang scheduling can be very effective with current technology.

1 Introduction

As parallel computers become more popular, there is a growing need for good schedulers that will manage these expensive shared resources. And indeed, many scheduling schemes have been designed, evaluated, and implemented in recent years [5,10].

Many papers investigate scheduling schemes from a system point of view, asking what the system can do to improve utilization and response time, but disregarding the effect on the user. As a result they sometimes advocate solutions that require users to depart from common practice, e.g. to write applications in a style that supports dynamic partitioning (i.e. the allocation may change at runtime) [30,20], rather than the prevalent SPMD style.

We take a different approach, and ask what the system can do given the constraint that users require jobs to execute on a fixed number of processors (as in SPMD). Within this framework, we compare variable partitioning, possibly with reordering of the jobs in the queue, with gang scheduling. We show that although gang scheduling suffers from more overhead than variable partitioning, it can lead to significant improvements due to its added flexibility. Indeed, gang scheduling can actually give better service (reduced response time) *and* improved utilization, so using it leads to a win-win situation relative to variable partitioning.

The results agree with actual experience on the LLNL Cray T3D, which employs a home-grown gang scheduler [12,17] (the original system software uses variable partitioning). When this scheduler was ported to the new Cray machine, utilization nearly doubled from 33.4% to 60.9% on average. Additional tuning has led to weekly utilizations that top 96%.

2 Approaches to Scheduling Jobs of Given Size

The schedulers of most commercial parallel systems use variable partitioning. The user specifies the number of processors to use at the time of submitting the job. The scheduler than carves out a partition of the required size, and dedicates it to the job for the duration of its execution. If the required number of processors is not available, the job is either rejected or queued. In most systems a time limit is also imposed, and if the job exceeds it it is killed.

The problem with this scheme is that scheduling decisions have a potentially large, persistent, and unpredictable impact on the future. Specifically, when a new job arrives, the system is faced with the following dilemma:

- if the new job can be accommodated, then scheduling it immediately will utilize unused resources, so it is good.
- however, if this job runs for a long time, and will block other jobs in the future, it may lead to more future loss than current gain. So maybe it should be left aside.

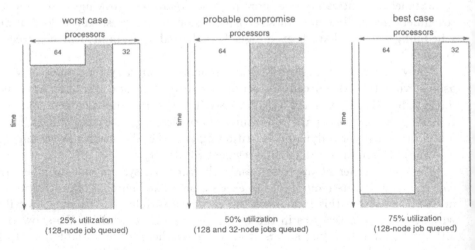

Fig. 1. *Example of the problems faced by variable partitioning.*

Consider the following simple case as an example (Fig. 1): a 128-node system is currently running a 64-node job, and there are a 32-node job and a 128-node job in the queue. The question is, should the 32-node job be scheduled to run concurrently with the 64-node job? Two outcomes are possible. If the 32-node job is scheduled and it terminates before the 64-node job, resource utilization is improved from 50% possibly up to 75%. But if the 64-node job terminates soon after the 32-node job is scheduled, and the 32-node job runs for a long time, the utilization drops from 50% to 25%. And, in order not to starve the 128-node job, it might be necessary to just let the 64-node job run to completion, and settle for 50% utilization.

As the future is usually unknown, there is no solution to this dilemma, and any decision may lead to fragmentation. Thus using variable partitioning may lead to significant loss of computing power [18,33], either because jobs do not fit together, or because processors are intentionally left idle in anticipation of future arrivals [26].

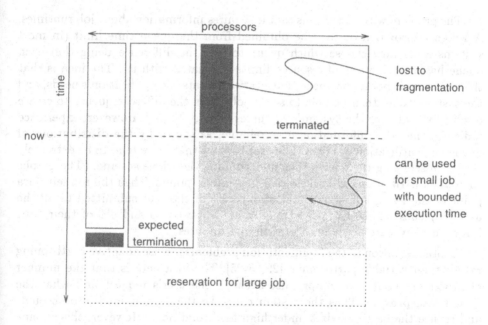

Fig. 2. *Runtime bounds on executing jobs allow reservations to be made for large jobs and then backfilling with smaller jobs to reduce fragmentation.*

The most common solution is to reorder the jobs in the queue so as to pack them more tightly [16]. One promising approach is to allow small jobs to move forward in the queue if they can be scheduled immediately. However, this may cause starvation of large jobs, so it is typically combined with allowing large jobs to make reservations of processors for some future time. Only *short* jobs are then allowed to move ahead in the queue (Fig. 2) [3,19].

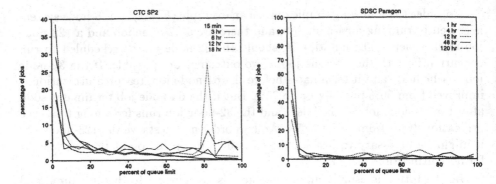

Fig. 3. *Job runtimes as a fraction of the batch queue time limit, showing that most jobs use only a fraction of the time limit, even for queues with very long limits. The plot for each queue limit is normalized independently.*

The problem with this idea is that it requires information about job runtimes. A rough approximation may be obtained from the queue time limit (in most systems users may choose which queue to use, the difference being that each queue has a distinct set of resource limits associated with it). The idea is that the user would choose the queue that best represents the application's needs, and the system would then be able to select jobs from the different queues to create a job mix that uses the system's resources effectively [31]. However, experience indicates that this information is unreliable, as shown by the distributions of queue-time utilization in Fig. 3. The graphs show that users tend to be extremely sloppy in selecting the queue, thus undermining the whole scheme. (The graphs show the distributions in buckets of 4 percentage points. Thus the top left data point in the left graph shows that about 38% of the jobs submitted to all the 3-hour queues on the Cornell SP2 only used between 0 and 4% of their time limit, i.e. they were actually shorter than 7 minutes.)

Another solution to the fragmentation problem is to use adaptive partitioning rather than variable partitioning [29,28,25]. The idea here is that the number of processors used is a compromise between the user's request and what the system can provide. Thus the system can take the current load into account, and reduce the partition sizes under high load conditions. However, this scheme also requires a change of user interfaces, albeit much less disruptive than dynamic partitioning.

The preferred solution is to use gang scheduling [22,7,8,27]. With gang scheduling, jobs receive the number of processors requested, but only for a limited time quantum. Then a "multi-context-switch" is performed on all the processors at once, and another job (or set of jobs) is scheduled instead. Thus all jobs can execute concurrently using time slicing, as in conventional uniprocessors. As a result, a scheduling decision only impacts the scheduling slot to which it pertains; other slots are available to handle other jobs and future arrivals. This adds flexibility and boosts performance.

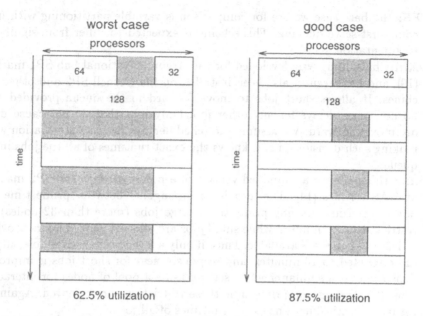

Fig. 4. *Example of how the flexibility afforded by time slicing can increase system utilization; compare with Fig. 1.*

Returning to the example considered earlier, the situation with gang scheduling is illustrated in Fig. 4. The 32-node job can safely run in the same time-slot with the 64-node job, while the 128-node job gets a separate time-slot. There is no danger of starvation. As long as all three jobs are active, the utilization is 87.5%. Even if the 64-node job terminates, leaving the 32-node job to run alone in its time-slot, the utilization is 62.5%. Naturally, a few percentage points should be shaved off these figures to account for context-switching overhead. Nevertheless, this is a unique case where time-slicing, despite its added overhead, can lead to better resource utilization than batch scheduling.

Using gang scheduling not only improves utilization — it also reduces mean response time. It is well known that mean response time is reduced by the shortest-job-first discipline. In workloads with high variability this is approximated by time slicing, because chances are that a new job will have a short runtime [24,23]. As production workloads do indeed exhibit a high variability [6], it follows that gang scheduling will reduce mean response time. Indeed, gang scheduling has even been advocated in conjunction with dynamic partitioning [21].

3 Simulation Results

3.1 The Compared Scheduling Schemes

In order to demonstrate the ideas described above, we simulate the performance of a multicomputer subjected to a realistic workload and using one of a set of different scheduling schemes. these are:

FCFS: the base case we use for comparison is variable partitioning with first-come-first-serve queuing. This scheme is expected to suffer from significant fragmentation.

Backfill: backfilling was developed for the Argonne National Lab SP1 machine [19], and has recently also been installed on the Cornell SP2 and other machines. It allows short jobs to move forward in the queue provided they do not cause delays for any other job. Only jobs that do not cause delay are moved forward. We assume the scheduler has perfect information when making such decisions, i.e. it knows the exact runtimes of all the jobs in the queue.

Prime: this policy is a simplified version of a policy used on the SP2 machine at NASA Ames [14]. The idea is to distinguish between prime time and non-prime time[1]: during prime time, large jobs (more than 32 nodes) are restricted to 10 minutes, while small jobs are allowed up to 4 hours provided at least 32 nodes are available. Thus, if only a few nodes are available, all jobs are restricted to 10 minutes, and responsiveness for short jobs is improved. This achieves a similar effect to setting aside a pool of nodes for interactive jobs [31]. During non-prime time these restrictions are removed. Again, we assume the scheduler knows the runtimes of all jobs.

Gang: gang scheduling with no information regarding runtimes. The jobs are packed into slots using the buddy scheme, including alternate scheduling [4]. Two versions with different scheduling time quanta are compared: one has relatively small time quantum of 10 seconds, so most jobs effectively run immediately, and the other has a time quantum of 10 minutes (600 seconds), so jobs may be queued for a certain time before getting to run.

3.2 Simulation Methodology

The workload model is an improved version of the model used in [4]. It is based on workload analysis from a number of production systems [6,15,32], and is characterized as follows (Fig. 5):

- The distribution of job sizes emphasizes small jobs and powers of two.
- The distribution of runtimes is a three-stage hyperexponential, where the relative weights of the three stages depend on the job size. This dependence is used to create a correlation between the job size and the runtime.
- The arrivals are Poisson, except for jobs that are re-run a number of times, in which case they are re-submitted immediately upon completion.

The simulation uses the batch means method to evaluate confidence intervals. Each batch includes 3333 job terminations. The first batch was discarded to account for simulation warmup. The length of each experiment (i.e. the simulation

---

[1] Our workload model does not include a daily cycle of job submittals — it is a continuous stream of jobs with the same statistical properties. Thus in our simulations the distinction is only in the scheduling policy, which is switched every 12 hours.

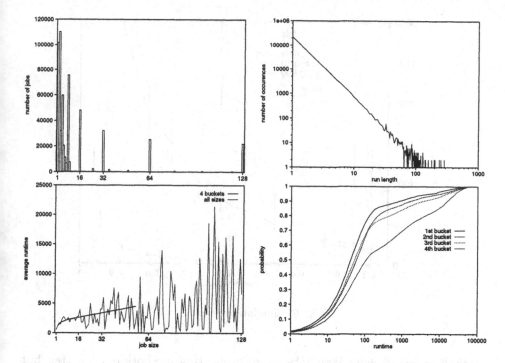

Fig. 5. *Statistical properties of the workload model: (a) distribution of job sizes (b) distribution of runlengths (number of repeated executions) (c) correlation of runtime with job size, for all sizes and when jobs are grouped into four buckets according to size (d) cumulative distributions of runtimes for the jobs in the four buckets.*

for each data point in the results) is at least 3 batches, or more as required so that the 90% confidence interval is no larger than 10% of the data point value, up to a maximum of 100 batches. Interestingly, simulations of all scheduling schemes except gang scheduling with short time quanta used all 100 batches, without a significant reductions in the confidence interval: it was typically in the range of 20-40% of the data point value. This reflects the very high variance present in the workload.

The sequence of job arrivals is generated once and reused for each data point and each scheme. Only the mean interarrival time is changed to create different load conditions.

The performance metric is the average slowdown. The slowdown for a given job is defined as the ratio between its response time on a loaded system (i.e. its queuing time plus run time and possible preempted time) and its runtime on a dedicated system.

3.3 Experimental Results

The results are shown in Fig. 6. As expected, FCFS saturates at extremely low loads, and even before saturation it tends to create very high slowdowns.

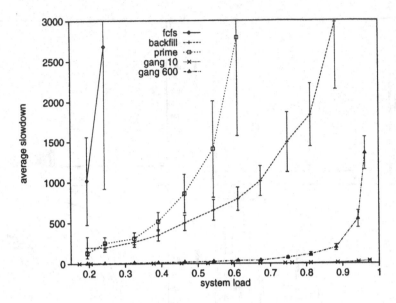

Fig. 6. *Simulation results.*

Backfilling and delaying large jobs to non-prime time are both much better, but backfilling can sustain a higher load and produces lower slowdowns. Attempts to improve the performance of the prime/non-prime policy by fiddling with its parameters (the threshold between small and large jobs, and the length of the prime shift) showed that it is relatively insensitive to the exact values of these parameters. However, it should be remembered that our workload model is not suitable for a detailed study of the prime/non-prime policy, because it does not include a daily cycle.

Gang scheduling, even with relatively long quanta of 10 minutes, takes the cake: the slowdowns are very low, and saturation is delayed until system load approaches 1. This agrees with the informal arguments presented in Section 2. While our simulations may be criticized for not modeling the overheads involved in gang scheduling — for example, the overhead of context switching and the effect of corrupting cache state — we feel that with long enough time quanta these overheads can be kept relatively low, so the main results remain valid.

4 Experience with Gang Scheduling on the Cray T3D

The default mode of operation for the Cray T3D is that of variable partitioning. Generally, jobs are allocated a partition of processors as soon as a suitable set becomes available. In the case where a job has waited for longer than some configurable period of time, the initiation of all other jobs is deferred until it begins execution. The partitions are held until the job completes and relinquishes them, effectively locking out any other use for those processors. With such a processor allocation mechanism, the computational requirements of long-running production jobs directly conflict with those of interactive code development work.

Goals in the development of the Gang Scheduler for the Cray T3D were:

- Provide better response for interactive jobs that are submitted directly
- Provide better throughput for batch jobs that are submitted through NQS
- Permit larger jobs to be executed
- Provide optimum throughput for specific jobs, as designated by management

While achieving all of these objectives would seem impossible, the initial utilization rate of 33.4% provided a great deal of room for improvement.

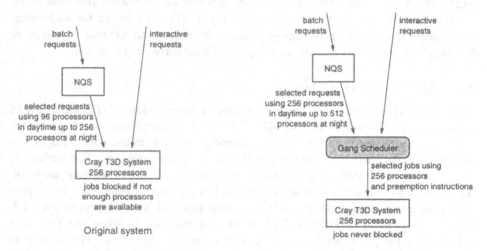

Fig. 7. *The place of the gang scheduler in the Cray T3D scheduling system.*

In a nutshell, our approach is as follows (Fig. 7). Originally, batch jobs were submitted via NQS and interactive jobs were submitted directly to the Cray system software. NQS buffered the jobs, and forwarded only few small jobs during the day, so that (hopefully) sufficient processors would be left free for interactive use. At night, NQS would submit enough jobs to fill the whole machine. With the gang scheduler, NQS fills the machine during the day and over-subscribes it during the night. The gang scheduler preempts jobs as necessary in order to provide timely service to higher-priority jobs, notably interactive jobs. This is a "lazy" form of gang scheduling: rather than performing a context switch across the whole machine at given intervals, specific jobs are chosen for preemption when an urgent need for processors arises.

Gang scheduling thus effectively creates a larger virtual machine, and meets the above objectives by:

- Time sharing processors for interactive jobs when experiencing an extremely heavy interactive workload

- Keeping processors fully utilized with batch jobs until preempted by an interactive or other high priority job
- Making processors available in a timely fashion for large jobs
- Making processors available in a timely fashion for specific jobs and making those jobs non-preemptable

Some might argue that interactive computing with a massively parallel computer is unreasonable, but interactive computing accounts for a substantial portion of the workload on the Cray T3D at Lawrence Livermore National Laboratory (LLNL): 79% of all jobs executed and 11% of all CPU cycles. The reason is that interactivity is used for code development and rapid throughput. A single interactive job can be allocated up to 25% of all processors and memory, and the aggregate of all interactive work will normally consume between zero and 150% of all processors and memory. While the Cray T3D is well suited for addressing the execution of grand challenge problems, we wanted to expand its range of functionality into general purpose support of interactive work as well.

4.1 Cray T3D Design Issues

The Cray T3D is a massively parallel computer incorporating DEC alpha 21064 microprocessors, capable of 150 MFLOPS peak performance. Each processor has its own local memory. The system is configured into nodes, consisting of two processors with their local memory and a network interconnect. The nodes are connected by a bidirectional three-dimensional torus communications network. There are also four synchronization circuits (barrier wires) connected to all processors in a tree shaped structure. The system at LLNL has 256 processors, each with 64 megabytes of DRAM. Disk storage is required to store the job state information for preempted jobs. This can be either shared or private storage space. We have created a shared 48 gigabyte file system for this purpose. The storage requirements will depend upon the T3D configuration and the amount of resource oversubscription permitted.

Without getting into great detail, the T3D severely constrains processor and barrier wire assignments to jobs. Jobs must be allocated a processor count which is a power of two, with a minimum of two processors (one node). The processors allocated to a job must have a specific shape with specific dimensions for a given problem size. For example, an allocation of 32 processors must be made with a contiguous block with 8 processors in the X direction, 2 processors in the Y direction and 2 processors in the Z direction. Furthermore, the possible locations of the processors assignments is restricted. These very specific shapes and locations for processor assignments are the result of the barrier wire structure. Jobs must be allocated one of the four barrier wires when initiated. The barrier wire assigned to a job cannot change if the job is relocated and, under some circumstances, two jobs sharing a single barrier wire may not be located adjacent to each other. The number of processors assigned to a job can not change during execution [2].

There are two fundamentally different ways of providing for timesharing of processors. The entire state of a job, including memory contents, register contents and switch state information can be written to disk. Alternately, the register and switch state information can be saved and the memory shared through paging. Saving the entire job state clearly makes context switches very time consuming, however, it can provide a means of relocating jobs to different processors and provide a means of preserving executing jobs over computer restarts. Sharing memory through paging can make for much faster context switches. Our system provides timesharing by saving the entire state of a job to disk. Cray does not support paging on this architecture because of the large working sets typical of programs executed and in order to reduce system complexity.

Timesharing by saving the entire state of a job to disk has an additional advantage as well. Given the T3D's constraints on processor assignment, the ability to relocate jobs with this mechanism clearly make it preferable. While the ability to preserve executing jobs over computer restarts has proven to be of some use, most programs complete in a few hours and can be restarted without substantial impact upon the system. Unfortunately, the high context switch time provides lower interactivity than would be desirable. It should also be noted that the system only supports the movement of a job's state in it's entirety. It is not possible to initiate state transfers on a processor by processor basis, although that capability would improve the context switch time.

The original version of this Gang Scheduler was developed for the BBN TC2000 computer. The BBN computer permitted programs to be assigned processors without locality constraints. Its timesharing through shared memory and paging was successful at providing both excellent interactivity and utilization [13,12].

4.2 Policy Overview

The T3D Gang Scheduler allocates processors and barrier circuits for all programs. In order to satisfy the diverse computational requirements of our clients, the programs are classified by access requirements:

- Interactive class jobs require responsive service
- Debug class jobs require responsive service and can not be preempted
- Production class jobs require good throughput
- Benchmark class jobs can not be preempted
- Standby class jobs have low priority and are suitable for absorbing otherwise idle compute resources

There are several class-dependent scheduling parameters to achieve the desired performance characteristics.

- Priority: Job classes are prioritized for service. We make interactive jobs higher priority than production jobs during the daytime and assign them equal priority at night.
- Wait time: The maximum time that a job should wait before (or between) processor access. This is used to ensure timely responsiveness, especially for interactive and debug class jobs. After a job has waited to be loaded for the

maximum wait time, an attempt will be made to reserve a block of processors for it. This processor reservation mechanism frequently preempts multiple small jobs to prevent starvation of large jobs.

- Do-not-disturb time multiplier: This parameter is multiplied by the number of processors to arrive at the do-not-disturb time, the minimum processor allocation time before preemption. A job will never be preempted before its do-not-disturb time is up. This allows the desire for timely response to be balanced against the cost of moving a job's state onto disk and back to memory (it is similar to the scheme proposed for the Tera MTA [1]). The do-not-disturb time multiplier should be set to a value substantially larger than the time required to move a job's state in one processor from memory to disk and back to memory. This time will vary with the disk configuration. On the LLNL T3D with 256 processors and 64 megabytes of memory each, the entire torus or processors can be repacked in about eight minutes, or one second per processor.
- Processor limit: The maximum number of processors which can be allocated to jobs of this class. This is used to restrict the number of processors allocated to non-preemptable jobs during the daytime.

Job Class	Priority	Wait Time	Do-not-disturb Time Multiplier	Processor Limit
Interactive	4	0 Sec	10 Sec	256
Debug	4	300 Sec	1 Year	96
Production	3	1 Hour	10 Sec	256
Benchmark	2	1 Year	1 Year	64
Standby	1	1 Year	3 Sec	256

Table 1. *Scheduling parameters for different job classes.*

The scheduling parameters currently being used during the daytime on weekdays are shown in Table 1. The time of one year is used in several cases to insure no preemption or an indefinite wait for some job classes.

Several non-class dependent scheduling parameters also exist to regulate computer-wide resource use.

- Large job size: The minimum number of processors requested by a job for it to be considered "large". We set this to 64 during daytime.
- Large processor limit: The maximum number of processors which can be allocated to "large" jobs at any time. Since "large" jobs can take a significant period of time to have their state moved between memory and disk, interactivity can be improved by restricting the number of processors allocated to them. Our limit is 192 during daytime.
- Job processor limit: The maximum number of processors which can be allocated to any single job. We use 256, i.e. we do not place such a limit.

- System processor limit: The maximum number of processors used by jobs either running or swapped to disk. This defines the degree of over-allocation; we use 576, i.e. an overallocation factor of 2.25. A limit is required to avoid filling the file system used for job state information. We are conservative in our allocation of this storage area because it is shared. Jobs will be queued, but not initiated to avoid exceeding this parameter. If an attempt is made to preempt a job when insufficient storage is available, that job will continue execution and no further attempts will be made to preempt it.

4.3 Job Scheduling Algorithm

We have implemented a two pass scheduling algorithm. The first pass checks for jobs which have waited for loading longer than their job class' maximum wait time. These jobs are viewed as having a high priority for loading and special measures are taken for loading them. If there is more than one such job, a list of these jobs is constructed then sorted by job class priority and within each priority value by the time waiting for loading. Each of these jobs is considered for loading in the sorted order. The processor requirement for the job will be compared against the scheduler's job processor limit. If the job's processor request cannot be satisfied, that job will no longer be considered a candidate for loading.

Multiple possible processor assignments for the job are considered. For each possible processor assignment, a cost is computed. The cost considers the number of nodes occupied by the potentially preempted jobs, their relative priority, and how much time remains in their do-not-disturb time. In no case will a job be preempted for another job of a lower priority class. Jobs of benchmark and debug class will never be preempted. If no possible processor assignment for loading the waiting job is located, its loading will be deferred. If a possible processor assignment is located, the lowest cost set of processors will be reserved for the exclusive use of this waiting job and jobs occupying those processors will be preempted when their do-not-disturb times have been exhausted.

Only one job will have processors reserved for it at any point in time. Once a set of processors have been reserved for a waiting job, the reservation of processors for other waiting jobs will be deferred until the selected job has been loaded. An exception is made only in the case that a higher priority class job exceeds its maximum wait time. For example, an interactive class job could preempt the reservation of processors for a production class job. The job with reserved processors can be loaded into other processors if another compatible set of processors becomes available at an earlier time. As soon as that job is loaded, the reserved processors are made generally available. This mechanism insures timely interactivity and prevents the starvation of large jobs.

In the second scheduler pass, other executable jobs are recorded in a list sorted by job class priority and within each priority by the time waiting for loading. Each job in the sorted list is considered for processor assignment. First the limits (job processor limit, large job limit, and job class limit) are checked to determine if the job should be allocated processors. Any job satisfying these limits will have its barrier wire circuit and processor requirements considered.

If the job can have its requirements met either with unallocated resources or resources which can be made available by preempting jobs which have exceeded their do-not-disturb time, it will have a barrier wire circuit and processors assigned. If a specific barrier wire is not requested, one of those available will be assigned. All four barrier wire circuits are considered for use and selected on the basis of lowest contention. More efficient relocation of jobs can be achieved by using all four barrier wire circuits.

The time required to save the state of a job on disk can be up to four minutes. Given this delay, it is not ideal to queue the loading of a job until the processors assigned to it are actually available. Whenever processors are actually made available, the job scheduler is executed again. This insures that when processors become available, they are assigned to the most appropriate jobs then available.

When a newly started job can immediately begin execution in a variety of possible sets of processor, a best-fit algorithm is used to make the selection. We also try to locate debug and benchmark class jobs, which can not be preempted, together in order to avoid blocking large jobs.

4.4 Client Interface

The default mode of operation for the Cray T3D requires all jobs, batch and interactive, to be initiated through a program called mppexec, which will accept as arguments the number of processors required, specific processor requirements, specific barrier wire requirements, etc. The Gang Scheduler takes advantage of this feature by creating a wrapper for mppexec which is upwardly compatible with it. The interface registers the job with the Gang Scheduler and waits for an assignment of processors and barrier circuit before continuing. On a heavily utilized computer, this typically takes a matter of seconds for small numbers of processors and possibly much longer for large jobs. The only additional argument to the Gang Scheduler interface is the job class, which is optional. By default, interactive jobs are assigned to the interactive job class, the TotalView debugger jobs are assigned to the debug class, and batch jobs are assigned to the production job class.

4.5 The Gangster Tool

We provide users with an interactive tool, called "gangster", for observing the state of the system and controlling some aspects of their jobs. Gangster communicates with the Gang Scheduler to determine the state of the machine's processors and individual jobs. Gangster's three-dimensional node map displays the status of each node (each node consists of two processing elements on the T3D). Gangster's job summary reports the state of each job, including jobs moving between processors and disk. Users can use gangster to change the class of their own jobs or to explicitly move their job's state to disk (suspending execution) or make it available for execution (resume).

A sample gangster display is shown in Fig. 8. This display identifies jobs in the system and assigned processors. The node map is on the left. A dot or letter

```
h  h  c  c  a  a  a  a  CLAS JOB-USER      PID  COMMAND   #PE BASE  W ST MM:SS
 h  h  c  c  a  a  a  a  Int  d - colombo   2976 icl1        8 100  1 R  42:44
h  h  c  c  a  a  a  a   Int  h - mshaw      9529 icf3d      32 020  2 R  00:33
h  h  c  c  a  a  a  a
                        Bmrk g - grote      9264 warpslav   32 200  1 R  00:20
 h  h  c  c  a  a  a  a
 h  h  c  c  a  a  a  a  Prod a - caturla   95396 moldy     128 400  2 R 107:35
 h  h  c  c  a  a  a  a  Prod b - colombo   98057 vdif        8 000  3 R  91:54
h  h  c  c  a  a  a  a   Prod c - wenski    98484 pproto6.   32 220  3 R  85:12
                        Prod e - colombo    8712 icl3        8 004  1 R   6:23
   b  d  g  g  a  a  a  a Prod f - colombo   8873 icl2        8 104  2 R   4:54
   b  d  g  g  a  a  a  a Prod i - dan       5684 camille    32 020  0 O  32:08
 e  f  g  g  a  a  a  a   Prod j - vickie   99393 kiten      64 400  3 O 132:59
 e  f  g  g  a  a  a  a

   b  d  g  g  a  a  a  a
   b  d  g  g  a  a  a  a
 e  f  g  g  a  a  a  a
 e  f  g  g  a  a  a  a
gangster:
```

Fig. 8. *Sample gangster display. The W field shows the barrier wire used. The MM:SS field shows the total execution time. The ST field shows the job's state: i = swapping in, N = new job, not yet assigned nodes or barrier wire, o = swapping out, O = swapped out, R = running, S = suspended, W = waiting job, assigned nodes and barrier wire.*

denotes each node (two processing elements on the T3D): a dot indicates the node is not in use, a letter designates the job currently occupying that node. On the right is a summary of all jobs. Node number 000 is in the upper left corner of the lowest plane. The X axis extends downward within a plane. The Y axis extends up, with one Y value in each plane. The Z axis extends to the right. This orientation was selected for ease of display for a 256 processor T3D configuration.

4.6 NQS Configuration

Jobs may be submitted to the Cray T3D interactively or via the NQS batch queuing system. Interactive jobs are limited to 64 processors and 2 hours. Prior to installation of the Gang Scheduler, our NQS batch system was configured to leave an adequate number of processors available for interactive computing during the day. This was changed when the Gang Scheduler was introduced, and now NQS fully subscribes the machine during the day. At night, it oversubscribes the machine by as much as 100% (Table 2).

Note that jobs requiring more than a four hour time limit were originally limited to 64 processors. Also note that substantial compute resources were sacrificed in order to insure processors for interactive computing. This was particularly noticeable in the early morning hours as the mpp-pe-limit dropped to 96 at 04:00 in order to insure the availability of 160 processors for interactive use at 08:00. Frequently this left many processors idle. Even so, under the occasionally heavy interactive workload, all processors would be allocated and interactive jobs experienced lengthy initiation delays.

Global limits:

Period	User Limit	Run Limit	Aggregate mpp-pe-limit
00:00 – 04:00	2 → 5	8 → 20	256 → 512
04:00 – 07:00	2 → 5	8 → 20	96 → 320
07:00 – 18:00	2 → 5	8 → 20	96 → 256-320*
18:00 – 24:00	2 → 5	8 → 20	192 → 320

Queue limits:

Queue Name	User Limit	Run Limit	Job Time Limit	Job Processor Limit	Aggregate mpp-pe-limit
pe32	1 → 3	4 → 8	4 h → 4 h	32 → 32	128 → 128
pe64	1 → 2	3 → 2-3*	4 h → 4 h	64 → 64	192 → 128-192*
pe64_long	2 → 2	2 → 2	19 h → 40 h	64 → 128	96 → 96-128*
pe128_short	1 → 1	4 → 4	15 m → 15 m	128 → 96	128 → 128
pe128	1 → 0-2*	1 → 1	4 h → 4 h	128 → 128	128 → 0-256*
pe256_short	1 → 0-1*	1 → 1	15 m → 15 m	256 → 256	256 → 0-256*
pe256	1 → 0-1*	1 → 1	4 h → 4 h	256 → 256	256 → 0-256*

*Varies by time of day and/or day of week

Table 2. *Changes made in NQS configuration parameters when the Gang Scheduler was introduced. User Limit is the maximum number of batch jobs a single user may have executing. Run Limit is the maximum number of batch jobs (from a certain queue) the system may have executing at one time. mpp-pe-limit is the maximum number of processors which the batch jobs may have allocate at one time.*

With the gang scheduler, NQS is now allowed to fully subscribes the computer and oversubscribe at night. The overallocation of processors permits the execution of larger jobs and makes more jobs available for fully packing the T3D's torus of processors. NQS jobs now relinquish their processors only as needed, not in anticipation of interactive work. During periods of heavy use, this improves our realized throughput substantially while preserving good interactivity. While average interactivity has decreased slightly due to interference from NQS jobs, the worse case startup time has dropped from tens of minutes to about one minute. This is still quite acceptable to our user community, especially when accompanied by a substantial increase in realized batch throughput. We also see a few jobs relocated to better utilize the available processors during periods of heavy use, especially when jobs requiring 64 or 128 processors exist.

4.7 Performance Results

In order to quantify the effect upon system throughput and interactivity under heavy load, we have continuously tabulate system performance with the Gang Scheduler. Before installing the Gang Scheduler, we did the same for the standard UNICOS MAX scheduler and the Distributed Job Manager (DJM). DJM is a gang scheduler developed by the Minnesota Supercomputer Center, which has undergone substantial modification for performance enhancements by Cray analysts at LLNL. All of the DJM code to accomplish job swapping is new. The enhanced version of DJM was used for testing purposes.

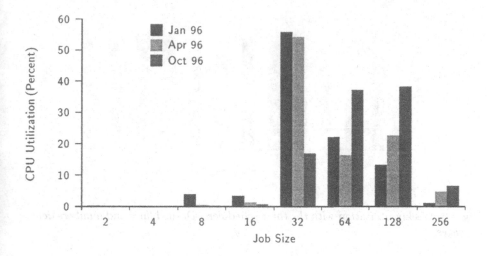

Fig. 9. *Changes in workload distribution due to use of the Gang Scheduler.*

Fig. 9 demonstrates the Gang Scheduler's ability to execute large jobs: note the dramatic improvement in throughput of 128 and 256 processor jobs. This charts the distribution of resources allocated to each job size as percentage of CPU resources actually delivered to customers. The percentage of gross CPU resources which are delivered to large jobs has increased by an even wider margin. The January 1996 period is the last full month of operation with the standard UNICOS MAX operating system. April is just after installation of the Gang Scheduler, and by October the workload had shifted to take advantage of its improved support for large jobs.

The best measure of success is probably actual throughput achieved. While utilization is quite low on weekends, the improvement in throughput at other times has dramatically improved with preemptive schedulers[2]. Fig. 10 summarizes utilization of processor resources over the course of several entire weeks. Over the longer term, utilization has improved even more dramatically while providing good interactivity, as shown in Fig. 11. CPU utilization reported is the percentage of all CPU cycles available which are delivered to customer computation. Weekly utilization rates have reached over 96%.

---

[2] While DJM would also have provided for good interactivity and throughput, it became available at the same time as our Gang Scheduler was completed and we felt that continued development of our Gang Scheduler was worthwhile. In addition, our Gang Scheduler provided the means to arbitrarily lock jobs into processors. This was important for us to be able to insure optimal throughput for jobs specified by our management.

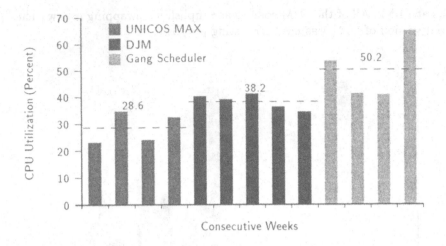

Fig. 10. *Weekly utilization with the three schedulers. Dashed lines and numbers denote averages.*

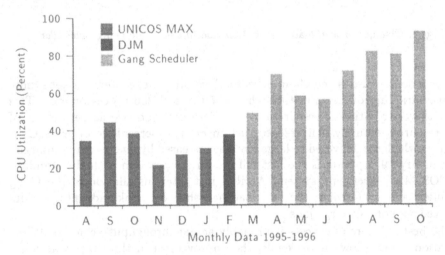

Fig. 11. *Monthly utilization with the three schedulers.*

Even though the improved utilization is impressive, this should not come at the expense of interactive jobs. To quantify this, we tabulated the slowdowns of interactive jobs, i.e. the ratio of the time they spent in the system to the time they actually ran. This was done for the period of July 23 through August 12. During this period, 2659 interactive jobs were run, using a total of 44.5 million node-seconds, and 1328 batch jobs were run, using a total of 289.4 million node-seconds.

The ratio of the *total* time all interactive jobs spent in the system to their *total* runtimes was 1.18, leading one to assume only 18% overhead. However, this

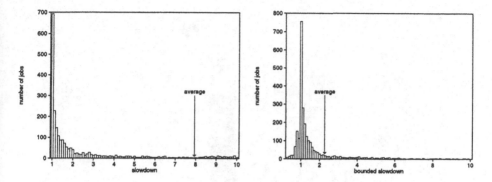

Fig. 12. *Histograms of slowdown and bounded slowdown of interactive jobs.*

is misleading, because slowdowns of individual jobs should be checked. The full distribution of slowdowns is plotted in Fig. 12. Actually, only the low part of the distribution is shown, as it has a very long tail, but most jobs have rather low slowdowns. The most extreme case was a one-second job that was delayed for just less than 23 minutes, leading to a slowdown of 1371. The average slowdown was determined to be 7.94.

While the high average slowdown is disappointing, it too is misleading. The problem is that many interactive jobs have very short runtimes, so a high slowdown may not be indicative of a real problem. Indeed, merely loading the application from disk typically takes about 0.5 seconds per processor used; thus a one second job running on 4 nodes will require two seconds of load time, for an optimal slowdown of 3, which is actually quite reasonable in this case. In order to counter the effect of short jobs, we also plot the *bounded slowdown* [11]. For long running jobs, this is the same as the slowdown. But for short jobs, the denominator is taken as the "interactivity threshold" rather than as the actual (very short) runtime. In processing the data for Fig. 12, we used a threshold of 10 seconds; the average bounded slowdown is then 2.27, and the tail of the distribution is also shorter.

4.8 Operational Characteristics

Figs. 13 to 15 portray the gang scheduler in operation. These figures are based on detailed logs of all jobs and all job preemptions during four months of production use, from June 1996 through September 1996.

It should be noted that only 7.5% of jobs that completed normally were ever preempted. Fig. 13 shows the likelihood of preemption as a function of the job size, and shows that different size jobs were preempted in roughly equal proportions. While most jobs were not preempted or were only preempted a small number of times, the maximal number of preemptions observed was pretty high: one job was preempted 77 times before completing. The histogram of number of preemptions is shown in Fig. 14.

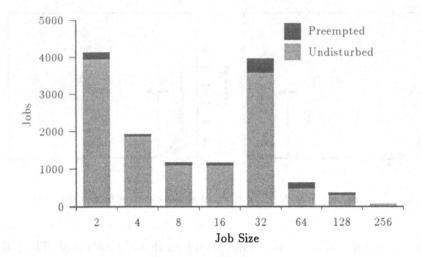

Fig. 13. *Likelihood of preemption for different job sizes.*

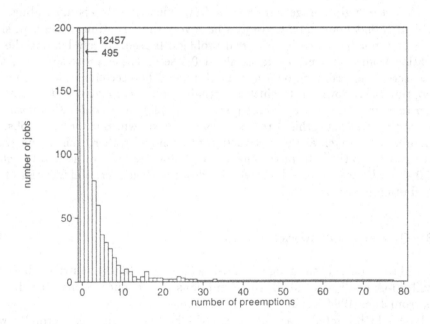

Fig. 14. *Histogram of the number of preemptions suffered by different jobs.*

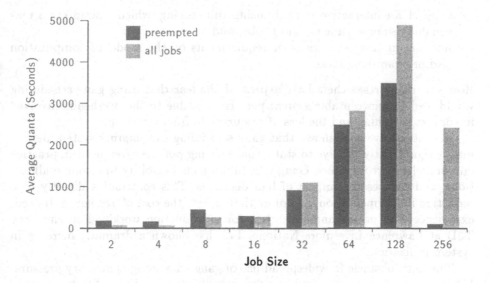

Fig. 15. *Average time quanta for different size jobs.*

Finally, we take a look at the average length of the time quanta for the different sizes. This is shown in Fig. 15, once for jobs that were actually preempted, and again for all jobs (i.e. including those that ran to completion without being preempted even once). As expected, use of the do-not-disturb time multiplier leads to larger average time quanta for larger jobs. (The 256-processor figure is a special case of only one job. Jobs of this size are normally not preempted.)

4.9 Future Development

While the Gang Scheduler manages the currently active jobs well, the NQS batch system selects the jobs to be started. It would be desirable to integrate the Gang Scheduler with NQS in order to more efficiently schedule all available jobs. Work is also planned for the gang scheduling of jobs across a heterogeneous collection of computers.

5 Conclusions

Gang scheduling has often been advocated based on its advantages of

- presenting jobs with an environment similar to that of a dedicated machine, thus allowing fine grain interactions based on user-level communication and busy waiting [9],
- allowing jobs with extreme requirements to share the system: a job that requires all the nodes does not have to wait for all previous jobs to terminate, nor does it delay subsequent jobs,

- support for interactive work by using time slicing, which guarantees a reasonable response time for short jobs, and
- not placing any restrictions or requirements on the model of computation and programming style.

However, many researchers have expressed the fear that using gang scheduling would lead to unacceptable system performance due to the overheads involved in context switching and the loss of resources to fragmentation.

In contrast, we have shown that gang scheduling can *improve* system performance significantly relative to static space slicing policies often used in practice on parallel supercomputers. Gang scheduling adds flexibility to resource allocations, and reduces the impact of bad decisions. This contributes directly to a reduction in fragmentation, and more than offsets the cost of overheads. Indeed, experience with using gang scheduling for a production workload on the Cray T3D at Lawrence Livermore National Lab has shown a dramatic increase in system utilization.

The main obstacle to widespread use of gang scheduling is memory pressure. If gang scheduling is performed at a fine granularity, all jobs need to be memory resident at the same time, so each has less memory available. The alternative is to swap jobs to disk when they are preempted, and swap them in again when scheduled. This is a viable approach, but it requires sufficient resources to be invested in adequate I/O facilities. The combination of demand paging and prefetching with gang scheduling remains an interesting topic for future research.

References

1. G. Alverson, S. Kahan, R. Korry, C. McCann, and B. Smith, "*Scheduling on the Tera MTA*". In *Job Scheduling Strategies for Parallel Processing*, D. G. Feitelson and L. Rudolph (eds.), pp. 19–44, Springer-Verlag, 1995. Lecture Notes in Computer Science Vol. 949.
2. Cray Research, Inc., *Cray T3D System Architecture Overview*. Order number HR-04033, Sep 1993.
3. D. Das Sharma and D. K. Pradhan, "*Job scheduling in mesh multicomputers*". In *Intl. Conf. Parallel Processing*, vol. II, pp. 251–258, Aug 1994.
4. D. G. Feitelson, "*Packing schemes for gang scheduling*". In *Job Scheduling Strategies for Parallel Processing*, D. G. Feitelson and L. Rudolph (eds.), pp. 89–110, Springer-Verlag, 1996. Lecture Notes in Computer Science Vol. 1162.
5. D. G. Feitelson, *A Survey of Scheduling in Multiprogrammed Parallel Systems*. Research Report RC 19790 (87657), IBM T. J. Watson Research Center, Oct 1994.
6. D. G. Feitelson and B. Nitzberg, "*Job characteristics of a production parallel scientific workload on the NASA Ames iPSC/860*". In *Job Scheduling Strategies for Parallel Processing*, D. G. Feitelson and L. Rudolph (eds.), pp. 337–360, Springer-Verlag, 1995. Lecture Notes in Computer Science Vol. 949.
7. D. G. Feitelson and L. Rudolph, "*Distributed hierarchical control for parallel processing*". *Computer* **23**(5), pp. 65–77, May 1990.
8. D. G. Feitelson and L. Rudolph, "*Evaluation of design choices for gang scheduling using distributed hierarchical control*". *J. Parallel & Distributed Comput.* **35**(1), pp. 18–34, May 1996.

9. D. G. Feitelson and L. Rudolph, *"Gang scheduling performance benefits for fine-grain synchronization"*. *J. Parallel & Distributed Comput.* 16(4), pp. 306–318, Dec 1992.

10. D. G. Feitelson and L. Rudolph, *"Parallel job scheduling: issues and approaches"*. In *Job Scheduling Strategies for Parallel Processing*, D. G. Feitelson and L. Rudolph (eds.), pp. 1–18, Springer-Verlag, 1995. Lecture Notes in Computer Science Vol. 949.

11. D. G. Feitelson, L. Rudolph, U. Schwiegelshohn, K. C. Sevcik, and P. Wong, *"Theory and practice in parallel job scheduling"*. In *Job Scheduling Strategies for Parallel Processing*, D. G. Feitelson and L. Rudolph (eds.), Springer Verlag, 1997. Lecture Notes in Computer Science (this volume).

12. B. Gorda and R. Wolski, *"Time sharing massively parallel machines"*. In *Intl. Conf. Parallel Processing*, vol. II, pp. 214–217, Aug 1995.

13. B. C. Gorda and E. D. Brooks III, *Gang Scheduling a Parallel Machine*. Technical Report UCRL-JC-107020, Lawrence Livermore National Laboratory, Dec 1991.

14. R. L. Henderson, *"Job scheduling under the portable batch system"*. In *Job Scheduling Strategies for Parallel Processing*, D. G. Feitelson and L. Rudolph (eds.), pp. 279–294, Springer-Verlag, 1995. Lecture Notes in Computer Science Vol. 949.

15. S. Hotovy, *"Workload evolution on the Cornell Theory Center IBM SP2"*. In *Job Scheduling Strategies for Parallel Processing*, D. G. Feitelson and L. Rudolph (eds.), pp. 27–40, Springer-Verlag, 1996. Lecture Notes in Computer Science Vol. 1162.

16. Intel Corp., *iPSC/860 Multi-User Accounting, Control, and Scheduling Utilities Manual*. Order number 312261-002, May 1992.

17. M. Jette, D. Storch, and E. Yim, *"Timesharing the Cray T3D"*. In *Cray User Group*, pp. 247–252, Mar 1996.

18. K. Li and K-H. Cheng, *"A two-dimensional buddy system for dynamic resource allocation in a partitionable mesh connected system"*. *J. Parallel & Distributed Comput.* 12(1), pp. 79–83, May 1991.

19. D. Lifka, *"The ANL/IBM SP scheduling system"*. In *Job Scheduling Strategies for Parallel Processing*, D. G. Feitelson and L. Rudolph (eds.), pp. 295–303, Springer-Verlag, 1995. Lecture Notes in Computer Science Vol. 949.

20. C. McCann, R. Vaswani, and J. Zahorjan, *"A dynamic processor allocation policy for multiprogrammed shared-memory multiprocessors"*. *ACM Trans. Comput. Syst.* 11(2), pp. 146–178, May 1993.

21. C. McCann and J. Zahorjan, *"Scheduling memory constrained jobs on distributed memory parallel computers"*. In *SIGMETRICS Conf. Measurement & Modeling of Comput. Syst.*, pp. 208–219, May 1995.

22. J. K. Ousterhout, *"Scheduling techniques for concurrent systems"*. In 3rd *Intl. Conf. Distributed Comput. Syst.*, pp. 22–30, Oct 1982.

23. E. W. Parsons and K. C. Sevcik, *"Multiprocessor scheduling for high-variability service time distributions"*. In *Job Scheduling Strategies for Parallel Processing*, D. G. Feitelson and L. Rudolph (eds.), pp. 127–145, Springer-Verlag, 1995. Lecture Notes in Computer Science Vol. 949.

24. R. C. Regis, *"Multiserver queueing models of multiprocessing systems"*. *IEEE Trans. Comput.* C-22(8), pp. 736–745, Aug 1973.

25. E. Rosti, E. Smirni, L. W. Dowdy, G. Serazzi, and B. M. Carlson, *"Robust partitioning schemes of multiprocessor systems"*. *Performance Evaluation* 19(2-3), pp. 141–165, Mar 1994.

26. E. Rosti, E. Smirni, G. Serazzi, and L. W. Dowdy, *"Analysis of non-work-conserving processor partitioning policies"*. In *Job Scheduling Strategies for Parallel*

Processing, D. G. Feitelson and L. Rudolph (eds.), pp. 165–181, Springer-Verlag, 1995. Lecture Notes in Computer Science Vol. 949.

27. B. Schnor, *"Dynamic scheduling of parallel applications"*. In *Parallel Computing Technologies*, V. Malyshkin (ed.), pp. 109–116, Springer-Verlag, Sep 1995. Lecture Notes in Computer Science vol. 964.

28. K. C. Sevcik, *"Application scheduling and processor allocation in multiprogrammed parallel processing systems"*. *Performance Evaluation* 19(2-3), pp. 107–140, Mar 1994.

29. K. C. Sevcik, *"Characterization of parallelism in applications and their use in scheduling"*. In *SIGMETRICS Conf. Measurement & Modeling of Comput. Syst.*, pp. 171–180, May 1989.

30. A. Tucker and A. Gupta, *"Process control and scheduling issues for multiprogrammed shared-memory multiprocessors"*. In *12th Symp. Operating Systems Principles*, pp. 159–166, Dec 1989.

31. M. Wan, R. Moore, G. Kremenek, and K. Steube, *"A batch scheduler for the Intel Paragon with a non-contiguous node allocation algorithm"*. In *Job Scheduling Strategies for Parallel Processing*, D. G. Feitelson and L. Rudolph (eds.), pp. 48–64, Springer-Verlag, 1996. Lecture Notes in Computer Science Vol. 1162.

32. K. Windisch, V. Lo, R. Moore, D. Feitelson, and B. Nitzberg, *"A comparison of workload traces from two production parallel machines"*. In *6th Symp. Frontiers Massively Parallel Comput.*, pp. 319–326, Oct 1996.

33. Q. Yang and H. Wang, *"A new graph approach to minimizing processor fragmentation in hypercube multiprocessors"*. *IEEE Trans. Parallel & Distributed Syst.* 4(10), pp. 1165–1171, Oct 1993.

Global State Detection Using Network Preemption

Atsushi Hori[1], Hiroshi Tezuka[1], Yutaka Ishikawa[1]

Tsukuba Research Center, Real World Computing Partnership,
Tsukuba Mitsui Building 16F, 1-6-1 Takezono, Tsukuba-shi, Ibaraki 305, JAPAN
e-mail:{hori,tezuka,ishikawa}@rwcp.or.jp
URL:http://www.rwcp.or.jp/

Abstract. Gang scheduling provides shorter response time and enables interactive parallel programming. To utilize processor resources on interactive parallel programs, the global state of distributed parallel processes should be detected. This problem is well-known as the "distributed termination problem." In this paper, we propose a practical method to detect a global state of distributed processes. There are two key methods for detecting a global state described in this paper. One is network preemption and the other is combining global state detection with gang scheduling by the nwtwork preemption. The proposed scheme is scalable, and the overhead for the detection of a global state is negligible. To implement our scheme, we extend our gang scheduler, SCore-D, to an operating system by implementing a system-call mechanism. We confirmed that our proposed global state detection scheme is very useful on SCore-D.

1 Introduction

Gang scheduling is considered to be effective especially for fine-grain parallel programs [17, 5]. Gang-scheduling is beneficial in that it can provide a shorter response time than batch scheduling. Hours of running time can be reduced to minutes on a parallel machine or a workstation cluster. Thus, gang scheduling enables some types of parallel applications to be interactive [6].

In UNIX, the state transition of a process is clearly defined. An idle state of a process means that a blocked system-call exists. However, the state transition of gang-scheduled processes can be different from that of sequential processes. For example, there could be a case where processes are gang-scheduled every time a system-call is blocked. This strategy requires a number of gang context switches proportional to the number of processors. Considering the overhead of gang context switches, this situation should be avoided. Therefore, it is desirable that the processes are gang-switched when every process is idle or blocked.

The detection of "no running process" in a set of communicating processes is well known as as the "distributed termination problem" and a number of algorithms have been proposed to tackle this [4, 16]. Essentially, there are two key points in detecting the global termination of a distributed parallel processes. One is to detect the termination of all processes. The other is to guarantee that no message for the processes in the communication network is present. If these predicates are true, then the processes are assumed globally terminated.

Some algorithms require extra *marker* messages to detect the non-existence of messages, some require counting the number of messages, and so on. Those additional mechanisms add extra overhead to the underlying computation.

Globally terminated or idling distributed processes should be detected by a parallel operating system. The operating system is responsible for not allocating processor resources in vain. These idling processes can be preempted and switched to another runnable distributed processes. Of course, a globally terminated process should be terminated by the operating system also.

We have developed a user-level parallel operating system, called SCore-D [10, 9], for workstation clusters. The key idea enabling gang scheduling in SCore-D is *network preemption*. Under SCore-D, distributed user processes can communicate by manipulating network hardware directly. When switching processes, the messages are flushed from the network. Then the flushed messages and the network hardware status are saved and restored on each processor.

We applied this network preemption technique to the global state detection problem. Each time processes are gang-switched, the saved network status is investigated on each processor. When every process is idle and there is no message in the saved network context, then the distributed processes are assumed to be globally terminated. The benefits of this method are that this method is scalable, the overhead to detect a global state is negligible, and there is no need of a special mechanism for the underlying computation.

Here, we modify the definition of global termination slightly by considering parallel operating systems. In addition to the conditions of detecting a global termination, if at least one blocked system-call exists, the distributed process is assumed to be globally idle. After the system-call is finished, the distributed processes are ready to run. Most of the blocking system-calls causing global idle situations are I/O operations. For a multi-threaded system, it could be argued that the blocking time can be hidden by scheduling other threads. Disk related I/O operations usually end within tens of milli-seconds, and there could be a sufficient quantity and/or length of threads in a distributed processes. However, there is also the case of waiting for human reaction; quite a problem if he or she has been out at a restaurant having a lunch. It is hard to imagine that there can always be a sufficient quantity and/or length of threads to fill several hours.

We implemented a system-call mechanism and some I/O devices in the SCore-D. In addition to the global termination detection, we also implemented global idle detection. Eventually, we confirmed that this global idle detection is very effective for maximizing the system throughput and for decreasing user frustration.

2 SCore-D Overview

At this time, the nature of parallel operating systems is still unclear, thus it is important to implement and evaluate any proposed parallel operating system functions. To match state-of-the-art hardware technology, fast development is crucial. Therefore development of a parallel operating system at the user-level is reasonable for parallel operating system research. SCore-D is a user-level parallel operating system on top of UNIX [10, 9].

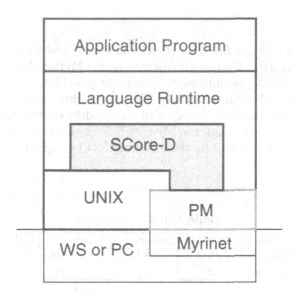

Fig. 1. Software structure of SCore-D

Figure 1 shows the software structure of SCore-D. A unique feature of SCore-D is that it is written in MPC++ [12], a multi-threaded C++. Although the runtime library of MPC++ is hidden in this figure, its runtime system has been developed for SCore-D. The runtime system of another parallel object-oriented language, OCore[15], is now supported by SCore-D.

Currently, SCore-D is running on both our workstation cluster (36 Sparc-Station 20s) and PC cluster [8] (32 Pentium PCs). Myrinet [3] is used as the inter-processor communication hardware in both clusters. We have developed a Myrinet driver software, called PM [20, 21]. PM supports not only low-level communication, but also some functions for network preemption. SCore-D is independent of both network hardware and the programming language of application programs. Also, we are now developing an Ethernet communication library.

To execute a user program, a user has to connect to a SCore-D server via TCP on the Ethernet and supply the required information to execute the user program. These include user ID, the current directory path, the executable file-name, number of processors, and so on. If the user program is linked with an appropriate runtime library, then all procedures take place in the runtime library. SCore-D then **forks** and **execs** user program over the processors. After the user processes are forked, the runtime library initializes the PM library according to the information passed from SCore-D, and the user program starts. For gang scheduling and job control, user processes are controlled via UNIX signals by SCore-D [10].

2.1 PM

PM consists of a Myrinet firmware (LANai program) and a low-level communication library [20, 21]. PM allows its users to access Myrinet hardware. Avoiding system-calls to UNIX and interrupts (whenever possible), we succeeded in reducing software overhead dramatically. The same technique can be found in FM [18]. Table 1 shows one-way latency and bandwidths on the SparcStation 20s (SS20) and PC-ATs. Although the Myrinet link has a bandwidth of 160 MB/s, PM's bandwidths are limited by the machines I/O bus speed.

Table 1. PM performance

Machine	Clock [MHz]	Latency [μs]	Bandwidth [MB/s]
SS20	75	8.0	38.6
Pentium	166	7.2	117.6

Table 2. PM interface

Send and Receive	
GetSendBuf	allocate send buffer
Send	send a message
Receive	check message arrival
PutReceiveBuf	free receive buffer
Network Preemption Support	
SendStable	confirm message arrivals
SaveChannel	save network context
RestoreChannel	restore network context
GetChannelStatus	return channel status

Table 2 shows a list of functions related to communication and network preemption. Communication with PM is asynchronous. To send a message, first a message buffer is allocated by calling GetSendBuf(). Next the runtime constructs or packetizes a message in the allocated buffer area. Then the message buffer is sent to a destination processor by calling Send(). This allocation and sending procedure can avoid extra memory copying. The receiving procedure is almost the same as the sending. The lower half functions in Table 2 are for network preemption and are used in SCore-D only. PM supports multiple communication channels. The function GetChannelStatus() is to obtain channel information including the number of messages waiting for sending and receiving.

Table 3. Context Save and Restore Time

SS20	save [μsec]	restore [μsec]
Send Full	3747	3002
Recv Full	7203	5201
Both Empty	1866	1094
Both Full	8963	7073
Pentium	save [μsec]	restore [μsec]
Send Full	2399	1843
Recv Full	4663	2955
Both Empty	938	365
Both Full	6118	4427

Table 3 shows the time required to save and restore network context. The time to save and restore depends on the number of messages and the total message size in a channel's receive and send buffers. In this table, "Send Full" means the send buffer contains 511 messages (49,056 bytes in total), and "Recv Full" means that the receive buffer contains 4,095 messages (65,520 bytes). Larger buffer size contributes to communication performance, however, it takes longer time to save and restore network context.

SCore-D initializes the Myrinet hardware and uses one channel for its interprocessor communications, while the user processes use the other channel. When SCore-D creates a new user processes, it resets the other channel for the user's inter-processor communication. With this multiple channel feature of PM, SCore-D and user process can share a Myrinet hardware. All the send and receive operations in PM are totally safe from preemption of the CPU, so that SCore-D can preempt user process at any time.

From the viewpoint of SCore-D, the functions listed in Table 2 are API. SCore-D does not assume there is a Myrinet interface, but does assume that there is a communication library having the same functions as defined in Table 2.

2.2 Network preemption

Since PM allows its users to access network hardware directly, the network hardware status is also saved and restored when switching processes. However, this is not enough. There is the possibility of receiving a message belonging to the process before switching. To avoid this, the messages in the network should be flushed before starting a new process.

PM uses a modified Ack/Nack protocol for flow-control. Although message delivery is reliable on Myrinet, a flow-control mechanism is still needed. The allocated sending message region is preserved until the corresponding Ack message is received. Note that these Ack/Nack messages are used for releasing or resending the corresponding message. The `Send()` function sends a message asynchronously. Thus, latency and bandwidth can be improved. We applied this protocol to the detection of message flushing. The `SendStable()` function returns if there is a message in transient.

When user processes are gang-scheduled, SCore-D first sends the UNIX signal `SIGSTOP` to all user processes. On each processor, SCore-D waits until the user process stops, then calls the `SendStable()` function to wait for the flushing of message sending from the node. The completion of flushing at each node is synchronized in a barrier fashion, and the flushing of user messages in a network is then complete. Subsequently, the network context on each processor is saved, and the network context of a new process is restored. After reloading a new network context, the execution of new processes is resumed by sending `SIGCONT` signals. Thus, the saving and restoring of network context is done at each processor. The control structure of sending signals can be a tree structure, and it takes a $log(N)$ order. Therefore, the implemented network preemption is scalable.

CM-5 has a hardware support for network preemption called *All-Fall-Down* [22]. When an operating system decides to switch processes, it sets a special hardware register to trigger the All-Fall-Down. In the All-Fall-Down mode, all messages in the network fall down to the nearest processor regardless of destination. To restore the network context, the fallen messages are reinjected into the network. Since the CM-5 network was not designed to preserve message order, the disturbance of message order by All-Fall-Down does not cause a problem. PM preserves message order. Message order is preserved even when network preemption takes place. PM also guarantees reliable communication. This message order preserving and reliable communication eliminates the needed software overhead to handling irregular situations.

Franke, et al. also implemented a gang-scheduler, called *SHARE* on an IBM SP-2 [7]. It also saves and restores network hardware context. The communication mechanism used in [7], however, did not guarantee reliable communication. The absence of reliability may not require the network preemption. When a context switch takes place and a message arrives at a wrong process, then the message is discarded and its sender must resend the message. The PM guarantees reliable communication, and this feature not only simplifies programming, but also contributes to the low-latency and high-bandwidth in communication as shown in Table 1. The PM's reliable and asynchronous features require extra mechanisms, such as the network preemption including global synchronization, for enabling gang scheduling. However, considering that the frequency of communication is much higher than that of gang scheduling, lower-overhead communication is desirable.

2.3 System-call mechanism

In [10], SCore-D is introduced as a gang scheduler. In addition, we have added a system-call mechanism and have implemented I/O mechanisms and other operating system functions. In this subsection, we will briefly introduce the system-call mechanism as implemented in SCore-D.

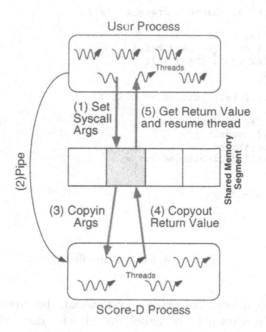

Fig. 2. System-call mechanism

SCore-D and a user process share a memory segment defined in the System V IPC. This memory segment is used to relay information to initialize a user process. The segment is also used for system-calls from user processes to SCore-D (Figure 2). The arguments for a system-call are copied into a region of a shared segment. SCore-D is notified of the existence of a service request via a UNIX pipe. SCore-D processes the request, and the result is copied to the same region.

2.4 Thread model

SCore-D assumes that user programs are written in a multi-threaded language and that the thread is implemented at the user-level. Figure 3 is an idle loop skeleton for such a thread runtime library. So that SCore-D can observe its status, an integer variable `idle_flag` is put in the shared memory segment to indicate whether the user process is idle or not, so that .

```
 1 void idle_loop( void )
 2 {
 3   char *recv_buf;
 4
 5   while( 1 ) {
 6     if( !Receive( channel, &recv_buf ) )
 7     {
 8       idle_flag = FALSE;
 9       process_message( recv_buf );
10       PutReceiveBuf( channel );
11       break;
12     }
13     if( syscall_cell->status == DONE )
14     {
15       idle_flag = FALSE;
16       syscall_count --;
17       enqueue_thread(
18         syscall_cell->thread );
19       break;
20     }
21     idle_flag = TRUE;
22   }
23   return;
24 }
```

Fig. 3. Skeleton of an idle loop

By suspending a thread invoking a system-call, the thread runtime system can obtain the benefits both of kernel threads and user threads[1]. SCore-D assumes that user programs run with a user-level thread runtime library. There is no need for a UNIX system-call to switch threads, and the runtime only suspends the thread invoking a system-call. In an idle loop, shown in Figure 3, a flag indicating the end of a system-call is checked. If a system-call is finished, then the runtime re-schedules the suspended thread. No thread is preempted when a system-call is done. Thus, our thread model can avoid the critical section problem discussed in the paper [1].

3 Global State Detection

Although the asynchronous nature of PM contributes to communication performance, it complicates the detection of a global state. The overhead to detect a global state should be as low as possible. Additional mechanisms needed in user programs are not ideal. Here, we propose a practical method to detect a global state by combining network preemption for gang scheduling and global state detection.

In Figure 3, the `idle_flag` variable is located in the shared memory segment. The `syscall_count` variable counts pending system-calls and is also located in the shared segment. Now, SCore-D can detect a global state in user's distributed processes each time the processes are gang-scheduled.

1. Suspend user distributed processes.
2. Preempt the network.
3. Gather message count information in preempted network context, the processes' activities, and the system-call count from each process.

As a result, if no message can be found in the preempted network, and there is no busy process, then the distributed processes are assumed to be either globally idle or terminated. Further, if there is no pending system-call, the processes are assumed globally terminated, otherwise the processes are globally idle.

The first two steps in the above procedure follow normal procedures for gang scheduling, and are nothing new in the detection of global states. Only the last step is modified. However, with normal gang scheduling, the last step is still needed to synchronize all network preemptions at each process. The overhead for the global state detection is only in adding extra arguments for the synchronizer. Thus the overhead for adding this global state detection mechanism is negligible; it preserves the scalability of network preemption.

The largest drawback of this proposed method is that a global state can be detected only when the distributed processes are gang-switched. This means that when a distributed processes becomes globally idle, the processors are idle for half of the time quantum in average. In many cases, users may expect a shorter response time with their interactive programs. To get this, the process switching must take place in a shorter interval. However, the shorter the interval, the larger the overhead. To answer the question of how often, we have to know how much overhead is incurred by the network preemption and the degree of user frustration concerning the intervals. The measured overhead of gang scheduling under SCore-D is shown in Section 4.

Generality

So far, we have been targeting multi-threaded programs. Here, it is assumed that the local idle state of a user process can be detected by SCore-D. The idle_flag in Figure 3 should be set with great care. The idle_flag is set before incoming message is consumed by PutReceiveBuf(), and before the system-call post-processing. Otherwise, a user program might be mistaken as being globally idle or terminated.

Imagine a program in which a single thread per processor is running on a distributed shared memory machine, and the program code is busy-waiting at a global flag that may be set by another process. The idle_flag can be set in the busy-wait loop. However, a problem can arise over the race between the setting of the idle_flag and the consuming of a remote-memory-write message. At the moment just after the message to set the flag arrives and when the code is about to check the flag, a preemption may occur. If there is no message in the network and all the other processes are idle, the program is mistaken as being in an idle state.

Thus, the generality of the proposed method of global state detection depends on the detection of a local state and timing of message consumption. Presently, we are targeting multi-thread programming environments and cannot go into further detail on shared memory programming models.

Load monitoring

One of the notable side effects of our scheme to detect a global state is the function of user load monitoring. SCore-D can sample the `idle_flag` variable while the user distributed processes are running. Activity indices of user's program on each processor can be calculated and collected.

Many commercially available parallel machines have some hardware support for monitoring its hardware. On Paragon, a program, called SPV, is used to display the load status of each processor and network [11]. Although the OS of Paragon provides a multi-user environment, the SPV program can only display the load information of the entire machine, and not of each user.

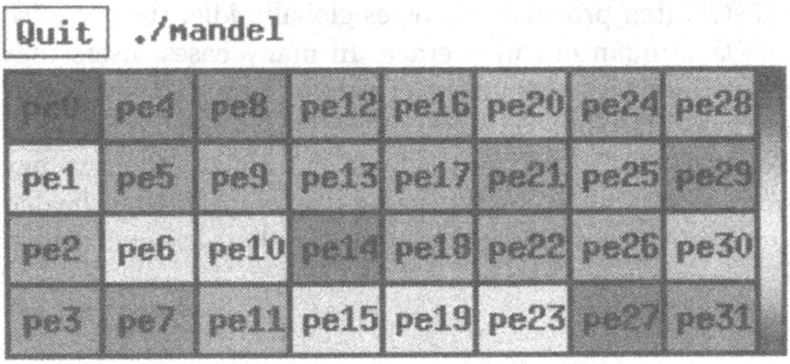

Fig. 4. Sample of activity window

In SCore-D, we implemented the load monitoring function by sampling the `idle_flag` flag. Figure 4 is an example of a window displaying the activities of a user program. The color of each "cell" in the window specifies the activity of a processor. Red means the busiest and blue means idle.

4 Gang Scheduling Overhead

The longer the time quantum, the lower the gang scheduling overhead. However, longer time quantums mean a longer response time and an increased possibility of idling processors. Thus the time quantum of gang scheduling is a trade-off between these and should be decided in accordance with the overhead.

We have developed two types of clusters. One is a workstation cluster consisting of 36 SparcStation 20s (Figure 5). The other is a PC cluster consisting of 32 PCs (Figure 6) [8]. Myrinet is used to interconnect the processors in each cluster.

Table 4 shows slowdown (overhead) due to gang scheduling, varying the time quantum, 0.2, 0.5, and 1.0 second. To measure the overhead, we run a special program in which barrier synchronization is iterated 200,000 times running on 32 processors. Evaluating with this special program, all possible gang scheduling overheads, including co-scheduling skew[2], can be included. The slowdown is compared with the same program running with a stand-alone runtime library (called SCore-S) of MPC++ . On the workstation and the PC cluster, the slowdown is 8.84 % and 4.16 % with the time quantum of half second, respectively. The overhead of the PC cluster is much less than that of workstation cluster. We suspect that this difference is dominated by a scheduling policy of the local Unix operating system[10].

Although the time quantum is relatively larger than that of Unix, granularities of execution time of parallel applications are considered to be larger than that of sequential applications. It is not reasonable to run a text editor on parallel machines. Scheduling tens of processors to echo one character is meaningless. Thus, even for interactive parallel programming, processing granularities triggered by input commands should be larger, and the time quantum around one second is still considered acceptable. The mechanism of the global state detection of distributed processes can utilize processor resource and can reduce users frustration with interactive parallel programs.

Table 4. Slowdown due to gang scheduling [%]

	Time Quantum [*Sec.*]		
	1.0	0.5	0.2
Workstation Cluster	6.96	8.84	28.7
PC Cluster	2.87	4.16	6.25

The overhead of gang scheduling under SCore-D is not small. Sampling the global state of a user program for each gang scheduling is assumed to be practical.

5 Related Works

The global state detection problem can also arise in the area of distributed databases [14], consistent checkpointing [19], and global garbage collection [13]. The famous Chandy and Lamport algorithm used to take a snapshot of a global

Fig. 5. Workstation cluster

Fig. 6. PC cluster

state [4] requires $O(n^2)$ messages, where n is the number of processors, to check a global state. Although the number of required messages can be reduced when network topology and router hardware knowledge are given [19], the detection mechanism should be triggered periodically. Another algorithm, proposed by Misra, used a *marker* message to guarantee the non-existence of messages in the network [16]. Passing one marker message at a time is required, and this marker message passing adds still extra overhead.

In most global detection algorithms proposed so far, it is assumed that messages in transient can not be observed. However, the proposed network preemption mechanism enables this with negligible extra overhead. As mentioned, global idle detection is especially effective for gang-scheduled interactive parallel programs. Thus, integrating a global state detection mechanism into a gang-scheduler is very natural. The message flushing mechanism implemented in PM is needed not only for the network preemption, but also for barrier synchronization. In data parallel programming model, barrier synchronization is used to guarantee that 1) the procedure on every processor has reached the synchronization point, and 2) remote memory write requests have been reflected to the destination memory area. To guarantee the latter item, the PM's message flushing mechanism can be applied. In this case, the proper arrivals of all sending messages should be guaranteed. In the case of network preemption, the non-existence of messages, including Ack/Nack messages, should be guaranteed, no matter if sent messages are properly received.

As described, the largest drawback of this proposed method is that the global state can only be detected at each time quantum. To investigate the global state, network preemption is sufficient, but the saving and restoring network status are not needed. A global state can be detected only by stopping the user processes and counting the flushed messages. More frequent investigation of global state than using gang switching can reduce the possible idle time. As shown in Table 3, it takes several milli-seconds to save and restore network context. This idea is feasible.

6 Concluding Remarks

We have discussed a practical method, implemented in SCore-D, of integrating global idle or termination detection with network preemption. The proposed method is scalable, and the overhead needed to detect a global state is negligible. However this method inherits the drawback of an off-line (or, sync-and-stop in terms of [19]) algorithm.

On shared memory model programs, our proposed method may not be applicable. However, global idle or termination detection is very important in utilizing processor resources on interactive parallel programs. Thus, global state detection should be implemented in a parallel operating system.

References

1. T. E. Anderson, B. N. Bershad, E. D. Lazowska, and H. M. Levy. Scheduler Activations: Effective Kernel Support for the User-Level Management of Parallelism. *ACM Transactions on Computer Systems*, 10(1):53–79, February 1992.
2. R. H. Arpaci, A. C. Dusseau, A. M. Vahdat, L. T. Liu, T. E. Anderson, and D. A. Patterson. The Interaction of Parallel and Sequential Workloads on a Network of Workstations. UC Berekeley Technical Report CS-94-838, Computer Science Division, University of California, Berekeley, 1994.
3. N. J. Boden, D. Cohen, R. E. Felderman, A. E. Kulawik, C. L. Seitz, J. N. Seizovic, and W.-K. Su. Myrinet: A Gigabit-per-Second Local Area Network. *IEEE Micro*, 15(1):29–36, February 1995.
4. M. Chandy and L. Lamport. Distributed snapshot: Determining global states of distributed systems. *ACM Transactions on Computer Systems*, 3(1):63–75, February 1985.
5. D. G. Feitelson and L. Rudolph. Gang Scheduling Performance Benefits for Fine-Grain Synchronization. *Journal of Parallel and Distributed Computing*, 16(4):306–318, 1992.
6. D. G. Feitelson and L. Rudolph. Parallel Job Scheduling: Issues and Approaches. In D. G. Feitelson and L. Rudolph, editors, *Job Scheduling Strategies for Parallel Processing*, volume 949 of *Lecture Notes in Computer Science*, pages 1–18. Springer-Verlag, April 1995.
7. H. Franke, P. Pattnaik, and L. Rudolph. Gang Scheduling for Highly Efficient Distributed Multiprocessor Systems. In *Frontier'96*, October 1996.
8. A. Hori and H. Tezuka. Hardware Design and Implementation of PC Cluster. Technical Report TR–96017, RWC, December 1996.
9. A. Hori, H. Tezuka, and Y. Ishikawa. User-level Parallel Operating System for Clustered Commodity Computers. In *Cluster Computing Conference '97*, March 1997.
10. A. Hori, H. Tezuka, Y. Ishikawa, N. Soda, H. Konaka, and M. Maeda. Implementation of Gang-Scheduling on Workstation Cluster. In D. G. Feitelson and L. Rudolph, editors, *IPPS'96 Workshop on Job Scheduling Strategies for Parallel Processing*, volume 1162 of *Lecture Notes in Computer Science*, pages 76–83. Springer-Verlag, April 1996.
11. Intel Corporation. *PARAGON Ssystem Performance Visualization Tools User's Guide*, January 1996.
12. Y. Ishikawa. Multi Thread Template Library – MPC++ Version 2.0 Level 0 Document –. Technical Report TR–96012, RWC, September 1996.
13. T. Kamada, S. Matsuoka, and A. Yonezawa. Efficient Parallel Global Garbage Collection on Massively Parallel Computers. In *Supercomputing Conference*, pages 79–88, 1994.
14. E. Knapp. Deadlock Detection in Distributed Database. *Computing Surveys*, 19(4):303–328, December 1987.
15. H. Konaka, Y. Itoh, T. Tomokiyo, M. Maeda, Y. Ishikawa, and A. Hori. Adaptive Data Parallel Computation in the Parallel Object-Oriented Language *OCore*. In *Proc. of the International Conference Euro-Par'96, Vol.I*, pages 587–596, 1996.
16. J. Misra. Detecting termination of distributed computations using markers. In *Second ACM Symposium on Principles Distributed Computing*, pages 290–294, August 1983.

276

17. J. K. Ousterhout. Scheduling Techniques for Concurrent Systems. In *Proceedings of Third International Conference on Distributed Computing Systems*, pages 22–30, 1982.
18. S. Pakin, M. Lauria, and A. Chien. High Performance Messaging on Workstations: Illinoi Fast Messages (FM) for Myrinet. In *Supercomputing'95*, December 1995.
19. J. Plank. *EFFICIENT CHECKPOINTING ON MIMD ARCHITECTURES*. PhD thesis, Printceton University, 1993.
20. H. Tezuka, A. Hori, and Y. Ishikawa. PM: A High-Performance Communicatin Library for Multi-user Parallel Environments. Technical Report TR–96015, RWC, November 1996.
21. H. Tezuka, A. Hori, Y. Ishikawa, and M. Sato. PM: A Operating System Coordinated High Performance Communication Library. In *High-Performance Computing and Networking '97*, 1997. to appear.
22. Thinking Machines Corporation. *NI Systems Programming*, October 1992. Version 7.1.

Performance Evaluation of Gang Scheduling for Parallel and Distributed Multiprogramming

Fang Wang[1]   Marios Papaefthymiou[2]   Mark Squillante[3]

[1] Yale University, New Haven CT 06520, USA
[2] University of Michigan, Ann Arbor MI 48109, USA
[3] IBM Research Division, Yorktown Heights NY 10598, USA

Abstract. In this paper we explore the performance of various aspects of gang scheduling designs. We developed an event-driven simulator of a vanilla gang scheduler that relies on the Distributed Hierarchical Control (DHC) structure. We also developed three variations of the vanilla gang scheduler that rely on a push-down heuristic and on two job-migration schemes to decrease response times by reducing processor idle time. We evaluated the gang schedulers on a compiled, one-month long history of jobs from the Cornell Theory Center that was scheduled by EASY-LL, a particular version of LoadLeveler with backfilling. Our results demonstrate the significant performance improvements that can be achieved with gang scheduling. They also show the performance impact of various aspects in the design of gang schedulers. We identify and discuss the potential benefits of several approaches for addressing a number of gang scheduling issues that, under certain workload conditions, become important in practice. Our techniques include heuristics for mapping jobs to processors and for choosing time quanta, block paging for reducing memory overheads, and the allocation of multiple time-slices to smaller jobs per timeplexing cycle.

1 Introduction

Resource management schemes have become essential for the effective utilization of high-performance parallel and distributed systems that are shared among multiple users. The main objective of resource schedulers is to achieve high overall system throughput, while at the same time providing some guarantee for the performance of individual jobs in the system. This is a particularly challenging task, given that typical workloads of multiprogrammed multicomputers include a large number of jobs with diverse resource and performance requirements.

The two basic mechanisms used in multicomputer schedulers are time-sharing and space-sharing. Time-sharing ensures that no job monopolizes the system's resources and can be suitable for scheduling jobs with relatively small processing requirements. A job may not require the attention of the entire system, however. Moreover, abundant empirical evidence indicates that program dependencies and communication costs may limit the degree of achievable parallelism (e.g., [2, 16]). In these situations, space-sharing can increase throughput by partitioning resources and reducing the underutilization of system partitions.

Gang scheduling is a flexible scheduling scheme that combines time-sharing and space-sharing with the goal of providing the advantages of both approaches, including high system throughput and low response times for short-running jobs. The roots of gang scheduling can be traced back to the coscheduling concept described in [18]. This two-dimensional division (in time and space) of resources among jobs can be easily viewed as having the resource allocations governed by a scheduling matrix, where each column represents a specific processor and each row represents a particular time-slice, or quantum. Each non-empty matrix entry (i,j) contains a job (or set of jobs), which represents the allocation of the jth processor to this job during the ith quantum. The set of entries containing the same job (or set of jobs) on a given row is called a partition. The number of partitions and the size of each partition can vary both within and across rows. When a job is submitted, it is assigned to a partition on a particular row. Each partition is allocated a specific time quantum associated with its row, with the possibility of having the partitions on a given row use different quantum lengths. When the time quantum for a partition expires, the resources are reallocated and the job(s) of the partition(s) on the next row are scheduled to execute on the system. Within each partition, resources may be dedicated or time-shared. Thus, gang scheduling supports time-sharing at the partition level and at the individual job level.

Gang scheduling encompasses a very broad range of schedulers depending on the particular schemes used for partitioning resources and for sharing resources within each partition. One particular approach is based on the distributed hierarchical control structure [4, 5, 6]. Within the context of the above description, this scheme can be logically viewed as having a scheduling matrix with $\log P + 1$ rows, where the ith row contains 2^i partitions each of size $P/2^i$, $0 \leq i \leq \log P$, and P denotes the number of system processors. A somewhat different approach, which can be conceptually viewed as a generalization of Ousterhout's original global scheduling matrix, has also been considered [13, 14].

Due to its promising characteristics, gang scheduling has attracted considerable attention in recent years. Gang schedulers based on the distributed hierarchical control structure [4, 5, 6] have been implemented for the IBM RS/6000 SP2 [8, 30] and for clusters of workstations [9, 29]. Similarly, another form of gang scheduling has been implemented on both the IBM SP2 and a cluster of workstations [13, 14]. The performance of gang scheduling schemes that use distributed hierarchical control has been analyzed from a queueing-theoretic perspective [21, 22]. Moreover, the performance of several gang scheduling algorithms has been studied by simulation on synthetically generated workloads [3, 7].

In this paper we present an empirical evaluation of various gang scheduling policies and design alternatives based on an actual parallel workload. Our focus is on the distributed hierarchical control approach to gang scheduling, although many of the principles and trends observed in this study are relevant to other forms of gang scheduling. Our study includes an examination of a vanilla gang scheduling scheme [4, 21] and two variations of this scheme that use *push-down* and *job-migration* heuristics to increase system throughput and decrease response times by minimizing idle partitions. These scheduling strategies are simulated under a workload that we obtained by post-processing a trace of the workload characteristics for one month at the Cornell Theory Center [10, 11, 12]. The original workload was scheduled on 320 processors of the IBM SP2 at Cornell's Theory Center using EASY-LL, an enhanced version of the basic LoadLeveler scheduler that uses backfilling to reduce the response times of jobs with small resource requirements [20].

The objectives of our evaluation study were to assess the effectiveness of different aspects of gang scheduling designs under a variety of heuristics for assigning jobs to processors and across a range of memory overheads. We investigated a greedy scheme for the vanilla and the push-down scheduler and two priority-based policies for migrating and redistributing jobs. In our experiments, both job-migration policies perform better than the vanilla and the push-down schemes. Our first job-migration scheme favors jobs with small resource requirements and achieves significantly shorter response times than EASY-LL for most job classes in the system. Our other job-migration policy favors large jobs and performs better than either EASY-LL or any of our gang scheduling schemes in most job classes with large resource requirements. For jobs with small resource requirements, however, EASY-LL outperforms this particular gang scheduler. As context-switch costs increase due to factors such as memory and communications overheads, the performance of the three gang scheduling policies degrades significantly, especially for short quanta. We propose an approach to effectively reduce the performance impact of such memory overheads as part of our study.

The remainder of this paper is organized as follows. We begin in Section 2 with a more detailed description of EASY-LL and the gang scheduling policies considered. In Section 3 we present the mechanisms examined for mapping jobs to processors. A brief overview of our simulator engine is given in Section 4. We describe the workload used in our study in Section 5, and continue with the presentation of our experimental results in Section 6. We then discuss in Section 7 some of the practical implications of our results, as well as approaches to improve gang scheduling performance and current ongoing aspects of our study. Our concluding remarks are presented in Section 8.

2 Scheduling policies

In this section we describe the scheduling policies examined in our study. We first present the notation and terminology used throughout this paper. We then give a brief overview of the EASY-LL scheduling scheme, followed by a description of the gang scheduling policies we considered.

2.1 Preliminaries

The basic parameters associated with serving any given job j is the *arrival time* α_j, the *dispatch time* β_j, and the *completion time* ϵ_j of the job. When this job is submitted to the system at time α_j, it is placed into a particular queue based on the scheduling policy. At time β_j, the job is moved from this queue to a specific partition and receives service for the first time. At time ϵ_j the job finishes its execution and exits the system. The (cumulative) amount of time for which job j actually receives service is its *service time* S_j.

A number of important performance measures are used to compare the different scheduling policies considered in our study. In particular, the job parameters $\alpha_j, \beta_j, \epsilon_j$ and S_j can be used to define the following performance metrics for the execution of job j:

- *response time* $\mathcal{R}_j$, where $\mathcal{R}_j = \epsilon_j - \alpha_j$
- *queueing time* Q_j, where $Q_j = \beta_j - \alpha_j$
- *execution time* $\mathcal{E}_j$, where $\mathcal{E}_j = \epsilon_j - \beta_j$
- *sharing time* $\mathcal{H}_j$, where $\mathcal{H}_j = \mathcal{E}_j - S_j$
- *waiting time* $\mathcal{W}_j$, where $\mathcal{W}_j = \mathcal{R}_j - S_j$

In these definitions, we have split "waiting time" (respectively, "service time") into two separate components $\mathcal{W}_j$ and Q_j (respectively, $\mathcal{E}_j$ and $\mathcal{H}_j$) to take the time sharing into account. Thus, the total waiting time $\mathcal{W}_j$ is the sum $Q_j + \mathcal{H}_j$ of the time spent waiting on the queue (Q_j) and the time that job j is swapped out ($\mathcal{H}_j$). Also, the execution time $\mathcal{E}_j$ is the sum $S_j + \mathcal{H}_j$ of the service time (S_j) and the sharing time during which job j is swapped out ($\mathcal{H}_j$).

2.2 EASY-LL

Our consideration here of the LoadLeveler and EASY-LL schedulers is based upon the use of the versions of these schedulers at the Cornell Theory Center when the workload traces used in our experiments were collected. This version of LoadLeveler schedules jobs in the order of their arrival times. The job at the head of the queue is dispatched and begins its execution as soon as sufficient resources become available in the system. LoadLeveler does not support preemption. Once a job begins its execution, it continues until it terminates. Thus, in LoadLeveler we have $\mathcal{W}_j = Q_j$ and $\mathcal{E}_j = S_j$. This LoadLeveler scheme may not be suitable for interactive execution, as system access is blocked for every job that arrives immediately after any single job with large resource requirements.

The EASY-LL scheduler is a variation of this version of the LoadLeveler scheme that uses a backfilling heuristic to improve response time for short-running tasks. When submitting their jobs to the system queue, users request a specific number of processors and provide an estimate of the execution times of their jobs on the requested resources. Whenever new resources become available or a new job is submitted, EASY-LL schedules the first job in the queue that fits within the available resources and whose execution does not delay the dispatching of any job ahead of it in the queue. Thus, small jobs can bypass larger jobs, provided they do not delay the execution of the larger jobs.

2.3 Vanilla gang scheduling

Generic gang scheduling under distributed hierarchical control views a parallel computing system as a collection of P identical processors and a hierarchy of

$L = \log P + 1$ different *classes* of jobs. At any time, the system is serving jobs from a specific class. When serving jobs of class i, the system is divided into $P/2^i$ *partitions* where each partition consists of 2^i processors. For example, a 256-processor system has 9 classes, where class 0 has 256 partitions each with one processor, class 1 has 128 partitions each with two processors, and so on. A first-come first-served queue is associated with each class from which the corresponding partitions select jobs for execution. An example of this hierarchical, binary-tree view of the gang scheduling system is illustrated in Fig. 1. Jobs are allocated to partitions in their corresponding classes according to a specific job assignment policy (described in Section 3).

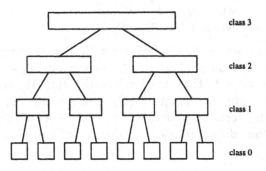

Fig. 1. Binary-tree view of an 8-processor multicomputer system under the distributed hierarchical control structure.

During the operation of the system, each class i is allocated a time-slice of certain length. Processors are dedicated to each of the L classes in a time-shared manner by rotating the time allocated to the job classes. The time interval between successive time-slices of the same class is called the *timeplexing cycle* of the system, which we denote by T. A system-wide switch from the current class i to the next class $i - 1$ (modulo L) occurs when at least one of the following two events becomes true:

- The time-slice of class i has expired.
- There are no jobs of class i in the system.

In the vanilla gang scheduling scheme, when the number of partitions in a class exceeds the number of jobs assigned to it, the excess partitions remain idle during the time-slice. Therefore, the system may be significantly underutilized in light load situations.

2.4 Gang scheduling with push-down

A simple variation of the vanilla gang scheduling scheme uses a push-down heuristic to reduce the number of idle partitions at any time. In push-down gang scheduling, every partition that is idle during its designated time-slice is reconfigured into two partitions for the class below it, each of which is half the size of the original partition. The partitions are reconfigured recursively until they find a job(s) from a class below that is allocated to the same set of processors. Thus, a fraction of the original partition's time-slice is allocated to jobs belonging to the class(es) below (i.e., it is "pushed down" to the lower partitions), and at any time the system may be serving jobs from more than one class. With push-down, the actual length of the timeplexing cycle is workload dependent. Assuming that no job finishes before the expiration of its quantum, the actual timeplexing cycle is equal to the maximum number of busy nodes in any path from the root to the leaves of the distributed hierarchical control tree.

2.5 Gang scheduling with job migration

The third gang scheduling policy we consider borrows characteristics from both the vanilla and the push-down schedulers. Under this policy, all jobs waiting in the queue of a class are scheduled to execute in the beginning of the corresponding time-slice. As is the case with push-down gang scheduling, idle partitions are assigned jobs from other classes according to some job assignment priority scheme. These jobs are free to execute on *any* idle partition, however. Therefore, gang scheduling with migration is more flexible and may result in fewer idle partitions than gang scheduling with push-down. In a manner similar to the vanilla gang scheduler, switches are system-wide and occur when the time-slice of the class expires. Thus, even though the system may not be serving any job from the class that corresponds to the active time-slice, jobs are reallocated in logical synchrony, and the timeplexing cycle remains fixed.

The overhead of such a migration scheme can be quite large. In our current study, we ignore this overhead and thus use the job-migration policy in our experiments to explore the upper bound on gang scheduling performance under distributed hierarchical control. A few methods for attempting to achieve the performance of this migration scheme in practice, such as *tree-packing*, are discussed in Section 7.

2.6 Processor counts that are not powers of 2

It is straightforward to embed the scheduling schemes described in the previous subsections in systems with 2^i processors. When processor counts are not powers of 2, however, there are several ways to implement the distributed hierarchical control structure. Fig. 2 illustrates the general approach that we adopted in our scheduling policies. For one time-slice during each timeplexing cycle, system resources are configured as a single 320-processor system. Subsequently, the 320 processors are partitioned into a 64-processor and a 256-processor system, each of which is viewed as a binary tree. With the push-down scheduling policy, the two trees proceed independently. With the job-migration policies, however, the switches in the two trees are synchronized. Due to their different heights, the two trees may be serving different classes at a time. In our implementations, when the 256-processor subtree is serving class 8 or 7, the 64-processor subtree is serving class 1 or 0, respectively. From class 6 and below, both trees serve the same class during each time-slice.

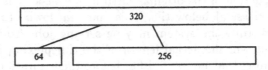

Fig. 2. Distributed hierarchical control structure for a 320-processor system.

3 Job assignment policies

An important component of every gang scheduling approach is the policy that it uses to assign dispatched jobs to partitions. This policy can have a profound impact on the performance of a gang scheduler, as we have found in our numerous experiments, and these performance issues are highly dependent upon the workload characteristics. So far, we have experimented with three policies for assigning jobs within each class. The first two policies are used together with the vanilla and the push-down scheduler. Under these policies, each job is assigned to a partition when it starts to execute for the first time and remains assigned to the same partition for the duration of its execution time. The third policy is used together with the migration scheduler and assigns jobs to partitions on every switch via different priority schemes.

Our first job assignment policy is a greedy, first-fit strategy that always starts from the leftmost branch of the tree and assigns each new job to the first available partition in that class. In a lightly loaded system, this scheme will load the left branch of the tree, while leaving the partitions on the right branch idle. Under these circumstances, the degree to which push-down can be applied on the right branch is limited, and thus it can become ineffective for the right branch.

The second policy we investigate is a very simple, "weight-oriented" allocation scheme. Every node in the tree is associated with a weight equal to the sum of the jobs allocated to that node and all its descendents in the tree. Node weights are updated whenever a job finishes or is dispatched to a partition in the tree. When assigning a job to a partition in class i, we select the one with the lightest weight node in the level i of the tree. Such a partition can be found by a straightforward tree traversal that recursively looks for the lightest branch at each level until it reaches level i. The lightest partition in the class has the smallest number of jobs allocated in level i and below. This scheme is a local optimization procedure that does not take into account the remaining service times of the currently dispatched jobs or future job arrivals. Moreover, the details of its definition are meant to work in unison with the push-down scheduler. Under a different approach, such as a push-up scheme, the weights and traversals should be modified to match the corresponding properties of the approach employed.

For gang schedulers that support job migration, we experimented with a simple job assignment policy that maps jobs to idle partitions in a greedy manner. During each time-slice, jobs waiting to execute in the queue of the corresponding class are dispatched. If processors remain idle, they are assigned jobs from other classes. Each time a job is dispatched, it may run on a different set of processors. Since it is assumed that there is no overhead for migrating jobs to different partitions (see Section 2.5), there is no loss of generality while obtaining the best gang scheduling performance. A straightforward job assignment strategy would be to impose a priority on the system's classes and to assign idle processors to jobs of other classes by considering these classes in decreasing priority. In our experiments, we investigated two extremes of this simple priority scheme. We looked at a top-down order that starts from the root and proceeds to the leaves, thus favoring jobs with large resource requirements. Conversely, we also studied a bottom-up approach that traverses classes from the leaves to the root, thus favoring jobs with small resource requirements.

4   Simulator

We developed an event-driven simulator engine to experiment with the various gang scheduling policies described above. Our simulator has four different events: job arrival, job completion, time-slice expiration, and context switch. All events are inserted into an event queue, and the earliest event in the queue is triggered first. In this section we outline the operation of our simulation and explain the design choices we made in order to simplify its implementation.

In general, when a class i job arrives, if class i is currently being served and has partitions available, the job is dispatched to an available partition according to one of the schemes described in Section 3. If no partition in class i is available, the job is inserted into the queue for class i.

If class i is currently not being served, the job is handled according to the specifics of the gang scheduling policy under consideration. In the vanilla policy, the job is simply inserted into the waiting queue for class i. With the push-down and job-migration policies, if there are available partitions in another class j that can have their class j time-slice pushed down to host the newly arrived class i job, the new job will be dispatched accordingly. If there is no available partition or no time can be pushed down, the job will be added to the class i queue.

When a job completes, its partition becomes available, and the weight associated with each node is updated. If there are jobs waiting in the queue of the current class, the available partition may be assigned to a new job according to one of the mechanisms described in Section 3. Otherwise, under the push-down and migration policies, the time-slice of the available partition is allocated to a job of another class in a manner similar to that described above for an arrival that finds the system serving another class while processors are idle.

When the time-slice of a class expires, every job that is currently executing is stopped and its remaining execution time is updated. Subsequently, a context switch event occurs. A context switch also occurs when all the partitions in a class become idle, and there are no jobs waiting in the queue. Thus, the time remaining in the quantum is not wasted idling.

The context switch event starts the execution of the jobs in the next class that are ready to run. Preempted jobs resume their execution, and jobs in the queue are dispatched if there are still partitions available. With push-down scheduling, if any partitions remain idle, their time-slices are pushed down for jobs in lower classes. In a similar manner, with the job-migration policy, idle partitions will be assigned jobs from the queues of higher or lower classes in the system.

In order to avoid a complex software implementation, we made a few simplifying assumptions in the simulation of the migration scheduler. First, our simulator dispatches new jobs only in the beginning of each time-slice. Thus, whenever jobs arrive or finish in the middle of a time-slice, our simulator does not take advantage of the possibly idle processors in the system. Second, our simulator does not account for the various overheads (e.g., communication, data transfer, system state, etc.) incurred for migrating jobs among processors. In view of the relatively light loads we experimented with, dispatching jobs only in the beginning of time-slices should not significantly change the trends of our performance results. Moreover, our second assumption yields an upper bound on the performance of gang scheduling under distributed hierarchical control, and we wanted to quantify this potential benefit under an actual workload. This and other related issues, including several mechanisms that can be used to reduce the cost of data transfers, are discussed further in Section 7.

5 Workload characteristics

We experimented with a collection of jobs that were submitted to the Cornell Theory Center SP2 during the month of August 1996. The execution of these jobs on the SP2 was managed by the EASY-LL scheduler described in Section 2.2. Our workload comprised 6,049 jobs that requested up to 320 processors and had nonzero CPU times. We categorized these jobs into ten classes according to their resource requirements. Each job requesting p processors was assigned to class i, where $2^{i-1} < p \leq 2^i$. This classification scheme facilitated the direct performance comparison of the gang scheduling policies with the EASY-LL scheduler on a 320-processor system.

The statistics of this workload are given in the table of Fig. 3. The first two columns of the table give the class number and the job counts in each class. The third column gives the average service time for the jobs in each class. This number is intrinsic to each job and the number of processors it executes on. The fourth and fifth columns give the average waiting and response time that was achieved for each class using the EASY-LL scheduler. The last column gives the normalized average response time for the jobs in each class. An interesting point about these data is that, with the notable exception of the uniprocessor class 0, the average response times increase almost monotonically with the number of processors in the class. Also, with the exception of class 8, the normalized response times increase monotonically with the number of processors.

class	jobs	S_j	W_j	R_j	R/S_j
0	2,408	16,854	9,105	25,959	1.5
1	515	18,100	12,122	30,222	1.7
2	669	9,571	10,315	19,885	2.1
3	582	3,563	13,946	17,510	4.9
4	848	8,822	24,947	33,768	3.8
5	465	9,008	69,157	78,165	8.7
6	420	93,189	93,040	102,359	11.0
7	74	12,168	128,895	141,062	11.6
8	45	300	146,141	146,441	488.4
9	23	5,912	147,240	153,153	26.0

Fig. 3. Job counts, service times, waiting times, response times, and normalized response times for the one-month workload from the Cornell Theory Center under EASY-LL. Service, waiting, and response times are measured in seconds.

6 Simulation results

Initially, we experimented with the vanilla gang scheduling policy. It soon became evident that this scheme was performing consistently and significantly worse than EASY-LL under the Cornell Theory Center workload. Since the vanilla scheduler switches all partitions in the same class synchronously, this relatively light parallel workload resulted in several idle partitions. We thus turned our attention to the other gang schedulers, due to their promising handling of idle partitions. In this section we discuss the results we obtained by simulating the push-down scheduler and our two job-migration policies on the one-month workload from the Cornell Theory Center. For the push-down policy, we only present the results we obtained with the weight-oriented job assignment policy, since it consistently outperformed the first-fit policy, as expected.

Figs. 4, 5, 6, and 7 give the performance of the gang scheduling schemes for context-switch costs of 1 second and 16 seconds. In each of these graphs, the y-axis gives the mean response time for the jobs in the corresponding class normalized by the mean service time for that class. The timeplexing cycle, which is given on the x-axis, is divided uniformly among the system's ten classes. We arrived at the worst-case context-switch cost of 16 seconds by assuming that the jobs have a 64MB working set on each processor [11] which must be loaded in its entirety at the rate of 1 page/millisecond for a page size of 4KB, given the characteristics of many parallel scientific applications [19] and the (potentially) large degree of multiprogramming with ten classes. Note that EASY-LL is not affected by the context-switch overheads of gang scheduling, and the corresponding curves in Figs. 4 – 7 represent the last column in the table of Fig. 3.

Our results show that the scheduling policy with migration from the leaves achieves shorter response times than EASY-LL for eight out of the ten classes. Recall that this migration policy favors jobs with smaller resource requirements. This results in better performance for the small job classes than that provided

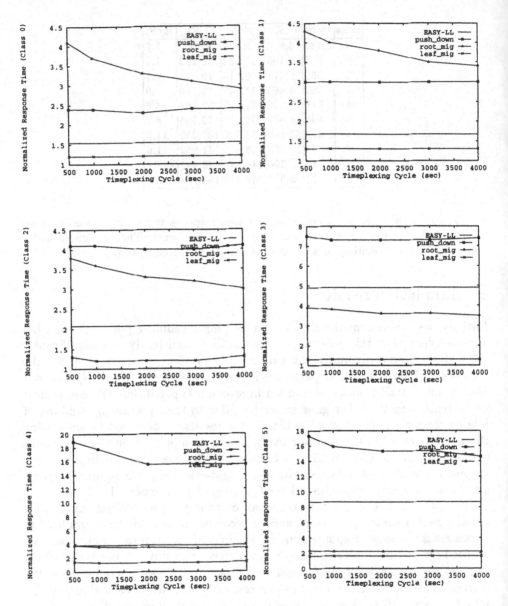

Fig. 4. Normalized response times of classes 0–5 for the push-down gang scheduler, the migration scheduler with jobs assigned from the root, and the migration scheduler with jobs assigned from the leaves. Quanta are allocated uniformly, and the context-switch cost for each class is 1 sec.

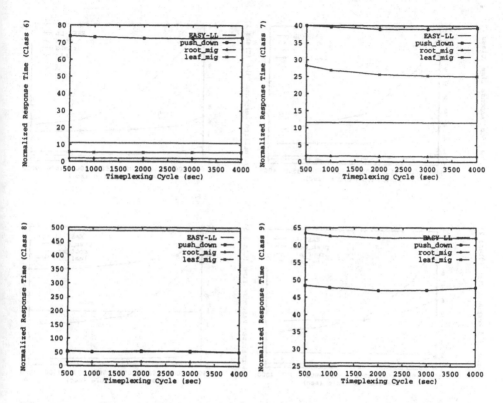

Fig. 5. Normalized response times of classes 6–9 for the push-down gang scheduler, the migration scheduler with jobs assigned from the root, and the migration scheduler with jobs assigned from the leaves. Quanta are allocated uniformly, and the context-switch cost for each class is 1 sec.

under EASY-LL, which also attempts to improve performance for jobs with smaller resource requirements via backfilling. In some cases, these performance improvements are quite significant, with a reduction in the normalized response times by factors that typically range between 2 and 4. Some of the larger job classes also receive improved performance under migration from the leaves in comparison to EASY-LL; e.g., the normalized response time of class 8 decreases by almost a factor of 10. However, the favoring of smaller job classes under migration from the leaves degrades the performance of classes 7 and 9 relative to EASY-LL, where our results show a decrease in normalized response time by about a factor of 3.

The job-migration policy that gives higher priority to the jobs closer to the root of the control tree outperforms EASY-LL for classes 5 through 8. Moreover, for sufficiently large timplexing cycles, this policy performs as well as EASY-LL for classes 3 and 4. In comparison with the migration policy that favors jobs at the leaves, this policy breaks even for class 5 and performs better for classes 6 and above. As expected, both job-migration policies achieve the same performance

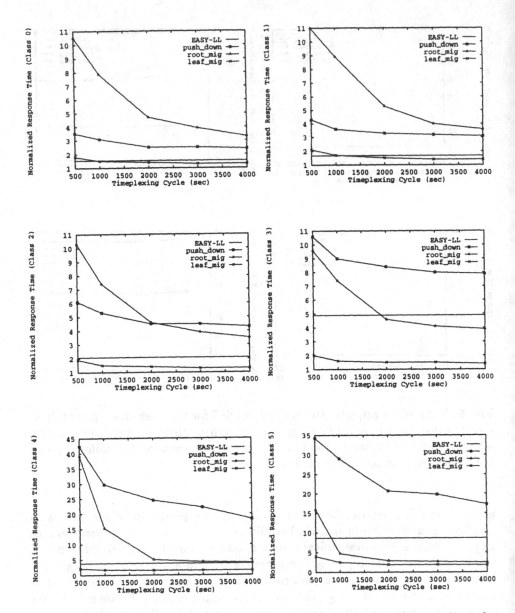

Fig. 6. Normalized response times of classes 0–5 for the push-down policy, the job-migration policy from the root, and the job-migration policy from the leaves. Quanta are allocated uniformly, and a worst-case context-switch cost of 16 sec is assumed for each class.

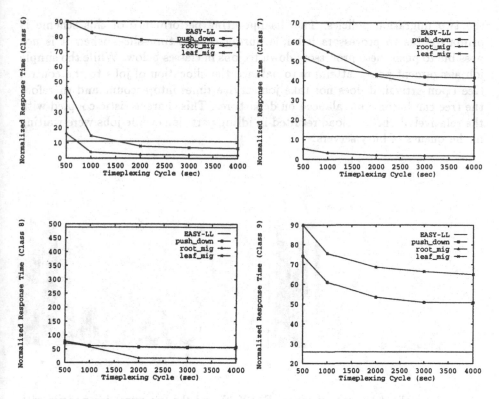

Fig. 7. Normalized response times of classes 6–9 for the push-down policy, the job-migration policy from the root, and the job-migration policy from the leaves. Quanta are allocated uniformly, and a worst-case context-switch cost of 16 sec is assumed for each class.

on class 9, since the timplexing cycle is fixed and the jobs in that class cannot fit in any smaller partition of the system. The gains achieved for the large classes by migrating jobs from the root come at a sometimes significant performance hit for the smaller classes, however. For classes 0 through 2, migration from the root performs worse than all the scheduling policies we considered.

As these results show, there is an important tradeoff with respect to the priority order used to fill otherwise idle slots in the control tree (via migration or other methods). This priority order should be reflected in the job assignment and other aspects of the gang scheduling policies. Moreover, performance benefits may be realized in various cases by exploiting adaptive (dynamic) schemes that adjust the priority order based upon the state of the system (as well as changes to this state). As a simple example, an adaptive migration scheme based on the extremes considered in this paper could consist of determining whether migration is performed from the root or the leaves on each timeplexing cycle based on the state of the system at the start of the cycle.

The push-down policy almost always performs worse than EASY-LL and the two migration policies. The disappointing performance of this scheme is primarily due to processors left idle during certain time-slices when it is not possible to push these processors down to jobs in classes below. While the simple job assignment policy attempts to balance the allocation of jobs to the control tree upon arrival, it does not take job service times into account and therefore the tree can become unbalanced on departures. This characteristic coupled with the relatively light workload resulted in idling partitions while jobs were waiting in the queues of busy servers.

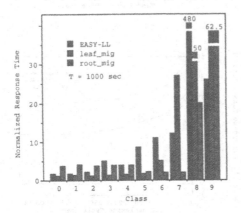 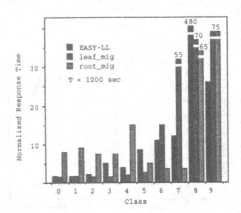

Fig. 8. Normalized response times for EASY-LL and the two migration policies with a timeplexing cycle equal to 1,000 sec. The context-switch costs are 1 sec for the left chart and 16 sec for the right chart.

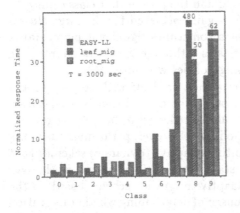 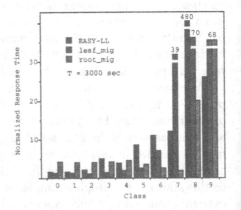

Fig. 9. Normalized response times for EASY-LL and the two migration policies with a timeplexing cycle of 3,000 sec. The context-switch costs are 1 sec for the left chart and 16 sec for the right chart.

Our simulations also show the performance degradation of the gang scheduling policies when the context-switch costs increase. For both values of context-switch overheads that we tried, however, the qualitative trends of our results are similar. The bar charts in Figs. 8 and 9 illustrate the effects of context-switch overheads on the performance of the job-migration schedulers. For low switch costs, the two job migration schemes underperform EASY-LL in several classes. When switch costs increase, however, the performance of both policies degrades, and the number of classes in which they outperform EASY-LL decreases. Performance degradation is more evident for short timeplexing cycles, since in this case context-switch costs become a significant fraction of each time-slice. We address in Section 7.1 ways to effectively reduce some of the dominant causes of this overhead.

7 Discussion

Our simulation results based on the Cornell Theory Center workload data have several important implications on gang scheduling strategies in practice. In this section, we discuss various aspects of these practical implications, as well as current ongoing aspects of our study.

7.1 Memory and paging overheads

Based on the simple analysis in Section 6 to estimate the context-switch memory overhead, as well as the corresponding response time results, memory and paging overheads can have a considerable impact on the performance of large-scale parallel systems that time-share their resources. We now discuss a particular strategy to significantly reduce and effectively eliminate these overheads for a general class of large-scale parallel applications. Our approach is based in part on the concept of *block paging*, which was introduced in the VM/SP HPO operating system [1, 25, 26] and extended in the VM/ESA operating system [23, 24]. A few other systems have since adopted some of these concepts, and related forms of prefetching have recently appeared in the research literature [15, 17]. We first provide a brief overview of the block paging mechanisms used in VM; the interested reader is referred to [1, 23, 24, 25, 26, 27, 28] for additional technical details. We then discuss our approach for addressing memory and paging overheads in large-scale parallel time-sharing systems, which is based on the VM mechanisms and extensions tailored to the parallel computing environments of interest.

The basic idea behind block paging is quite simple: the system identifies sets of pages that tend to be referenced together and then pages each of these sets into memory and out to disk as a unit. This strategy generalizes previous paging and swapping methods in that defining the block size to be 1 page yields demand paging and defining the block size to be the entire working set yields swapping. Block sizes in between these two extremes provide additional degrees of freedom to optimize various performance objectives.

The primary motivation for the block-paging mechanisms in VM was to improve the response times of interactive jobs by amortizing the cost of accessing disk over several pages, thus reducing the waiting time and processor overhead of demand paging techniques and reducing the number of times the paging paths need to be executed. For example, it is shown in [23, 24] that the delay to fetch a single page from a particular IBM 3380 disk configuration is 29ms, whereas the delay to fetch 10 pages from a simpler 3380 configuration is 48ms.

The VM paging system gathers various data and employs a number of algorithms exploiting these data for the creation and dynamic adjustment of page blocks. These algorithms attempt to identify pages that are referenced together. To identify such pages with temporal (and address) affinity, the VM algorithms are applied locally to each address space rather than globally across all address spaces. The page replacement algorithms therefore work on a per address-space basis to select pages of similar age and last-reference for similar treatment and eventual placement on disk. In this manner, the time (and space) affinity of pages is used to create blocks of pages that will be written to and read from disk as a unit, subject to the constraint that the block size is tailored to the characteristics of the particular disk(s) employed in the system. As a specific example, the average block size on VM systems is between 9 and 12 pages with a range of 2 to 20 pages [23, 24]. When a page is fetched from disk as part of a block and is never referenced during the block's residence in memory, then the VM algorithms subsequently eliminate the page from the block. In certain cases, the system also chains together related page blocks for additional optimizations.

When a page fault occurs and the page is part of a block, the VM system issues the I/O request(s) in a manner that attempts to bring this particular page into memory as fast as possible. A program controlled interrupt is associated with the frame assigned to this faulting page, which signals when the required page is in memory. Once this interrupt occurs, the system makes the faulting process ready, therefore allowing it to be immediately scheduled. The remainder of the page block continues to be fetched in parallel with the (possible) execution of the process, thus overlapping the I/O and computation *within* an application. All pages in the block are initially marked as not referenced, with the exception of the one causing the original page fault. This page status information together with other temporal (and address) affinity information are used to minimize failures in accurately predicting future page co-reference and to dynamically maintain page blocks. The analysis in [28] shows that the VM paging algorithms are very effective in maintaining appropriate page blocks (e.g., a page is incorrectly placed in a block – in the sense that it is brought in as part of the block but never referenced – less than 13% of the time in practice) and extremely effective at minimizing the impact of disk performance on interactive response times.

There are two basic approaches to address the performance issues related to the memory management component of large-scale parallel environments in general [19], and especially in systems that time-share their resources. One approach consists of allocating jobs to partitions such that the memory requirements of all jobs on each node of the partition fit within the memory available on that node, thus avoiding the memory overhead problem. This approach can severely limit (or eliminate altogether) the degree of time-slicing, however, and for large-scale parallel computing environments such as the Cornell Theory Center workload considered in our study, it is impossible within the context of the distributed hierarchical control schemes described in Section 2. Another basic approach consists of developing memory management schemes to reduce the performance impact of these memory overheads. In the remainder of this section, we sketch one such approach based in part on block paging.

For each application being executed on a node, the operating system gathers data and employs algorithms much like those in VM for the creation and dynamic adjustment of page blocks. When there is a context-switch to a previously executing job and that job encounters a page fault, the operating system issues an I/O request to bring in the faulting page as quickly as possible and sets a program controlled interrupt[4] on the page frame allocated to the faulting page. As soon as the page is brought into memory, the system returns to the execution of this job and the remaining pages of the block are brought into memory in parallel with the execution of the job. Given the memory reference characteristics of many scientific applications [19], the operating system can continue to bring into memory a number of page blocks that are chained to the faulting page block based on time (and space) affinity. The optimal number of additional page blocks that should be brought into memory depends upon the quantum length allocated to the job (and estimates of the program behavior that could be provided by the compiler). Since the scheduling system controls this parameter, it can work together with the memory management system (possibly together with additional compiler support) to employ a reasonable estimate of the best number of chained blocks to fetch into memory for the current time-slice. These page blocks will replace page blocks already in memory. Once again, since the scheduling system controls the time-slice ordering of the execution of the jobs, it can convey this information to the memory management system so that the page replacement policies displace page blocks that are guaranteed to not be referenced for the longest period of time, thus minimizing the amount of page faults encountered by the system. In this manner, the memory management system can effectively set up a pipeline in which the fetching of the set of pages required by a job during its current time-slice and the corresponding writing of memory-resident page blocks to disk (when necessary) are overlapped with useful computation for the job.

7.2 Quanta allocation

A key parameter of any time-sharing policy is the quantum length assigned to each class of jobs. We have used, and continue to use, an analytic approach [21, 22] to gain insights into this problem with which heuristics can be developed for practical gang scheduling policies. A simple resulting heuristic is based on

---

[4] The system could also have the job spin on an event associated with the page fault being satisfied, depending upon which is more efficient for the given hardware platform.

the relative utilization of the resources by each class. More formally, we define the relative utilization for class i over a particular interval of interest as $\rho_i \equiv (\lambda_i 2^i)/(\mu_i P)$, where λ_i and μ_i are the mean arrival and service rates for class i over the interval, respectively. We then define the simple heuristic of allocating quanta lengths of $(\rho_i/\rho)T$ to each class i, where T is the timeplexing cycle and $\rho \equiv \sum_i \rho_i$. Note that this approach assumes that time-slices assigned to each class i are primarily consumed by jobs of class i over the time period of interest.

To examine the benefits and limitations of this approach, we ran a number of simulations comparing the above heuristic with the uniform approach (i.e., the quantum length for each class is T divided by the number of classes) where the period of one day was used (a finer granularity of four hours was also examined). In order to estimate the expected per-class relative utilization, we adjusted the quantum of each class every day based on the class' utilization the day before. The simple intuition behind this allocation policy is that system utilization may exhibit some form of "temporal locality" in which partitions that are used more heavily than others over a given time interval are likely to continue to do so over the next interval. In fact, comparisons between this approach and using the actual relative utilization for each day (obtained by an off-line analysis of the trace data) demonstrated only small differences in the mean response times realized for each class. In our preliminary simulations, we therefore set the quantum of class i for day d equal to $(\rho_i(d)/\rho(d))T$, where these parameters are as defined above with the addition of the parameter d.

Our preliminary simulation results suggest that this quanta allocation heuristic can work quite well for heavier load situations in which each class has a non-negligible amount of work, as the system resources are being allocated to equalize the work brought to the system by each class. On the other hand, this approach is not appropriate for (nor is it intended for) migration-based gang schedulers (and to a lesser extent, push-down schemes) under lighter loads, since in this case the classes are grabbing resources assigned to each other and the relative utilization is not very representative of the actual allocation of resources. Hence, one possible solution is to have the system use the ρ-based heuristic during heavier load situations, and then switch to a uniform quanta length policy when the load drops below certain thresholds. We are currently studying such approaches in more detail.

Another important aspect of quanta allocation was also observed based upon our queueing-theoretic gang scheduling analysis [21, 22]. In particular, the setting of these policy parameters in gang scheduling systems must address the complex tradeoff between providing preferential treatment to short-running jobs via small quanta lengths at the expense of larger delays for long-running jobs. By allocating multiple quanta to shorter-running job classes for each quantum allocated to longer-running job classes, the system can generalize the optimization problem at hand and provide additional flexibility to optimize various performance objectives. We are currently working on variations of the basic gang scheduling policy in which certain classes are allocated more than one time slice during each timeplexing cycle and they are executed out of order. For example, instead of visiting classes in the order < class-0, class-1, ..., class-8 >, the scheduler could execute a timeplexing cycle order < class-0, class-1, class-2, class-0, class-3, class-4, class-0, ..., class-8 >. We believe that such policies can be used to significantly improve the performance of job classes with smaller processing requirements while not degrading considerably the performance of jobs with larger processing requirements.

7.3 Job assignment schemes

As previously noted, the migration scheme considered in our experiments provides an upper bound on gang scheduling performance for the actual workload considered. We have been working on a tree-packing scheme that exploits *parasite allocations* (somewhat similar to the alternative scheduling in [3]) by assigning jobs to partitions in the tree that maximize the number of processors kept busy throughout the timeplexing cycle. Much like the migration scheme, this approach uses a priority-based mechanism for choosing among multiple assignments that are equal with respect to keeping processors busy. We are also developing a push-up gang-scheduling policy that is similar to our push-down policy. When two sibling partitions are idle during their designated time-slices, they can be combined to serve jobs in the higher class. When both push-up and push-down scheduling is used, the idle time-slice may be passed either up or down, depending on which class has the largest number of outstanding jobs. Of course, a broad variety of other criteria can be applied depending on the specific performance objectives that are set forth for the scheduling policy. We are in the process of adding these schemes to our simulator and will be evaluating how well they perform relative to the job-migration method.

Another area we are currently investigating concerns different mechanisms for assigning jobs to partitions in a balanced manner. Different functions or algorithms may be required for the different policies (vanilla, push-up, push-down). Moreover, during the assignment of a job in class i, the values at level i as well as its parents and immediate children could be used to determine which half of the tree the job should be allocated on. Finally, it would be interesting to prove the optimality of job assignment mechanisms under simple service time and arrival time assumptions for the jobs in the system.

8 Conclusions

In this paper we evaluated the performance of various aspects of several gang scheduling approaches and compared them with EASY-LL. We developed an event-driven simulator of the various policies and evaluated their performance by applying them on an actual parallel workload from the Cornell Theory Center. Our experimental results demonstrate the performance benefits, trade-offs, and limitations of alternative gang scheduling designs under the specific workload conditions we considered. We proposed several approaches for addressing different aspects of gang scheduling in practice and presented evidence for the potential benefits of some of these approaches. We are continuing to explore these and other issues related to different forms of gang scheduling in large-scale and/or distributed parallel computing environments.

Acknowledgments

We gratefully acknowledge and thank the Cornell Theory Center (CTC), and especially Steve Hotovy, Joseph Skovira and Joseph Riordan, for providing us with the workload data from its SP2; we also thank Steve Hotovy for several fruitful discussions about this data. We thank Pratap Pattnaik from the IBM T. J. Watson Research Center (WRC) for several helpful discussions; we also thank Russ Miller and Bill Tetzlaff from WRC for fruitful discussions on the details of VM's block paging mechanisms, and we thank Liana Fong from WRC for information on the LoadLeveler and EASY-LL schedulers.

References

1. T. Beretvas and W. H. Tetzlaff. Paging enhancements in VM/SP HPO 3.4. Technical Report TB GG22-9467, IBM Washington Syst. Center, May 1984.
2. D. L. Eager, J. Zahorjan, and E. D. Lazowska. Speedup versus efficiency in parallel systems. *IEEE Trans. Comp.*, 38:408–423, March 1989.
3. D. G. Feitelson. Packing schemes for gang scheduling. In *Job Sched. Strategies for Parallel Processing, D. G. Feitelson and L. Rudolph (eds.)*, pages 89–110. Springer-Verlag, 1996. LNCS Vol. 1162.
4. D. G. Feitelson and L. Rudolph. Distributed hierarchical control for parallel processing. *Computer*, pages 65–77, May 1990.
5. D. G. Feitelson and L. Rudolph. Mapping and scheduling in a shared parallel environment using distributed hierarchical control. In *Proc. International Conf. Parallel Processing*, volume I, pages 1–8, August 1990.
6. D. G. Feitelson and L. Rudolph. Gang scheduling performance benefits for fine-grain synchronization. *J. Parallel and Distr. Comp.*, 16(4):306–318, December 1992.
7. D. G. Feitelson and L. Rudolph. Evaluation of design choices for gang scheduling using distributed hierarchical control. *J. Parallel and Distr. Comp.*, 35:18–34, 1996.
8. H. Franke, P. Pattnaik, and L. Rudolph. Gang scheduling for highly efficient distributed multiprocessor systems. In *Proc. Frontiers'96*, 1996.
9. A. Hori, H. Tezuka, Y. Ishikawa, N. Soda, H. Konaka, and M. Maeda. Implementation of gang-scheduling on workstation cluster. In *Job Sched. Strategies for Parallel Processing, D. G. Feitelson and L. Rudolph (eds.)*, pages 126–139. Springer-Verlag, 1996. LNCS Vol. 1162.
10. S. G. Hotovy. Workload evolution on the Cornell Theory Center IBM SP2. In *Job Sched. Strategies for Parallel Processing, D. G. Feitelson and L. Rudolph (eds.)*, pages 27–40. Springer-Verlag, 1996. LNCS Vol. 1162.
11. S. G. Hotovy. Personal communication. 1997.
12. S. G. Hotovy, D. J. Schneider, and T. O'Donnell. Analysis of the early workload on the Cornell Theory Center IBM SP2. In *Proc. ACM SIGMETRICS Conf. Measurement and Modeling of Comp. Syst.*, pages 272–273, May 1996.

13. N. Islam, A. Prodromidis, M. S. Squillante, L. L. Fong, and A. S. Gopal. Extensible resource mangement for cluster computing. In *Proc. International Conf. Distr. Comp. Syst.*, May 1997.

14. N. Islam, A. Prodromidis, M. S. Squillante, A. S. Gopal, and L. L. Fong. Extensible resource scheduling for parallel scientific applications. In *Proc. Eighth SIAM Conf. Parallel Processing for Scientific Comp.*, March 1997.

15. T. Kimbrel, A. Tomkins, R. H. Patterson, B. Bershad, P. Cao, E. W. Felten, G. A. Gibson, A. R. Karlin, and K. Li. A trace-driven comparison of algorithms for parallel prefetching and caching. In *Proc. USENIX Symp. Operating Syst. Design and Implementation (OSDI)*, pages 19–34, October 1996.

16. V. M. Lo. Heuristic algorithms for task assignment in distributed systems. *IEEE Trans. Comp.*, 37(11):1384–1397, November 1988.

17. T. C. Mowry, A. K. Demke, and O. Krieger. Automatic compiler-inserted I/O prefetching for out-of-core applications. In *Proc. USENIX Symp. Operating Syst. Design and Implem. (OSDI)*, pages 3–17, October 1996.

18. J. K. Ousterhout. Scheduling techniques for concurrent syst.. In *Proc. Third International Conf. Distr. Comp. Syst.*, pages 22–30, October 1982.

19. V. G. Peris, M. S. Squillante, and V. K. Naik. Analysis of the impact of memory in distributed parallel processing systems. In *Proc. ACM SIGMETRICS Conf. Measurement and Modeling of Comp. Syst.*, pages 5–18, May 1994.

20. J. Skovira, W. Chan, H. Zhou, and D. Lifka. The EASY-LoadLeveler API project. In *Job Sched. Strategies for Parallel Processing, D. G. Feitelson and L. Rudolph (eds.)*, pages 41–47. Springer-Verlag, 1996. LNCS Vol. 1162.

21. M. S. Squillante, F. Wang, and M. Papaefthymiou. An analysis of gang scheduling for multiprogrammed parallel computing environments. In *Proc. Annual ACM Symp. Parallel Algorithms and Architectures (SPAA)*, pages 89–98, June 1996.

22. M. S. Squillante, F. Wang, and M. Papaefthymiou. Stochastic analysis of gang scheduling in parallel and distributed syst.. *Perf. Eval.*, 27&28:273–296, 1996.

23. W. H. Tetzlaff. Paging in the VM/XA system product. *CMG Trans.*, 66:55–64, 1989.

24. W. H. Tetzlaff. Paging in VM/ESA. In *Proc. CMG'91 Conf.*, pages 723–734, 1991.

25. W. H. Tetzlaff and T. Beretvas. Paging in VM/370 operating systems. *CMG Trans.*, 53:65–76, 1986.

26. W. H. Tetzlaff, T. Beretvas, W. M. Buco, J. Greenberg, D. R. Patterson, and G. A. Spivak. A page-swapping prototype for VM/HPO. *IBM Syst. J.*, 26:215–230, 1987.

27. W. H. Tetzlaff and R. Flynn. A comparison of page replacement algorithms. In *Proc. CMG'92 Conf.*, pages 1136–1143, 1992.

28. W. H. Tetzlaff, M. G. Kienzle, and J. A. Garay. Analysis of block-paging strategies. *IBM J. Res. and Devel.*, 33(1):51–59, January 1989.

29. F. Wang. *Multiprogramming for parallel and distributed systems*. PhD thesis, Computer Science Department, Yale University, 1997.

30. F. Wang, H. Franke, M. Papaefthymiou, P. Pattnaik, L. Rudolph, and M. S. Squillante. A gang scheduling design for multiprogrammed parallel computing environments. In *Job Sched. Strategies for Parallel Processing, D. G. Feitelson and L. Rudolph (eds.)*, pages 111–125. Springer-Verlag, 1996. LNCS Vol. 1162.

Author Index

Springer
and the
environment

At Springer we firmly believe that an
international science publisher has a
special obligation to the environment,
and our corporate policies consistently
reflect this conviction.
We also expect our business partners –
paper mills, printers, packaging
manufacturers, etc. – to commit
themselves to using materials and
production processes that do not harm
the environment. The paper in this
book is made from low- or no-chlorine
pulp and is acid free, in conformance
with international standards for paper
permanency.

Springer

Lecture Notes in Computer Science

For information about Vols. 1–1238

please contact your bookseller or Springer-Verlag